Doing Theology
for the Church

Essays in Honor of KLYNE SNODGRASS

Doing Theology for the Church

Essays in Honor of KLYNE SNODGRASS

Edited by REBEKAH A. EKLUND and JOHN E. PHELAN JR.

WIPF & STOCK · Eugene, Oregon

DOING THEOLOGY FOR THE CHURCH
Essays in Honor of Klyne Snodgrass

Copyright © 2014 Covenant Publications. All rights reserved. Except for
brief quotations in critical publications or reviews, no part of this book may
be reproduced in any manner without prior written permission from the
copyright holder. Covenant Publications, 8303 W. Higgins Rd., Chicago, IL
60631, (773) 784-3000.

Unless otherwise noted, biblical citations are taken from New Revised
Standard Version Bible, copyright 1989, Division of Christian Education
of the National Council of the Churches of Christ in the United States
of America. Used by permission. All rights reserved.

Wipf & Stock
An Imprint of Wipf and Stock Publishers
199 W. 8th Ave., Suite 3
Eugene, OR 97401

www.wipfandstock.com

ISBN 13: 978-1-4982-0535-1
ISSN: 0361-0934, *The Covenant Quarterly*, Vol. LXXII, Nos. 3-4,
August and November 2014

Library of Congress Cataloging-in-Publication Data

Doing theology for the church : essays in honor of Klyne Snodgrass/
   edited by Rebekah A. Eklund and John E. Phelan Jr.
   pages cm
   Includes bibliographical references.
   ISBN-13: 978-1-4982-0535-1
   1. Bible. New Testament. 2. Jesus Christ—Parables. 3. Bible
Gospels. 4. Bible. Epistles of Paul. 5. Women clergy. 6. Snodgrass, Klyne.
I. Title.
BS2395 D665 2014

Design by David R. Westerfield

Printed in the United States of America

KLYNE R. SNODGRASS

Contents

Foreword

I am privileged to have encountered Klyne Snodgrass as both his student and his colleague at North Park Theological Seminary. When I came under his tutelage as a student, he was fresh from St. Andrews with his PhD in New Testament studies. As a young professor he was intense and rigorous; fair, yet unrelenting. As I view him now, from the vantage point of dean of the seminary, he is still all of those things and more.

A scholar's scholar, he is renowned around the world for his work in the New Testament. His work in the parables, the hermeneutics of identity, and Ephesians just scratch the surface of his contribution to biblical studies. However, from my bookend perspectives I want to recognize what might be his most enduring contribution to North Park Theological Seminary, to its faculty and generations of students, and to the community of pastors in the Evangelical Covenant Church: his clarion call to "be faithful."

Concise and lean, like much of his writing, his directive to students and colleagues to "be faithful"—to the text, to the church, to each other, and most importantly, to Christ—is reinforced by his admonition that "in the end it's all we have." Most students and colleagues have heard him declare this command to be faithful as an imperative for the call of Christian life and, particularly, for those called to ministry. This wonderful collection of writings in Klyne's honor is a testimony to his own faithful and fruitful life as a scholar, and as a master teacher. In honoring him, we must also recognize the impact he's made on North Park, the school to which he's given his vocational life, its community of scholars and a generation of students.

In attempting to capture the essence of Klyne's work among us I came across this quote from John Steinbeck: "I have come to believe that a great teacher is a great artist, and that there are as few as there are any other great artists. Teaching might even be the greatest of the arts since the medium is the human mind and spirit."

In this volume we celebrate the high artistry of one of our own, spoken in the classroom, written on the page, held in many minds and hearts. Thank you, good friend and colleague. Every blessing for the next part of the journey.

David Kersten
North Park Theological Seminary
Chicago, Illinois

Tribute

I consider it a great honor to write about Klyne Snodgrass. I graduated from North Park Theological Seminary in 1993 and yet, more than twenty years later, Klyne's kind, wise, and insightful scholarship holds a prominent place in my pastoral identity. I use many of Klyne's published works in my own study as a pastor, and I love that his voice, laced with that distinctive southern drawl, so clearly resonates in my head while I read.

Who among his students does not remember the crushing workload of our first New Testament encounter with Klyne? I remember laughing with incredulity when Klyne urged us to spend twenty hours a week maintaining our Greek skills in the midst of our other pastoral responsibilities. While I'm sure that few of us have heeded that request, I know I remain indebted to Klyne for his deep commitment to God's word, to knowing it well, to understanding the issues, to living with tension—all in order to ultimately proclaim the good news of Jesus Christ well, encourage deeper discipleship among Christ's followers, and to grow in our love for God's word. Klyne's passion for understanding the text in order to lead others in ministry lingers. It was never just about being a scholar; it was always about knowing Christ and preparing us to help others know Christ better.

Klyne was clear about his expectations for us as teachers of God's word. He instilled in his students a deep responsibility for careful scholarship to honor the place of privilege that the pulpit holds for pastors. Klyne's own love for God's word, for the complexities of the original Greek, and his deep interest in equipping us to live with the tensions that Scripture presents motivated me to treat the text with care, to do my homework, seeking the full depth of meaning of a text. Klyne's outstanding scholarship speaks for itself. I am in awe when I consider how privileged I was to sit in his classroom and enjoy his gifts firsthand.

But beyond that gift of sitting in Klyne's classroom, it is his friendship that touches me even more. Yes, even twenty years later, I feel a warm and abiding connection to Klyne as a friend and colleague that is powerful and profoundly meaningful. Klyne was a demanding professor, yet he was also deeply compassionate. He cared about our studies but he was also genuinely invested in our lives. His door was open to us to talk about our life concerns, our pastoral identity, and the personal struggles that sometimes emerged for young seminary students. He modeled an impressive scholarship, but even more impressive was his modeling of pastoral care and concern for the person.

Perhaps the most significant way he combined these two qualities was through his care and concern for women in pastoral ministry. Klyne has been a great advocate for women in pastoral leadership through the years. His careful and thoughtful biblical scholarship has allowed others a platform from which to teach and minister to lay people regarding this often controversial issue. Klyne's affirmation of women in pastoral leadership, rooted in sound biblical scholarship, moved the women in ministry conversation away from being a liberal versus conservative issue. By offering such solid biblical evidence for the participation of women in all roles of the church, Klyne has challenged those who hold traditionally male-only models of leadership to reconsider their position based on what Scripture truly says about women in the Bible and the early church. Klyne does not shy away from the so-called "problem texts" regarding women's leadership. Instead he carefully exegetes them, revealing new ways of understanding the original context of these texts to challenge previous assumptions and urge today's church to come to better conclusions about the role of women in pastoral leadership. All of this is based on careful biblical scholarship, coupled with Klyne's deep desire to see all of God's children discover and use the full giftedness that God has granted them.

At one time I thought I would name my firstborn after Klyne, so deep was my gratitude toward him! I ended up not having children so I could not fulfill that desire, but I know that when I hear Klyne's name, read something he has written, hear him speak or teach, or have the privilege of enjoying a chat with him, I am filled with the deepest gratitude a student can have for a professor and feel the warmth of a friendship that has been formed over years of meaningful connection and learning. Klyne will always have a presence in my life and I know I am a better pastor and person because of him.

Jodi Mullen Fondell
Stockholm, Sweden

Tabula Gratulatoria

Joel M. Anderle, *Peabody, Massachusetts*
Dennis M. Anders, *Huntley, Minnesota*
Craig and Dorothy Anderson, *Plantation, Florida*
Frances M. Anderson, *St. Petersburg, Florida*
Philip and Karna Anderson, *Hovland, Minnesota*
Robert M. Anderson, *Boulder Junction, Wisconsin*
Greg and Hilary Applequist, *South Euclid, Ohio*

Matthew Bach, *Angels Camp, California*
Jung Chi Back, *Leonia, New Jersey*
Dwight and Lois Baker, *New Haven, Connecticut*
Dave and Martha Benedict, *Bemidji, Minnesota*
Bradley Bergfalk, *Omaha, Nebraska*
Bob and Judy Bergquist, *Bedford, New Hampshire*
Keith and Cynthia Bergstrom, *Eagle River, Alaska*
Deborah C. Blue, *Calumet Park, Illinois*
Dan Boyce, *Visalia, California*
Paul and Marlene Bramer, *Toronto, Ontario*
Christian B. Breuninger, *Santa Rosa, California*
Howard Burgoyne, *Cromwell, Connecticut*
Michael Burke, *Chico, California*

Aune M. Carlson, *Chicago, Illinois*
Dennis K. Carlson, *Farmington Hills, Michigan*
LeRoy L. and Colleen I. Carlson, *Chicago, Illinois*
Russell Carlson, *Muskegon, Michigan*
Linnea and Kip Carnes, *Mason, Ohio*
Bill and Laurie Clark, *Hinsdale, Illinois*
Tom and Lynda Collins, *Madison, Wisconsin*

Alan S. Dean, *Red Oak, Iowa*
Jo Ann Deasy, *Moon, Pennsylvania*
Paul and Gretchen de Neui, *Chicago, Illinois*
Tom and Celeste Dierenfeld, *Loveland, Colorado*
Robert and Dorothy Dvorak, *Bradenton, Florida*

Nancy Ebner, *Indian Orchard, Massachusetts*
Marc and Sarah Eix, *Manistee, Michigan*

George B. Elia, *Yarmouth Port, Massachusetts*

Kurt Fredrickson, *Simi Valley, California*
Jim and Kathy Fretheim, *Bemidji, Minnesota*
Tim Fretheim, *Port Coquitlam, British Columbia*

Jim Gaderlund, *Mountain View, California*
Scot and Meagan Gillan, *Naperville, Illinois*

Whitney Hall, *Lowell, Massachusetts*
Cherie Harris, *Olympia Fields, Illinois*
Peter Hawkinson, *Wilmette, Illinois*
Paul and Hope Hedberg, *Homewood, Illinois*
Tim and Colleen Heintzelman, *Gahanna, Ohio*
Eric R. Hillabrant, *Blue Island, Illinois*
Betty and Fredrick Holmgren, *Chicago, Illinois*
Dean and Robin Honnette, *Martinez, California*
Robert and Yvonne Huse, *Strathmore, Alberta*

Herbert and Phyllis Jacobsen, *Lords Valley, Pennsylvania*
Daron and Kristin Jagodzinske, *Poulsbo, Washington*
Jesus People USA Covenant Church, *Chicago, Illinois*
Daniel F. Johnson, *Hilmar, California*
Douglas W. and Mary J. Johnson, *Santa Barbara, California*
Evelyn M. R. Johnson, *Park Ridge, Illinois*
LeRoy and Carole Johnson, *Glenview, Illinois*
S. Jerome Johnson, *Plymouth, Minnesota*
Timothy L. Johnson and Kari B. Lindholm-Johnson, *Chicago, Illinois*
Todd and Susan Johnson, *La Canada, California*
Rodger L. Jorgenson, *Rockton, Illinois*
Neil and Sharol Josephson, *Pitt Meadows, British Columbia*

Thomas and Janice Kelly, *Mexico City, Mexico*
James and Susan Knight, *Harbert, Michigan*
Bruce Knofel, *Seward, Alaska*
Jason and Daryl Knudeson, *Rosamond, California*
Paul and Linda Koptak, *Chicago, Illinois*

Michael and Melissa Langer, *Glen Ellyn, Illinois*
Paul and Elisabeth Larsen, *Rancho Mirage, California*
John K. Larson, *Batavia, Illinois*
Karl and Kristina Larson, *Aurora, Nebraska*

Ken Larson, *Wixom, Michigan*
Margaret A. Larson, *Two Harbors, Minnesota*
Steven P. Larson, *Brooklyn Park, Minnesota*
Todd and Wendy Larson, *Wheaton, Illinois*
Jonah J. Lee, *Morton Grove, Illinois*
Max and Su Lee, *Chicago, Illinois*
Jonathan and Jill Lind, *Park Ridge, Illinois*
Kevin and Peggy Lockett, *Eielson Air Force Base, Alaska*
Richard and Valerie Lucco, *Chicago, Illinois*
Sandy Lund, *Minneapolis, Minnesota*
Janet Lundblad, *Des Plaines, Illinois*

Ronald Magnuson, *Three Oaks, Michigan*
Katherine Burns Martinez, *Loveland, Colorado*
John Martz, *Arvada, Colorado*
Paul R. and Vicki H. Marxen, *Oshkosh, Wisconsin*
Greg and Charlotte Mesimore, *Chicago, Illinois*

Chester L. (Chet) Nelson, *Otis Orchards, Washington*
Chris and Sharon Nelson, *Oberlin, Kansas*
Eloise and LeRoy Nelson, *Northbrook, Illinois*
Jerome Nelson, *Evanston, Illinois*
Roger and Marilyn Nelson, *Chicago, Illinois*
Tom and Nancy Nelson, *Dennis, Massachusetts*
Edward Newton, *Portland, Oregon*
Monty Newton, *Westminster, Colorado*
David and Marilyn Noreen, *Westminster, Colorado*
Jerry and Nancy Nugent, *Voorhees, New Jersey*

Don and Amanda Olson, *Chicago, Illinois*
Mark and Doreen Olson, *Chicago, Illinois*
José João Orr, *Emo, Ontario*
Joel J. Osterlund, *Mahtowa, Minnesota*
Amy Oxendale, *Chicago, Illinois*

Karen L. Palmatier, *Quincy, Massachusetts*
Mark Pattie, *Lino Lakes, Minnesota*
Joel and Adria Pearson, *Chicago, Illinois*
Mark Pearson, *Westbrook, Maine*
Jim and Arlys Persson, *Westminster, Colorado*
Curt and Martie Peterson, *Park Ridge, Illinois*
G. Verle Peterson, *Spring Valley, California*

Judy Peterson, *Eagan, Minnesota*
John E. and Dawn Phelan, *Arlington Heights, Illinois*
J. Christopher and Janet Pickett, *Crystal Lake, Illinois*
Douglas C. Pierce, *Dassel, Minnesota*
Bob and Marilyn Poor, *Northbrook, Illinois*
Carolyn Poterek, *Seattle, Washington*

Nancy B. Reed, *Spring Valley, California*
Jim Ressegieu, *La Vista, Nebraska*

Reynold Samundsen, *Batavia, Illinois*
John H. Satterberg, *Edina, Minnesota*
Dan and Toni Schwabe, *Wyoming, Minnesota*
George A. and Claire E. Scranton, *Seattle, Washington*
Ben Searway, *Riverbank, California*
Stephen and Kathleen Sharkey, *Quincy, Massachusetts*
Paul E. Springer, *Turlock, California*
Cathy and Jim Stanley-Erickson, *Harleysville, Pennsylvania*
Linda and Philip Stenberg, *Balsam Lake, Wisconsin*
James Stone, *Martensville, Saskatoon*
Andrew Stonina, *Stephenson, Michigan*
Jim and Carol Sundholm, *Vashon, Washington*
Steven and Barbara Swanson, *Ekeren, Belgium*
Tammy Swanson-Draheim, *Omaha, Nebraska*

Mark and Valeri Tao, *Chicago, Illinois*
Robert K. Tenglin, *Palatine, Illinois*
Melanie Tornquist, *Evanston, Illinois*

Andrew Vanover, *Grand Rapids, Michigan*
Charles and Sharon Vaughan, *Reidsville, North Carolina*

Kirsten Wagenius, *St. Cloud, Minnesota*
Charles D. Wahlstrom, *Lakewood, Washington*
Gary Walter, *Palatine, Illinois*
Lois and John Weborg, *Princeton, Illinois*
Wayne Weld, *Spring Valley, California*
Mark and Alice Westlind, *Chicago, Illinois*
Glen V. Wiberg, *Golden Valley, Minnesota*
J. David Wood, *Rockford, Illinois*
Bert Wright, *Fort Collins, Colorado*

Preface

I (Jay) remember vividly the first time I met Klyne Snodgrass. I was finishing up my doctoral work at Northwestern University and was exploring filling in for Klyne at North Park Theological Seminary while he was on sabbatical. I had been attending a Covenant church for some years and had heard Klyne's name mentioned frequently. I knew he was a fellow Tennessean and, of all things, a Southern Baptist! I did not yet know of his prowess on the basketball court. That afternoon he was sporting a rather vivid black eye—the result of an overly enthusiastic elbow thrown by a seminarian. I was to learn over time that Klyne was as apt to throw an elbow as to receive one. I was also to learn over time that however fearsome Klyne could be on the basketball court, he was a gentle, compassionate, kind-hearted teacher beloved of students and colleagues alike.

Klyne was also a demanding, rigorous teacher. I (Rebekah) can recall my astonishment (and maybe a bit of dismay) after my first look at the famous New Testament syllabus. I can also vouch for how thoroughly and deeply trained I was in the exegesis of the New Testament under Klyne's steady guidance. His rigorous preparation served me well as I later pursued doctoral studies at Duke Divinity School. Like many of his students, I can say that Klyne's classes were the most formative of my seminary years. Because I also worked for three years as Klyne's teaching assistant, I felt honored to count Klyne as a mentor and, over time, as a friend. Klyne and his wife, Phyllis, generously opened their home to me and to countless other students.

In fact, a steady stream of students have always found their way to his door—and have all found a warm welcome. Klyne has nursed struggling students through their exegesis papers and mentored young scholars contemplating doctoral studies. He has also sustained and encouraged colleagues in Nyvall Hall, around the United States, and in nearly every part of the globe.

Klyne has made an enormous contribution to the Evangelical Covenant Church. It is fair to say that without his advocacy for and writing on the biblical basis for women in pastoral ministry, the struggle for women's ordination in the church would have been longer and more bitter. Klyne was (and is) deeply respected by both the "left" and the "right" sides of the denomination, and his rigorously biblical approach to the issue educated, encouraged, and enlightened the entire Covenant Church. But this is only one of many contributions to the life and health of the church universal. In addition to his work with the

Covenant Church in the United States, he has taught, lectured, and preached in sister churches in Latin America, Europe, and Asia. He has been among the most highly regarded lecturers at meetings of the International Federation of Free Evangelical Churches.

Klyne has also been a scholars' scholar. His massive study of the parables, *Stories with Intent*, is already a classic. But his interests and contributions have been significant and wide-ranging, as the bibliography included in this volume attests. For many years he has shepherded the North Park Symposium on the Theological Interpretation of Scripture and edited the journal *Ex Auditu*, which publishes the papers presented there. This conference brings together scholars, students, and practitioners to do theological reflection for the church. It brings scores of world-class scholars to North Park Theological Seminary to engage in often intense conversations about the relevance of their work for the life and mission of the church. The symposium is, in fact, a perfect reflection of the life, teaching, and scholarship of Klyne Snodgrass. His has always been a scholarship in service of the church and its mission. He has always insisted that students first pay attention to the *text* and then address that text to the *church*. His scholarship has never been self-referential or addressed narrowly to the scholarly community. It has always been scholarship for the sake of the gospel.

Most recently, Klyne has been pursuing a question: "What is the gospel?" It's a deceptively simple question. He's been asking students in his capstone course at North Park to answer it. In fact, one could argue that his entire career—and his life—is an attempt to answer that question and then to live faithfully according to the answer. Along the way, he's wrestled with a number of related questions: What is a parable? What is the kingdom of God? Whom does God call into ministry, and how? Where do we get our identity (or identities) from? Who are we in Christ?

The scholars who contributed essays to this *festschrift* all reflected in deep and thoughtful ways on these and other questions. To try to do justice to the breadth of Klyne's interests, we asked scholars to contribute essays in areas that related to a significant area of Klyne's current or past research: 1) the gospels and parables; 2) the apostle Paul, especially his views on the law; 3) inner-biblical interpretation, or how to read the whole Bible as a coherent whole, from Genesis through Revelation; 4) women and ministry; and 5) identity, which is the topic of his current research. Everyone who participated was eager to honor Klyne, and gave generously of their time through the work printed here. The breadth of scholars represented—both men and women, long-time colleagues and former students, from Chicago to South Africa—testify to the impact and significance of Klyne's research as well as the collegial friendships he has forged.

In addition to those who wrote essays, this book has been a labor of love undertaken by many friends. Paul Koptak's careful and insightful editorial work (and timely reminders) kept us organized and on schedule. We would also like to thank Ed Gilbreath for his support, Evy Lennard for typesetting the project, David Westerfield for his design work, and Jane Swanson-Nystrom for additional support and editorial oversight. Finally, we extend our thanks to the publication committee: Zach Martinez, Andy Meyer, and Steve Spencer.

It is with deep gratitude to our friend Klyne that we present this volume to honor his many contributions: seen and unseen, known and unknown; to the lowliest student and most exalted scholar; to academy and church. We recognize his enduring legacy in his superb scholarship and in the lives and ministries of thousands of students who continue to prepare to preach and teach in churches and classrooms across the country and around the world. His compassionate rigor has marked us all, faculty, staff, and students, and for that we are deeply thankful. In presenting this volume to Klyne we also honor his wife, Phyllis, who, along with Klyne, welcomed generation after generation of students into their home. And we offer it with the hope and confidence that his contributions will continue to nurture both the academy and the church for years to come.

REBEKAH A. EKLUND
JOHN E. PHELAN JR.

GOSPELS AND PARABLES

Jesus Laments (or Does He?)
The Witness of the Fourfold Gospel

Rebekah A. Eklund

Look at all the works of the Most High: they go in pairs, one the opposite of the other.[1]

The crucifixion of Jesus is at the heart of the gospel proclamation, yet each gospel narrates it in a significantly different way. The four accounts do not agree on the signs that accompany Jesus's death or the final words that Jesus speaks. More pressingly, the Gospels portray Jesus approaching his impending death in strikingly divergent ways: does he die in anguished abandonment, crying out to God? Does he die peacefully, relinquishing his soul in trust to the Father? Does Jesus lament from the cross, or doesn't he?

Until the rise of modern historical-critical methods, interpreters accepted the four gospel narrations of Jesus's crucifixion, including his last words from the cross, as complementary accounts of the same event. Patristic, medieval, and Reformation exegetes assumed that Jesus spoke all the words attributed to him, and that different evangelists simply chose different words to report. Until the Reformation era, apparent tensions in the emotions of the last words were often resolved by assigning Jesus's fear, doubt, and suffering to his humanity, and Jesus's powerful mastery of events to the Son's divinity. Ambrose writes: "As being man, therefore, He speaks, bearing with Him my terrors, for when we are in the midst of dangers we think ourself abandoned by God. As man, therefore, He is distressed, as man He weeps, as man He is crucified."[2]

An important shift occurred in the modern era, with the rise of historical-critical scholarship: scholars began to question whether Jesus in fact did speak all seven of the last words. The theory of Markan priority (widely accepted by the mid-1800s) led many to privilege the cry of forsakenness as the only (possibly) authentic word. Thus scholars solved the "problem" of divergences in the crucifixion accounts in an entirely different way than their predecessors—through treating the Lukan and Johannine words as reflections of the evangelists' particular theological emphases. Once one hypothesizes that the "historical" Jesus has not spoken all the last words attributed to him, the problem of how to resolve the tensions in his final words simply disappears: the differences are traced not to Jesus himself but to the evangelists.

In the last several decades, some scholars have suggested alternative approaches, which seek to use the strengths of the available historical-critical tools while reaffirming the traditional stance that the Scriptures "provide a true and faithful vehicle for understanding the will of God."[3] Since I take this to be an apt description of the work of Klyne Snodgrass, this essay explores this third path, and is modeled in part on Brevard Childs's case studies of parallel but divergent accounts of the same event in the Gospels (each case study begins with "pre-modern" exegesis, then considers historical-critical methods, and finally models what Childs calls a canonical approach).[4] My essay also seeks to extend Childs's important work, in part by appealing to Snodgrass's concept of the "creative tension" inherent to the Christian life, and by finding that tension within the pattern of lament itself (anguished cries for help *together with* trust in the midst of distress). With a nod to Hans Frei's reflections on the coherent identity of Jesus Christ, I suggest that the pattern of lament is one intratextual way to hold together the diverse crucifixion accounts as harmonious portraits of a single death.[5] Finally, I briefly consider the theological interpretation of Scripture: how do these texts, when read together, lead the reader into deeper discipleship, into wisdom, into greater love of God and neighbor?

Harmonizing the Last Words

Until the modern era, the principle of unity guided most biblical interpreters: the diverse texts of Scripture, Old and New Testaments, bore witness to the one Triune God. In many ways, the problem of difference—the divergences in the four gospel accounts of the life of Jesus—is a modern problem. On the other hand, the plurality of the Gospels created a challenge for the church from the very beginning. Witness the early and enduring popularity of Tatian's Diatessaron (ca. 170), and the vehemence of Theodoret's attempt to stamp out its use.[6] While the early church resisted the efforts at harmonization represented by the Diatessaron, and insisted on retaining the diverse witnesses of the four evangelists, gospel harmonies persisted well into the 1700s. Although the impulse toward harmony always remained strong, it was held in relative check by the fourfold gospel collection of the canon.

The obvious differences among the four accounts provided ammunition to Christianity's critics, and the seven last words were no exception. Crucifixion accounts posed a special challenge since each evangelist reports the scene with significant variations. In his *Harmony of the Gospels*, Augustine defends the Gospels against charges that the evangelists contradict one another. Chapter 18 of the *Harmony* is thoroughly titled: "Of the Lord's successive utterances when he was about to die; and of the question whether Matthew and Mark are in harmony with Luke in their reports of these sayings, and also whether these three evangelists are in harmony with John."[7] Augustine concludes that Jesus did speak all the utterances reported by the four Gospels, and that all four are in essential harmony. Ambrose of Milan and Bonaventure follow much the same strategy, noting that the Gospels record different last words but emphasizing that Jesus spoke them all.[8]

Other exegetes defend the unity of the four accounts of Jesus's last words by highlighting common themes, such as the motif of the fulfillment of Scripture (Aquinas) or, more often, the theme of Jesus giving up his life willingly (Augustine, Origen, Chrysostom).[9] Origen draws parallels between Jesus "giving up his spirit" (Matthew 27:50), committing his spirit to God's hand (Luke 23:46), and handing over his spirit (John 19:30), treating all three texts as representations of the singular notion that Jesus does not merely die but entrusts himself to God.[10] Likewise Chrysostom takes the "loud voice" of Matthew 27:50 as evidence that Jesus has laid down his life of his own accord (citing John 10:18, "No one takes [my life] from me, but I lay it down of my own accord. I have power to lay it down, and I have power to take it up again").[11] In fact, John 10:18 functions as a hermeneutical key that opens the other crucifixion texts.[12]

Because the theme of voluntary self-giving is more explicit in Luke and John, focusing on this theme effectively brings the accounts of Matthew and Mark into closer alignment with Luke and John. This is a fairly common strategy, in part due to an impulse to subordinate Jesus's human responses—especially his fear and doubt, more apparent in Mark and Matthew—to his divinity, which is more apparent in John. Exegetes also frequently narrate Jesus's mastery of his fear as an example to be followed. Chrysostom, for example, narrates the cry of abandonment in Mark and Matthew as an expression of Christ's piety, since it is a quotation of Scripture: clearly, it is a simple task to interpret the Lukan and Johannine cries likewise as expressions of trust and piety.[13]

The assumption that Christ spoke all seven last words raises another question: in what order did he speak them? For Augustine, this is hardly a crucial issue; he assumes that the evangelists sometimes felt free to alter the "literal," chronological order of events in their retellings of Jesus's life. Therefore, although he accepts that Jesus spoke all the last words reported by the Gospels, he makes no serious attempt to place them in a particular order.[14] Other exegetes describe the order in which they believe Jesus spoke all the words, but they achieve no consensus on that point. Bonaventure begins with, "I thirst"; Tatian's Diatessaron opens with, "Today you shall be with me in Paradise"; Ambrose and Saint Bridget of Sweden place the cry of forsakenness last.[15] The familiar present-day order (most likely established either by the Jesuit priest Roberto Bellarmine in 1618 or the Jesuit priest Alonso Mesia ca. 1687) begins with "Father, forgive them…" and ends with "Into your hands…."[16] Commentators sometimes offer reasons for placing the words in a certain order, revealing that the ordering of the words is in fact its own kind of interpretive act. Ambrose, for example, although he initially discusses the cry of forsakenness as the third word, describes it again as the final word, spoken immediately before Jesus's death as the sign of "the withdrawal of the Godhead."[17]

In the Reformation era, John Calvin represents a particularly interesting attempt to "harmonize" the synoptic accounts (Calvin does not include John in his analysis). Like Augustine, Calvin interprets the "loud cry" uttered by Jesus just before he dies in Matthew 27:50 and Mark 15:37 as the "loud cry" of Jesus quoting Psalm 31:5 in Luke 23:46.[18] Whereas Augustine makes this identification without elaborating on it, Calvin explores the connection further, using the wider context of Psalm 31. Calvin interprets Jesus's cry of Psalm 31:5 (in Luke's account) as evidence that Jesus's faith remains unshaken "although He was sore shocked with many violent trials." In fact, Calvin reads the Lukan prayer "Into your hands I commit my spirit" as if it were spoken in the context of Matthew 27:50: "There is no doubt that Christ, in the anguish of the temptations that beset Him, let out this cry at last with a deep and burning effort."[19] Calvin paraphrases the quotation of Psalm 31:5 as Jesus saying, "Although according to the flesh, *I feel no help from You*, yet that will not prevent My resting My spirit in Your hands and, without anxiety, taking support from the hidden protection of Your goodness."[20]

This interpretation of Jesus's prayer neatly harmonizes Luke's account with Mark and Matthew's quotation of Psalm 22:2 and the cry of abandonment. To do so, Calvin draws on the wider context of Psalm 31, reading the quotation of verse 5 [Psalm 30:6 LXX] through the lens of verse 9 [Psalm 30:10 LXX] ("Be gracious to me, O LORD, for I am in distress; my eye wastes away from grief, my soul and body also"). Calvin notes that in Psalm 31 David is "continually beset with many deaths" but yet "boasts that [his soul] is safe from every danger" once he entrusts his soul to God as its guardian.[21] In the same way, Jesus who is beset on every side with danger and death entrusts his soul to God. In this way, Calvin points the way toward seeing lament as the undergirding theme of Jesus's last words.

In general, then, interpreters from the patristic, medieval, and Reformation eras have the same basic tendencies with respect to the last words: to assert that Jesus spoke all seven last words, to read all seven for their underlying theological coherence, and (until the Reformation) to assign the various words to either Jesus's humanity or his divinity. Pre-modern interpreters recognize that the evangelists have their own theological purposes and inclinations, but they rarely focus on the particular functions of the last words in their wider gospel contexts. Furthermore, it is somewhat more common for pre-modern interpreters to favor the portrayals of John (for example, by appealing to John 10:18), although Calvin is an important exception to this rule. Calvin represents an additional impulse that becomes important to a canonical reading, which is to invoke the wider context of the lament psalms in order to read the accounts together.

Historical-Critical Approaches

The confident insistence of Augustine and Calvin that Christ prayed all the words from the cross attributed to him by the four Gospels began to wane in the eighteenth and nineteenth centuries. Instead, as Benjamin Jowett's famous insistence that the Bible be read just like any other book gained ascendancy, scholars increasingly questioned the relationship between the gospel accounts and history.[22] It began to seem "historically improbable" that Jesus spoke all seven of the traditional last words from the cross.[23] From the vantage point of Markan priority, modern historical-critical interpreters have tended to treat Jesus's "cry of forsakenness" as the only authentic cry from the cross.[24] Sometimes even this conclusion is questioned: perhaps Jesus merely cried out in a loud voice, and the church (in the form of the Markan evangelist) placed Psalm 22's first line in his mouth.[25] The other three accounts are then read in light of Mark. Matthew has closely followed Mark's account, as usual. Luke has dropped the quotation of Psalm 22 but retained the tradition that Jesus prayed from a lament psalm by substituting words from Psalm 31. And John follows his own independent path, choosing (or reporting) words that display the Son in perfect union with the will of the Father. It is generally assumed that Mark is closest to the historical Jesus and thus has the best chance of reporting what Jesus "actually" said from the cross.

Of course, difficulties with the historical Jesus quests have been well-documented.[26] Nobody seems able, in the end, to sort out precisely where history ends and theological interpretation begins. As Snodgrass notes, "The old methods attempting to strip off layers of ecclesial accretions to get back to the message of Jesus have proved a dead end too burdened by methodological uncertainties and the subjectivity of the particular scholar."[27] This chastened confidence has led many scholars to be more cautious about deciding which words Jesus "really" said and which he did not.[28]

Historical-critical approaches have had two other primary effects with regard to the last words. First, if pre-modern approaches highlight unity, historical-critical tools enable interpreters to isolate and emphasize the unique voices of each evangelist, a task that allows each of the four to be heard at "full volume" before integrating them or seeking the sense of Scripture as a whole.[29] Canonical reading seeks to hear the "cry of forsakenness" in light of the cry "It is finished" only once it has been heard in the context of Mark 1:1–16:8.[30]

Second, if one studies the last words along a continuum of historical development, beginning with Mark and ending with John, it appears that Mark has preserved the starkest form of lament, followed closely by Matthew, whereas Luke and John's accounts contain the least amount of obvious lament (if any at all). In other words, historical-critical reading of the Gospels seems to reveal a bias or a trajectory *away* from a lamenting Jesus in the earliest Christian tradition. "Thus Luke and John, taming the wilder elements of the text, inaugurate the dominant trend in the history of the interpretation of the earliest version of the pericope. That is, the domestication of the text begins almost immediately."[31]

There is certainly an element of truth in this narrative; it is hard to deny that John's account, lacking the Gethsemane narrative and any obvious lament from the cross, portrays a less sorrowful Jesus than Mark. Yet this trajectory is not as straightforward as it first appears. From our modern vantage point, we might assume that early Christians (like Luke and John) avoided Jesus's despairing cry from the cross because they were embarrassed by it. But as Mark Goodacre points out, "Mark is not in the least 'embarrassed' by this cry. It is an ideal means of expressing plausibly the horror of the cross at the same time as reaffirming, by quoting the Psalms, that it is in God's will."[32] Furthermore, when one places the last words in their fuller narrative contexts, Matthew and Mark (however subtly in Mark's case) contain notes of triumph and vindication, and both Luke and John layer their passion narratives with allusions to the lament psalms. Upon closer scrutiny, then, the concept of a "trajectory" away from lament turns out not to be a trajectory at all, but something much more complex.

In this case, the often helpful preoccupation with the evangelists' particularities has led scholars to assume a kind of difference that is simply not present, at least not in such a simple form. For example, it is not uncommon to find biblical scholars making claims about the "domestication" of the gospel, or describing the upward tilt of Christian doctrine away from Jesus's humanity and toward his divinity. Larry Hurtado and Peter Head, among others, have called these assumptions into question.[33] Jesus's lament from the cross in Mark does not *necessarily* indicate a low Christology; likewise, Jesus's triumphant declarations from the cross in John do not *necessarily* represent an aversion to lament per se.

Indeed, at this point we should pause and consider what is intended by the term "lament." The word is often taken as a synonym for mourning, or perhaps anguished dissatisfaction. But lament in its Old Testament context entails something much richer and more precise: a form of speech directed toward God that presumes a God who keeps promises, and calls upon that God to keep those promises in the midst of distress. While this form of address to God pervades the Old Testament, its distinct pattern occurs most clearly in the Psalms, which provide the basis for many of Jesus's last words. It is this very pattern of lament that enables seeing in the last words from the cross what Childs calls "a canonical harmony."

A Canonical Approach

Unlike standard historical-critical impulses, canonical reading shares with pre-modern approaches a basic trust that the Scriptures provide a truthful and sufficient witness to Jesus Christ. As a corollary, this implies that no individual gospel (whether Mark or John) is sufficient *on its own*.[34] D. Moody Smith argues, for example, that "John makes sense best, and makes proper theological sense, only when it is viewed in light of the Synoptic Gospels."[35] A canonical approach, then, assumes that one must take into account all of the last words, and that they will make the best sense when read together, alongside one another.

Earlier, I suggested that pre-modern readers tended to approach the "problem" of tensions between the last words primarily through assigning differences to the two parts of Jesus's nature (human and divine), whereas modern strategies assign differences not to Christ's complex person but to the evangelists. If the four passion narratives are diverse portrayals of one person, the problem of difference reappears: how do all these last words, with all their different forces and functions within their respective contexts, cohere in a single person? And, is there a way to discover this coherence through the inner logic of the four Gospels themselves, without recourse to later Christological controversies over the two natures (as illuminating as those controversies were)?

Francis Watson suggests that the decision to accept a fourfold gospel achieves "a delicate dialectical balance...between diversity and coherence." Subtracting from the four undermines diversity—the richness of the divine self-disclosure—whereas adding to the four undermines coherence.[36] The differences among the four accounts are reconfigured not as a problem to be solved but as a gift of abundance, an indication of "the infinite richness of the divine self-disclosure."[37] Mark and John, in all their apparent incompatibilities, are faithful portraits of the one person Jesus of Nazareth and how he died.

I offer here a necessarily abbreviated tour of the function of the last words in their respective contexts, which reveals the pattern of lament that undergirds all four passion narratives, and thus indicates an intratextual way that each account contributes to a complex but coherent portrait of Jesus's death. Although a canonical reading properly begins with Matthew, beginning with Mark accepts the theory of Matthew's dependence on Mark, thereby borrowing a useful historical-critical tool that allows us to see both Mark and Matthew's particularities more clearly.

Mark 15:34. "My God, my God, why have you forsaken me?" (cf. Psalm 22:1). In Mark's account, Jesus's final cry is the opening line of a Davidic lament psalm, the invocation (*my God*) and the complaint (*why?*) about God's absence. Alongside the fear and trembling silence of the women at the empty tomb, the Markan last word emphasizes the darkness and distress of Jesus's death—but also the irony of Jesus's true identity as Messiah and King, the truth *known to the reader* that the empty tomb signifies the resurrection of Jesus and thus his vindication—that Jesus is precisely the one whom God has not ultimately forsaken. Of course Mark's Gospel famously ends on a note of uncertainty and lacks any resurrection appearances. But the resurrection in Mark is "the veiled center toward which the action moves...the open mystery not actually included in the narrative, which nonetheless serves as the narrative's mainspring."[38] Does Jesus lament in Mark? Yes, with a shout.

Matthew 27:46. "My God, my God, why have you forsaken me?" (cf. Psalm 22:1). Matthew accompanies Jesus's final cry with a surplus of eschatological signs and makes more explicit what Mark leaves hidden by including Jesus's resurrection appearances and the women's joy alongside their fear at the empty tomb. Does Jesus lament in Matthew? Yes, but the context makes the note of vindication somewhat more pronounced.

Luke 23:34, 43, 46. "Father, forgive them; for they do not know what they are doing."[39] "Truly I tell you, today you will be with me in Paradise." "Father, into your hands I commend my spirit." In Luke, Jesus speaks three times from the cross: first to forgive his enemies, next to assure the penitent criminal on the cross nearby that he would join Jesus in Paradise, and finally with a quotation of Psalm 31:5. This gives Jesus's final words in Luke's account a much more complex set of functions than in Matthew or Mark. Taken as a whole, they portray Jesus as fully in command. He forgives his enemies, recalling his earlier instructions to "love your enemies...pray for those who abuse you" (Luke 6:27-28). Jesus's gracious word to the penitent criminal reinforces the criminal's recognition that "Jesus's crucifixion is a precursor to his enthronement," and demonstrates that "God's plan comes to fruition through, not in spite of, the crucifixion of Jesus, so that Jesus is able to exercise his regal power of salvation in death as in life."[40] The final word, by which Jesus willingly gives himself over to death, is a close quotation of Psalm 31:5 (Psalm 30:6 LXX).

Although Psalm 31, like Psalm 22, is a Davidic lament, Jesus's quotation from Psalm 31 is from one of the trusting sections of the psalm, obscuring its nature as a lament—unless the reader knows the whole psalm. As Calvin noticed, the wider context of the psalm aligns the quotation of Psalm 31 more closely with Jesus's quotation from Psalm 22 in Mark and Matthew. For example, consider verse 13b of Psalm 31: "They scheme together against me, as they plot to take my life"; and verse 22 echoes a sense of separation from God: "I had said in my alarm, 'I am driven far from your sight.'" Does Jesus lament in Luke? Surprisingly, yes, if we hear the wider context of Psalm 31, and if we remember that the lament of Israel always (with the one exception of Psalm 88) includes trust in God in the midst of distress.

John 19:26-27, 28, 30. "Woman, here is your son.... Here is your mother." "I am thirsty." "It is finished." As in Luke, Jesus speaks three times from the cross in John (the first two lines being grouped together as a single "last word"). Also like Luke, the last words in John portray Jesus directing events, even as he dies. The first phrases seem fairly straightforward (although they have sometimes been interpreted allegorically): Jesus arranges a new kinship of care between his mother and his beloved disciple. The next two words are more enigmatic, admitting to multiple interpretations (a situation appropriate to a gospel that delights in puns and double-meanings). Jesus *thirsts*, most straightforwardly "in order to fulfill [*teleioō*] the Scripture" (John 19:28), most likely Psalm 69:21 (but cf. Psalm 69:3). Like Psalm 22 and Psalm 31, Psalm 69 is a Davidic lament, and it too contains pleas for deliverance from death (v. 15) and from enemies (vv. 14, 18-19). Like Psalm 22, it ends on a triumphant note: "For God will save Zion..." (v. 35). Psalms 69 and 22 both contain complaints about thirst, although neither uses Jesus's word for thirst (*dipsō*); Psalm 69 connects the motif of thirst to waiting with tears for God's deliverance. Jesus's thirst thus hints at God's absence, admittedly in a much more subtle way than the cry of forsakenness in Mark and Matthew.[41] And, in John's context, the reader would surely note the painful irony of the one who offered living water to others now thirsting in advance of his death (John 4:13-14; 7:37-38).

"It is finished [*teleō*]" is generally taken as a final, triumphant declaration that Jesus has accomplished everything the Father gave him to do, but even this simple line evokes, ever so faintly, echoes of the lament psalms. Perhaps it hints at the "*eis to telos* [unto/for the end]" of the inscription in the Greek title of Psalm 22 and 69.[42] Jesus's proclamation that "it is finished" also resonates intriguingly with the ending of Psalm 22: "he has done it!" (Heb. *kî 'āśâ*; Gk. *hoti epoiēsen ho kurios*). This is likewise a very faint echo. Even if the evangelist himself did not intend the allusion, however, it provides a fascinating canonical frame to the allusions to Psalm 22, beginning with the first verse in Matthew and Mark and concluding with the final verse in John.

Joel Marcus draws a theological connection between the first and final words, the two last words usually considered to be the greatest opposites: "It is finished" and "My God, my God, why have you forsaken me?" Pointing to early Christian convictions that Jesus "enters the darkness of the old age in order that humanity might live in light of the new," Marcus writes: "The cry of dereliction, then, is in a strange way the Markan counterpart to the Johannine cry of triumph, 'It is finished!' (John 19:30)—the goal has been achieved, humanity has been redeemed, and Jesus can therefore die."[43]

Does Jesus lament in John? At first glance, and when compared to Mark, not at all. But on more thorough examination, even John quietly evokes the language of lament. The impulse of pre-modern interpreters to find common theological themes in the four accounts thus resurfaces even when investigating the unique functions of each of the last words. Most importantly for the purposes of this essay, the guiding pattern of the lament psalms is apparent in all four accounts, especially when the four are viewed alongside one another. The unity of the gospel witnesses to Jesus's last words emerges precisely through their different voices—not in spite of them.

The canonical order reveals the typical pattern of lament, from the complaint and invocation of Mark and Matthew, to the trust and praise of Luke and John. In one sense, then, John completes the pattern of lament that Mark begins. One might note other key thematic or theological commonalities: for example, Jesus's voluntary renunciation of power and acceptance of suffering and death, as Origen observed. Although this theme is sharper in Luke and John, it appears in Mark and Matthew as well (Matthew 26:53-54; Mark 10:32-34, 45). Nonetheless, it is difficult not to allow Luke and John to overpower Mark and Matthew at this point—or vice versa. If pre-modern interpreters tended to favor John's portrayal of Jesus's death, the modern tendency, particularly from the mid-twentieth century onward, has been to privilege Mark.

Balancing the Tensions

As Snodgrass writes: "Tension permeates our faith. Every truth that we know is balanced by another truth that seems to be moving in the opposite direction."[44] Jesus dies in lonely lament, asking God why he has been forsaken; Jesus dies entrusting his soul into the loving hands of his Father. This is the full breadth of the lament pattern, from anguished complaint to stubbornly trusting praise; it represents the "peaceful and creative" tension that is part of belonging to Christ.[45]

If John insists, in creative tension with Mark 15:34, that the Father is *always* with the Son (John 16:32), Mark tugs the reader in the other direction, back into the darkness of Jesus's death, and the silence of God, a little longer. The canon keeps these two voices in constant conversation with one another, as it does with so many other scriptural tensions. While discussing the danger of sectarianism and schism in 1 John, Richard Hays points to "the corrective witness of the canon." That is, "[1 John's] testimony brings some important matters into sharp focus; however … its testimony needs to be supplemented and counterbalanced by other witnesses," including Paul, Luke, and 1 Peter.[46] In the same way, Mark and John can be corrective witnesses to one another. Reading the cry of forsakenness and the cry of triumph with one another guards the church from a theology that distorts too far in one direction or another, whether Arian or Docetic.[47]

Liturgy and the Last Words

Might it also matter *how* we read the last words together? Richard Burridge argues that Jesus's cry in Mark 15:34 should *not* be read together with John 19:30, at least in liturgies: "Both [cries] represent the culmination of their respective gospel's portraits and theologies. We cannot enter into the horror of the first, nor feel the power of the second, if they are narrated together in liturgy."[48] While the point about the integrity of each evangelist's portrait and purpose is well-taken, let us examine for a moment what happens when they *are* narrated together. The modern order of the words (listed just below) was likely established by the end of the seventeenth century; for almost three hundred years, many people have encountered the last words in this order, whether in the "Three Hours' Devotion" services popular in the 1800s (and which continue today), musical settings such as Joseph Haydn's 1796 *Die sieben letzten Worte unseres Erlösers am Kreuze*, or recently published meditations on the seven last words.[49]

The now traditional order of Jesus's last words runs as follows:

1. Father, forgive (Luke)
2. Today in paradise (Luke)
3. Behold your son/mother (John)
4. My God, why? (Matthew and Mark)
5. I thirst (John)
6. It is finished (John)
7. Into your hands (Luke)

This order begins with three confident assertions, turns to two plaintive cries, and ends with two final declarations. This is obviously not the only way to narrate the last words together, as the fifteen centuries-long discussion about ordering the words demonstrates. But it reveals that the last words can indeed change in force and function when abstracted from their narrative contexts and placed into conversation with one another. For example, in this order, the cry of forsakenness is "enfolded within" the Lukan cries (as the outer frame) and the Johannine cries (the inner frame).[50] Does placing the cry of forsakenness in the middle mute its force by burying it inside Luke and John's witness, or does it make it the hinge of all the last words, the turning-point of the crucifixion?

The Hermeneutics of Obedience

Discovering the pattern of lament that interweaves these texts is one way to hold these texts together in all their difference, and a way that respects the intratextual echoes within the texts themselves. Lament is most pronounced in Mark and Matthew, is present in a changed key in Luke, and is subtly but perhaps most deeply embedded in John. When we hear all their voices raised together, in all their distinctiveness, we hear the one complex chorus of the fourfold gospel. A more musical friend has suggested to me that the laments in the last words are like the French horn section in an orchestra: you might not hear them until someone teaches you how to listen for them. Or, perhaps the four Gospels are different arrangements of the same symphony; each arrangement has French horns, but they are louder in Mark than they are in John.

In the end, though, does it matter whether Jesus laments or not? Klyne Snodgrass reminds us that "we have not understood a text until we understand what it seeks to accomplish in its hearers."[51] What do the last words accomplish in the reader who seeks to shape her life around them? This is a question that is almost certainly easier to answer in a worship service, or around a kitchen table, rather than in an essay; but an initial answer returns to the function of the last words in their respective contexts. Each evangelist narrates the identity of Jesus through a particular set of theological lenses: Son of God, King of Israel, beloved Son of the Father, light in the darkness, God-with-us, Son of Man; and in each case Jesus's true identity is "climactically manifested" in the crucifixion and resurrection.[52] As Marcus observes, the purpose of Mark and John meet at precisely this point: the demonstration that Jesus's death accomplishes God's purposes for the redemption of the world. Thus we have misunderstood any of the last words if we fail to read them within this overarching horizon—if the last words point to anything other than the obedient Son who renounced power and accepted death, and the faithful God who vindicated this Son by raising him from the dead.

If theological interpretation of Scripture trains us in deeper love of God and our neighbors, we might think about reading the last words alongside some of those neighbors—a convicted criminal in a re-entry program, or a family enduring a drought, or a mother who has just buried a son, or a mother who has just adopted a new son, or a neighbor who wonders whether God is present in the midst of daily gun violence. Samuel Wells suggests that the church must be a diverse community in order to hear the Scriptures in all their diversity: "If there is no foreigner, no resident alien among the congregation, will the stories [of Esther and Daniel] be heard in the same way?…How can Christians hear the parable of Dives and Lazarus if they do not know in their fellowship with one another the pain of class difference and economic inequality?"[53] Can we hear the cry of forsakenness in all its anguish unless we are in relationship with those who feel themselves forsaken? Or the word assuring the penitent thief of Paradise unless we break bread with people enduring the weight of guilt and condemnation?

A life shaped by the last words might display the same pattern of lament that Jesus's last words themselves reveal: a life characterized by both struggle with God and trust in God. A life that dwells within the tensions of the Christian life—an unpredictable journey with a God of steadfast love—and does not resolve them for us. Fleming Rutledge recalls the words of a man who spoke out of the grief of losing his only son: "The Christian life is lived in between— in between *My God, my God, why hast thou forsaken me?* and *Father, into thy hands I commend my spirit.*"[54]

Endnotes

1. Ecclesiasticus (Sirach) 33:15, quoted in Klyne Snodgrass, *Between Two Truths: Living with Biblical Tensions* (Eugene, OR: Wipf & Stock, 1990), 14.

2. Ambrose, *Of the Christian Faith* 2.7.56, in *Nicene and Post-Nicene Fathers,* Second Series, vol. 10, ed. Philip Schaff and Henry Wace (Peabody, MA: Hendrickson, 1994), 230. So also Chrysostom, *Homilies on the Gospel of Saint John,* in *Nicene and Post-Nicene Fathers,* First Series, vol. 14, ed. Philip Schaff (Peabody, MA: Hendrickson, 1994), Homily 85, esp. p. 318. Origen suggests this solution in *De Principiis,* but in *Contra Celsus,* he attributes Jesus's willing prayer, "Nevertheless, not as I will, but as Thou wilt" to the "readiness of spirit which existed in His humanity"; see Origen, *De Principiis,* in *Ante-Nicene Fathers,* vol. 4, ed. Alexander Roberts and James Donaldson, 2.6.2, pp. 281-82; and Origen, *Against Celsus,* in *Ante-Nicene Fathers,* vol. 4, 2.25, p. 442.

3. Brevard Childs, *The New Testament as Canon* (Philadelphia: Fortress Press, 1984), 37. For a thorough exploration of canonical criticism, see *Canon and Biblical Interpretation,* Scripture and Hermeneutics Series, vol. 7 (Grand Rapids: Zondervan, 2006). See also John Webster, "Canon," in *Dictionary for Theological Interpretation of the Bible,* ed. Kevin Vanhoozer (Grand Rapids: Baker Academic, 2005), 97-100.

4. Childs, *The New Testament as Canon,* 157-209.

5. Hans Frei, *The Identity of Jesus Christ* (Philadelphia: Fortress Press, 1975).

6. See Helmut Merkel, *Die Pluralität der Evangelien als theologisches und exegetisches Problem in der Alten Kirche* (Bern: Lang, 1978); Oscar Cullmann, "The Plurality of the Gospels as a Theological Problem in Antiquity," in *The Early Church,* ed. A. J. B. Higgins (London: SCM Press, 1956); Bruce M. Metzger and Bart D. Ehrman, *The Text of the New Testament,* 4th ed. (Oxford University Press, 2005), 131-34.

7. Augustine, *Harmony of the Gospels, in Nicene and Post-Nicene Fathers,* First Series, vol. 6, ed. Philip Schaff (Peabody, MA: Hendrickson, 1994), 205.

8. Saint Ambrose of Milan, *Exposition of the Holy Gospel According to Saint Luke*, trans. Theodosia Tomkinson (Etna, CA: Center for Traditionalist Orthodox Studies, 2003), 432; Bonaventure, *Works of St. Bonaventure: Commentary on the Gospel of John*, trans. Robert J. Karris (St. Bonaventure, NY: Franciscan Institute, Bonaventure University, 2007), 934.

9. Aquinas, *Commentary on the Gospel of John, Chapters 13-21*, ed. Daniel Keating and Matthew Levering, trans. Fabian Larcher and James A. Weisheipl (Washington DC: Catholic University of America Press, 2010), 245-46.

10. *Zur Überlieferung der Matthäuserklärung des Origenes*, ed. Erich Klostermann and Ernst Benz (Texte und Untersuchungen zur Geschichte der altchristlichen Literatur, Bd. 47, Heft 2; Leipzig: J. C. Hinrichs, 1931). Excerpts translated into English in *Matthew 14-28*, Ancient Christian Commentary on Scripture, vol. 1b, ed. Manlio Simonetti (Downers Grove, IL: InterVarsity Press, 2002), 295-96.

11. *Chrysostom: Homilies on the Gospel of Saint Matthew*, in *Nicene and Post-Nicene Fathers*, First Series, vol. 10, ed. Philip Schaff (Peabody, MA: Hendrickson, 1994), 521.

12. Augustine, *Homilies on the Gospel of John*, in *Nicene and Post-Nicene Fathers*, First Series, vol. 7, ed. Philip Schaff (Peabody, MA: Hendrickson, 1994), 119.19, p. 434; Chrysostom, *Homilies on the Gospel of Saint John*, Homily 85, p. 318; Chrysostom, *Homilies on the Gospel of Saint Matthew*, Homily 88, p. 521. Cf. Ambrose, *Of the Christian Faith*, in *Nicene and Post-Nicene Fathers*, Second Series, vol. 10, ed. Philip Schaff and Henry Wace (Peabody, MA: Hendrickson, 1994), 6.51, p. 230.

13. *Matthew 14-28*, 295; *Saint Ephrem's Commentary on Tatian's Diatessaron*, trans. Carmel McCarthy (Oxford: Oxford University Press, 1993), 316.

14. Augustine, *Harmony of the Gospels*, 206.

15. Bonaventure, 934; Ambrose, *Exposition of the Holy Gospel According to Saint Luke*, 432; *The Diatessaron of Tatian*, in *Ante-Nicene Fathers*, vol. 9, ed. Allan Menzies, trans. Hope W. Hogg (Peabody, MA: Hendrickson, 1994), 123.

16. Roberto Bellarmine wrote *De Septem Verbis Christi* in 1618. For Mesia, see Herbert Thurston, "Historical Introduction," in Alonso Mesia, *The Devotion of the Three Hours' Agony on Good Friday* (London: Sands & Co., 1899), 7-12.

17. Ambrose, *Exposition of the Holy Gospel According to Saint Luke*, 432.

18. Augustine, *Harmony of the Gospels*, 205; cf. Calvin, *A Harmony of the Gospels: Matthew, Mark and Luke and the Epistles of James and Jude*, Calvin's New Testament Commentaries, vol. 3, trans. A. W. Morrison (Eerdmans, 1972), 210.

19. Calvin, 210.

20. Ibid., 209-10, emphasis added.

21. Ibid., 210.

22. See Hans Frei, *The Eclipse of Biblical Narrative* (New Haven: Yale University Press, 1974); Michael Legaspi, *The Death of Scripture and the Rise of Biblical Studies* (Oxford; New York: Oxford University Press, 2010).

23. Gérard Rossé, *The Cry of Jesus on the Cross* (New York: Paulist Press, 1987), 28.

24. Ibid., 328 n.2; Raymond Brown, *The Death of the Messiah*, vol. 2 (New York: Doubleday, 1994), 1085-88.

25. E.g., Rudolf Bultmann, *History of the Synoptic Tradition* (New York: Harper & Row, 1968), 281, 313.

26. Mark S. Goodacre, "Scripturalization in Mark's Crucifixion Narrative," in *The Trial*

and Death of Jesus, ed. Geert van Oyen and Tom Shepherd (Leuven: Peeters, 2006), 33-47; Dale Allison, *Constructing Jesus* (Grand Rapids: Baker Academic, 2010).

27. Klyne Snodgrass, "The Gospel of Jesus," in *The Written Gospel*, ed. Markus Bockmuehl and Donald A. Hagner (Cambridge: Cambridge University Press, 2005), 32.

28. E. P. Sanders, *Jesus and Judaism* (London: SCM Press, 1985), 1-22; cf. Allison, 436.

29. Robert W. Wall, "The Significance of a Canonical Perspective of the Church's Scripture," in *The Canon Debate*, ed. Lee Martin McDonald and James A. Sanders (Peabody, MA: Hendrickson, 2002), 533.

30. In Klyne's Introduction to the New Testament class, he often reminded us, "There are three things that matter when interpreting the New Testament: context, context, and context."

31. Kevin Madigan, "Ancient and High-Medieval Interpretations of Jesus in Gethsemane: Some Reflections on Tradition and Continuity in Christian Thought," *Harvard Theological Review* 88, no. 1 (1995): 161.

32. Goodacre, "Scripturalization in Mark's Crucifixion Narrative," 47.

33. Larry Hurtado, *How on Earth Did Jesus Become a God? Historical Questions about Earliest Devotion to Jesus* (Grand Rapids; Cambridge, U.K.: Eerdmans, 2005); Peter Head, *Christology and the Synoptic Problem* (Cambridge, U.K.: Cambridge University Press, 1997).

34. Childs, *The New Testament as Canon*, 116; Denis Farkasfalvy, "The Apostolic Gospels in the Early Church," in *Canon and Biblical Interpretation*, 116-17.

35. D. Moody Smith, "The Fourth Gospel in Four Dimensions: Should Their Being Together in the New Testament Make a Difference in Their Interpretation?" in *The Fourth Gospel in Four Dimensions* (Columbia, SC: University of South Carolina Press, 2008), 206.

36. Francis Watson, "Are There Still Four Gospels?" in *Reading Scripture with the Church*, ed. A. K. M. Adam, Stephen E. Fowl, Kevin J. Vanhoozer, and Francis Watson (Grand Rapids: Baker Academic, 2006), 109.

37. Ibid., 107, cf. John Milbank, who describes the triune God as a peaceful harmony of difference, in *Theology and Social Theory* (Malden, MA; Oxford, U.K.: Blackwell, 1993), 6, 424. Not all canonical or theological interpreters agree on this point.

38. Frei, *The Identity of Jesus Christ*, 34 n.17.

39. Several important early manuscripts lack this verse, including P75, B, and D; it is the original reading of א, but is rejected in a later correction. It is plausible that a scribe omitted it in anti-Judaic resistance to the image of Jesus forgiving the Jews who crucified him. No significant variant exists for Acts 7:60, where Stephen prays similar words; because of the multiple parallels between Jesus's and Stephen's deaths, this strengthens the possibility that Luke 23:34 was an original tradition. For a detailed study, see Joshua Marshall Strahan, *The Limits of a Text: Luke 23:34a as a Case Study in Theological Interpretation* (Winona Lake, IN: Eisenbrauns, 2012).

40. Joel B. Green, *The Gospel of Luke*, New International Commentary on the New Testament (Grand Rapids: Eerdmans, 1997), 823.

41. Other scholars have noted the possible thematic or even structural connections between the two cries: J. M. Spurrell, "Interpretation of 'I thirst,'" *Church Quarterly Review* 167/ 362 (1966): 12-18; Leonard Theodor Witkamp, "Jesus's Thirst in John 19:28-30: Literal or Figurative?" *Journal of Biblical Literature* 115/3 (1996): 507-8.

42. Mark George Vitalis Hoffman, *Psalm 22 (LXX 21) and the Crucifixion of Jesus* (Ann Arbor, MI: U.M.I., 1997), 426, 427 n.37.

43. Joel Marcus, *Mark 8-16*, The Anchor Yale Bible, vol. 27A (New Haven; London: Yale University Press, 2009), 1064. Marcus also points to other textual factors, such as the echoes of Amos 8:9-10 in Mark 15:33, to suggest that "while Jesus may feel abandoned by God, he remains the cherished offspring of a loving father" (ibid., 1062).

44. Snodgrass, *Between Two Truths*, 14.

45. Ibid., 16, 25, 32-34.

46. Richard B. Hays, "The Palpable Word as Ground of *Koinōnia*," in *Christianity and the Soul of the University: Faith as a Foundation for Intellectual Community*, ed. Douglas V. Henry and Michael D. Beaty (Grand Rapids: Baker Academic, 2006), 31, 32.

47. This has some bearing on the controversies over patripassianism, if only in the observation that "suffering God" theologies (e.g., Jürgen Moltmann) usually rely exclusively on Mark 15:34, whereas defenders of divine *apatheia* tend to privilege the Johannine (and Lukan) portrayals of Christ.

48. Richard Burridge, *Four Gospels, One Jesus?*, 2nd ed. (Grand Rapids; Cambridge, U.K.: Eerdmans, 2005), 165.

49. The 1965 Methodist Book of Worship still contains a "Three-Hour Service of Devotion" for Good Friday (pp. 102-8). Contemporary meditations include Stanley Hauerwas, *Cross-Shattered Christ: Meditations on the Seven Last Words* (Grand Rapids: Brazos Press, 2005); Richard Neuhaus, *Death on a Friday Afternoon: Meditations on the Last Words of Jesus from the Cross* (New York: Basic Books, 2000); Fleming Rutledge, *The Seven Last Words from the Cross* (Grand Rapids; Cambridge, U.K.: Eerdmans, 2005); William H. Willimon, *Thank God It's Friday: Encountering the Seven Last Words from the Cross* (Nashville: Abingdon Press, 2006).

50. David Hart writes, "And the terrible distance of Christ's cry of human dereliction, despair, and utter godforsakenness—'My God, My God, why hast thou forsaken me?'—is enfolded within and overcome by the ever greater distance and always indissoluble unity of God's triune love: 'Father, into thy hands I commend my spirit.'" David B. Hart, "No Shadow of Turning: On Divine Impassibility," *Pro Ecclesia* 11/ 2 (2002): 205.

51. Klyne Snodgrass, "Exegesis," in *Dictionary for Theological Interpretation of the Bible*, 204.

52. Frei, *The Identity of Jesus*, 33.

53. Samuel Wells, *God's Companions: Reimagining Christian Ethics* (Malden, MA; Oxford: Blackwell, 2006), 157, 158.

54. Rutledge, *Seven Last Words*, 77.

Film as Parable
What Might This Mean?

Robert K. Johnston

In April 1910, the minister of South Congregational Church in New Britain, Connecticut, the Rev. Herbert A. Jump, proposed that it would be good if his church purchased motion-picture equipment so that the citizens of the city, many of foreign birth, might have the motion picture as an adjunct to their religious education.[1] Two months later the ex-mayor of the city, who attended the church, generously offered to endow thirty film screenings on Sunday evenings, including the purchase of all necessary equipment. And though the proposal got substantial publicity along the East Coast, and though Jump spent considerable time researching the subject and choosing the movies, visiting both studios and the censorship board, and consulting with exhibitors and social workers, his church board decided the project was too controversial (their term was "unwise") to pursue at that time and the screenings were abandoned. Moreover, Jump soon found himself needing to move on to another congregation, this time in Oakland, California.

Though it didn't work out for Jump in Connecticut, the pastor thought the information he had garnered could still be useful to other churches, so even before he left, Jump published a pamphlet entitled *The Religious Possibilities of the Motion Picture*.[2] In it, he not only provided information concerning how to put on such a series (complete with a sample film list), but after reminding his readers that quartet singing and Bibles printed in the vernacular were also rejected as worldly in earlier days, he sought to justify the use of film in the church as "a religious tool" by appealing to Jesus's use of parables in his ministry. In this way, he hoped to disarm the mood of antagonism that he no doubt had experienced at South Church and that he assumed would be present elsewhere as well.

In particular, Jump referenced Jesus's parables by telling the dramatic story of the Good Samaritan (Luke 10:30-37). He observed in the pamphlet that just as with movies, (1) the story was taken not from religious sources but from contemporary experience; (2) it was exciting in character and "thus interesting even to the morally sluggish"; and (3) it had realistic and morally negative features in it ("crime, accident, ignorance, sin") that made it (4) "true to life." And yet, the parable exhibited the heart of the gospel. Asked Jump, "Has it not urged more men [sic] into lives of ministry and helpfulness than any piece of literature of equal length which the race has ever known?"[3] Jump concluded his plea by saying the films that had value for religious education today were like the parables of Jesus.

Jump would not be the last to make the comparison between movies and parables. Nor was he the last to have the comparison dismissed without much of a hearing. Kenneth Morefield, for example, writing on August 7, 2013, for the website christianitytoday.com quotes only to dismiss the comments of conservative writer Carol Iannone in *First Things* about *The Last Temptation of Christ*, which was celebrating the twenty-fifth anniversary of its release. Said Morefield, "She stressed the good intentions of the artists, however misguided the results. Kazantzakis, 'in order to speak to modern man,' she said, must make Jesus 'to bear the infirmities of our age—the doubt, the angst, the fear and trembling, the existential dread, and yes, even the sexual obsessiveness.' She quotes Scorsese's [the director's] own desire to create, like Kazantzakis, 'a parable that is fresh and alive.'" But Morefield will have none of this. He says, "It's not a living parable," only a confused film about Jesus.[4]

"Parable" Described

How would we decide if Morefield is correct? By what criteria might a film be considered a parable? What makes a film a parable, or, in the case of Morefield, not a parable? Certainly it has been common to make such a comparison over the last hundred years, ever since Jump first proposed the analogy. And certainly Jump's four descriptors—that film, like parable, is based in the everyday, is exciting, realistically depicts life, and seeks to convey truth—remain. Iannone seems to have had this in mind as well. But are such similarities sufficient to make certain films parabolic? Does such a description capture the heart of parable as Jesus used them? Or is there more at work here? Or again, should Scorsese's disorienting, even subversive, portrayal of Jesus disqualify it as a parable? What should be fundamental criteria for abandoning the notion of a film as modern-day parable? Certainly Jesus's parables often functioned subversively, undermining contemporary religious authority.

Klyne Snodgrass's magisterial volume *Stories with Intent: A Comprehensive Guide to the Parables of Jesus* (2008) provides us a helpful set of descriptors around which parables might be understood.[5] In his introduction to Jesus's parables, Snodgrass begins by recognizing more generally the power of story. He notes that stories are compelling to the hearer.

> Discourse we tolerate: to story we attend.... Stories are one of the few places that allow us to see reality.... There, to a degree we cannot do in real life, we can discern motives, keep score, know who won, and what success and failure look like.... The storyteller is in control so that we are forced to see from new angles and so that the message cannot be easily evaded.... From this "other world" we are invited to understand, evaluate, and, hopefully, redirect our lives.[6]

Stories should not be confused with the raw data of plot. Instead, the storyteller has a point of view—an intention, a perspective he or she thinks important. Otherwise the narrator would not bother to tell the tale. Perhaps the agenda is to entertain; or perhaps, as with parables, it is to convince or to portray truth (or even falsehood). But there is always intention.

But if stories also have intention, what, then, makes a story a parable? The definition of a biblical "parable" has proven elusive. Snodgrass gives his readers a sampling of some of his favorite descriptions: "A parable is a literary creation in narrative form designed either to portray a type of character for warning or example or to embody a principle of God's governance of the world and men [sic]" (T. W. Manson).[7] Parables "are the natural expression of a mind that sees truth in concrete pictures rather than conceives it in abstractions.... At its simplest the parable is a metaphor or simile drawn from nature or common life, arresting the hearer by its vividness or strangeness, and leaving the mind in sufficient doubt about its precise application to tease it into active thought" (C. H. Dodd).[8] Parables are "the conjunction of a narrative form and a metaphoric process" (Paul Ricoeur).[9]

Or perhaps better, thinks Snodgrass, using the definition of fable—the genre to which parable belongs—is this first-century description: a parable is "a fictitious saying picturing truth" (Theon).[10] Still better, writes Snodgrass, is his own adaptation of Marianne Moore's description of poetry: "parables are imaginary gardens with real toads in them" (Moore).[11]

Key to each of these descriptions, argues Snodgrass, is the role of indirect communication. Parables are expanded analogies, referring outside themselves and compelling interest by the power of their stories, thereby attending to meaning in a new way. The goal of a parable is not to convey information (about common life), but to invite meaning.

Such description might make it seem that "parable" and story are synonyms. But no, writes Snodgrass, "a parable is not merely a story."[12] It is a particular kind of story. "A parable is an expanded analogy used to convince and persuade."[13] As such, it is one type of story. Continues Snodgrass:

> If meaning is the value assigned to a set of relations, parables provide new sets of relations that enable us (or force us) to see in a fresh manner. Parables function as a lens that allows us to see the truth and to correct distorted vision. They allow us to see what we would not otherwise see, and they presume we *should* look at and see a *specific* reality. They are not Rorschach tests; they are stories with an intent, analogies through which one is enabled to see truth.[14]

As Jesus told them, parables are brief, marked by simplicity and symmetry, focusing on humans and describing their everyday life, often containing elements of reversal. They are "mirrors of reality—angled at different degrees—designed often to shock and arrest and move people to response."[15] That is, as parables construct surprising worlds of meaningful life, they not only subvert and disrupt, they create and construct. In the words of Paul Ricoeur, they "reorient by disorienting."[16] Again, let us have Snodgrass provide a final description: "A good parable creates distance, provokes, and appeals. By creating distance it gives the hearer/reader [viewer] space to reconsider; one has no sense of needing to defend one's turf. By provoking the parable requires new channels of thought, and by appealing the parable seeks decisions that bring behavior into line with the teller's intent."[17]

Film Described as Parable: Three Recent Articles

Just as with story more generally, not all films function in this way. But some do! Turning to three recent articles that use parable as a defining metaphor for describing a film's religious possibilities, it will be helpful to locate the heart of parable as these film critics currently use it. Then, having compared present usage with Snodgrass's summative descriptions of Jesus's parables, we will be able to conclude this brief foray into intertextual studies by positing as parable Marc Forster's *Stranger than Fiction* (2006). The movie portrays in story form the interaction of free will and providence, subverting through irony and hyperbole modernity's trust in what can be measured and inviting viewers in the process to attend to life's meaning in new ways.

In 2001, Robert Palma of Hope College published in *Perspectives* his article, "Theological Parables in Paul Schrader's Films."[18] Referencing not only Schrader's corpus of movies but also his influential book, *Transcendental Style in Film* (1972), Palma argues that in Schrader's movies he has tried to embody a transcendental style through the use of a parabolic form in which viewers confront the Holy by "progressing from abundant to sparse artistic means," thus building spiritual momentum. He believes Schrader uses Jesus's parables as operative paradigms for depicting human mystery. In particular, thinks Palma, Schrader has himself described "the artistic pertinence of parables when he describes 'a film of spiritual intent' as needing 'to have an everyday and a disparity.'"[19] Where myth supports what we think and feel, parable "undermines and questions the very ground on which we stand." With Schrader, this has meant consistently creating parables of the biblical story of the fall and its fallout—*Hardcore* (1979), *American Gigolo* (1980), *Affliction* (1997), *Light of Day* (1987), *Raging Bull* (1980), *Taxi Driver* (1976), *Light Sleeper* (1992). Schrader, that is, has tried to subvert our dominant myths, both as a culture and as a church. Concludes Palma: "In his filmmaking Paul Schrader has indicted religious and moral legalism, petty piety, and cheap grace. In their place, he presents parables of stark sin...but also rays of grace and hope breaking from sparse means... [V]iewers may even confront the Holy One who stands in judgment over a fallen world."[20] In this way, Palma defines film parables in this article about Paul Schrader as sparse stories of the everyday that create disparity and invite a new moral vision by offering glimpses of grace. Undermining our ordinary take on reality, they function as subversive speech.

In 2002, Jeremy Punt, a South African biblical scholar, published "The Prodigal Son and *Blade Runner*."[21] In this intertextual study, Punt explores the analogies between the animosity between two sons and their father in Luke's parable of the prodigal son and a similar animosity between a creator-father and his creation-children in the movie *Blade Runner*. More particularly, and following the lead of Larry Kreitzer, Punt wishes to reverse the hermeneutical flow between these texts, encouraging non-confessional readings of confessional texts by letting the movie as parable broaden and challenge traditional biblical interpretations.[22] By linking a movie rooted in anguish and anger with this biblical parable, Punt is able to explore additional perspectives present in Luke's Gospel (a father is marginalized by his younger son; the younger son finds himself marginalized in a pigsty; and an older brother tries to define himself as marginalized in the family). He highlights how "both animosity and reconciliation interrelate with vulnerability (both) within literary text and movie script."[23]

Of particular importance for our purposes is Punt's working definition of parable:

Three elements are stressed in modern parable theory. Parables combine the qualities of narrative, metaphor, and brevity. A parable must tell, in as short a space as possible, a story with a double meaning. One meaning will usually be quite clear on the surface of the narration. Another, and presumably deeper meaning, or other, and possibly multiple meanings lie hidden within the complexities of the narrative, and these challenge or provoke the recipient to interpretation.[24]

Here is a description of Punt's argument in his article. The story of *Blade Runner* is able to break open new meanings within the biblical parable related to animosity and vulnerability, allowing readers/viewers to entertain, not only in *Blade Runner* but in the prodigal son, a different set of questions. In this way, the movie as parable not only entertains, but it engages dominant cultural ideas with lingering questions.

A third use of "parable" to describe film is Christopher Deacy's 2002 article in the *Journal of Contemporary Religion*, "Integration and Rebirth through Confrontation: *Fight Club* and *American Beauty* as Contemporary Religious Parables."[25] Deacy, a leading scholar in the emerging field of theology and film, discusses the religious significance of two iconic American films by understanding them as potent religious parables. In both movies, the directors wrestle with "the efficacy of confrontation as a means of attaining redemption from the disconnectedness and estrangement that characterize the lives of their protagonists."[26] According to Deacy, both films function through their parabolic structure as adroit adult satire, critiquing the values and preoccupations of contemporary western culture. But these two movies do not simply raise questions concerning the spiritual and normative values of the West abstractly. Rather, both movies leave an indelible imprint on many of their viewers, as what some mistakenly perceive as two nihilistic and sado-masochistic movies turn out instead, thinks Deacy, to have a "profound and inescapably religious dimension" at their core.[27] Both movies, like the biblical parables they parallel, are "capable of engulfing and overwhelming—even transforming—the audience" as the audience response on IMDb (Internet Movie Database) bears witness.[28] For Deacy, Jesus's parables are short, essentially fictional narratives, used to reveal religious, symbolic, and transcendental truths and values about the human condition, its aspirations and potentialities. Different than myth, writes Deacy, "the *parable* is meant to provoke us, challenge us, and transform us, reminding us of our limits and limitations, and laying the groundwork for the possibility of *transcendence*." Parables are, that is, "*human* renderings and allegories of stories that encapsulate, stimulate, and pave the way for transcendental insight."[29] Here is how both *Fight Club* and *American Beauty* act upon their audience. As one reviewer commented, they have "the rare ability to make you stop and think about your own life."[30] It is true that both films operate thematically in religious-parabolic terms. Both enact our spiritual blindness—caused by our sense of disconnectedness and dislocation—and our desire to see anew. But it is not the overt religious themes, the surface level analogies, that matter. As with other parables, it is not these movies' content, but their effect, stimulated by deeper, more universal social and psychological undercurrents, that matters most. Writes Deacy: "The appropriation of particular religious terms and teachings in *Fight Club* and *American Beauty* thus transcends mere textual analysis, and could, in essence, be construed as the gateway through which an audience can come to a fuller understanding of how to address some of the core problems that pertain to the human condition."[31] In both of these movies, in fact, the audience is directly addressed. Though they might not fully understand what the protagonists are talking about, as Lester says to the viewers in a final voiceover in *American Beauty*, "But don't worry....You will someday."

Film as Parable: Some Working Criteria

Here, then, in Snodgrass's synoptic review of biblical scholarship on the parables of Jesus, and in these three recent examples of film criticism that makes use of the notion of parable to describe a film's intent, we have overlapping descriptions of how film as parable might be understood. Despite their particular emphases, something like consensus is apparent, though those dealing with film's affective power tend perhaps to emphasize that aspect of parable more than many biblical scholars. Four criteria can be identified:

1. Parables are brief stories rooted in everyday life.
2. Parables are compelling ("exciting") stories, arresting the attention of their audience by inviting them to see reality from a new angle, the distance thus created allowing the audience to enter fully into the story, their defenses being lowered in the process.
3. Parables do not convey information, but through indirect communication, through the metaphoric process, invite their audience into meaning, as spiritual truth about the human condition is portrayed and revealed.
4. As such, parables are meant to function subversively, undermining contemporary religious attitudes, beliefs, and/or authority (disorienting) even while inviting, teasing, provoking new truth and/or transcendental insight (reorienting). As such, parables are meant to challenge and perhaps even transform their audience. It is not their content but their effect that matters most.

Film as parable tells its narrative sparsely (usually in less than two hours). As metaphor, it has levels of meaning, the surface story being taken from everyday life, but its underlying meaning opening up to symbolic and even transcendental insight. Subverting our ordinary take on reality, there is in the depiction of our lives a disparity that suggests the need for (an)other deeper meaning(s). In the process, film as parable leaves its imprint on the viewers; it provokes, enlightens, and can even transform.

A Decade of Award-Winning Movie Parables

Consider, for example, several recent years of award winning movies. In 2004, the movies that won the Academy Award for Best Picture and for Best Foreign Language Picture were *Million Dollar Baby* and *The Sea Inside*. Both told stories whose plot centered around euthanasia, but whose meaning actually drilled deeper, focusing on the nature of human life itself. Other movies from that year included *Eternal Sunshine of the Spotless Mind* and *Sideways*. Each captured its viewers' attention by showing reality from a new angle. And both bore down below the surface of the story, subverting regnant understandings of life's meaning, provoking and inviting new truth in the process. In 2005, all five Academy Award nominees were stories that also invited their viewers to see reality from a new angle, seeking not merely to convey information but to suggest a deeper meaning concerning the human condition—*Crash, Capote, Good Night and Good Luck, Munich,* and *Brokeback Mountain*. To this list of parabolic movies from 2005 might be added Woody Allen's *Match Point* and Danny Boyle's *Millions*. Paul Haggis, writer and director of *Crash,* as well as writer of both *Million Dollar Baby* and the 2006 Oscar nominated *Letters from Iwo Jima,* said of his work on *Crash* that he wanted to "cause people to walk out and then argue about the film on the sidewalk.…I think we're all [meaning all the directors up for an Oscar with him in 2006] seeking dissension, and we love to affect an audience."[32] Like other parables, it was not the presence of certain themes that was thought most important by Haggis, but the movie's ability to effect transformation in the audience.

In 2006, award winning movies that invited parabolic interpretation included *Babel, Little Children, The Last King of Scotland, The Lives of Others,* and even *Little Miss Sunshine*. In 2007 *Juno* proved to be not just a quirky story about unwed teenage pregnancy but a parable that invited viewers to consider the sanctity of human life. (Similarly, *Knocked Up* and *Waitress* were two other movies from 2006 that challenged cultural expectations through story lines that rejected abortion and invited and teased out a reevaluation of the sanctity of life.) Also in 2007, *No Country for Old Men* and *The Bourne Ultimatum* told stories that despite their differences both shocked readers into reconsidering whether some humans are beyond redemption. Paul Thomas Anderson's masterful *There Will Be Blood* also presented viewers with a parable—a story whose plot centered on the consequences of greed, whether in oil or in religion, but more deeply forced viewers also to consider our country's involvement in Iraq and Christianity's sometime lust for power. Who are we really as Americans?

In every case, these were movie stories with intent, stories that left interpretation open to the viewer much as Jesus's parables did (and do), but also stories that invited viewers not just to be edified—to learn something—but to be transformed by what they saw. Invited into the lives of characters dealing with life's enigmas and extremities, the audiences of these movies were not merely entertained; they were also shaped by what they saw. For it was the intention of these filmic storytellers to challenge us as viewers—even to seek our transformation, as their stories (1) of everyday life (2) grabbed our attention, (3) inviting a thick interpretation that challenged our regnant understandings, and (4) opened us up to transformative, and at times transcendent, insight.

An Example of Film as Parable: *Stranger than Fiction*

But having suggested this cross-section of parabolic films, it will be helpful in conclusion to test our fourfold description by drilling deeper, by exegeting in some detail a recent movie that might be described as a parable. For could it not be that the descriptor "parable" as applied to a given film is simply being used suggestively to evoke a spiritual aura, or to highlight the teaching of human themes, in the process investing in that film a certain spiritual authority? That is, could it not be, when all is said and done, that "parable" when applied to film is more a tonal word—one lacking real content or specificity, one used only to create a certain pious effect? My argument is that this is not the case. But reflection in some detail on *Stranger than Fiction* (2006) will allow us to assess whether specific characteristics can be assigned to film as parable.[33]

An everyday story. Life often can become lost in routine—the same route to work; the same coffee at Starbucks; even the same pew at church! Harold Crick (Will Ferrell), the main character in Marc Forster's wonderfully droll movie, *Stranger than Fiction,* is simply an extreme example of the lives many of us lead. Everything has been reduced to a mathematical formula in his life— Crick counts the number of strokes he takes to brush his teeth each morning and the number of steps he walks to the bus stop.[34] His constant companion is his watch, which helps him compulsively track the minutes he spends at lunch and on coffee breaks. Harold, not surprisingly, works as an auditor for the IRS.

That grabs the viewer's attention. Except for his friend Dave at work, Harold speaks to few people. He spends most of his life alone. Then one day, he begins to hear a woman's voice speaking in his head and narrating his own life. The narrator turns out to be Karen Eiffel (a superb Emma Thompson), an accomplished, although reclusive, mystery writer with eight novels to her credit. Her latest, *Death and Taxes* (life's two "givens"), has remained unfinished for a decade because she cannot figure out an appropriate way to kill off her main character—a plot twist that has become a trademark in each of her other stories. Desperate to overcome her writer's block, she is the perfect complement to Harold's neurosis. When we first meet her, Eiffel is balancing on the edge of her desk trying to imagine jumping off a roof. She sits in the rain with Penny Escher (Queen Latifah), her personal assistant, watching cars pass over a bridge and imagining an accident. But an ending to her novel does not present itself.

The movie goes back and forth between the stories of these two lonely, neurotic people. But actually, it is only one story, for the main character in Eiffel's story is none other than Harold Crick. At first the voice in his head is simply a nuisance. But then he hears the woman say, "Little did he know it would lead to his imminent death." Such foreshadowing would grab anyone's attention. It certainly does Harold. Is his life trajectory destined?

Inviting a metaphoric interpretation that challenges regnant understandings. The basic tension in the movie is thus clearly drawn: Is the story Karen's or Harold's? Who is really in control? Is the story character driven, or is it rooted in the point of view of the narrator? Is Harold a puppet, or is he free to act? Free will or providence? Harold is desperate to know, and Karen is paralyzed to act. Harold, thus, seeks the advice of a psychiatrist (Linda Hunt) who diagnoses him as a schizophrenic. He challenges her diagnosis by asking: "But what if I'm part of a story, a narrative?" to which she responds facetiously, "I don't know, I'd send you to someone who knows literature." So Harold lands at the door of Professor Jules Hilbert (Dustin Hoffman), an expert in literary theory. Hilbert gives Harold a test to narrow down the genres and archetypes of his story, and then suggests that Harold try to figure out whether his life is a tragedy or a comedy. The exchanges between Harold and the professor are filled with clever, understated humor. Viewers both laugh and groan as the teaching profession is skewered. It is a delight (even for me, a professor by trade).

And so the movie's set-up is complete. On one level, it is a story about the artistic process. Following up on his wonderful exploration of the imagination in *Finding Neverland*, a fictional account of J. M. Barrie, the creator of Peter Pan, director Marc Forster "asks" what happens when an artist comes to care about her creation so much that her affection begins to color the shape of her imaginative creation. Is there a necessary shape to a story, a narrative arc that the creator must follow? Or do a character's actions and attitudes invite the plot to develop in surprising ways?

Opening viewers up to transformative and at times transcendent insight. Such questions are not simply pedantic and abstract, to be left in the literature classroom; rather, they also have to do with our own stories. Are our stories told by a master storyteller? Are our personal stories defined as "comedies" or "tragedies" apart from our own efforts, or do we give shape to our destinies? Or can it be both? The movie's literary conceit turns out to be the context for reflection on the narrative shape of our own lives: free will or providence?

The movie's surface story is not only about the artistic process, however. It is also about love—about the compelling power of a new affection. Harold discovers love while auditing Ana Pascal (Maggie Gyllenhaal), a Harvard Law School dropout turned baker. Even as they spar, the chemistry between Harold and Ana is delightful. When Harold finally gives in and eats one of Ana's chocolate chip cookies, the sensuality of the moment is palpable. We watch Harold's slow transformation as he realizes that life is not work and work is not life. Harold gives Ana an assortment of "flours" (pun intended); he asks her out on a date and plays her a two-chord song he has just learned on his guitar. Harold might be a beginner, but he knows life can be fuller. Somehow schedules no longer matter and his watch no longer controls.

But *Stranger than Fiction* is more than its surface narrative; it invites and compels a thicker interpretation. The movie might remind some, for example, of the book of Ecclesiastes. Wisdom (Professor Hilbert), fame (Karen Eiffel), and work (Harold Crick) prove vain, ephemeral, meaningless. Life cannot be parsed; it is more than a formula. Nevertheless, we are reminded that two are better than one, and that life is a gift to be savored—like freshly baked cookies with a glass of milk.

It should be clear that this Will Ferrell movie is a far cry from his comedic portrayals of an elf (*Elf*, 2003), a race-car driver (*Talladega Nights*, 2006), and an ice skater (*Blades of Glory*, 2007). Perhaps this is why the film was largely ignored when it first came out. Those expecting the broad, physical, sophomoric humor of Ferrell that was honed on *Saturday Night Live* were either disappointed or stayed away. True, the movie abounds in humor, but here it serves a larger purpose and remains understated and ironic (think of Bill Murray in *Lost in Translation* [2003], Jim Carrey in *The Truman Show* [1998], or Adam Sandler in *Punch Drunk Love* [2002]). Intelligent, poignant, heartfelt, real—this parable invites our personal introspection and response.

We will all die. That is a given. The question is only, how then should we live? And who is in charge of providing answers to this query? These are the questions that Harold Crick must face, even as they become the viewer's questions as well. As the movie ends, we hear the narrator in a voiceover addressing his audience, while incidents from Harold's life appear on the screen:

> Sometimes when we lose ourselves in fear and despair, in routine and constancy, in hopelessness and tragedy, we can thank God for Bavarian sugar cookies [we see Ana bringing Harold cookies in the hospital where he has landed after sav-

ing a boy who was about to be hit by a bus]…for a familiar hand on the skin [Ana touches Harold], or a kind and loving gesture [Harold sends his friend Dave to his dream—Space Camp], or a subtle encouragement [Karen is given non-smoking patches by her assistant Penny], or a loving embrace [the boy on the bicycle is hugged by his father], or an offer of comfort [by coworkers of the bus driver who hit Harold], not to mention hospital gurneys [which are shown], and nose plugs [Hilbert swims with them], and uneaten Danish, soft spoken secrets [Harold and Ana whisper in bed], and Fender Stratocasters [Harold plays this guitar in a store], and maybe the occasional piece of fiction [Harold reading Eiffel's manuscript on the bus]. And we must remember that all these things, the nuances, the anomalies, the subtleties, which we assume only accessorize our lives, are in fact here for a much larger and nobler cause. They are here to save our lives. I know the idea sounds strange, but I also know it happens to be true.

So a movie that asks the question, "What is the meaning of Harold Crick's life?" answers by recognizing that as someone else is providentially in charge of the story, best for all of us to enjoy while we can our portion in life, both its big and small pleasures. As Harold discovered, we need to give thanks for Bavarian sugar cookies (and for the one who baked them), for these are the gifts that offer meaning in our short little lives.

This article is offered as a small expression of thanks to Klyne Snodgrass for his long-time friendship and hospitality. Klyne's generosity of spirit toward others, combined with his rigor in scholarship and pedagogy, is a rare combination that has taught me much. His commitments to family, friends, and faith continue to be personally inspirational. Thanks, Klyne.

Endnotes

1. For a fuller description of these events, see Terry Lindvall, *The Silents of God: Selected Issues and Documents in Silent American Film and Religion, 1908-1925* (Lanham, MD: Scarecrow, 2001), 7-8, 44-78.

2. Ibid., 44-78.

3. Ibid., 56.

4. Kenneth R. Morefield, "Last Temptation Turns Twenty-Five," *Christianity Today*, accessed August 9, 2013, http://www.christianitytoday.com/ct/2013/august-web-only/last-temptation-of-christ.html.

5. Klyne Snodgrass, *Stories with Intent: A Comprehensive Guide to the Parables of Jesus*

(Grand Rapids: Eerdmans, 2008).

6. Ibid., 1.

7. Ibid., 7.

8. Ibid.

9. Ibid., 8.

10. Ibid.

11. Ibid.

12. Ibid., 2.

13. Ibid., 9.

14. Ibid., 8.

15. Ibid., 30-31; cf. 17-22.

16. Paul Ricoeur, "Love and Justice," in *Figuring the Sacred: Religion, Narrative, and Imagination* (Minneapolis: Fortress, 1995), 329, quoted in Matthew Rindge, "Narratives of Disorientation, Stories of Subversion: The Rhetorical Power of Jesus' Parables," (unpublished manuscript), 27.

17. Ibid., 21.

18. Robert J. Palma, "Theological Parables in Paul Schrader's Films," *Perspectives* (August/September 2001): 13-15, 18.

19. Ibid., 14.

20. Ibid., 18.

21. Jeremy Punt, "The Prodigal Son and *Blade Runner*: Fathers and Sons, and Animosity," *Journal of Theology for Southern Africa* 128 (July 2007): 86-103.

22. See Larry Kreitzer, *Pauline Images in Fiction and Film: On Reversing the Hermeneutical Flow*, The Biblical Seminar 61 (Sheffield: Sheffield Academic Press, 1999).

23. Punt, "Prodigal Son and Blade Runner," 103.

24. Ibid., 95.

25. Christopher Deacy, "Integration and Rebirth through Confrontation: *Fight Club* and *American Beauty* as Contemporary Religious Parables," *Journal of Contemporary Religion* 17, no. 1 (2002): 61-73.

26. Ibid., 61.

27. Ibid., 62.

28. Ibid., 66.

29. Ibid., 67.

30. Cosmo Landesman, quoted in ibid.

31. Ibid., 71.

32. Paul Haggis, quoted in *Newsweek*, February 6, 2006, 62.

33. A shorter version of this reflection on *Stranger than Fiction* was first written for a review in *The Covenant Companion*, November 2007, 26-27. I have adapted it for my purposes here, but the basic fourfold parabolic shape remains as originally written.

34. The filmmaker has even chosen historical names for his characters who were associated with mathematics in real life: Crick discovered DNA; Eiffel was the architect of the Eiffel Tower; Escher is an artist known for fantastic linear designs; even Hilbert might be a

reference to mathematician David Thilbert, whose ideas influences quantum mechanics. See Peter Chattaway, "Stranger than Fiction," *Christianity Today*, accessed December 6, 2006, http://www.christianitytoday.com/movies/reviews/2006/strangerthanfiction.html.

The Wheat and the Weeds,
the Kingdom, and the World

Darrell L. Bock

At the center of Jesus's teaching is the kingdom of God. It is one of the few topics on which there is virtually absolute consensus about Jesus. It also is a major topic of his parables. Klyne Snodgrass's *Stories with Intent* lists six parables whose main topic is the kingdom (growing seed, wheat and weeds, mustard seed, leaven, treasure, and pearl).[1] However, other parables also contain the kingdom as a topic because the kingdom makes us accountable to God. So, all of the parables about future eschatology also connect to this theme (net, faithful and unfaithful servant, ten virgins, talents or minas, sheep and the goats). It is this "claim on the world" dimension of the kingdom I wish to address, exploring how the New Testament idea of the kingdom as arrival is sometimes underappreciated, as is its claim on the world. This means that our conception of the kingdom may need to be both narrowed and broadened simultaneously.

The Kingdom as Arriving

Sometimes the claim is made that the kingdom of God has always been with us. In one sense, this is certainly the case. The Old Testament in particular affirms, especially in the Psalter, the rule of God, an expression of the fact that God sits over the universe as creator. So we read in Psalm 45:6 that "Your throne, O God, endures forever and ever. Your royal scepter is a scepter of equity...." Psalm 103:19 declares: "The Lord has established his throne in the heavens and his kingdom rules over all." In other texts such as Psalm 114:2, Israel is called God's kingdom. Yet Psalm 145 goes cosmic again, as verses 11-13 affirm: "They shall speak of the glory of your kingdom, and tell of your power, to make known to all people your mighty deeds, and the glorious splendor of your kingdom. Your kingdom is an everlasting kingdom, and your dominion endures throughout all generations."

So there is a sense in which God's existence as the creator and ruler of heaven means his kingdom is always with us. But the creation is dysfunctional. God's right to rule is not recognized by all. Creation is out of kilter. Nevertheless, the faithful have hope that alignment and peace might one day be restored. This stands behind and anticipates the hope of the kingdom and the Old Testament promises. Those who had such hope sensed the kingdom was not yet what it should be. This kind of hope is vividly expressed in Daniel 2, where a kingdom made not with hands replaces the strangely described and terrifying kingdoms of the world (Daniel 2:44). The hope of a universal restoration and accountability enhances the picture of the saints' vindication, expressed in the imagery of the Son of Man receiving authority from the Ancient of Days in Daniel 7.

This background is important because it means that what the kingdom has been is not what the kingdom will be. The disjunction produced the hope for a better world, a more comprehensively visible manifestation and acknowledgment of God's presence in it. The hope of this promised kingdom's arrival means that whatever the kingdom was and has been is not all the kingdom will be. There was a longing for something more, something Jesus noted that kings and prophets had longed to see (Matthew 13:17; Luke 10:24). When John the Baptist said the kingdom of God is near, he invoked this hope. When Jesus teaches through the parables, he raises this expectation.

Usually, when people speak of God's kingdom we equate it with the church: we bring people into the kingdom, or we expand the kingdom, or we help the kingdom to grow. I would argue that the kingdom, at least in some of its dimensions, is bigger than the church. It has a claim on the world. In fact, that claim is part of the premise for preaching the kingdom and taking that message into the world. When John and Jesus announce the kingdom's arrival, it is not merely a place where people are called out of the world to come into this new arriving hope; it is also a reality whose shadow and presence extends to fill the creation, making it imperative that every soul responds to its coming.

The Parable of the Wheat and the Weeds

We see this hope expressed most clearly in the parable of the wheat and the weeds. Snodgrass asks: "Is this a parable about the mixed nature of the church, as is often assumed?" The question connects with the observation just made that often we equate kingdom and church. When we do so, we may be missing something. Another question Snodgrass raises about this parable in Matthew 13 also applies: "What is the relation of the kingdom of heaven (v. 24), the world (v. 38), the kingdom of the Son of Man (v. 41), and the kingdom of the Father (v. 43)?"[2] Fortunately, this parable is one of the few that has an interpretation tied to it, so some elements of what we are exploring are given to us for reflection.[3] After all, that is what parables seek to do, to move us to contemplate, ponder, and meditate over the meaning and importance of what Jesus is teaching.

Before Jesus gets to this parable, he has noted how the parables about the kingdom in Matthew 13 disclose mysteries about the kingdom. Surely one of those mysteries is that the kingdom is arriving, but evil is not being eradicated with its coming. That awaits a later time, as this parable also affirms. The eschatological hope among Second Temple Jews who looked for something more to come expected the kingdom's arrival to mean the defeat of evil, an anticipated immediate defeat. One can see this hope in texts like 1QS 4:15-26 or Psalms of Solomon 17:21-23.

Snodgrass notes that many read this parable as being about the mixed nature of the church community. Interestingly, this kind of interpretation ranges from critical New Testament scholars to conservative interpreters, including dispensational commentators. Also interesting are the almost opposite points made from that reading. Daniel Patte argues that the vocation of fighting evil in the church is prohibited by this teaching.[4] On the other hand, some dispensationalists argue that we should not be surprised about the presence of evil in the church, even as one contends for its righteousness and purity in resisting evil.[5] Their point is not that resistance should not be undertaken, but that eradication of evil will not come completely until the end.

But is this kind of mixed-community reading even on the right track? Snodgrass states it clearly: "The parable is not about the mixed character of the church but about the fact that the righteous and sinners coexist in the world—even when the kingdom is present."[6] I would like to tweak this correct and crucial observation a bit. I would argue that the kingdom does not merely come in alongside a divided world, it invades it and casts its shadow over all of it. There is an effective presence of God's rule in the kingdom that takes place among those who opt into it by faith and enter into the kingdom. But the claim and reach of the kingdom in terms of its presence and accountability extends across the entire creation. The background of kingdom hope and how it addressed creation's dysfunction through redemption, as mentioned at the start of this essay, cannot be forgotten when one reads Matthew 13.

So where does this emphasis on the kingdom's claim on the world come from? It is found by observing one crucial part of the parable's interpretation:

that the field where the kingdom is active is the world (Matthew 13:38). Two groups of people exist in this field: people of the kingdom and people of the evil one. However, the people of the evil one are not outside the kingdom's reach and accountability, for it is in the judgment at the end that all will be made to answer for the kingdom's presence. Judgment, wherever it appears in Scripture, is always about the reestablishment of justice and peace in a dysfunctional world, the righting of a listing ship. It is cosmic in scope and has the nations in view, not just Israel alone. It is this slot into which this parable and this detail fit. Matthew 24:30-31 is parallel in this regard.

We are arguing that the "parable makes an implicit claim for the authority of the Son of Man over the world."[7] However, we also would suggest that this authority is one the Son of Man has because he has authority over the kingdom, received from the Father. So although the kingdom is an entity distinct from the world, it is an entity invading the world and gradually casting its shadow over it, a shadow that one day the Son of Man will make quite apparent when the light of a righteous judgment shines on everyone with darkness purged. This leads me to reject Snodgrass's idea that the kingdom of the Son of Man is somehow proleptic and incomplete because evil is not eradicated yet. This is where I want to tweak his exemplary treatment of this text. As he so clearly states, "its primary teaching is that the kingdom is present despite the presence of evil *and* that evil will be dealt with at the judgment."[8] What we see here is what we always see with Jesus's kingdom teaching: the kingdom comes in stages and reflects a process by which the arrival of consummation takes place over time. I would wish to add one additional point more explicitly to the key theme—although evil is present and present to the end, it is accountable to the kingdom and its king, so the kingdom has a claim on the world it enters to restore.[9] In the next section, I will argue how the imagery of this parable coheres with other kingdom parable ideas. Its meaning becomes clear in the narrative sequence of additional kingdom parables.

The Parables of the Mustard Seed and the Leaven

It is interesting and no accident that the parables that intervene between the parable of the wheat and weeds and the giving of its interpretation are the parables of the mustard seed and of the leaven (Matthew 13:31-35). These parables picture how the kingdom starts surprisingly and mysteriously as something small, but eventually becomes either a large place of residence or that which permeates the whole. Each parable makes the point that what starts out seemingly insignificant and small ends up being big.

It seems wise to ask if the intervening role of these parables interacts with the parable of the wheat and weeds. The suggestion is that they do. They depict the process of the kingdom's arrival to its consummation. The move is from a seemingly small presence with a shadow of accountability on the world to covering that world. In the end, Jesus is saying the kingdom will be the place to reside, just as birds seek shelter in tree branches, and it will be the only place to reside, as the kingdom in the end will permeate the entire "loaf" of existence. If we ask why the parables of the mustard seed and leaven are located between the telling of the parable of the wheat and weeds and its interpretation, this link connects the dots.

This means that the kingdom is a place in the midst of the world, but its reach extends outside of itself. One has to deal with the kingdom whether one opts in or not. One day the kingdom will deal with all the earth's inhabitants, whether they are righteous or evil. It also means one can distinguish between where the kingdom is active and effective—among its followers—and where its authority extends—having a claim on all. The dynamic helps to explain why the mission of those in the kingdom is to proclaim the kingdom message, to sow seed in the field of the world to those outside of it but within its authority. The hope is that they will enter into the place where God's rule is experienced in deliverance, not judgment. The kingdom then has two dimensions: one of benefit to those who enter into it and one of authority that extends even over those who refuse to enter in or are not a part of the effective kingdom that comes from responding to it.

Conclusion

At the opening of my essay I noted how our understanding of the kingdom may need narrowing and broadening at the same time. It needs narrowing in that the claim of the promised kingdom is not the same as the universal kingdom claim of the Old Testament, although it moves along a trajectory that connects to that universal claim. What comes with Jesus is new, but it also is restorative. This restorative element reveals where the broadening occurs. For not only does the kingdom program, small as it is at the start, look to restore and reflect God's claim of universal authority, it extends that claim to every creature of God and will show that scope at the consummation. The kingdom is bigger than the church. It has a real claim on the world.

The kingdom is about God's invasion into his disruptive creation to redeem what has been lost. The parable of the wheat and weeds gives us a glimpse of how Jesus showed the comprehensive extent of this restorative kingdom program. The introduction of one feature not commonly present in his parables, that the field is the world, is no minor detail. Fortunately it was interpreted as present for us, disclosing key elements of the mystery of the kingdom. The kingdom does not eradicate evil immediately, but it still makes a claim on all until the time of consummation. The kingdom is not merely arriving in the world, it is invading it and is in the process of manifesting itself across the whole of the creation, whether one accepts it or not. The hope is that many will see and respond to their creator, in part because they sense they are his creatures made in his image. Regardless, the promised kingdom of God brings justice and shalom one day because it is a place where all will render an account. It may start as a little leaven, but one day the kingdom will be in the whole of creation. Here is one very profound reason why Jesus's kingdom message was for the world, because the kingdom enters into the world to contend for its well-being and cast the authoritative shadow of God's presence over it. This story is about God's mission as well as mystery. Truly this parable is a story with intent.

Endnotes

1. Klyne Snodgrass, *Stories with Intent: A Comprehensive Guide to the Parables of Jesus* (Grand Rapids: Eerdmans, 2008), Contents. All citations are from the Kindle version and reflect its pagination.

2. The two questions presented in this paragraph are from *Stories with Intent*, 191.

3. The sower and net are the other parables with interpretation.

4. Daniel Patte, *The Gospel According to Matthew* (Philadelphia: Fortress, 1987), 194.

5. A simple check of notes in the Scofield Bible on Matthew 13 will find this reading.

6. Snodgrass, 202.

7. Ibid., 211.

8. Ibid., 212, emphasis his.

9. This idea is implicit in what Snodgrass says, but I think it is actually part of what makes the parable so important—an explanation of how the kingdom enters the world and why evil is not eliminated with its coming.

PAUL

Faith Working through Love (Galatians 5:6)
The Role of Human Deeds in Salvation in Luther and Calvin's Exegesis[1]

Stephen J. Chester

Twentieth-Century Exegesis of Galatians 5:6 in Relation to Luther and Calvin's Exegesis

In his 1988 monograph *Obeying the Truth*, John Barclay explains what he perceives as the reasons for the comparative neglect of chapters 5 and 6 of Galatians and their ethical content in twentieth-century exegesis:

> [I]t is a by-product of the "Lutheran" theological consensus. If one considers that the main thrust of Paul's attacks on "works of the law" is against human works and achievement, one is apt to conclude that his specific ethical instructions are merely an appendix or, perhaps, an attempt to prevent himself from being misunderstood as antinomian. To give these instructions any more integral place would be to admit that Paul also is concerned to promote works.[2]

The force of the charge can be illustrated by looking at the exposition of Galatians published in 1981 by the great Luther scholar and theologian Gerhard Ebeling (1912-2001). In *The Truth of the Gospel*,[3] chapters 1-4 occupy more than 230 pages, whereas chapters 5-6 occupy a mere 25 pages. Ebeling treats Galatians 5-6 as *parenesis*, ethical exhortation that is an integral part of Paul's letter, and genuinely important in that theology must always be lived, but that nevertheless is subsidiary to the earlier doctrinal sections of the letter. Ebeling does note some new accents in 5:1-12, including the introduction of *agapē* (love) at 5:6, and he does highlight the connection back to 2:20 where Paul speaks of Christ's love displayed in the self-giving of the cross. Yet these observations are not at all extensive and the impression is left that Paul's argument is already essentially complete at the end of Galatians 4.

The irony of this recent episode in the history of interpretation is that it is quite anomalous in a longer perspective. It is the purpose of this essay to argue that early Protestant exegesis is far more concerned than is often allowed to embrace Paul's concern to promote works. For far from downplaying works in Galatians 5-6 in general, or more particularly experiencing embarrassment at Paul's use of the verb *energeō* ("I work, I effect") in Galatians 5:6, it mattered profoundly to Luther, Calvin, and other early Protestant interpreters to insist loudly and at length that faith works. In their view this is an essential aspect of the nature of faith without which faith is not truly faith. In his *Table Talk* from the year 1533, Luther is recorded as expressing this succinctly: "Paul's view is this: Faith is active in love, that is, that faith justifies which expresses itself in acts."[4] Luther's opinion had already been memorably rendered into English by Tyndale, who in 1525 had translated Galatians 5:6 with the words, "For in Jesu Christ nether is circumcision eny thynge worth nether yet uncircumcision but fayth which by love is myghty in operacion."[5]

Faith Formed by Love: Medieval Exegesis of Galatians 5:6

The reason for the strength of this insistence that justifying faith is inherently active is not hard to find. It lies in the history of medieval exegesis of the verse. Confronted by the need to coordinate the statements of James that faith without works is dead (2:17) and that even the demons believe and tremble (2:19) with Paul's statements here in Galatians 5:6, medieval interpreters developed a distinction between two different kinds of faith: formed and unformed. From Peter Lombard in the twelfth century onward, unformed faith is understood as a cognitive acceptance of the facts of the gospel which does not of itself justify. It is "a 'quality of mind' (*qualitas mentis*) but one that remains 'unformed' because it lacks the shaping effect of love or charity."[6] This unformed faith soon becomes identified with what is received in the sacrament of baptism and the transition to a formed faith is identified with the sacrament of penance: "Forming faith meant persuading people to put the faith into practice by way of charity or penance, and restraining or absolving them from mortal sin."[7] The distinction correlates perfectly with medieval understandings of justification in which the Christian always remains rooted in the grace received at baptism but must cooperate with this grace in producing good works in order eventually to merit heaven on the basis of what he or she has become. It is thus only faith formed by love that can be identified with justifying faith, because only formed faith can act in meritorious ways as part of the Christian's lifelong journey towards righteousness.

This pattern can be seen in the exegesis of the very greatest of Paul's medieval interpreters. Thomas Aquinas perceives the role of faith within the process of justification as that of the gift of beatifying knowledge. It is a foretaste of the knowledge of God that will be possessed in eternal life.[8] In his exegesis of Galatians 5:6, Aquinas takes faith working through love to refer to "faith, not unformed, but the kind that worketh by charity: 'Faith without works is dead' (James 2:26). For faith is a knowledge of the word of God 'That Christ may dwell by faith in your hearts' (Ephesians 3:17)—which word is not perfectly possessed or perfectly known unless the love which it hopes for is possessed."[9] The right kind of faith is clearly here a personal knowledge in relationship and not simply a factual knowledge, but Aquinas does not deal with this tension by refusing to categorize solely factual knowledge as faith, or arrive at a similar destination by terming it dead faith. Instead Aquinas refers to faith that is "unformed," clearly implying that only faith formed by love justifies, and also raising the possibility of faith that is in some sense truly faith but which is of lesser value and which does not justify. Aquinas has here moved exegetically beyond the widespread insistence, stretching back to Augustine, that faith never comes alone and into a distinction between two kinds of faith: one formed by love and capable of meritorious deeds, the other lacking this formation and incapable of merit. To read Galatians 5:6 in this way thus provided the starting-point for a crucial theological distinction: "all the masters followed essentially one scriptural text (Galatians 5:6)."[10] Yet once one text was read in this way, it also proved possible to apply the distinction to other texts. Paul's statement at Romans 1:17 that in the gospel the righteousness of God is revealed "from faith to faith" is identified by Nicholas of Lyra in the fourteenth century with the transition from unformed to formed faith. Aquinas himself did not reach this particular exegetical conclusion, but he had insisted that Paul's quotation of Habakkuk 2:5, "The righteous shall live by faith," refers to faith formed by love.[11]

Faith That Works: The Reformation Reaction to Medieval Exegesis of Galatians 5:6

From very early in his career Luther is robust in dismissing as misguided the entire distinction between unformed and formed faith. In his *Lectures on Romans* in 1515 he rejects Nicholas of Lyra's interpretation of Romans 1:17. In his first Galatians commentary, published in 1519, Luther suggests in his remarks on Galatians 5:6 that Paul simply intends to indicate that faith only exists if it is sincere and genuine: "Therefore he who hears the Word of God sincerely and clings to Him in faith is at once also clothed with the Spirit of love, as Paul has said above, 'Did you receive the Spirit by works of the law, or by hearing with faith' (Galatians 3:2)? For if you hear Christ sincerely, it is impossible for you not to love Him forthwith, since He has done and borne so much for you."[12] By the time of his Galatians commentary of 1535, Luther expresses similar sentiments at much greater length. He finds it monstrous that his opponents teach that unformed faith is at once both a divine gift and yet not able to justify since it requires to be formed by love: "Who could stand for the teaching that faith, the gift of God that is infused in the heart by the Holy Spirit, can coexist with mortal sin…to believe this way about infused faith is to admit openly that they understand nothing about faith."[13] He also appeals to what he regards as the basic sense of Paul's words: "Paul does not make faith unformed here, as though it were a shapeless chaos without the power to be or to do anything; but he attributes the working itself to faith rather than to love.…He does not say 'Love is effective.' No, he says: 'Faith is effective.' He does not say: 'Love works.' No, he says: 'Faith works.' He makes love the tool through which faith works."[14] Although Luther does not say so, these points clearly rely on taking the participle *energoumenē* as middle rather than passive. If passive it could be taken as saying that faith "is made effective through love." Yet while some patristic writers do take the participle as passive the majority of commentators in all eras, including most pertinently the Latin of the Vulgate itself, and therefore also many medieval advocates of the doctrine of faith formed by love, take it as middle.[15] Luther's argument is that when the participle is so taken as middle in voice, Paul's words do not easily speak of faith as something passive or unformed but as something active and working.

With minor variations Luther's arguments are made again and again by other early Protestant commentators. There is a shared repeated insistence that what their opponents called unformed faith is not faith at all. Melanchthon is typical when he writes in 1521 that, "For pedagogical reasons I used to call that which was acquired and incomplete, 'historical faith'; now I do not call it faith at all, but merely opinion.…That Parisian quality, which is even in the godless and in despisers of God, cannot be called faith."[16] Calvin writes in the 1541 French edition of the *Institutes* that, "the consent of faith is of the heart rather than of the head, of the affection rather than of the understanding. For that reason faith is called obedience, which the Lord prefers to all other service (Romans 1[5])."[17] Of course, having insisted that faith works while also teaching that justification is not by works, the Reformers do have to explain how they hold together these two convictions. Calvin expresses the case concisely in his *Commentary on Galatians*: "It is not our doctrine that the faith which justifies is alone. We maintain that it is always joined with good works. But we contend that faith avails by itself for justification."[18] That faith alone justifies but that justifying faith is never alone and always brings with it good works is a refrain frequently repeated. Good works characterized by love are either integral to justification or distinct but inseparable from it, even though such works are never an effective cause of justification. The relationship between faith and love found in medieval exegesis has been reversed. In medieval interpretation faith was initially unformed and lacking in vitality and true faith followed on from the presence of love. But for the Reformers it is true faith that comes first and produces works of love. Luther writes that true and living faith "arouses and motivates good works through love....He who wants to be a true Christian or to belong to the kingdom of Christ must be truly a believer. But he does not truly believe if works of love do not follow his faith."[19]

This distinction between faith as alone justifying and justifying faith as never remaining alone but always producing good works is safeguarded exegetically by the insistence, which appears prominently in the remarks of both Luther and Calvin, that at Galatians 5:6 Paul is *not* in fact here discussing justification. When Paul speaks of waiting for "the hope of righteousness" in the previous verse (5:5), Luther interprets the statement as eschatological. It is the hope of future freedom from the sin that during their earthly lives clings to the flesh of those who have already been justified. Calvin seems to imply something similar when he says that Paul's words probably "denote perseverance: 'Let us continue steadfastly in the hope (*fiducia*) of righteousness which we obtain by faith.'"[20] Thus the noun *dikaiosunē* (righteousness) here has a specific ethical meaning that distinguishes it from other uses of the term by Paul in discussions of justification. In contrast, for the Reformers *pistis* (faith) is always simply true and living faith or it is not faith, but its consistency is to be understood against the backdrop of its relevance to all aspects and phases of Christian existence. Luther says that "Paul is describing the whole of the Christian life in this passage: inwardly it is faith toward God, and outwardly it is love or works towards one neighbor. Thus a man is a Christian in a total sense: inwardly through faith in the sight of God, who does not need our works; outwardly in the sight of men, who do not derive any benefit from faith but do derive benefit from works or from our love."[21] Thus the works of love produced by faith do not count before God in relation to justification, but in Luther's view this by no means empties them of significance since they are of the essence of Christianity in the relationship of the believer with other human beings. Calvin produces a similar emphasis on the all-embracing nature of faith through the sharpness of his distinction between justification and sanctification and an assertion that faith is just as relevant to sanctification as it is to justification: "But we deny that true faith can be separated from the Spirit of regeneration. When we debate justification, however, we exclude all works."[22]

It is therefore plain that the Reformers' antipathy to works is specific and focused. They object to any and all attributions of merit to works in relation to justification. Here work is irrelevant and righteousness is to be received passively as a gift from God. This does not mean, however, that works or human activity are being denigrated in general or that passivity is being enshrined in general as the correct disposition for human beings to adopt in relation to God. For while righteousness is passive, and while Luther makes central to his famous preface to the 1535 Galatians commentary the distinction between this and the false active righteousness taught by his opponents, the faith that justifies is inherently active and working. To receive passive justifying righteousness is in fact to be equipped to work: "When I have this righteousness within me, I descend from heaven like the rain that makes the earth fertile. That is, I come forth into another kingdom, and I perform good works whenever the opportunity arises."[23] Luther makes it clear that aside from this righteousness of faith he does not accord any general valuation to working or not working in his comment that, "Whatever there is in us besides Him (Christ)—whether it be intellect or will, activity or passivity etc.—is flesh not Spirit."[24] What matters as regards human conduct is not any particular quality as a disposition but rather how it is related to Christ.

Faith That Works in Christ: Galatians 5:6 and Union with Christ

To say this takes us, for both Luther and Calvin, to the Christological heart of the matter. In his 1535 commentary Luther establishes the priority of Christology long before he gets to 5:6 by attacking the distinction between formed and unformed faith in his comments on Galatians 2:16. He says of the scholastic theologians that:

> Where they speak of love, we speak of faith. And while they say that faith is the mere outline but love is its living colors and completion, we say in opposition that faith takes hold of Christ and that He is the form that adorns and informs faith as color does the wall. ... It takes hold of Christ in such a way that Christ is the object of faith, or rather not the object but, so to speak, the One who is present in the faith itself. Thus faith is a sort of knowledge or darkness that nothing can see. Yet the Christ of whom faith takes hold is sitting in this darkness as God sat in the midst of the darkness on Sinai and in the temple.[25]

Thus Luther's exegetical scheme is clear. At 2:16ff. Paul speaks of human faith as it relates to God and to justification. Faith justifies because it unites the believer with Christ, because it places the believer in Christ Jesus. At 5:6 Paul speaks in contrast of faith as it expresses itself in love of neighbor. Yet the faith spoken of is the same faith in both contexts. It is faith in which Christ is present and it is because of that presence that faith is able to work through love. The words "in Christ Jesus" with which 5:6 begins are therefore truly significant. Union with the one "who loved me and gave himself for me" (2:20) makes faith living and empowers the work of the Christian in loving the neighbor. For Luther, the structure of Paul's statements about faith in Galatians expresses the programmatic statement that he had made in 1520 in his tract *The Freedom of a Christian*: "a Christian lives not in himself, but in Christ and his neighbor. Otherwise he is not a Christian."[26]

Luther was to maintain this position even when close colleagues chose a different emphasis. For a number of reasons in the early 1530s, Philipp Melanchthon worried that Luther's way of stressing that which faith does risked implying that the works involved contributed to justification. Without wavering in his rejection of the scholastic distinction between formed and unformed faith, Melanchthon began to formulate justification in an exclusively relational manner.[27] For Melanchthon the crucial element is not so much that Christ is present in faith, but rather that on account of the merit of Christ's sacrificial death, the person of faith is declared innocent by God. Paul's forensic metaphors are thereby made central to understanding justification and the works performed by faith are rendered distinct from justification. They belong to a consequent aspect of renewal or sanctification and are not part of justification. In this sanctification that results from justification, faith works, and the believer is empowered by the indwelling of the Holy Spirit, but there is little direct response either here or in Melanchthon's account of justification to Paul's vocabulary of participation in Christ. The first and foremost reason that works must be done by the believer is the necessity of compulsion: "For although it is one thing to speak of compulsion, yet there does remain in force the eternal ordering of the immutable God that the creature shall render obedience to the will of God."[28] It is essential that works are done if faith is to be retained "because the Holy Spirit is driven out and grieved when we permit sins against conscience."[29] Faith can never be without works for Melanchthon, but unlike Luther he does not claim that to be active in works is a constitutive part of justifying faith.

That this is so for Luther can be seen most clearly from a dialogue with Melanchthon dating from 1536.[30] Rejecting all temptation to separate the works of the believer from justification, Luther seeks to explain his belief that the righteousness of works is necessary:

> It is necessary, however, not by a legal necessity, or one of compulsion, but by a gratuitous necessity, or one of consequence, or an unalterable condition. As the sun shines by necessity, if it is a sun, and yet does not shine by demand, but by its nature and its unalterable will, so to speak, because

it was created for the purpose that it should shine so a person created righteous performs new works by an unalterable necessity, not by legal compulsion. For to the righteous no law is given. Further, we are created, says Paul, unto good works... it is impossible to be a believer and not a doer.[31]

Luther returns to this point of the nature of the believer again and again. It is not that believers are made good by their works, but rather that their works are accepted because they are offered by believers. And if justifying faith is present then good works will result: "believers are new creatures, new trees; accordingly, the aforementioned demands of the law do not apply to them, *e.g., faith must do good works,* just as it is not proper to say: *the sun must shine, a good tree must produce good fruit, 3 + 7 must equal 10.* For the sun shines *de facto,* a good tree is fruitful *de facto,* 3 + 7 equal 10 *de facto.*"[32] Because faith works or it is not faith, so works cannot be excluded from discussion of justification by faith for "faith is a work of promise, or a gift of the Holy Spirit.... necessary, in order that the Law be fulfilled, but it is not obtained by the Law and its works."[33]

Calvin too expresses the central importance of union with Christ in his objections to the distinction between formed and unformed faith. Unformed faith is a simple impossibility:

> For, since faith receives Christ as He is offered by the Father—and He is offered, not only for righteousness, forgiveness of sins, and peace, but also for sanctification [1 Corinthians 1:30] and as a fountain of living water—faith certainly cannot properly know Him without grasping the sanctification of His Spirit. Or indeed, if someone wants to hear this even more clearly, faith is located in the knowledge of Christ, and Christ cannot be known without the sanctification of His Spirit; it follows that faith must never be separated from a good affection.[34]

In a sermon on Galatians 5:6 Calvin says that "Jesus Christ is the Redeemer. Faith means that each of us knows him to be our redeemer. Is this possible unless the Lord Jesus lives and reigns within us, causing his love to burn within us, that we might give ourselves solely to him?"[35] This strong sense that faith unites with Christ is also expressed in Calvin's comments on Galatians 2:20 where he says simply that "faith makes us partakers of everything it finds in Christ."[36] Christ is both righteous and holy and it is in union with him that righteousness and sanctification are received by the believer. That sanctification is by faith serves again to make the point that for Calvin as for Luther either faith works or it is not faith.

There are nevertheless certain differences between the two Reformers that must be noted. Unlike Luther, Calvin distinguishes clearly between justification, which he defines in strongly forensic terms, and sanctification. Works he assigns to sanctification. Yet justification and sanctification are for Calvin indissolubly linked and simultaneous aspects of union with Christ, the one never to be received without the other. Good works are not part of justification but they are always alongside justification and in union with Christ are not simply consequences of justification. Because justification and sanctification are in this way twin aspects of union with Christ, Calvin can speak of good works as a condition of salvation. Good works are not simply organic, with good trees automatically producing good fruit. This means that Calvin can give full weight to texts in which Paul stresses the obligation of believers to grow in obedience. When Paul says at 2 Corinthians 7:1 that he and his readers should "cleanse ourselves…making holiness perfect in the fear of God," Calvin comments: "It is of the very nature of God's promises that they summon us to sanctification, just as if God had inserted an implied condition."[37] At Philippians 3:10, where Paul expresses the wish to share in Christ's sufferings in order to attain the resurrection from the dead, Calvin says bluntly: "Let everyone, therefore, who has become through faith a partaker of all Christ's benefits, acknowledge that a condition is presented to him—that his whole life be conformed to His death."[38] Of course it is axiomatic for Calvin that the true believer will satisfy this condition of works. Calvin holds that the good works of the believer are fully those of the believer, for the exercise of the believer's will is essential to them. He also holds that such works are not in any sense meritorious, for the renewed will that enables such good works is the work of the Holy Spirit. The only explanation possible for blatant disregard for holiness is that a person is not genuinely a believer and has not truly been justified and renewed. Thus although the believer's good works are not meritorious and are not an effective cause of justification, they are for Calvin essential to salvation.

Yet despite such significant differences and the different theological concepts that embody them, Calvin's sense of the exegetical shape of Galatians remains similar to that of Luther. At 5:6 Paul speaks of sanctification, having spoken earlier in 2:16-21 and elsewhere of justification, but the faith involved is the same faith. It is living and works through love because it unites with Christ. Although there is for both Luther and Calvin a sense that 5:6 belongs to a different part of the argument from Paul's earlier discussion of justification by faith, they could not characterize the difference as that between doctrinal argument and *paranesis* or ethical instruction.[39] For them, the centrality of faith to the unfolding of Paul's argument in Galatians ensures that, although never an effective cause of justification, works of love remain either a constitutive part of justification (so Luther) or intimately and inseparably connected to justification (so Calvin). Like justification itself, works of love are Christologically grounded.

Faith That Works and Social Location

Finally, there is also for both Luther and Calvin a sociological pattern to the works that faith performs through love. Paul's assertion that what counts in Christ Jesus is not circumcision or uncircumcision but faith working through love prompts Luther to comment that

> [Paul] does not say: "That which makes a Christian is a cowl or fasting or vestments or ceremonies." But it is true faith toward God, which loves and helps one's neighbor—regardless of whether the neighbor is a servant, a master, a king, a pope, a man, a woman; one who wears purple, one who wears rags, one who eats meat, or one who eats fish. Not one of these things, not one, makes a man a Christian; only faith and love do so.[40]

Such statements are connected for Luther to his sense that divine love is not based on the nature of its object or on the potential of that object to become something good and lovable even if it is currently not so. In contrast to merely human or fleshly love, divine love is oriented not towards what is good and lovable, but instead towards what is bad or evil, and gives itself in spite of the unlovable nature of its object. This, of course, is what Christ did for human beings in his incarnation and crucifixion.[41] Therefore faith in which Christ is present and that works through love will have the same disinterested quality. In *Freedom of a Christian* Luther argues that "faith is truly active through love [Galatians 5:6], that is, finds expression in works of the freest service, cheerfully and lovingly done, with which a man willingly serves another without hope of reward; and for himself is satisfied with the fullness and wealth of his faith."[42]

In his preaching on Galatians 5:6 Calvin similarly argues that the contrast between a false regard for either circumcision or uncircumcision and a right emphasis upon faith working through love constitutes a rejection of the pomp of papist ceremonies. What counts is to love neighbor in truth and sincerity. He has already argued that the hope of righteousness in 5:5 implies that while God sees believers in Christ as without spot or stain, "Other folk scarcely condescend to look at them, except to give a fleeting glance…there is no pomp, no special show in the righteousness that comes from the Lord Jesus Christ.…It implies complete poverty."[43] This reflects the fact that for Calvin sanctification has two aspects: mortification and vivification. For the self that existed before faith to be put to death involves not only the crucifying of sinful desires but also sharing in Christ's suffering. Believers can expect their experience in the present life to be characterized by humiliation. The sociology of faith working through love is therefore highly polemical. In contrast to self-indulgent papist pomp the true believers concentrate on free service of neighbor (so Luther) and in contrast to self-indulgent papist pomp the true believers are not praised by the world but share in the rejection experienced by Christ (so Calvin). Nevertheless, despite the unhelpfulness of the polemic from a twenty-first century perspective, there remains a serious exegetical and Christological point. The direction in which faith works through love is first of all resolutely downwards towards what is low and despised because that is the direction of incarnation and crucifixion.

Conclusions

Our consideration of Luther and Calvin's exegesis of Galatians 5:6 therefore leads us to three conclusions.

1. In insisting that faith works, the two Reformers are not eliminating good works or human actions from their soteriology or expressing any general suspicion of works. In their view justifying faith always works, and no one is saved without works, even if it is also true that works do not justify. They retain works as integral even as they strive to ensure that works can never be regarded as an effective cause in justification.

2. The two Reformers' exegesis of Galatians 5:6 shows that for them faith is the key integrating term or concept in Paul's argument in the letter. It binds Paul's advice about Christian conduct to Christology no less than it binds his teaching about justification to Christology. Their treatment of 5:6 provides no warrant for later "Lutheran" approaches that subordinate *parenesis* to doctrine and therefore treat Galatians 5-6 as a subsidiary section of the letter. Luther and Calvin's exegesis provides no basis for such approaches.

3. For the two Reformers faith works through love in a way that has sociological characteristics. There is no doubt that in expressing this they pay insufficient attention to the Jewish context of early Christianity, and furthermore that they use anti-Catholic polemic rightly unacceptable in a contemporary context. Yet they do also insightfully highlight a cruciform pattern to the way in which faith behaves that is often neglected in contemporary exegesis of the verse.

None of this proves that Luther and Calvin's exegesis of Galatians 5:6 is correct. However, it does demonstrate that their exegesis must be treated on its own merits and cannot be dismissed on the grounds that their teaching about justification entailed a general hostility toward works self-evidently incompatible with Paul's teaching.[44] Like the apostle, they take the place of works in salvation with the utmost seriousness.

Endnotes

1. Earlier versions of this essay were presented at the conference on "Galatians and Christian Theology" (St. Andrews, 2012) and to the Chicago Society of Biblical Research (October 2013). I am grateful to all those who offered comments and asked questions on those occasions.

2. John M. G. Barclay, *Obeying the Truth: Paul's Ethics in Galatians* (Minneapolis: Fortress, 1988), 7. Barclay here intends "Lutheran" to denote a particular tradition of interpreting Paul in modern scholarship and not as a denominational label.

3. Gerhard Ebeling, *The Truth of the Gospel: An Exposition of Galatians*, trans. D. Green (Philadelphia: Fortress, 1985). Ebeling acknowledges in his foreword that the treatment is uneven, but comments that "in the latter part of the Epistle, the interpretation could go more rapidly without skipping essentials than at the beginning or in the middle" (x-xi). Hans Dieter Betz, *Galatians* (Philadelphia: Fortress, 1979) influentially also treats Galatians 5-6 as "exhortation," but with rather different implications for the significance of the material: "The final argument, and the cutting edge of the letter, is identical with Paul's exhortation and with his theory of ethics" (32). Betz, "The Literary Composition and Function of Paul's Letter to the Galatians," *New Testament Studies* 21 (1975): 353-79, adopts the position advocated by H. Cancik, that "scholarly argument is facilitated not only by 'descriptive' language, but by 'prescriptive' as well, so that *parenesis* cannot be regarded as a 'Kümmerform,' which is deficient of logic and merely applies the result of rational theory" (375).

4. *LW* 54:74 = *WA* Tr 1:199, 10-12 (No. 458). References to Luther's texts are to the English translation (abbreviated *LW*) Philadelphia Edition, *Luther's Works*, ed. J. Pelikan and H. T. Lehmann (Philadelphia & St. Louis: Concordia, 1955-86) and to the Latin and German Weimar Edition (abbreviated *WA*), *D. Martin Luthers Werke: Kritische Gesamtausgabe* (Weimar: H. Böhlaus Nachfolger, 1883-1993). References to *WA* Tr are to the subsection within the Weimar Edition dealing with the Table Talk (Tischreden). Those to *WA* Br are to the subsection dealing with Luther's correspondence (Briefswechsel).

5. *The New Testament: A Facsimile of the 1526 Edition Translated by William Tyndale* (Peabody, MA: Hendrickson, 2008).

6. John Van Engen, "Faith as a Concept of Order in Medieval Christendom," in *Belief in History: Innovative Approaches to European and American Religion*, ed. Thomas Kselman (Notre Dame: University of Notre Dame Press, 1991), 19-67 (33). See 31-36 for a fuller account of the distinction between unformed and formed faith upon which I rely here.

7. Van Engen, "Faith as a Concept of Order in Medieval Christendom," 35.

8. J. P. Torrell, *Saint Thomas Aquinas*, trans. R. Royal (Washington, DC: Catholic University of America Press, 1996-2003), 2:322-6.

9. F. R. Larcher, O.P., *Commentary on Saint Paul's Epistle to the Galatians by St. Thomas Aquinas* (Albany, NY: Magi, 1966), 156. For Larcher's translation with accompanying Greek and Latin text, see http://dhspriory.org/thomas/SSGalatians.htm#52 (cited September 30, 2013). See also the comments of J. K. Riches, *Galatians through the Centuries* (Oxford: Blackwell, 2008), 249-51. Riches also comments, 258-9, on the appropriation of this tradition of interpreting Galatians 5:6 at the Council of Trent.

10. Van Engen, "Faith as a Concept of Order in Medieval Christendom," 34.

11. For Larcher's unpublished translation, see http://nvjournal.net/files/Aquinas_on_Romans.pdf (cited September 30, 2013). The relevant comments are in Lecture 6, para. 104-08.

12. *LW* 27:336 = *WA* 2:567, 7-11.

13. *LW* 27:28 = *WA* 40.2:35, 14-19.

14. *LW* 27:29 = *WA* 40.2:36, 8-14.

15. Riches, *Galatians through the Centuries*, 262.

16. Philip Melanchthon, "Loci Communes Theologici," in *Melanchthon and Bucer*, ed. Wilhelm Pauck (Philadelphia: Westminster, 1969), 91-2 = CR 21:162. This is the 1521 first edition of Melanchthon's theological textbook intended to offer to students an alternative to the *Sentences* of Peter Lombard. The Latin text (abbreviated *CR*) is *Philippi Melanthonis opera quae supersunt omnia*, ed. K. Bretschneider and H. Bindseil (28 vols; *Corpus Reformatorum*, vols. 1-28; Halle: Schwetschke, 1834-1860).

17. John Calvin, *Institutes of the Christian Religion: 1541 French Edition*, trans. Elsie A. McKee (Grand Rapids: Eerdmans, 2009), 193 = *IRC* (1541), 556. The French text (abbreviated *IRC*) is Institution de la religion chrétienne 1541, ed. O. Millet (Geneva: Droz, 2008).

18. *Comm. Gal.* 5:6; *CNTC* 11:96 = *OE* 16:120, 1-4. The English translation (abbreviated *CNTC* 11) is *The Epistles of Paul the Apostle to the Galatians, Ephesians, Philippians, and Colossians*, Calvin's New Testament Commentaries, vol. 11, trans T. H. L. Parker (Grand Rapids, Eerdmans, 1965). The Latin text (abbreviated *OE* 16) is *Ioannis Calvini Opera exegetica volumen XVI: Commentarii in Pauli Epistolas ad Galatas, ad Ephesios, ad Philippenses, ad Colossenses*, ed. H. Feld (Geneva: Droz, 1992).

19. *LW* 27:30 = *WA* 40.2:37, 14-17.

20. *Comm. Gal.* 5:5; *CNTC* 11:95 = *OE* 16:118, 26-7.

21. *LW* 27:30 = *WA* 40.2:37, 26-30.

22. *Comm. Gal.* 5:6; *CNTC* 11:96 = *OE* 16:120, 5-8.

23. *LW* 26:11 = *WA* 40:51, 21-23.

24. *LW* 27:25 = *WA* 40.2:30, 20-21.

25. *LW* 26:129-30 = *WA* 40:228, 27–229, 18.

26. *LW* 31:371 = *WA* 7:69, 12-13.

27. For a fuller account of Melanchthon's views and their evolution, see Stephen J. Chester, *Righteousness in Christ: Paul, the Reformers, and the New Perspective* (Grand Rapids: Eerdmans, forthcoming), chapter 6.

28. Philip Melanchthon, *Loci Communes* 1543, trans. J. A. O. Preus (St. Louis, MO: Concordia, 1992), 103 = *CR* 21:775.

29. Melanchthon, *Loci Communes* 1543, 103 = *CR* 21:775.

30. This discussion is not included in the major English translations of Luther's Works. However, an obscure translation can be found in the anonymous "Cordatus' Controversy with Melanchthon," in *Theological Quarterly* 11, no. 4 (1907): 193-207. It appears in the *Corpus Reformatorum* as a supplement: *Philippi Melanchthonis Epistolae, Iudicia, Consilia, Testimonia Aliorumque ad eum Epistolae quae in Corpore Reformatorum Desiderantur*, ed. H. E. Bindseil (Halle: Gustav Schwetske, 1874), 344-48. See also WA Tr 6:148, 29–153, 15 (German text) and *WA* Br 12:191-94 (Latin text). See the analysis offered in Martin Greschat, *Melanchthon neben Luther: Studien zur Gestalt der Rechtfertigungslehre zwischen 1528 und 1537* (Wittenberg: Luther, 1965), 230-42 and in Mark Seifrid, "Luther, Melanchthon, and Paul on the Question of Imputation," in *Justification: What's at Stake in the Current Debates?*, ed. M. Husbands and D. Treier (Downers Grove: IVP, 2004), 137-52.

31. "Cordatus' Controversy with Melanchthon," 199 = Bindseil (ed.), 346.

32. "Cordatus' Controversy with Melanchthon," 202 = Bindseil (ed.), 348.

33. "Cordatus' Controversy with Melanchthon," 201 = Bindseil (ed.), 348.

34. John Calvin, *Institutes of the Christian Religion: 1541 French Edition*, 193-4 = *IRC* (1541): 556-7.

35. John Calvin, *Sermons on Galatians*, trans. K. Childress (Edinburgh: Banner of Truth Trust, 1997), 486 = *CO* 50:680-1. The Latin text (abbreviated *CO*) is *Ioannis Calvini opera quae supersunt omnia*, ed. G. Baum, E. Cunitz, and E. Reuss (59 vols; Corpus Reformatorum, vols. 29-87; Brunswick: Schwetschke, 1863-1900).

36. *Comm. Gal.* 2:20; *CNTC* 11:43 = *OE* 16:56, 19-20.

37. *Comm. 2 Cor.* 7:1, *CNTC* 10: 93 = *OE* 15:119, 6-8. The English translation (abbreviated *CNTC* 10) is *The Second Epistle of Paul the Apostle to the Corinthians and the Epistles to Timothy, Titus, and Philemon*, Calvin's New Testament Commentaries vol. 10, trans T. A. Smail (Grand Rapids: Eerdmans, 1964). The Latin text (abbreviated 15) is *Ioannis Calvini Opera exegetica volumen XV: Commentarii in secundam Pauli Epistolam ad Corinthios*, ed. H. Feld (Geneva: Droz, 1994).

38. *Comm. Phil* 3:10, *CNTC* 11:276 = *OE* 16:357, 13-15.

39. Such a distinction is not in and of itself alien to early Protestant exegesis, since both Melanchthon and Calvin recognize a transition by Paul to primarily ethical modes of argument at the beginning of Romans 12. However, there is nothing in Calvin's commentary on Galatians to suggest that he discerns a similar transition in Galatians 5. Luther's opening statement in relation to Galatians 5 is that "As he approaches the end of the epistle, Paul argues vigorously and passionately in defense of the *doctrine* of faith and of Christian liberty against the false apostles" (my emphasis, *LW* 27:3 = *WA* 40.2, 1, 15-16). Where Luther discerns a transition to exhortation is not at 5:1 but at 5:13 (see *LW* 27:47 = *WA* 40.2:59, 20-23).

40. *LW* 27:31 = *WA* 40.2:38, 27-31.

41. See T. Maneerma, *Two Kinds of Love: Martin Luther's Religious World* (Minneapolis: Fortress, 2010).

42. *LW* 31:365 = *WA* 7:64, 34-7.

43. Calvin, *Sermons on Galatians*, 479 = *CO* 50:674-5.

44. Although often obscured, the positive dimension of the Reformers' relationship to works and the significance for this of Galatians 5:6 has sometimes been explicitly recognized. From within Lutheranism, see especially George W. Forell, *Faith Active in Love: An Investigation of the Principles Underlying Luther's Social Ethics* (New York: American Press, 1954), 70-111.

Ancient Mentors and Moral Progress According to Galen and Paul

Max J. Lee

G alen of Pergamum, though a familiar figure in classical philosophy, has received only a limited treatment in the field of New Testament studies. Although Galen wrote more than 170 (extant) treatises (many of which have been assembled in the ongoing series *Corpus Medicorum Graecorum*), biblical scholars interested in the cultural interface of Galen's essays with the discourse of early Christianity have tended to focus on Galen's description of medicine in the ancient world,[1] on his criticism of Christianity in the second century CE,[2] on his account and critique of Stoic self-mastery,[3] on his analysis of the organizational structures of the philosophical schools and their possible comparison with Christian discipleship circles,[4] or most recently on a rediscovered treatise by Galen for its own sake without any reference to the New Testament.[5] With few exceptions, little attention has been paid to Galen's own account of moral transformation, especially as it is described in his treatise *De Affectuum Dignotione* (*On the Passions of the Soul*; henceforth *Aff. Dig.*).[6]

In this essay, I will give a sketch of Galen's program for moral transformation and then focus especially upon the social structures, the mentor-disciple relations that support the program. The essay ends by demonstrating how Galen's account of moral transformation can help illuminate Paul's discourse on imitation in 1 Corinthians.

Galen's Program for Moral Transformation

In his introduction (*Aff. Dig.* 1.1.1–1.2.21),[7] Galen tells the reader that the treatise is a response to a friend's inquiry on how one could control human emotions or passions (*pathē*/*pathēmata*). Despite Galen's claim elsewhere in the treatise that he has no philosophical allegiance to any one sect (8.32.19-21), it is the Peripatetic School and the Academy who arguably have had the most influence upon his understanding of moral progress.[8] Galen's view of moral progress follows the Peripatetic framework in this way: Galen assumes the general structural pattern that desire leads to action, action to patterns of conduct, and conduct to the formation of character.[9]

Emotions, experienced in moderation and under the guidance of reason, function to motivate and strengthen a person to perform virtuous actions and develop virtuous character. Yet excessive emotions, unchecked by reason, can dangerously drive a person to take a wrong course of action. For Galen, as a Platonist, while emotions can be irrational (i.e., the product of the soul's irrational or desiderative part), an error (*hamartia*/*hamartēma*) is a false judgment or wrong choice stemming from the *rational* part of the soul plus its corresponding wrong action (1.2.1-12).[10] In short, the passions can incapacitate reason and spur a person to make bad choices and err (3.5.14-24). Galen, in fact, argues that many tragic figures in the plays of Euripides are prone to error precisely because they make crucial life-changing decisions in the heat of anger, lust, revenge, and the like. The constant repetition of errors in moral action can result in the development of vice (*kakia*) and ultimately in the formation of a completely intemperate person (*ho akolastos*).[11]

Thus a vicious cycle begins to emerge. The passions spur a person to perform errors and eventually help catalyze vicious character. Continuing the cycle, a person's intemperate character also makes one much more susceptible to the power of the passions. So, for example, a person who repeatedly displays anger and acts on it becomes an angry person; yet at the same time, a person with a volatile personality tends to act angrily anyway and only reinforces one's angry character with angry behavior (4.12.5–4.16.4). In short, *what we do* determines *who we are*, but *who we are* also determines *what we do*. This Middle Platonic cycle of vicious behavior sounds very Peripatetic, and probably stems from a classic Aristotelian paradox that states that we are morally responsible for our actions, but *not fully* responsible for our states of character.[12] Irrational behavior becomes almost addictive at this stage, and the intemperate person is said to be a fatally sick person (6.22.8-16).[13]

So, how does a Platonist break this vicious cycle of "bad actions develop bad character" and "bad character produces bad actions"? The road to moral progress and the reversal of vicious character begins with the pursuit of three inter-related projects modeled on Plato's classic tripartite division of the soul:[14]

1. Debilitate the desiderative part (*to epithumētikon*) of the soul: Galen argues that the power of the passions can be crippled into a small and weak state (*mikra te kai asthenēs*) by denying the desiderative part those bodily impulses that feed it. Bodily impulses are curbed through the ascetic denial of physical pleasures (*hēdonai*), especially food, drink, and sex (6.21.13–6.24.10).

2. Train the spirited part (*to thymoeidēs*) of the soul: Galen advises an angry person to make a conscious effort to train (*askein*) the spirited part of the soul to obey reason. The way one trains the spirited part of the soul is to take the opposite course of action from what anger wants to take (6.20.20–6.21.13).

3. Empower the rational part (*to logistikon*) of the soul: Galen insists that we can strengthen the power of the rational faculty or mind through learning philosophy (8.31.23–8.33.11).

Galen's advice throughout his treatise on how one implements the above three-part program is often practical and very much within the power of the agent to perform. At times, the instructions appear overly simplistic. In *Aff. Dig.* 5.16.5–5.17.3, for example, Galen counsels the person struggling with anger to begin by refusing to punish immediately a disobedient slave until one's temper has first subsided and even then only to take disciplinary action appropriate to the slave's offense.[15] To help overcome greed and weaken the desiderative part, Galen suggests following his own example of charity: that is, paying off other people's debts, or sharing one's own clothing with slaves, or spending one's money on noble pursuits such as funding prospective writers and buying books (9.37.7–9.38.2). To strengthen the rational part of the soul, Galen advises that we memorize the maxims and teachings of the ancient philosophers twice daily, once in the morning and again in the evening (6.25.3-15).

Will such practical courses of action actually result in moral progress? Yes, but only if they are carried out daily over a long period of time. In case a person might become frustrated at one's apparent lack of progress, Galen encourages the reader:

> [1] Even if you should not become much better, be satisfied if in the *first year* you have advanced and shown some small measure of improvement. If you continue to withstand your passion and to soften your anger, you will show more remarkable improvement during the *second year*; then, if you still continue to take thought for yourself, you will notice a tremendous growth (*megalēs auxēseōs*) in the dignity of your life in the *third* year, and after that, in the *fourth*, the *fifth*,

and so on. A man does everything for many successive years that he may become a good doctor, or rhetorician, or grammarian, or geometrician. Is it so shameful for you to toil for a long time in order that you may one day be a good human being (*anthrōpos agathos*)?[16]

Galen insists that moral progress is a lifetime process (*di' holou tou biou*) involving several years of intense behavioral modification (*askēsis*; cf. 3.10.23–4.11.14). A person may struggle tremendously for the first or second year of training, but as time goes on, one will gain greater self-mastery over the passions as the passions become controlled by appropriate and virtuous actions. That is, the moral transformation of a vicious soul into a good human being (*anthrōpos agathos*) seems to be a tenable goal but only after many years of consciously reversing the growth or build-up of vice.

Especially interesting is Galen's use of the term *auxēsis* and its cognate *auxanō* to describe how both virtue and vice (cf. 10.42.8–10) grow or increase. The term *auxanō* can be translated one of several ways: "to increase in power," "augment," "grow," or "build up."[17] Concerning Galen's specific use of the term in *Aff. Dig.*, Harkins prefers to translate *auxanō* as "to wax strong," an old idiom for steady growth.[18] Harkins's translation is an appropriate one, for Galen appears to understand vicious character as something that grows slowly and reinforces itself over time, and the only way to counteract the growth is to build on top of it, that is, the rubbing-away of vice through the rubbing-in of virtuous character. Galen's program is, in fact, the process of employing a counter cycle (i.e., moderate emotion → virtuous action → virtuous character) to reverse the vicious one (i.e., passion → vicious action → vicious character) that has already "waxed strong" in the life of an intemperate person.

Moral Mentors and Frank Friends in the Greco-Roman World

Having outlined Galen's system of moral transformation above, I now move to the social structures that support the whole program. One major barrier to moral progress is the inability of people, especially beginners in philosophy, to see their own passions, errors, and vices. Galen explains the importance of self-knowledge in the following way:

> [2] It is likely that we do err (*hamartanein*) even if we ourselves think that we do not, and we can deduce this from what follows: we see that all people suppose that they themselves are altogether without error (*anamartētous*) or that their errors are few, mild, and infrequent....but I have seen that those men who suppose that they are excellent and who do not entrust this evaluation to others, they are the very

ones who stumble frequently into the gravest errors. When I was young, I thought that the Pythian dictum "Know thyself" (*gnōnai heauton*) was held in praise without good reason because it did not require some great action. Later in life, I discovered that this dictum was rightly praised, for only the wisest person (*ho sophōtatos*) can know himself (*heauton gnoiē*) accurately, and no other can do this accurately, though a person may have better or worse knowledge of oneself than another.[19]

[3] As Aesop says, we have two sacks suspended from our necks; the one in front is filled with the faults of others; the one behind is filled with his own. This is the reason why we see (*blepomen*) the faults of others but those which *concern* ourselves remain invisible to us. All people admit the truth of this. And Plato explains the reason behind it [cf. *Leg.* 731E]. He says: "The lover is blind (*typhloutai*) concerning the object of his love." Therefore, if each of us loves oneself most of all, one necessarily becomes blind concerning oneself. How, then, will a person see (*ophsetai*) his or her own evils? How will one know when he or she is in error (*pōs hamartanōn gnōsetai*)? Both Aesop's myth and Plato's word demonstrate to us that the [self-] discovery of one's own errors is practically hopeless. For unless a person can separate oneself from self-love (*philein...heauton*), the lover must be blind to what he or she loves [namely, oneself]. Thus, I do not expect the person who reads this book to consider, by oneself, how to discover one's own errors; even if a person should make as extensive an examination into one's own errors as one could, the person would find it difficult to discover them.[20]

In the above texts [2] and [3], Galen likens self-knowledge (*gnōnai heauton* [2]; *hamartanōn gnōsetai* [3]) to seeing (*blepomen* [3]; *ophsetai* [3]), and an ignorance of one's own errors and evil character to a kind of philosophical or metaphysical blindness (*typhloutai* [3]). Quoting a maxim of Plato, Galen further explains that the reason for the blindness of most people in regards to their own errors is self-love (*philein heauton* [3]); for just as a lover is blind to the errors of the beloved, so a person is blind to one's own faults because that person loves oneself most of all. Only the wisest (*ho sophōtatos*; [2]) can judge correctly.[21]

So, how does the beginner of philosophy hope to make any sort of progress if he or she cannot even see one's own passions, errors, and vices which together impede moral transformation? In answer to this anticipated question, Galen advocates a certain set of personal relationships or social structures that enable a person to see oneself more accurately and that function to support one's moral progress. That is, he advises that the person have: (1) *frank friends* who will point out, expose, and criticize the errors to which one is blind, and (2) *a moral mentor* who will not only frankly criticize but also function as a moral or ethical paradigm after which the student can model oneself.

Concerning the first set of relationships, that is, the frank friend, much work has already been done by recent New Testament scholarship.[22] In contrast to the flatterer (*ho kolax*) who mimics friendship but only seeks his or her own welfare, the true friend (*ho philos*) seeks the welfare of the befriended (*ho philoumenos*) and epitomizes that concern through the proper use of frank criticism (*parrēsia*). Edward O'Neil, in his analysis of Plutarch's concept of friendship, lists some eight characteristics of a genuine friend.[23] However, he points out that the proper use of frank criticism is arguably the most important distinguishing quality of the friend.[24] Troels Engberg-Pedersen further adds that a true friend neither ignores the errors of the befriended, nor applies frank criticism indiscriminately, but rather first stings (*dēgma*) the befriended by pointing out his or her faults, and later ameliorates the pain of the rebuke with reassuring words and actions.[25]

We can find a similar discussion by Galen concerning the frank friend's role in exposing the errors and vices of the befriended in several passages throughout *Aff. Dig.*[26] In fact, not only does Galen consider "the person who shows us our every defect" (*ton mēnysanta tōn plēmmeloumenōn hekasta*) as "the greatest friend" (*philon megiston*), but he also calls the frank friend a personal "savior" (*sōtēra*).[27] In a tone similar to Plutarch, Galen insists that we show "gratefulness, not to those who flatter us, but to those who severely rebuke us."[28] For Galen, the need to have a frank critic is an absolutely essential prerequisite to moral progress, whether the corrector is a friend or a moral mentor.[29]

Having described the role of the frank friend, who is generally a social *equal* or *peer* of the befriended,[30] I now focus my discussion upon the moral mentor who stands at a *higher* level of moral expertise than the philosophical trainee. The mentor, like the friend, is a frank critic of a person's passions, errors, and vices. However, the key difference between the mentor and friend lies in the former's demand for imitation (*mimēsis*). That is, the student of philosophy must imitate the virtuous actions of the mentor and follow the tutor or overseer as one's paradigm. In ancient discourse, there is no explicit call for a person to imitate a friend (although the call to imitation may be implicit). In contrast, the trainee is explicitly charged to follow his or her teacher's example. Galen lists the qualifications and role of the wise moral mentor as follows:

[4] But concerning the recognition of one's own errors (*peri tēs diagnōseōs tōn idiōn hamartēmatōn*), and since it is not possible for beginners to recognize these errors by themselves, we shall appoint others to watch over (*heterous...epoptas*) beginners. These [= the overseers] will be themselves well-trained (*tous askountas*) and secondly have the power to recognize (*dynamenous gnōnai*) the errors and passions from which they have been made free (*apēllagēsan hamartēmatōn kai pathōn*) and [thirdly, to see] whatever is lacking for perfection.[31]

[5] Thus, a person needs to find some mature figure (*presbytēn*) who can see (*blepein*) these [vices] and urge the elder to expose with frankness (*meta parrēsias*) all [our errors]. Then, when the elder tells us of some fault, let us first be immediately grateful to him or her.[32]

[6] As I said before, let that person [i.e., the one seeking moral progress] set over oneself some overseer and tutor (*epoptēn tina kai paidagōgon*), who on every occasion will remind, rebuke sharply, urge, and spur the person forward to pursue better things; [the tutor does this] by making himself or herself in all things a paradigm (*paradeigma*) of what he or she says and urges. By [the tutor's] words, the person will be able to build in oneself a soul that is both free and noble.[33]

In the texts [4]–[6] above, Galen explains that the mentor or tutor (*paidagōgos* [6]; *epoptēs* [4, 6]) must be: (1) someone who can see (*blepein* [5]) or recognize (*diagnōsis / gnōnai* [4]) both the vices of the student and the virtuous qualities which the student lacks in reaching perfection; (2) someone who is him or herself well-trained (*askountōn* [4]) and has already been set free of the very errors and passions (*apēllagēsan hamartēmatōn kai pathōn* [4]) which he or she exposes in the student; (3) preferably someone who is more mature and older in years (*presbytēs* [5]); (4) a model or paradigm (*paradeigma* [6]) that the philosophical trainee can imitate. In other words, the moral mentor should be one who is already wise, or at the very least, one who is further along in moral progress so he or she can blamelessly lead the student to the same point of moral maturity which the tutor has achieved.

Plutarch specifically employs the term *mimēsis* and its cognates to punctuate the need for emulating or imitating the mentor (*Virt. prof.* 84C). He also adds that the conduct of the good and perfect person (*praxesin andros agathou kai teliou*; *Virt. prof.* 84D) acts as a sort of moral mirror (*esoptra*; 85B) to the beginning student of philosophy, who, upon seeing the example of the peda-gogue, is "pricked" (*daknomenos*) in his or her conscience by his or her own moral deficiencies (84D). Yet the virtuous character of the sage also becomes a source of hope for the trainee. For in the sage, the trainee witnesses a living example that moral transformation is attainable (84D). Otherwise, the person may become too discouraged at one's own lack of progress and give up moral training altogether (76F-77B).

Elsewhere in *Aff. Dig.* (5.18.25–5.19.10), Galen provides a further descrip-tion of the relationship between philosophical trainee and mentor. The trainee is not to be annoyed when he or she is rebuked, and even if the disciple thinks the mentor or friend is making a false charge, one is called to wait and see if the mentor may end up being correct. We are, after all, according to Galen, blind, and it just may be our blindness that prevents us from seeing our errors. The student, even if falsely reprimanded, can gain a great deal from the rebuke because the hidden anger and resentment that is brought up to the surface through such a rebuke is now exposed, and the trainee can see the utter "ugli-ness of soul" (*tēs psychēs aischros*; 5.19.9) that lay underneath. Lastly, the trainee should avoid seeking political office because then no one would want to correct a person in a position of power. As Galen humorously remarks: "In these times [it is hard to] find a [Cynic like] Diogenes [of Sinope] who will proclaim the truth even to a wealthy man or king" (3.10.10-13).

The Apostle Paul as a Moral Mentor and Father to the Corinthians

Concerning the need for moral mentors as frank critics and exemplars, Galen's discussion on the social structures necessary to support moral progress helps us to understand the concept of *imitatio Pauli* found in the Corinthian correspondence (1 Corinthians 1:18–4:20) and to interpret other Pauline texts on imitation (Philippians 3:17; 1 Thessalonians 1:6; 2:14; cf. Ephesians 5:1). Michaelis, after surveying Greek classical literature, the Septuagint, the Pseude-pigrapha, Philo and Josephus, demonstrated that the language of mimesis is a unique contribution of Paul relatively unknown outside of Hellenism. Except for a few apocryphal texts in the Septuagint (Wisdom 4:2; 9:8; 15:9; 4 Mac-cabees 9:23; 13:9) and the works of some Diaspora Jewish writers such as Philo (*Decal.* 111; *Virt.* 168; *Spec. Leg. IV,* 73; *Mos. I,* 158) and Josephus (*Ant.* 8.316; 12.203; 17.97) who were familiar with Greco-Roman philosophical discourse, *mimēsis* finds its most prolific use in the wider Greek-speaking world and not in Jewish sources.[34] Since Michaelis's work, Betz has affirmed that the concept of imitation has no antecedent in the Hebrew Scriptures.[35] While to eliminate Jewish influence altogether is too hasty (given the possibility that Diaspora Jews may have adapted the concept of imitation into their literature using words outside of the *mimēsis* lexical group), the studies by Michaelis and Betz nevertheless point to the prospect that understanding Paul requires us to move beyond his Jewish context and into the more broadly conceived framework of Greco-Roman culture.

Recalling Galen's list of qualifications concerning the moral mentor (i.e., the *paidagōgos*, *epoptēs*, and *presbytēs*), I noted that the function of the mentor in the Greco-Roman world was to remind, frankly criticize, and even sharply rebuke one's students for their passions, errors, and vices. The mentor provided in himself or herself a model (*paradeigma*) for the student to emulate (*mimeomai*). It is striking, therefore, that Paul's admonition to "be imitators of him" is set in the context of comparing himself to both a pedagogue and a father of the Corinthian church. In 1 Corinthians 4:14-16, Paul states: "I am writing these things not to shame you, but to admonish you as my beloved children (*tekna*). For though you might have countless pedagogues (*paidagōgous*) in Christ, you do not have many fathers (*pateras*). Yet in Christ Jesus I begat (*egennēsa*) you through the gospel. Therefore, I urge you, become imitators (*mimētai*) of me!"[36]

When Paul tells the Corinthians that they might have numerous tutors (*paidagōgous*) in Christ but not many fathers (*pateras*), he is acknowledging elements of both continuity and discontinuity between the two metaphors. In other words, there are elements of continuity between how a Greco-Roman pedagogue or tutor treats his students (*mathētai*) and how a father relates to his children (*tekna*), but also distinctive features to each relationship. Paul assumes all the responsibilities that a Greco-Roman pedagogue would have for his disciples (4:15), but he is also *more than* a pedagogue.

As a moral mentor, Paul rebukes the Corinthians for their immaturity, calling them fleshly and infantile (3:1). Paul even uses the same metaphor of a whip that Galen employs in *Aff. Dig.* to describe the kind of disciplinary action that he may take if the congregation does not respond to his admonitions. In *Aff. Dig.* 6.14.25–6.15.18, Galen relates the humorous story of how a young Cretan man was so distraught over his hot temper that he asked Galen to flog him (*mastigoun*) with his belt strap in penance for having injured a slave in a fit of rage. Galen's response was to admonish (*parekaloun*) him over his vices. Commenting on the experience, Galen states: "This is the way that I obviously whipped him but not in the manner that he had requested" (6.15.16-17).[37] Here Galen uses the metaphor of flogging to describe the painful experience of having one's errors exposed.

In a very similar sounding exhortation, Paul closes his discourse in 1 Corinthians 4:14-21 with the enigmatic phrase: "For the kingdom of God depends not upon talk but upon power. What would you wish? Shall I come to you with a rod/whip (*en rhabdō*) or with love in a spirit of gentleness?" (4:20-21). The rod of discipline that Paul threatens to use if the Corinthians do not conform to his written admonishments is a metaphorical or rhetorical rod; and given Galen's use of the same metaphor, it is very possible that Paul's rod is a reference to the kind of harsh verbal admonishments with which he will flog the Corinthians if he were to visit them in person and find that they were still in a state of division.

So far, I have shown elements of continuity between the role of a sage as a pedagogue or moral mentor to his students and Paul's role as a spiritual father to the Corinthian church. Paul is all the things that a pedagogue is, but he is also something much more. Like a pedagogue, he exposes the sins/errors of his disciples and becomes a model of imitation for them; however, like a father, Paul's duties extend beyond just blasting his spiritual children for their faults or admonishing them toward virtuous conduct. There is a distinctive use of the father metaphor that must now be explored.

First, the image of father connotes his apostolic *authority* as the founder or the one who has begotten the church at Corinth through his missionary activities. Elizabeth Castelli has argued that in Roman antiquity, the relationship between father and son was almost totalitarian. She insists that the paternal role in Greco-Roman society is a "role possessing total authority over their children."[38] So she sees Paul's call to self-imitation as a strategy of power. Mimesis is an ingenious way for Paul to procure power because no matter how one defines imitation, the copy will always be inferior to the original. Paul will always be in a greater position to those who emulate him.[39]

However, Larry Yarbrough's later study on the parent-child relations within Greco-Roman households asserts that past despot images for parents are misplaced. Certainly, there were always potential abuses of parent roles in any society. However, often enough, fathers and mothers in Roman civilization associated with their children strong feelings of *intimacy*. Obedience is certainly also an important aspect of parent-children relations but not necessarily the predominant one.[40] Paul himself appears to stress *both* the authoritative and affectionate aspect of his relationship with the Corinthians when he admonishes them but as "beloved" children (4:14). Throughout 1 Corinthians 1-4, Paul alludes to several paternal and maternal images. Paul has begotten them through the gospel (4:15), feeds them with *kerygma* (i.e., milk not solid food; 3:1-2), serves them (4:1), loves them (4:14), admonishes them (1:10; 4:16), teaches them (4:17), and if necessary will discipline them (4:20-21). As a spiritual father, he strikes a proper balance between his role as an authority figure and as a nurturer.[41]

To the above observations on the distinctive features of the father-image (i.e., his authority and affection), I would add a third distinctive: the *permanent* commitment that a father has toward a child is far beyond the *temporary* commitment a pedagogue has towards his student. The pedagogue is usually a slave of the family whose duty was to escort the youth or child to and from school, act as a temporary custodian for the child's safety, and superintend the youth's conduct. When the young man grew older, the pedagogue was no longer needed.[42] Galen has described the moral mentor as a philosophical pedagogue, or as one who teaches and superintends the moral development of his disciples on their way toward becoming mature, virtuous people. Yet Galen also acknowledges the temporary role of pedagogues and contrasts them with the lasting influence of his own father.

In *Aff. Dig.* 3.6.17–3.7.16, Galen proposes the following experiment: to find some stranger to correct one's faults over a short period of time during several days. Ideally, one can find a frank friend or moral mentor with whom one can maintain a long-term association, but because such relationships are rare, Galen proposes a short-term training program. Since the moral mentor, in this case, does not have any real commitment to the student, the student must take initiative to pursue the counsel of the mentor. The student must vigilantly urge the mentor to reveal the truth, especially because the temporary mentor may not want to disclose what passions he or she sees in the student. Galen explains the reason for the reluctance as either being the result of negligence or a lack of concern (3.7.11) or because he does not wish to be hated (3.7.13-14). After all, the temporary mentor has no real investment in a person, and so the student must be pro-active in seeking the truth.

In contrast, Galen devotes an entire chapter in his treatise (*Aff. Dig.* 8) to a discussion on how much he had gained from his own father throughout a lifetime of training. Galen recounts with fond recollection that "I was most fortunate to have had the least irritable, the most just, the most devoted, and the most generous of fathers" (8.31.11-12). Using his father as an example, Galen goes on to explain that children imitate such things as the virtues from their fathers (*tauta mimoumenous*; 8.31.22).

The contrast between the short-term relationship with a pedagogue and a lifetime of learning from one's father is striking. When Paul tells the Corinthians that "you might have ten thousand tutors in Christ…but I am your father through the gospel" (4:14-15), Paul is stressing his long-term and permanent commitment to a church that is not only divided amongst themselves, but arguably are in rebellion against him as the founding pastor of their community.[43] The nature of Paul's long-term commitment to the Corinthians as a father, in contrast to the short-term pedagogue, provides an important insight in the nature of power relations between himself and his congregation.

As noted above, Castelli has accused Paul of using mimesis discourse to broker authority for himself in a way that is forced, manipulative, and harmful to his target audience. Underlying Castelli's thesis is the assumption that all forms of power-over are inherently oppressive.[44] Is Paul brokering power for himself when he is employing mimesis language? To Castelli's credit, her study forces the interpreter to take seriously how Paul's call to imitation as a father places him in a position of authority over his church. Yes, the language of imitation does provide Paul with power over his congregation.

But is this use of power harmful and manipulative? No. Here I would disagree with Castelli and instead argue (following Thomas Wartenberg's field theory of social power) that not all forms of power-over are oppressive. There are *positive* ways to exercise power-over that are *transformative* and beneficial to both the dominant and subordinate agents.[45] The two chief examples of transformative uses of power-over that Wartenberg analyzes are the nurturing model of a parent with his or her child[46] and the learning model of a teacher with his or her student.[47] In the former model, what makes their relationship transformative rather than domineering are the elements of *trust* and *permanent commitment* exercised by both agents. It is difficult to place ourselves under the authority of another if we feel that the person has no real commitment to us. Children accept the authority of their parents and trust them, precisely because the parents love them in the context of relationships that are long-term. When children eventually mature and grow, the relationship remains but its content changes. Children become less dependent on their parents, and the power differential decreases over time.[48]

Paul as a spiritual father to the Corinthians does not seek a relationship with his congregation in which they remain permanently immature and only infants in Christ. Instead, he hopes to see them grow to become coworkers in God's field, as he and Apollos are (3:1-15). One day, he hopes, the Corinthians can indeed eat solid food and share in the same ministry. But lest we misunderstand Paul and think that the apostle to the Gentiles is advocating a purely social system for moral transformation, we must take seriously his discourse that it is the power of God (*dynamis*; 1 Corinthians 2:3-5; 4:19-21) that transforms human existence and not the social structures themselves.

Using the horticulture metaphor, Paul insists on a correspondence between divine and human agency in the moral transformation of Christians. It is a process that systematic theologians have traditionally called "sanctification." In 1 Corinthians 3:5-8, Paul states:

> What then is Apollos? What is Paul? Servants through whom you came to have faith (*episteusate*) as the Lord assigned to each [a task]. I planted, Apollos watered, but God grew [it] (*ho theos ēuxanen*). So then, neither the one who plants nor the one who waters is anything, but it is God who makes things grow (*ho auxanōn theos*). The one who plants and the one who waters have the same purpose, and each will receive

> a reward according to one's labor. For we are fellow servants
> of God; you are God's field (*geōrgion*), God's building.

Paul's mapping of the horticulture metaphor is precise: God is the author of transformation and growth, Paul and Apollos are the co-laborers who help facilitate the growth by planting and watering, and the church is the vineyard or field in which God's transforming activity takes place. But interestingly enough, what exactly is God causing to grow? Some commentators have argued that the church is both the field where God works and the seed that God causes to grow.[49] However, it is more likely that what God causes to grow is the faith and moral character of the Corinthians as they live out their Christian lives. Recalling that Galen applied the term *auxanō* to describe how virtue (and vice) can grow and build up in the life of a philosophical trainee (see *Aff. Dig.* 4.15.18–4.16.4), it seems very likely that Paul used the horticulture metaphor to describe the development of virtuous or godly character in the Christian believer.

The distinction (in comparison with Galen) is at the point of agency. It is *God* who causes the growth and transformation. Where Galen's program of moral progress depends on human agency and the power of reason over the irrational parts of the soul, Paul clearly argues that without divine intervention, human beings cannot change.[50]

Conclusion

According to Galen and Paul, there is simply no moral progress without human authority. The need to have someone over us to expose our faults, errors, and vices is a proposition that both Galen and Paul affirm. It is arguably a value that was shared by most people in the broader cultural milieu of the Greco-Roman world. What made Paul's discourse on imitation distinctive was his use of paternal imagery to demonstrate his long-term commitment to his congregation. Even more important was Paul's utter dependence on God as the ultimate agent of moral transformation.[51]

Endnotes

1. Howard Clark Kee, *Medicine, Miracle, and Magic in New Testament Times* (New York: Cambridge University Press, 1986).

2. Robert Wilken, *The Christians as the Romans Saw Them*, 2nd ed. (New Haven: Yale University Press, 2003).

3. Stanley Stowers, *A Rereading of Romans: Justice, Jews, and Gentiles* (New Haven: Yale University Press, 1994); Emma Wasserman, *The Death of the Soul in Romans 7: Sin, Death, and the Law in Light of Hellenistic Moral Psychology* (Tübingen: Mohr-Siebeck, 2008), 42-44.

4. Loveday Alexander, "IPSE DIXIT: Citation of Authority in Paul and in the Jewish and Hellenistic Schools," in *Paul Beyond the Judaism/Hellenism Divide*, ed. Troels Engberg-

Pedersen (Louisville: Westminster John Knox Press, 2001), 103-27; idem, "Paul and the Hellenistic Schools: The Evidence of Galen," in *Paul in His Hellenistic Context*, ed. Troels Engberg-Pedersen (Minneapolis: Fortress, 1995), 60-83.

5. Clare Rothschild and Trevor Thompson, "Galen: 'On the Avoidance of Grief,'" *Early Christianity* 2/1 (2011): 110-29.

6. Even studies by classical scholarship are limited to a few key works: R. J. Hankinson, "Actions and Passions: Affection, Emotion, and Moral Self-Management in Galen's Philosophical Psychology," in *Passions and Perceptions: Studies in Hellenistic Philosophy of Mind: Proceedings of the Fifth Symposium Hellenisticum*, ed. J. Brunschwig, et al., (Cambridge: Cambridge University Press, 1993), 184-222; Pierluigi Donini, "Psychology," in *The Cambridge Companion to Galen*, ed. R. J. Hankinson (Cambridge: Cambridge University Press, 2008), 184-209; and Christopher Gill, *Naturalistic Psychology in Galen and Stoicism* (Oxford: Oxford University Press, 2010), 243-329.

7. The Greek text of *De Affectuum Dignotione* is taken from Ioannes Marquardt, et al., eds., *Claudii Galeni Pergameni Scripta Minora* (vol. 1; Leipzig: Teubner, 1884–1893; repr. by Amsterdam: Adolf M. Hakkert, 1967). The English translation of *De Affectuum Dignotione* is modified from Paul Harkins, *Galen on the Passions and Errors of the Soul* ([Columbus]: Ohio State University Press, 1963). All citations from *Aff. Dig.* have the following convention: *chapter no.: page no.: line no.* according to the Teubner edition.

8. Hankinson, "Actions and Passions," 191, 198-204; *pace* Gill, *Naturalistic Psychology in Galen and Stoicism*, 279-80, who thinks Galen's psychology is based on his medical sense of human physiology and only secondarily to Platonic-Aristotelian tenets.

9. Hankinson, "Actions and Passions," 201-3.

10. Cf. Galen, *Pecc. Dig.* 1.45.10-12; 2.49.9-20; PHP 4.2.25.

11. Hankinson, "Actions and Passions," 187 n. 14, 189-91.

12. Ibid., 201-203; Susan Sauvé Meyer, *Aristotle on Moral Responsibility: Character and Cause* (Cambridge: Blackwell Publishers, 1993), 126-29.

13. Cf. Galen, *PHP* 5.2.35-42, 5.3.21-31; Plato, *Soph.* 227D-228B; Plutarch, *Sera* 551C-E.

14. Plato, *Resp.* 4.436A-439E; *Tim.* 69D-70E; 77B-C; 89E.

15. See also Galen, *Aff. Dig.* 4.12.23–13.3. Cf. Plutarch, *Cohib. ira* 455B-E, who, like Galen, says that the best way to "dethrone anger as one would a tyrant" is to keep quiet and not intensify the passion by acting on it (455B). Plutarch gives the same advice as Galen, not to punish slaves in anger nor to punish one's children in the midst of rage (459A).

16. Aff. Dig. 4.15.18–4.16.4; Eng. trans. follows Harkins, p. 41 (italics mine).

17. H. G., Liddell, R. Scott, H. S. Jones, *A Greek-English Lexicon*, 9th ed. with revised supplement (Oxford: Oxford University Press, 1996), s.v. *auxanō*, 277. In the New Testament corpus, *auxanō* and its cognates not only describe a quantitative increase in number or amount (e.g., Acts 6:7, 7:17, 12:24, 19:20; 1 Corinthians 3:6-7; 2 Corinthians 9:10, 10:15; Colossians 1:10, 2:19), but the term is also used to describe the organic growth of plants and physical development of children (e.g., Matthew 6:28, 13:32; Mark 4:8; Luke 1:80, 2:40, 12:27, 13:19; for spiritual growth, see also: Ephesians 2:21, 4:15; 1 Peter 2:2; 2 Peter 3:18).

18. See Harkin's Eng. trans. on p. 67 (= *Aff. Dig.* 10.42.9) and p. 58 (= *Aff. Dig.* 7.33.1).

19. *Aff. Dig.* 2.2.22–2.3.12; Eng. trans. follows Harkins, p. 29.

20. *Aff. Dig.* 2.4.11–2.5.6; Eng. trans. follows Harkins, pp. 30-31.

21. Plutarch also argues that the beginning of moral transformation is knowing oneself

(*gnōthi seauton*) in *Adul. amic.* 48E-49B; cf. *Virt. prof.* 78E.

22. See, e.g., John T. Fitzgerald, ed., *Friendship, Flattery, and Frankness of Speech: Studies on Friendship in the New Testament World*, Novum Testamentum Supplement 82 (Leiden: Brill, 1996); idem, ed., *Greco-Roman Perspectives on Friendship*, Society of Biblical Literature Resources for Biblical Study 34 (Atlanta: Scholars Press, 1997).

23. Edward O'Neil, "Plutarch on Friendship," in *Greco-Roman Perspectives on Friendship*, 105-22.

24. Ibid., 116.

25. Engberg-Pedersen, "Plutarch to Prince Philopappus on How to Tell a Flatterer from a Friend," in *Friendship, Flattery, and Frankness of Speech*, 61-79; cf. O'Neil, "Plutarch on Friendship," 113.

26. See, e.g., *Aff. Dig.* 5.18.10-25; 5.19.10-20; 3.8.18-3.9.10.

27. *Aff. Dig.* 5.18.23-25.

28. *Aff. Dig.* 5.19.19-20.

29. See the purpose statements of *Aff. Dig.* by Galen in the beginning and conclusion of the treatise (2.3.27–2.4.11; 2.5.2-13; and 10.43.26–10.44.11).

30. O'Neil, "Plutarch on Friendship," 107; Engberg-Pedersen, "Plutarch to Prince Philopappus," 64-68; 76-79.

31. *Aff. Dig.* 6.26.14-20; Eng. trans. follows Harkins, p. 52.

32. *Aff. Dig.* 7.27.22-25; Eng. trans. follows Harkins, p. 53.

33. *Aff. Dig.* 10.41.5-11; Eng. trans. follows Harkins, p. 66.

34. Wilhelm Michaelis, s.v. *mimeomai*, in *Theological Dictionary of the New Testament*, ed. G. Kittel, et al., trans. G.W. Bromiley (Grand Rapids: Eerdmans, 1967), 4.659-74.

35. Hans Dieter Betz, *Nachfolge und Nachahmung Jesu Christi im Neuen Testament* (Tübingen: Mohr-Siebeck, 1967), 3; 139-42; 186-87.

36. All English translations of New Testament texts are the author's.

37. English translation follows Harkins, 41.

38. Elizabeth Castelli, *Imitating Paul: A Discourse of Power* (Louisville: Westminster/John Knox Press, 1991), 101.

39. Ibid., 21-22; 110; 122-23.

40. O. Larry Yarbrough, "Parents and Children in the Letters of Paul," in *The Social World of the First Christians: Essays in Honor of Wayne E. Meeks*, ed. L. M. White, et al. (Minneapolis: Fortress Press, 1995), 132-33.

41. Jin Ki Hwang, *Mimesis and Apostolic Parousia in 1 Corinthians 4 and 5: An Apologetic-Mimetic Interpretation* (Lewiston, New York: Edwin Mellen Press, 2010), 93-101.

42. Georg Bertram, s.v. *paideuō, ktl.*, in *Theological Dictionary of the New Testament*, 5.596–603; Anthony Thiselton, *The First Epistle to the Corinthians*, New International Greek Testament Commentary (Grand Rapids: Eerdmans, 2000), 370.

43. Gordon Fee, *The First Epistle to the Corinthians*, New International Commentary on the New Testament (Grand Rapids: Eerdmans, 1987), 6-15.

44. Castelli, *Imitating Paul*, 35-58.

45. Thomas Wartenberg, *The Forms of Power: From Domination to Transformation* (Philadelphia: Temple University Press, 1990), 183-201.

46. Ibid., 185-93.

47. Ibid., 203-21.

48. Ibid., 210-21.

49. Thiselton, *The First Epistle to the Corinthians*, 301-7.

50. Ibid., 303-4.

51. This essay is a revised, shorter version of a paper presented to the Hellenistic Moral Philosophy and Early Christianity Section at the 2005 Society of Biblical Literature meeting in Philadelphia under the older title "Lending Nature a Helping Hand: An Examination of Galen's Treatise *De Affectuum Dignotione in Reference to Pauline Christianity*." It is part of my larger book project: *Moral Transformation in Greco-Roman Philosophy of Mind: Mapping the Moral Milieu of the Apostle Paul and His Diaspora Jewish Contemporaries* (Tübingen: Mohr-Siebeck, forthcoming 2015).

The Metaphor of Adoption in Paul's Letters

Richard N. Longenecker

One of the exegetical enigmas of our day is how to understand the Greek word *huiothesia* (sonship, adoption) in Paul's letters. It is not found in the Greek version of the Jewish Scriptures (i.e., the Septuagint/LXX). Nor is it paralleled by any cognate expression in the Hebrew text of the Jewish Scriptures (i.e., the Masoretic Text). Further, there is no parallel of either thought or expression in the literature of Second Temple Judaism. Nor is the term used elsewhere in the New Testament outside of the letters of Paul. And in the Pauline corpus of letters the term appears only five times: first in Galatians 4:5; then three times later in Romans 8:15, 23, and 9:4; and finally in Ephesians 1:5.

It may be said, therefore, that the use of the metaphor of "adoption" in speaking of the relationship of God's people to God himself was unique to Paul—though the presence of the term in the "sending formula" of Galatians 4:5, as well as in what seems to be a traditional listing of features set out in Romans 9:4-5 as constituting the special status of Jews (beginning with *hōn hē huiothesia*, "theirs is the adoption"), suggests that *huiothesia* as characterizing the relationship of God's people to himself would have been understood by both Jewish and Gentile believers in Jesus.

The Term "Adoption" in the Parlance of the Greco-Roman World

There have been a number of significant studies on the laws pertaining to the adoption of children (principally of a male child) in the Greco-Roman world.[1] And the following features having to do with these laws are particularly important to note: (1) that an adopted son was taken out of his previous situation and placed in an entirely new relationship to his new adopting father, who became his new *paterfamilias*; (2) that an adopted son started a new life as part of his new family, with all of his old relationships and obligations cancelled; (3) that an adopted son was considered no less important than any other biologically born son in his adopting father's family; and, (4) that an adopted son experienced a changed status, with his old name set aside and a new name given him by his adopting father.

Undoubtedly most (if not all) of these features pertaining to the adoption of a son into a Gentile family of the Greco-Roman world would have come to the fore in the minds and consciousness of Paul's hearers in his mission to pagan Gentiles in the eastern portion of the Roman Empire when they heard him speak about a Christian's new status as being "adopted" by God. Likewise, it may be presumed that they would have come to the fore in the consciousness of his Christian addressees at Rome, as well as in that of his own converts to whom he wrote in the province of Galatia and in the city of Ephesus.

"Adoption" as a Familial Term

It needs to be noted that "adoption is fundamentally a relational and familial [i.e., related to a family] metaphor," and that the term *huiothesia* is one that "Paul borrowed from the Roman socio-legal context of his day"[2] and filled with theological significance in his proclamation of the Christian gospel to pagan Gentiles. The adoption of a child was not a Jewish practice.[3] So Paul would presumably not have taken over either the concept or the word *huiothesia* from his Jewish heritage or his Jewish-Christian background. Yet he used the term five times in his letters as a metaphor for what God has done through the work of Jesus Christ. Evidently he believed that it would be meaningful as a metaphor of spiritual familial relationships (1) to pagan Gentiles to whom he proclaimed the Christian message in his missionary outreach to Gentiles in various eastern provinces of the Roman Empire; (2) to his own Gentile converts to Christ living in the Roman province of Galatia (cf. Galatians 4:5); (3) to Gentile believers in Jesus living in the city of Ephesus and its environs (cf. Ephesians 1:5); and (4) to his Christian addressees at Rome to whom he wanted to present the essence of his own apostolic proclamation in a fashion that they would understand (cf. Romans 8:15, 23; 9:4).

In this new relationship of having been adopted by God into his family, Paul proclaims that we as believers in Jesus "cry out" (*krazomen*) in response to

God: "Abba, Father" (*abba ho patēr*). There have been numerous attempts to identify exactly what Paul had in mind when he spoke of Christians as "crying out" to God as "Father." Frequently it has been suggested that this "crying out to God as Father" should be understood in the context of the early Christians praying the Lord's Prayer, which begins with the familial affirmation "Our Father."[4] Others, however, have postulated that Paul had in mind either some portion of an early Christian confession, or some early Christian baptismal formula, or, perhaps some other early Christian liturgical formulation of his day, or some prominent ecstatic utterance that had been expressed in early Christian worship. But as C. E. B. Cranfield has quite rightly observed in stating his own opinion:

> The true explanation is surely rather the simple one that *krazein* is used again and again in the LXX of urgent prayer, being so used in Psalms alone more than forty times (e.g., 3.4 [LXX: 5]; 4.3 [LXX: 4]; 18.6 [LXX:17.7]; 22.2, 5 [LXX: 21.3, 6]; 34.6 [LXX: 33.7]). It is used to represent several different Hebrew words. So here it is best taken to denote an urgent and sincere crying to God irrespective of whether it is loud or soft (or even unspoken), formal or informal, public or private.[5]

Paul closes this final paragraph of his contextualized proclamation in Romans 8:1-17 with the following twofold declaration: that it is "the Spirit himself" (*auto to pneuma*) who "testifies with our spirit" (*summartyrei to pneumati hēmōn*) that "we are children of God" (*esmen tekna theou*), as he says in verse 16; and, that "since we are children" (*ei tekna*), we are "also heirs of God" (*kai klēronomoi theou*) and "co-heirs with Christ" (*sunklēronomoi Christou*), as he states in verse 17. Thus as those who are "in Christ Jesus," and therefore also "in the Spirit," believers in Jesus have come to experience a more intimate and far more truly filial relationship with God than could ever have been experienced under the "covenantal nomism" of the religion of Israel that God provided for his people, as expressed throughout the Jewish Scriptures. For now as God's own people, who are "in Christ Jesus" and live "by the Spirit," Christians can address God directly as "Father" (*abba ho patēr*) and are able to enjoy all of the benefits of being "children of God" (*tekna theou*). They are also, as Paul indicates in 8:18-30, involved in the advance of God's program of "salvation history" by "sharing in his [Christ's] sufferings in order that we may also share in his [Christ's] glory."[6]

The Significance of the Metaphor of Adoption in Romans 8:15

A major presentation of Paul's gospel proclamation is that found in Romans 8:1-17. In the materials of 8:1-11 Paul has been building up to the theme of believers in Jesus as being "children of God" (*tekna theou*). The hortatory material of 8:12-13, however, while vitally important, has somewhat broken the fuller development of that theme of believers as God's children. Therefore, in 8:14-17 he fills out the details of that important theme by (1) quoting what appears to be an early Christian confessional affirmation: "All who are led by the Spirit of God, they are sons [and daughters] of God" (*houtoi huioi theou eisin*); (2) referring to the Greco-Roman laws of "adoption" and using that socio-legal family situation of antiquity as a metaphor for the God-given status of a believer in God's family; (3) highlighting the work of the Spirit in bringing about a believer's new status as a child of God and in witnessing to the believer of the reality of this new family relationship; and (4) speaking about the results of being God's sons and daughters as including being "heirs of God and co-heirs with Christ" and as sharing "in his [Christ's] sufferings in order that we may also share in his glory."

A major contribution to the understanding of a Christian's new status, which has been established by God through the work of Jesus Christ and the ministry of the Spirit, was set out by Joachim Jeremias in his concise little book *The Central Message of the New Testament* of 1965 and his more extensive and detailed monograph *Abba: Studien zur neutestamentlichen Theologie und Zeitgeschichte* of 1966.[7] Jeremias observed (1) that while the word "father" (*'ab* in both Hebrew and Aramaic) was employed widely among Jews for an ancestor and other respected persons, the emphatic vocative form of "father" was used by Jewish children in an affectionate manner with respect to their own human fathers; (2) that Jesus used this form of address in his Gethsemane prayer to God his Father in Mark 14:36; and (3) that this use of "Abba" by Jesus provides the key to the new relationship that exists between God and his people throughout the New Testament presentations of the Christian gospel.[8] Further, the fact that in Mark 14:36, Romans 8:15, and Galatians 4:6 the Aramaic term "Abba" (*abba*) is immediately followed by the Greek term "Father" (*patēr*) indicates that such an affectionate consciousness of intimate relationship with God was widespread among early believers in Jesus, whether Aramaic or Greek speaking, and the fact that the Greek form of the expression is articular, that is, that it reads *ho patēr* ("the father"), suggests that the Greek form of the expression, as well as its Aramaic counterpart, should be understood as a vocative of address that carries an emphatic nuance.[9]

In such a family relationship, with God as our Father and believers in Jesus as God's adopted "sons and daughters," everything changes! Picking up from his use of the imagery and language of slavery in Romans 6:16-18 and 7:14, Paul declares here in Romans 8:15: "You did not receive a spirit that makes you a slave again to fear. Rather, you received a spirit of adoption by God as his sons and daughters, by which we cry out 'Abba, Father.'"

Paul's two uses of *pneuma* ("spirit") in the two clauses of this verse could be viewed (either or both) as referring to God's Holy Spirit, and so capitalized. More likely, however, they should both be understood as signifying "the activating or essential principle influencing a person,"[10] and therefore not capitalized. Thus the believer in Jesus lives his or her life in an entirely new environment—that is, no longer activated by the principle of "slavery to sin," which results only in fear, but activated by the principle of *huiothesia*, that is, by the reality of having been "adopted by God as his sons and daughters." It is this new factor of life that makes all the difference in one's Christian experience—not that "of slavery again unto fear" (*douleias palin eis phobon*), but that "of adoption (*huiothesias*) as his [God's] sons and daughters."

An Appeal for a Greater Appreciation of the Metaphor of Adoption in Paul's Proclamation

Christian biblical theology has most often focused on (1) the person and work of Jesus as Israel's promised Messiah, (2) the message of the New Testament as being the fulfillment of the religion of Israel in the Old Testament, and (3) the soteriological expressions "righteousness," "justification," "redemption," and "propitiation" ("expiation" or "sacrifice of atonement") as expressing the essence of the Christian proclamation. These are matters that have constituted the central themes in the theologies and writings of not only the church fathers of the first five centuries of Christian history, but also the Protestant reformers of the fifteenth and sixteenth centuries. This includes, of course, the vast majority of orthodox Christian theologians, preachers, teachers, and writers today. These are, in fact, the foundational themes of earliest Christian proclamation, expressed at many places and in various ways throughout the whole of the New Testament. They certainly, therefore, must be viewed as having been of great importance to the earliest Jewish believers in Jesus, to those influenced by early Jewish Christianity (as were, as we believe, the Christians at Rome), and to various other Christians scattered throughout the ancient world (as were the believers in Jesus in Ethiopia and elsewhere in North Africa). Further, they have been central features in the theologies of most of the "established" churches of the western world, whether Catholic, Orthodox, or Protestant.

What needs also to be recognized, however, is that while Paul fully agrees with all of these important matters (as I will attempt to highlight in a forthcoming Romans commentary in explicating Section I of his letter to the Christians at Rome, that is, 1:16–4:25), what he presents in 5:1–8:39, he considered his "spiritual gift" to his Roman addressees. He gave to those believers in Jesus at Rome this gift "so as to make you [i.e., them] strong" (1:11) and "so that we [i.e., both the believers at Rome and Paul] may be mutually encouraged by each other's faith, both yours and mine" (1:12). This form of Christian proclamation the apostle viewed as being uniquely his own contextualized presentation of the Christian message (cf. his use of the expression "my gospel" in Romans 2:16 and 16:25).

That "spiritual gift" of understanding and experiencing the "good news" of the Christian gospel in terms of its personal, relational, and participatory features, as presented in Romans 5:1–8:39, comes to quite explicit focus in the materials of Romans 8:1-17, where Paul sets out (1) the pronouncement of "no condemnation" for those who are "in Christ Jesus" (as in 8:1); (2) the themes of life "in Christ Jesus" and life "in the Spirit" (as in 8:2-8); (3) the experience of "Christ by his Spirit" being in and controlling the Christian (as in 8:9-11); and (4) the ethical imperative that is involved in the proclamation of the Christian gospel and in commitment to Jesus Christ (as in 8:12-13). But Paul also includes in that focus (5) what it means to be a "child of God," using the Greco-Roman familial metaphor of "adoption" as a meaningful illustration of what all of those four previous declarations mean for a Gentile hearer or reader who had been brought to God by means of the salvific work of Jesus, the message of the Christian gospel, and the ministry of the Spirit (so 8:14-17).

Paul is not presenting in Romans 8:1-17 some type of "second blessing," "deeper life," or "higher life" theology, as has sometimes been advocated for Christians in certain circles today. Rather, he is calling on believers in Jesus to understand and experience the Christian gospel, not just in the traditional manner of Judaism and early Jewish Christianity—that is, by highlighting the forensic terms "righteousness," "justification," "redemption," and "propitiation" ("expiation" or "sacrifice of atonement"), as, evidently, the Christians at Rome were doing. Rather, building on the truths of these forensic realities, he calls them to move forward in their Christian lives to an understanding of the meaning of "peace (i.e., *shalom*, completeness) with God" and "reconciliation to God" (as he sets out in 5:1-11). Finally, he encourages them to come to appreciate and experience the vitally important personal, relational, and participatory features of the Christian message of "life in Christ Jesus," "life in the Spirit," and "Christ by his Spirit" being in and controlling the Christian.

There is no doubt that Christians today need to do the following: focus their attention on Christ Jesus as their Savior and Lord; understand their Christian faith as rooted in the Scriptures of the Old Testament; see the lines of continuity that can be drawn between the proclamation of Christian gospel, as declared in the New Testament, and God's dealings with his people in the religion of Israel, as portrayed in the Old Testament; and, finally, appreciate the basic meanings and further New Testament developments of such soteriological terms as "righteousness," "justification," "redemption," and "propitiation" ("expiation" or "sacrifice of atonement"), both in Judaism and in early Jewish

Christianity. Such topics and such studies are certainly of great importance for all contemporary believers in Jesus. Yet the Christian religion is not just to be understood as the fulfillment of Jewish expectations about a promised Messiah and a Christocentric explication of Old Testament teachings.

Paul is proclaiming in his letter to believers in Jesus at Rome that the Christian message comes to its apex in what he presents to them as his "spiritual gift" in Romans 5:1–8:39—in particular, his proclamation in 8:1-17 of (1) "no condemnation" for those who are "in Christ Jesus," (2) new life "in Christ Jesus" and "in the Spirit," (3) "Christ by his Spirit" being in and controlling the Christian, and (4) the ethical imperative that must always be understood as being part-and-parcel of Christian proclamation and of commitment to Jesus Christ, together with (5) Paul's highly significant use of the metaphor of adoption, as drawn from the parlance of the Greco-Roman world, which highlights in rather dramatic fashion a number of major nuances (as enumerated earlier in this article) of what it means for believers in Jesus to be adopted (*huiothesia*) by God into his family.

It is this personal, relational, and participatory message of Romans 8:1-17 —including all that he proclaimed by his use of this familial metaphor of adoption in Galatians 4:5; Romans 8:23 and 9:4; and Ephesians 1:5—that Paul proclaimed to Gentiles in his missionary activities throughout various eastern provinces of the Roman Empire. Further, it was this personal, relational, and participatory message that he wanted believers in Jesus at Rome to both appreciate and accept as their own Christian experience, with the fervent hope that on the basis of their acceptance of such an understanding of the Christian gospel they would join with him by their prayers and financial support in a further outreach to Gentiles in Spain (and probably elsewhere in the western regions of the Roman Empire). It is this personal, relational, and participatory message that ought also to be a major feature today in the life and experience of all believers in Jesus, as an essential part of every truly "biblical theology," and at the heart of all Christian proclamation and teaching.

Endnotes

1. See, especially, W. J. Woodhouse, "Adoption (Roman)," in *Encyclopedia of Religion and Ethics*, ed. J. Hastings (Edinburgh: T & T Clark, 1908), 111-14; W. W. Buckland, *A Textbook of Roman Law from Augustus to Justinian* (Cambridge: Cambridge University Press, 1963), 124-28; J. M. Scott, *Adoption as Sons of God: An Exegetical Investigation into the Background of ΥΙΟΘΕΣΙΑ in the Pauline Corpus* (Tübingen: Mohr, 1992); A. Berger, B. Nicholas, and S. M. Tregarri, "Adoption," in *The Oxford Classical Dictionary*, ed. S. Hornblower and A. Spawforth (Oxford: Oxford University Press, 2003), 12-13; 54-57; J. Stevenson-Moessner, *The Spirit of Adoption: At Home in God's Family* (Louisville: Westminster /John Knox, 2003); T. J. Burke, *Adopted into God's Family: Exploring a Pauline Metaphor* (Downers Grove: InterVarsity Press, 2006); and idem, "Adopted as Sons (*huiothesia*): The Missing Piece in Pauline Soteriology," in *Paul: Jew, Greek, and Roman*, ed. S. E. Porter (Leiden: Brill, 2008), 259-87.

2. Quoting two of T. J. Burke's concluding statements in the "Summary" section of his book *Adopted into God's Family*, 194.

3. Yigal Levin, "Jesus, 'Son of God' and 'Son of David': the 'Adoption' of Jesus into the Davidic Line," *Journal for the Study of The New Testament* 28/4 (2006): 423.

4. So, e.g., O. Cullmann, *Christology of the New Testament*, 208-9; G. Kittel, "ἀββᾶ," *Theological Dictionary of the New Testament*, 1.6; J. Jeremias, *New Testament Theology, I: The Proclamation of Jesus*, trans. J. Bowden (London: SCM, 1971), 191-97; as well as a host of others.

5. C. E. B. Cranfield, *Romans* (Edinburgh: T & T Clark, 1980), 1.399.

6. All translations are the author's.

7. J. Jeremias, *The Central Message of the New Testament* (London: SCM; New York: Scribner's, 1965); idem, *Abba: Studien zur neutestamentlichen Theologie und Zeitgeschichte* (Göttingen: Vandenhoeck & Ruprecht, 1966).

8. See J. Jeremias, *Central Message*, esp. 9-30; idem, *Abba*, esp. 15-67, English translation: *The Prayers of Jesus* (London: SCM, 1967), 11-65; see also idem, *New Testament Theology, I* 61-68, 197.

9. On *abba ho patēr* as an emphatic vocative, see H. D. Betz, *Galatians* (Philadelphia: Augsburg Fortress, 1979), 211; also D. Zeller, "God as Father in the Proclamation and in the Prayer of Jesus," in *Standing Before God: Festschrift J. M. Oesterreicher*, ed. A. Finkel and L. Frizzell (New York: KTAV, 1981), 122-25.

10. Quoting definition 5a of the word "spirit" in *Merriam Webster's Deluxe Dictionary*, Tenth Collegiate Edition.

(Re)reading Paul
Jewish Reappraisals of the Apostle to the Gentiles

John E. Phelan Jr.

Paul has always had his critics. They lurk behind the more polemical parts of his letters. Paul is not gentle with them: "I wish those who unsettle you would castrate themselves!" (Galatians 5:12). Even his friends found Paul at times perplexing: "[Paul's]...letters [contain] some things [that are] hard to understand, which the ignorant and unstable twist to their own destruction, as they do the other scriptures" (2 Peter 3:16). But Paul became for Christians *the* apostle. His letters would make up a significant portion of the New Testament, and for what was to become Christianity, his vision, however misunderstood, would become normative. The church's greatest thinkers, from Augustine in the formative years, to Luther and Calvin during the Reformation, to Karl Barth in the modern era, have laid their theological superstructures on a Pauline (or at least a supposed Pauline) foundation.

The amount of scholarly work done on Paul in the last two hundred years alone has been staggering. And yet, the apostle remains as elusive and perplexing as ever. Paul is vilified and adored; seen as a misogynist and a liberator, as patriarchal and egalitarian, as Christianity's first great theologian and as the betrayer of the simple message of Jesus. And Paul is a, or perhaps *the*, battleground for Jews and Christians. For Jews Paul has not been the *apostle*, but the *problem*. While since the nineteenth century, at least, Jewish scholars have been able to reappropriate Jesus as a Jew, Paul is another matter.[1] For many, if not most Jews, it has been "Jesus, yes! Paul, never!"

Jews take issue with Paul not simply because his approach to the Jewish law is unacceptable and his understanding of Jesus's nature perplexing but, according to Jonathan Sacks, the chief rabbi of the United Synagogue in the United Kingdom, because he was "the architect of a Christian theology which deemed that the covenant between God and his people was now broken.... Pauline theology demonstrates to the full how remote from and catastrophic to Judaism is the doctrine of a second choice, a new election. No doctrine has cost more Jewish lives."[2] Christian theologian George Lindbeck would, to a certain extent, agree, insisting that "the understanding of the church as the replacement of Israel is the major ecclesiological source of Christian anti-Judaism."[3] Many contemporary scholars would *not* agree that Paul is the architect of so-called "supersessionism."[4] To read Paul in this way is for many to misread him and, ultimately, misuse him.

Be that as it may, it is fair to say that reclaiming Paul the Jew is an uphill climb for most Jews! Daniel Langton offers this sobering assessment: "In contrast to the figure of Jesus, who has, in the main, been reclaimed as a good Jew of one sort or another, Paul remains an object of hostility and suspicion. While there have been a number of scholarly exceptions to this rule, one should not expect him, whose likening of the Law to 'sin' and 'death' still echo down the centuries, to enjoy a more general Jewish reclamation any time soon."[5] Nevertheless, over the last few decades some Jewish thinkers have been taking another look at Paul. In this they have been aided by Christian scholars' willingness to reappraise their own views of Judaism in general and first-century Judaism in particular. Christian reappraisals of Judaism have led in turn to a reappraisal of Paul's thought by Jews and Christians alike. In what follows I will consider six books written by Jewish scholars and published in the last sixty years that reclaim Paul the Jew to one extent or another. But first I will explore the factors in the nineteenth and early twentieth centuries that informed their reflections on Paul.

Paul in the Nineteenth and Early Twentieth Centuries

The nineteenth century in Europe brought with it the development of sophisticated forms of anti-Semitism. This was not the anti-Semitism of superstitious peasants, but the intellectualized loathing of Jews by both Christian and anti-Christian thinkers. In some cases it is what has been called "anti-Christian anti-Semitism." The Jews were blamed not only for being Jews, but also for giving the world Christianity and particularly the Roman Catholic Church! This strain of anti-Semitic thought was also frequently anti-Paul. Hans Joachim Schoeps cites two examples, one Christian, one definitely not Christian.

Friedrich Nietzsche despised Paul. For him Paul was the "eternal Jew *par excellence.*" According to Nietzsche Paul "shattered essential and original Christianity." He was "a genius in hatred, in the vision of hate, in the ruthless logic of hate. What has not this nefarious evangelist sacrificed to his hatred! He sacrificed first and foremost the Savior, he crucified him on his cross." Paul, "that morbid crank," is responsible for the "falsification of true Christianity."[6]

For Paul de Lagarde, renowned German orientalist, biblical scholar, and anti-Semite, Paul was responsible for the "transformation and falsification of original Christianity." De Lagarde shows himself an heir of Marcion when he writes:

> Paul brought into the church for us the Old Testament, under the influence of which the gospel, as far as was possible, perished. Paul favored us with the Pharisaic mode of interpreting scripture, which proves everything from everything, and has ready resources for discovering in the text the meaning that has to be discovered, then boasting that it follows only the word of Scripture. Paul brought home to us the Jewish theory of sacrifice and all that depends on it; the whole Jewish understanding of history was foisted on us by him.[7]

From this it is a short road to the Aryan Jesus and truncated Bible of the National Socialists.[8]

Such analyses led to the search for alternative origins for Paul's thought outside of Judaism. Surely Paul, Protestantism's great hero, did not bring about the destruction of the gospel! Surely Paul did not foist on the early church the perverse and peculiar ways of the Jews! Nineteenth- and early twentieth-century liberalism sought to disconnect Paul from both the Jews and Christian orthodoxy. For the so-called history of religions school, Paul's theological sources were not Jewish at all, but Hellenistic. Many Jewish thinkers found this analysis congenial. Paul's strange deviations from "normative" Judaism could be explained by his being a heterodox Hellenistic Jew. According to Langton: "As German Christian scholarship emphasized Paul's role in injecting pagan elements into the religion of Jesus, it comes as no surprise that the prominent American Reform rabbi, Kaufman Kohler…found Gnostic influences and Hellenistic religions to account for many of Paul's teachings."[9]

Martin Buber and Leo Baeck

Perhaps the most important early twentieth-century figure to attach Paul to Hellenism was Martin Buber. In his book *Two Types of Faith*, Buber "argued that Judaism and Christianity represented two entirely different forms of religion, even if they were historically intertwined."[10] Hellenistic Judaism, Buber argued, distorted Judaism by associating the God of Israel with the notion of "fate." "For Paul (and other Hellenistic Jewish writers), the fusion of Hellenistic fate with the Jewish belief in God created an enormous chasm between human beings and God, and, thereby, a need for reconciliation."[11] Although Paul's theology was rooted in a form of Judaism—it was a distorted form.[12]

For Leo Baeck the religion of Paul was a form of "romanticism." He wrote, "Christianity accepted the inheritance of ancient—Greek and oriental—romanticism. At an early date, the traditional national religion of the Hellenic lands had been joined by a victorious intruder, probably from the north: another religion, phantastic and sentimental—the Dionysian or Orphic cult.... It had all the traits of romanticism: the exuberance of emotion, the enthusiastic flight from reality, the longing for experience."[13] Paul combined this Hellenistic romanticism with the power of Judaism to create a merger of "Orient and Occident."[14] In Paul's thought, "Judaism and paganism were now reconciled and brought together in romanticism, in the world of mystery, of myth, and of sacrament."[15] In the end, according to Baeck, faith for Paul was everything. Human beings could effect nothing; all was by God's intention, God's grace. He concludes, "the conception of the finished man which appears here—truly the child of romanticism for which truth is only a living experience—became one of the most effective ideas of the entire Pauline doctrine."[16]

Pamela Eisenbaum argues that Baeck's understanding of Paul's theology is entirely mediated by Luther. For Paul people are not understood as ethical beings, in that they are not subjects who act, but "objects who are acted upon, either by God's grace or by sin, and thus they are not accountable for their actions."[17] There could be nothing more at variance with traditional Judaism than this. Eisenbaum argues that Baeck and Buber's views of Paul were distorted because "they took for granted the typical German Protestant understanding of Paul....For Luther and the German Protestants who followed in his interpretive path, Paul's theology represents the pinnacle of human religiosity; for Buber and Baeck, it is the nadir. Buber and Baeck used Paul as a lens to critique Christianity, just as their Christian contemporaries used him to critique Judaism."[18]

The apparent ethical indifference, the vision of a passive human acted on by either fate or God without reference to their own actions, was anathema to Jews like Buber, Baeck, and Joseph Klausner, another critic of Paul. The latter concludes his book *Jesus and Paul* with these words: "It is permissible to say—of course with certain reservations—that it was not Jesus who created (or more correctly, founded) Christianity, but Paul. Jesus is the source and root of Christianity, its religious ideal, and he became all unconsciously its lawgiving prophet." But, he continues, it was Paul who "made Christianity a religious system different from both Judaism and paganism, a system mediating between Judaism and paganism but with an inclination toward paganism."[19]

Paul at Mid-Century

In the middle of the twentieth century things began to change. It may seem that the so-called "new perspective" on Paul sprang newly formed from the minds of Krister Stendahl and E. P. Sanders. But this overlooks the significant work of scholars like Johannes Munck of Denmark and W. D. Davies of Wales, who did much of his teaching and scholarship in the United States.[20] In fact, Stendahl in his foreword to Munck's *Christ and Israel* says, "it was reading this book more than twelve years ago which for the first time opened my eyes to Paul and his mission."[21] Munck laid the groundwork for Stendahl's programmatic essays in *Paul among Jews and Gentiles* and for the substantial rethinking of Paul's understanding of the Jewish people reflected in the "new perspective."[22] Both scholars took Paul's Jewish and even rabbinical background seriously. At the same time, Jewish scholars were also beginning a reappraisal of Paul, in part in reaction to the work of Stendahl and Davies.

H. J. Schoeps and Samuel Sandmel

H. J. Schoeps's *Paul: The Theology of the Apostle in Light of Jewish Religious History* came out at the same time as Munck's *Paul and the Salvation of Mankind.* Schoeps was a German Jew who taught at Erlangen University. For Schoeps, "the theology of the Apostle Paul arose from overwhelmingly Jewish religious ideas. In the age of tense Messianic expectation, Saul the Pharisee, following the religious convictions which came to him as a result of his Damascus experience and believing that the Messianic event had occurred, corrected traditional eschatology and refashioned it by means of the apocalyptic teaching about two aeons."[23] Paul's messianic expectations were all understandable within the Judaism of his day. On the other hand, Schoeps argued that Paul's Christology came from a combination of Jewish and pagan ideas. And that "by his doctrine of Christ's divinity Paul oversteps the bounds of Judaism, which has never known the idea of a divine Messiah, and has never attributed soteriological functions to the Messiah."[24]

Paul also misconstrued the law by separating the Torah from the covenant. "The law as a whole, resting on the covenant relationship, had ceased to be a living and personal possession for Paul the Diaspora Pharisee and Septuagint Jew." This led Paul to the question, "senseless for a Jew, whether the law as a whole was 'fulfillable.'"[25] For Schoeps, then, however important Paul's Jewish origins, his Diaspora Judaism and identification of Jesus as Messiah led him to misconstrue the law and God's covenant with Israel. Schoeps further argued that Paul "fixed the relationship of the new people of God to the old by maintaining that the election had been transferred to God's new Israel, the Messianic church formed of Jews and Gentiles."[26] So, for Schoeps, however Jewish Paul was, however rooted his expectations were in the Messianic expectations among the Jews of his day, he fundamentally misrepresented the Jewish position on the law and the covenant, and believed that God had thrust the "old people" of God aside for the new.

A second important voice is that of Samuel Sandmel who published *The Genius of Paul* in 1958. Sandmel was an American Jew with an unusual academic pilgrimage. According to his son David Fox Sandmel, Dean Harvie Branscomb III of Duke University encouraged Samuel Sandmel to pursue a degree in New Testament.[27] Sandmel subsequently taught at Vanderbilt University and Hebrew Union College–Jewish Institute of Religion where he served as professor of Bible and Hellenistic Literature (it being unlikely that Hebrew Union College would have a professor of New Testament!). Shortly before his untimely death in 1979 he moved to the University of Chicago as the Helen A. Regenstein Professor of Religion. He was a major interpreter of Christianity for the Jewish world and made a significant contribution to Jewish Christian dialogue. He was, perhaps not surprisingly, a close friend of Krister Stendahl, who called him "a gift of God to both Jews and Christians."[28]

Sandmel insists that "Paul in his own mind has not deviated from Judaism; it is these opaque Jews who do not share his conviction who have deviated and gone astray."[29] Nevertheless, Sandmel wonders, "what was there about Paul or his environment which questioned the continued validity, indeed the eternity of the Law of Moses?"[30] Sandmel, like Schoeps, thinks it is Paul's origin in Diaspora Judaism that accounts for his misunderstanding and abandonment of the law. Diaspora Judaism, remote from the temple, steeped in pagan surroundings, faced challenges unthinkable in remote Jerusalem.

In fact, "the living Judaism of Paul and his contemporaries was scarcely identified with the Biblical religion."[31] Paul (and Philo, for that matter) reduced the law, Torah, to "laws." But "to Palestinian Jews, and their spiritual descendants, the word Torah never had so restricted a connotation; they equated *Torah* with our word 'revelation.' While they would have conceded that the Torah was a revelation which *included* 'law,' they would properly have denied that revelation and 'law' were interchangeable."[32]

Sandmel is not impressed with W. D. Davies's attempts to locate Paul's thought in Palestinian Judaism. "Davies' book is an admirable book, indeed, a great one—and one with which I disagree almost one hundred per cent."[33] He sees little connection between Paul and what would become rabbinic Judaism. For Sandmel as for Scheops, Paul, the Diaspora Hellenized Jew, fundamentally misunderstands his own tradition and therefore offers a distorted view of the function of Torah within Judaism.

Scheops and Sandmel represent a generation of Jewish scholars who were more willing to acknowledge Paul's essential Jewishness. Both clearly located Paul's thought within the Judaism of his day, even if that Judaism, Diaspora

Judaism, deviated from "normative Judaism" in significant ways. In this way they can account for Paul's essential Jewishness as well as for the ways Paul misunderstands and misrepresents the Torah and the covenant. Subsequent scholarship, however, has questioned the once ironclad distinction between Hellenistic and Palestinian Judaism. According to John J. Collins, due to the extensive Hellenization within Palestine, "the old distinction between 'Palestinian' Judaism and 'Hellenistic' (=Diaspora) Judaism has been eroded to a great degree in modern scholarship."[34] He continues, "Diaspora Judaism, no less than its counterpart in the land of Israel, had its frame of reference in the Torah."[35] Paul's apparent deviations from Judaism cannot be explained with reference to his origins in the Diaspora. Furthermore, in subsequent years both Jewish and Christian scholars began to wonder if Paul's apparent misreading of the law and the covenant had more to do with Protestantism than Hellenism!

New Perspective for Jews and Christians

The story has by now been told many times. A sea change in the way Paul is read began with a slim book of essays by Krister Stendahl. He argued that Paul had been misunderstood for generations because he had been read through the experience of Luther and "the introspective consciousness of the west."[36] Paul did not agonize over his inability to keep the law, in fact, he had a rather "robust conscience"—or as my old teacher A. C. Sundberg used to put it, a "robust ego"![37] Furthermore, his so-called conversion was more of a "call" than a conversion. Paul was not a Jew who "converted" to another religion or *started* a new religion. He was a Jew who, like the prophets of old, experienced the call of God.[38] Protestants, Stendahl insisted, have read Paul the Jew not in his own terms, but in terms of Martin Luther's internal struggles with late medieval Catholic piety.[39]

Stendahl's book was based on lectures he did in the 1960s although the book itself was not released until 1976. A year later E. P. Sanders published *Paul and Palestinian Judaism: A Comparison of Patterns of Religion.* The book changed the conversation on Paul forever. He argued that Christians have misread Judaism as a religion of legalists determined to pursue salvation via "works righteousness." On the contrary, "God chose the Jews as his elect people and gave them the Torah to live by as their covenant obligation. God rewards obedience and punishes transgression. The Torah includes provisions for forgiveness and atonement. Those who maintain their covenant membership through obedience to Torah will be saved by God's grace." Jews, in other words, did not believe that their works made them righteous before God in the sense that Christians had claimed. It was the mercy of God's election of and his covenant with Israel that assured Israel of salvation.[40] Sanders thus called the entire framework of Protestant Pauline interpretation into question.

Sanders's book, along with his subsequent works, produced a cottage industry for Sanders fans and Sanders critics. As Pamela Eisenbaum puts it, "Sanders's book is one of those rare works whose influence on subsequent scholarship is difficult to overstate."[41] Christian scholars like James Dunn and N. T. Wright, taking their cue in part from Sanders, reassessed every part of Paul's thought in light of Sanders's reassessment of Judaism. And Jewish scholars have done the same. Scholars like Alan Segal, Daniel Boyarin, Mark Nanos, and Pamela Eisenbaum have been able to come to Paul from a fresh Jewish perspective, assured of a more favorable hearing from both Jews and Christians than they may have had before Stendahl and Sanders.

Alan Segal and Daniel Boyarin

Alan Segal was for many years a professor of Jewish studies at Barnard College. He is best known for his book *Paul the Convert*, published in 1990.[42] Segal points out that Paul "is one of only two Pharisees to have left us any personal writing" and the "only first century Jew to have left confessional reports of mystical experiences (2 Corinthians 12:1-10)." In fact, Paul "should be treated as a major source in the study of first century Judaism."[43] A bit later he says that in light of this "it is a pity that few Jewish writers have attempted to understand Paul. Because of the polemical context that forms the basis of Paul's letters, Christianity has been sadly bereft of all but the most daring of Jewish scholars' observations of Paul."[44] Thankfully, since Segal published his volume in 1990, this has begun to change.

Segal focuses on Paul's mystical/apocalyptic experience, arguing for a link in Judaism between mystical experience and apocalyptic speculation. Paul, for Segal, represents this important stream of Judaism. He even suggests that Paul's Christology is not alien to the Judaism of his day: "The identification of Jesus with the manlike appearance of God is both the central characteristic of Christianity and understandable within the context of Jewish mysticism and apocalypticism."[45] Segal not only sees continuity with contemporary Jewish apocalyptic mysticism, he sees a profound connection with what would become rabbinic Judaism. He explores Romans 11, a text that would become increasingly important in Jewish assessments of Paul. He notes the strange ambiguity in Romans 9-11. On the one hand, "Paul implies that only those who accept Christ will be saved," but he never actually says so! Instead, "he surprisingly asserts the rabbinic notion that all Israel will be saved (11:26)." Segal continues, "rather than merely abandon the unbelieving members of the Jewish community, Paul asserts that God's promises to them are still intact: 'For the gifts and call of God are irrevocable' (11:29)."[46] Paul's angry words in Galatians about agitators who are attempting to impose the law on his Gentile converts, are changed to words of alarm in Romans when he begins to see what could happen to the Jews in a majority Gentile community. Contemporary Christians who read Paul's words in defense of a threatened minority in their own situation of comfortable majority misuse those words and undermine Paul's purpose. For Segal, then, Paul's "conversion," his Christology, and even his understanding of the covenant are firmly rooted in the varieties of first-century Judaism, including the stream that led to rabbinic Judaism.

Daniel Boyarin, in his 1994 volume *A Radical Jew*, echoes Segal's concern that Paul has been neglected as a source for exploring first-century Pharisaic Judaism.[47] He would also like "to reclaim Paul as an important Jewish thinker. On my reading of the Pauline corpus, Paul lived and died convinced he was a Jew living out Judaism. He represents, then, one option that Judaism could take in the first century."[48] Nevertheless, Paul represents a serious challenge to Boyarin as a Jew. Paul's vision was a universal one that included both Jews and Gentiles. "While Paul's impulses toward the founding of a non-differentiated, non-hierarchical humanity were laudable in my opinion, many of its effects in terms of actual lives were not. In terms of ethnicity, his system required that all human cultural specificities—first and foremost, that of the Jews—be eradicated, whether or not the people in question were willing."[49] The outcome of this would be inevitably the "merging of all people into the dominant culture."[50]

All this places Boyarin in an almost intolerable tension: "the claims of difference and the desire for universality are both—contradictorily—necessary; both are equally problematic." The necessity of tolerance, solidarity, and equality in a world characterized by difference cannot be underestimated. But "just as surely the insistence on the value of ethnic—even genealogical—identity that the Rabbis put forth cannot be ignored or dismissed because of the reactionary uses to which it can and has been put."[51] Boyarin wants to reclaim Paul as an "internal critic of Jewish culture" and not as the founder of a new religion. To view him as a founder of a new religion is to "marginalize" him, when his critique is needed for both Judaism and Christianity.[52]

Boyarin appreciates the rereading of Paul "undertaken in the wake of the treatises of Krister Stendahl, W. D. Davies, and his student E. P. Sanders.... Perhaps, not surprisingly, this book [*A Radical Jew*] is part of the movement to thoroughly discredit the Reformation interpretation of Paul and particularly the description of Judaism on which it is based." Boyarin argues that this Reformation reading is not only unsupportable in scholarly terms, but an "ethical scandal as well, and one that does Christianity no credit." Paul does offer a critique of Judaism, he says, but not "the slanderous libel that Luther accused him of."[53] It should be said that later Jewish scholarship on Paul would not be so sure that Paul was the sort of critic of Jewish particularity Boyarin imagined him to be. Both Eisenbaum and Mark Nanos are convinced that Paul was perfectly happy for Jews to remain Jews in all their particularity in spite of Paul's insistence that Jews and Gentiles are now "one in Messiah."

Mark Nanos and Pamela Eisenbaum

One of the most interesting contemporary Jewish interpreters of Paul is Mark D. Nanos, who teaches at the University of Kansas. His book *The Mystery of Romans*, published in 1996, was the winner of the National Jewish Book Award for Jewish-Christian Relations.[54] Nanos denies that Paul rejected the continuing election of Israel or sought to undermine Jewish adherence to To-rah. "This study," Nanos writes, "finds the Paul behind the text of Romans to be a practicing Jew—'a good Jew'—albeit a Jew shaped by his conviction in Jesus as Israel's Christ, who did not break with the essential truths of the Judaism(s) of his day, who was committed to the restoration of his people as his first and foremost responsibility in the tradition of Israel's Deuteronomic prophets."[55] We are a long way here from Baeck, Buber, and Klausner, or, for that matter, Schoeps and Sandmel!

For Nanos the problem that Paul faces in Romans is very different from the one he addresses in Galatians. In the latter text the threat is from Jews who want to make sure Paul's Gentile converts are properly integrated into Israel through circumcision and Torah keeping. In Romans, Paul is concerned with a majority Gentile community of Jesus followers who are marginalizing the Jews in their community. Nanos insists that the Jews Paul is concerned with in Romans are not Jewish followers of Jesus, but Jews proper. He imagines that the Gentile and Jewish followers of Jesus are still part of the synagogues of Rome. Gentiles, overly liberated from the Jewish law not only create offense, but undermine Paul's mission "to the Jew first."[56]

The most succinct account of Nanos's understanding of Paul is found in the *Jewish Annotated New Testament*.[57] He argues that Paul continued to be a Torah practicing Jew. He did not think that Jews who did not yet follow Jesus as Messiah were "outsiders to God's family." Jewish privileges were intact as far as Paul was concerned (see Romans 9:4-5). Nanos thinks that Paul expected that all Jewish Christ followers would remain faithful to their Jewish covenant identity by the observance of Torah.[58] He even argues that both Paul and Jewish synagogue officials understood him to be under the authority of the synagogue since Paul was subjected to the discipline of the synagogue (see 2 Corinthians 11:24). Nanos makes the idiosyncratic suggestion that the "powers that be" in Romans 13 are not the imperial governing authorities, but the Roman synagogue authorities![59] In short, as I once heard Jewish New Testament scholar Amy-Jill Levine say, "Mark Nanos's Paul is so Jewish my daughter could date him."

Pamela Eisenbaum's book *Paul Was Not a Christian* has already been cited several times in this article. Eisenbaum teaches New Testament at Iliff School of Theology in Denver. Like Boyarin, Eisenbaum sees Paul addressing issues critical to her self-understanding as a Jew: "I have come to regard Paul as a Jew who wrestled with an issue with which many American Jews wrestle: how to reconcile living as a Jew with living in and among the rest of the non-Jewish world."[60] Also like Boyarin, she is wary of Paul's solution but understands the power of critique. Like Nanos she believes "Paul was a Jew before and after his experience of Christ." She agrees with Stendahl that Paul was "called rather than converted."[61] She insists that "Paul's belief in Jesus would not have branded him a heretic—a pain in the neck perhaps, but not a heretic."[62]

On the two major issues of Torah and covenant, she argues first that Paul's audience was made up of Gentiles, so everything he says about the law applied to *them*, unless specified otherwise. As many have noted, Paul's morality, even as it applied to his Gentile converts, was thoroughly Jewish and rooted in the Torah. Although there were certain aspects of Torah observance that Paul thought unnecessary for his Gentile converts, "Paul never speaks against Jews' observance of Torah—never."[63] Furthermore, the law is not meant to condemn humanity; it serves a positive pedagogical function. She argues that Paul is not as cynical about human capacity to obey God and do good as Luther, Calvin, and their followers would be. From this it follows that "the doing of good works is not the opposite of faith."[64] Finally, "Gentiles do not need to be circumcised to be in accord with Torah. But they *are* obligated to be in accord with Torah."[65] Nanos and Eisenbaum, unlike many Jewish readers of Paul before them, see Paul not as an opponent and critic of the law but as an upholder of the law for both Jews and Gentiles in their separate ways.

To the question, "Does God have two plans of salvation, one for Jews and another for Gentiles?" Eisenbaum seems to say both yes and no. There is only one God who shows mercy on all. The right question is not, "How will I be saved? Rather it is [Paul's] answer to the question, how will the world be redeemed and how do I faithfully participate in the redemption?"[66] Paul does not, she argues, "collapse Jew and Gentile into one generic mass of humanity. All will be kin; none will be strangers but the Gentile will not become Jew, and the Jew will not become Gentile."[67] She concludes, "I think everyone can agree that Paul's message was about grace. Why is it necessary to put limits on this grace? Let's let Paul's message of grace stand as it is."[68]

Conclusions

How has Pauline scholarship in particular and the Christian world in general benefited from a Jewish (re)reading of Paul? Alan Segal, as noted above, thought it a pity that so few Jewish writers had attempted to understand Paul. This reluctance to study the person many thought their great enemy left Christianity "sadly bereft of all but the most daring of Jewish scholars' observations of Paul." The more favorable views of Jews and Judaism emerging in the wake of concerted interfaith dialogue following the horrors of the Second World War, along with the reappraisal of Paul's relationship to Judaism by Stendahl, Sanders, and company, have made it possible for many more Jewish scholars to study and comment on Paul. The distinguished list of contributors to the *Jewish Annotated New Testament* bears eloquent witness to this new openness. Scholars like Shaye J. D. Cohen, Alan Gregerman, Susannah Heschel, Amy-Jill Levine, and David Fox Sandmel are making significant contributions to the understanding of the New Testament. For this Christian scholars can only give thanks. Reading Paul and, for that matter, any part of the New Testament "with Jewish eyes" can provide fresh insight into that profoundly Jewish text.

Eisenbaum alludes to a second benefit of the Jewish (re)reading of Paul. She viewed Paul through her American Jewish experience—an experience that includes teaching at a Christian institution. As a Diaspora Jew and then a Jew following Jesus as Messiah, Paul faced a similar struggle and question as Eisenbaum. How does one live as a Jew in a culture that does not support one's way of being? Paul's attempts to carve out a space for Jews and Gentiles to worship and work together in the shadow of a frequently hostile Roman imperial system offered Eisenbaum a model for reflection and emulation. As Eisenbaum profited from considering Paul's struggle to remain faithful to his vision and his God, Christians in an increasingly secular and hostile environment can benefit from the long experience of marginalization suffered by the Jews. Christianity has often struggled to maintain itself as a minority culture. The Jewish experience of faithfulness in the most hostile of circumstances offers Christians hope. For Christians, (re)reading Paul from the margins could be a salutary experience!

Third, the recent Jewish interpreters of Paul have also shown that both Christians and Jews share additional common struggles and questions. As Boyarin notes, both traditions struggle with the tension between universalism and particularity and the risk of being absorbed by the majority culture. Both constantly ask what it means in individual circumstances to be obedient to God. Both wonder what it might mean for the world to be redeemed and what their respective communities might do to collaborate with God in that redemption. Both wonder how God can honor the covenant promises made to Israel while including the Gentiles in the conversation.

Finally, both groups can now acknowledge that the New Testament actually belongs to both communities. For Jews, the New Testament bears witness to the nature of Judaism in the first century. It contains books written by Jews and for Jews facing situations not unfamiliar to contemporary Jews. In light of this, Christians must recognize that they are "reading someone else's mail" and could use a partner to add the other half of the conversation. Jews are still justly wary of Paul and his Christian readers. But courageous and competent Jewish readers of Paul are helping both Jews and Christians to see the apostle to the Gentiles in a different and more positive light. Perhaps both communities, (re)reading Paul together, can profit from his passion and wisdom in an increasingly hostile political and religious setting.

For more than twenty years Klyne Snodgrass has been my colleague at North Park Theological Seminary. We have taught together, written together, traveled together, and worshiped together. Klyne has been a consummate scholar, a generous and congenial colleague, a valued intellectual sparing partner, and an able consultant. Since his office is only one door away from mine, we are frequently in and out of one another's office sharing questions, opinions, complaints and books. In fact, he quite unknowingly helped me with ideas for this paper! Klyne has been a scholar's scholar and a teacher's teacher. It has been an enormous privilege to co-edit this volume and make this small offering in honor of his years of scholarship, teaching, and friendship. May God grant you years of joy, dear friend.

Endnotes

1. For a brief account of this reappropriation see Susannah Heschel, "Jesus in Modern Jewish Thought," in *The Jewish Annotated New Testament*, ed. Amy-Jill Levine and Marc Zvi Brettler (Oxford: Oxford University Press, 2011), 582-85. See also her *Abraham Geiger and the Jewish Jesus* (Chicago: University of Chicago Press, 1998).

2. Cited in Daniel R. Langton, "Paul in Jewish Thought," *The Jewish Annotated New Testament*, 586.

3. George Lindbeck, "What of the Future? A Christian Response," in *Christianity in Jewish Terms*, ed. Tikva Frymer-Kensky et al. (Boulder, CO: Westview Press, 2000), 358.

4. Ibid., 358, 359.

5. Langton, "Paul in Jewish Thought," 587.

6. H. J. Schoeps, *Paul: The Theology of the Apostle in the Light of Jewish Religious History*, trans. Harold Knight (Philadelphia: Westminster Press, 1959), 276, 277.

7. Ibid., 277.

8. See Susannah Heschel, *The Aryan Jesus: Christian Theologians and the Bible in Nazi Germany* (Princeton: Princeton University Press, 2010).

9. Langton, "Paul in Jewish Thought," 586.

10. Pamela Eisenbaum, *Paul Was Not a Christian* (New York: HarperCollins Publishers, 2009), 57.

11. Ibid.

12. An excerpt from Buber's *Two Types of Faith* is found in *Jewish Perspectives on Christianity*, ed. Fritz A. Rothschild (New York: Crossroad Publishing Company, 1990), 143-53.

13. Leo Baeck, "Romantic Religion," in *Jewish Perspectives on Christianity*, 60-61.

14. Ibid., 62.

15. Ibid., 64.

16. Ibid., 67.

17. Eisenbaum, *Paul Was Not a Christian,* 56-57.

18. Ibid., 58.

19. Joseph Klausner, *From Jesus to Paul* (New York: The Macmillan Company, 1943), 581.

20. See Johannes Munck, *Christ and Israel,* trans. Ingeborg Nixon (Philadelphia: Fortress Press, 1967) and *Paul and the Salvation of Mankind,* trans. Frank Clarke (Richmond, Virginia: John Knox Press, 1959); and W. D. Davies, *Paul and Rabbinic Judaism* (London: SPCK, 1958) and *Jewish and Pauline Studies* (London: SPCK, 1984).

21. Munck, *Christ and Israel,* vii.

22. Krister Stendahl, *Paul among Jews and Gentiles* (Philadelphia: Fortress Press, 1976).

23. Schoeps, *Paul,* 259.

24. Ibid.

25. Ibid., 260.

26. Ibid., 261.

27. See David Sandmel's biographical essay on his father in Samuel Sandmel, *We Jews and Jesus* (Woodstock, VT: SkyLight Paths Publishing, 2006), vii-xiii. The original publication date of *We Jews and Jesus* was 1965.

28. Ibid., ix.

29. Samuel Sandmel, *The Genius of Paul* (Philadelphia: Fortress Press, 1979), 30.

30. Ibid.

31. Ibid., 46.

32. Ibid., 47.

33. Ibid., 223.

34. John J. Collins, "Early Judaism in Modern Scholarship," in *The Eerdmans Dictionary of Early Judaism,* ed. John J. Collins and Daniel C. Harlow (Grand Rapids: Eerdmans, 2010), 16-17.

35. Ibid.

36. Stendahl, *Paul Among Jews and Gentiles,* 78-95.

37. Ibid., 81.

38. Ibid., 7-23.

39. Ibid., 83-86.

40. Mark A. Chancey, "Sanders, Ed Parish," in *Eerdmans Dictionary of Early Judaism,* 1191-2.

41. Eisenbaum, *Paul Was Not a Christian,* 64.

42. Alan F. Segal, *Paul the Convert* (New Haven: Yale University Press, 1990).

43. Ibid., xi.

44. Ibid., xv.

45. Ibid., 44. See also Daniel Boyarin, *The Jewish Gospels* (New York: The New Press, 2012) and Peter Schafer, *The Jewish Jesus* (Princeton: Princeton University Press, 2012).

46. Segal, *Paul the Convert,* 280.

47. Daniel Boyarin, *A Radical Jew: Paul and the Politics of Identity* (Berkeley: University of California Press, 1994), 2.

48. Ibid.

49. Ibid., 8.

50. Ibid.

51. Ibid., 10.

52. Ibid., 12.

53. Ibid., 11.

54. Mark D. Nanos, *The Mystery of Romans* (Minneapolis: Fortress Press, 1996). See also Mark D. Nanos, *The Irony of Galatians* (Fortress Press, 2002) and Mark D. Nanos, ed., *The Galatians Debate* (Peabody, MA: Hendrickson Publishers, 2002).

55. Nanos, *The Mystery of Romans*, 9.

56. Ibid., 12-16.

57. Mark D. Nanos, "Paul and Judaism," in *The Jewish Annotated New Testament*, 551-54. See also his commentary on Romans in the same volume.

58. Nanos, "Paul and Judaism," 552.

59. Nanos, *The Mystery of Romans*, 289-336.

60. Eisenbaum, *Paul Was Not a Christian*, 3.

61. Ibid.

62. Ibid., 8.

63. Ibid., 224.

64. Ibid., 233.

65. Ibid., 239.

66. Ibid., 252.

67. Ibid., 255.

68. Ibid.

Justification by (Covenantal) Faith to the (Covenantal) Doers
Romans 2 within the Argument of the Letter

Nicholas Thomas Wright

Nearly twenty years ago Klyne Snodgrass published an article on Romans 2 in which he emphasized that Paul, like the Jews of his day, believed in a final judgment according to works.[1] Noting that Romans 2 has often been "lost in the shuffle" as commentators whisk across Romans 1:18–3:20, assuming that the whole passage simply demonstrates universal sinfulness, Snodgrass pointed out no fewer than five ways in which, he says, "more time has been spent explaining the text *away* than explaining it."[2] First, Paul is speaking only hypothetically about law-keepers; in 3:9-20 he declares the category empty. Second, Paul is speaking in 2:14-15 and 2:25-29 of "Gentile Christians who fulfil the law through faith in Christ and a life in the Spirit"—a position taken by many, including the present writer. Third, the passage consists of unsorted elements from Paul's Jewish past; fourth, it simply contradicts things Paul says elsewhere; fifth, 2:14-15 means merely that Gentiles will be judged according to the "law" which they have—and, as in the first option, that judgment will be negative.[3] Klyne will not be surprised that I want to revisit this question, and in particular to try yet one more time to convince him that the second of these explanations is not "explaining the text away," at least in relation to 2:25-29, but is actually getting to its very heart. I have of course written about these questions in various places before, but there are good reasons for wanting to mount a fresh argument of a particular kind.[4]

A parable occurs to me, as it might when thinking of Klyne Snodgrass and his work. Several years ago, before the time of mobile telephones, Klyne offered to pick me up at Chicago's O'Hare Airport as I arrived at the start of a lecture tour. We somehow failed to arrange a definite meeting place. I found myself on an upper level from which I could see the road below, and I saw Klyne driving by, more than once, looking out of his car window to see where I was. I was as frustrated, and helpless, as he must have been. Eventually we both hit upon the only solution. We went, independently, to old-fashioned phone booths, and called his wife, Phyllis, who was waiting patiently at home. She, as a *dea ex machina* to our annoying little drama, was able to tell us how to find one another, which we duly did.

The reason I tell this story is that my present argument is not aimed so much at Snodgrass's denial that Romans 2:14-15 and Romans 2:25-29 refer to Gentile Christians, though it is that as well. It is primarily aimed, from the other end as it were, at the sharp disjunction between the first two main sections of Romans (chapters 1-4 and 5-8) which has been characteristic of Pauline scholarship for over a century, and which still emerges in various forms. On the one hand, there are many commentaries in the broadly Lutheran tradition which still treat Romans 1-4 as the heart of Romans and, with that, the heart of Paul: this is where he teaches "justification by faith," and everything else, including chapters 5-8, is seen in this tradition as footnotes and "implications" for that central doctrine. On the other hand, many, following Albert Schweitzer, have seen Romans 5-8 as offering not just a different doctrine of salvation but a different *kind* of doctrine of salvation, and have said that this is the real heart of his thought. For Schweitzer, this meant that "justification" was a "subsidiary crater" within the "main crater," which was (what he called) "Christ-mysticism," and what subsequent generations have variously labelled in terms of "participation," "incorporation," and the like.[5] For E. P. Sanders, this was the real heart of Paul's thought, though it remained more opaque to research than people usually suppose—a challenge some have taken up.[6] And for Douglas Campbell, the first section of Romans (chapters 1-4) was intended by Paul, not as a statement of his own position, but as a sketch of a misleading view which he then corrects in chapters 5-8.[7] Over against these views, I want first to point out that there is a much greater and more intimate connection between chapters 1-4 and 5-8 than is normally supposed; then to argue that the whole of chapters 1-8, not simply chapters 1-4, has to do with "justification," and that what Paul says about "being in Messiah" and about the Spirit in chapters 6-8 are part of the depth dimension of that, not expressions of a different type or scheme of theology; third, to suggest, once more against Klyne Snodgrass and others, that when we read Romans 2 as a whole in this light there are excellent reasons for supposing that the picture of "Gentiles who do the law," certainly in 2:25-29 and possibly also in 2:14-16, are indeed Gentile Christians who are indwelt by the Spirit. There are one or two necessary spin-off points to be made as well, most obviously to argue that, in reinforcing Snodgrass's point about Paul believing in final judgment according to works, I am not in any way undermining, but rather giving full depth to, Paul's argument about present justification by faith.

A couple of preliminary points by way of introduction. First, I have argued elsewhere that the normal reading of Romans 2:17-29, and in particular 2:17-24, is simply wrong.[8] Paul is not here addressing a legalistic Jew (still less a "bigot," as in Robert Jewett's extraordinary classification) who thinks that he is somehow able to avoid the charge of sin.[9] Paul is addressing the Jew, perhaps his own former self as a strict Pharisee, who claims that, granted that the Gentile world is really as bad as it appears, *it is Israel's vocation to put things right*, by being "a guide to the blind, a light to people in darkness, a teacher of the foolish, an instructor for children" (2:19-20). Israel is the answer to the plight of the world. And the point of 2:17-29 is *that Paul agrees with this theological position*, but explains that Israel's covenant failures have apparently put the Israel-shaped saving plan in jeopardy. As the ancient prophets insisted, Israel is incapable of fulfilling the role of rescuing the world from the plight sketched in Romans 1:18–2:16. Scornful commentators have often accused Paul of gross overstatement, as though he were saying that all Jews steal, commit adultery, or rob temples as a way of trying to "prove that all were sinful," but this misses the point. Nor is it simply that "he asked the Jew if he practised what he taught."[10] He does indeed draw the conclusion in 3:10-20 that all are "under the power of sin," but within that wider argument of 1:18–3:20 the second half of chapter 2 is making a very different point. *Israel is indeed God's plan for the world's salvation, but Israel as it stands under the prophetic critique cannot fulfil this vocation.* This whole dimension is usually ignored, but it makes all the difference. It is strongly confirmed by the line of thought in 3:1-9, which makes much better sense on this reading than on any other—and by the emphasis in 3:21-26 on the Messiah's faithfulness as the means by which God's covenant faithfulness has after all been displayed in saving action. This is how the One God has kept his covenant promises to Abraham: through Israel's representative, the Messiah, and his salvific death. About these things we cannot now speak in detail, except to say that this creates a very different context for 2:25-29 to the one normally imagined—which may perhaps then play back even into 2:14-16, though that is more difficult. One cannot simply assume that the two passages are parallel.

The second preliminary point is that in offering this very brief analysis of Romans 1-8 I am not at all marginalizing chapters 9-11 and 12-16, as sometimes used to be done. In fact, just as the argument of chapters 6-8 nests within the larger argument about justification which runs from chapter 1 all the way to chapter 8, so chapters 1-8 themselves nest within the larger argument about the faithfulness of God which runs from chapter 1 to chapter 11, so that Paul is able to sum up at 10:6-11 the view of justification for which he had previously argued. And chapters 1-11, constituting a single if complex theological argument, are themselves put to the service of Paul's missionary and ecclesial agendas in chapters 12-15, with the summary at 15:7-13 functioning as the closing theological statement before the travel plans and greetings (not themselves without theological interest) in 15:14–16:27.

Back, then, to the difficulty of communicating between the upper and lower decks of O'Hare Airport. One entire theological world, it seems, has been standing on the upper deck, marooned in Romans 1-4, unable to make contact with the argument that is circulating around the lower deck called Romans 5-8. Has Paul really written a letter with two such different schemes more or less unable to meet up?

It would be nice at this stage to propose that some particular element in Romans 5—love, say, or grace—might play the exegetical role that corresponds to the role played by Phyllis Snodgrass in the original story. We will come back to that, but my point here is a somewhat different one: when we examine what Paul is actually saying, not least in Romans 2 itself, we find that the argument which reaches its conclusion in chapter 8 is not simply one that was launched in chapter 6 or even in chapter 5. It was one that was launched at least in chapter 2, if not in chapter 1. In other words, the impression of the arguments being stuck on different levels is an optical illusion. They are in fact different sections of the same level, and there is an all-important walkway in between them. (This point could equally be made, and has often been made, by pointing out that in Galatians 2-4 Paul employs most of the theological tools on display in Romans 1-11, but they are not there separated out. They appear to belong naturally together.)

The most obvious clue to the close linkage between 1-4 and 5-8 is found in the verbal and thematic ties between Romans 2 and Romans 8. Paul, I suggest, is consciously and explicitly providing in chapter 8 the long-range answers to the questions raised by chapter 2. The link is clearest in the legal language; for here, in chapters 2 and 3 in particular, *and then again in chapter 8*, Paul exposes to view the "forensic" dimension of his theology of justification. Despite the regular attempts to systematize his doctrine across the three letters in which it appears, neither Galatians 2-5 nor Philippians 3:2-11, the other main "justification" discussions, make the "forensic" dimension explicit—which is not to say that Paul does not hold it at that point, only that, as so often in theology, it is impossible to say everything all the time.

There is of course a danger in highlighting any single element of Paul's soteriology. The history of theology is littered with overblown schemes which have tried to elevate one aspect into providing the framework for the whole. But here it is Paul who is highlighting the "law court" image. In 2:1-16 it could hardly be clearer, with "God's judgment," *to krima tou theou*, awaiting all people, not least those who try to pre-empt it with their own words of judgment (2:1-3); with "the day of anger, the day when God's just judgment [*dikaiokrisias*] will be unveiled" (2:5), doing for the whole world what a just judge must do, that is, judging all alike, without partiality [*prosōpolēmpsia*] (2:11); with the sentence of condemnation on the one hand and the sentence of vindication, "justification" indeed, on the other (2:13); with the law being upheld, with witness being borne, and with God himself acting as judge through Jesus the Messiah (2:12-16).[11] If Paul had wanted to avoid the impression that he was describing a law court scene, he could hardly have done a worse job.

This motif, however, is interestingly absent from 2:17-29. The only sign of the law court theme is the single reference in verse 27 to "people who are by nature uncircumcised, but who fulfil the law" who will "pass judgment" on the circumcised who break the law. That links 2:17-29 into the larger "law court" scenario, but the section does not by itself add to, or significantly develop, that picture. The further development happens in 3:9-20, where Paul declares that he has "already laid down this charge" that all alike are "under the power of sin" (3:9). The inclusion of Jews within this charge, which is not the main point of 2:17-29, is implicit in 1:18–2:16 (that is another question we cannot examine here) and then explicit in 3:10-18, since "whatever the law says, it is speaking to those who are 'in the law'" (3:19), in other words, to Jews, since Gentiles are "outside the law" and do not possess it as their birthright, as he has already said in 2:12-14. Thus Scripture itself, quoted at length in 3:10-18, demonstrates that Jews join the Gentiles in the dock, where the "legal" or forensic language comes to its height. The purpose of the law saying what it does (shades, here, of Galatians 3:22) is "that every mouth may be stopped, and the whole world may be brought to the bar of God's judgment" (3:19). Once again, we cannot escape Paul's relentless build-up of legal language. If you want to avoid "forensic" soteriology, you had better not read Romans at all. The judge will issue a verdict, as in 2:5-11; but if what counts for the defendants is "the works of the law," then, as Psalm 143:2 says, on that basis "no mere mortal can be declared to be in the right before God." What the law brings is "the knowledge of sin." Even the wide-ranging word "knowledge," *epignōsis*, may itself here carry an echo of the law court (3:20).

But why has Paul invoked a law court scene at such length? Here the ways divide—and here we are near one of the heavily defended frontiers in contemporary debates about atonement. Ever since Anselm at least, a good deal of western theology has elevated some kind of legal framework into the controlling position. However, though that scheme claims its primary biblical legitimacy from Romans, it fails to take account of the way in which Paul's careful set-up of the law court scene is itself in the service of, and is held in place by, the larger motif of the *covenant*.[12] As I have argued elsewhere, when Paul speaks of the righteousness of God, which I have translated as the "covenant justice" of God in Romans 1:17 and 3:21, he is using language whose biblical resonances are not just "relational" in some general sense but more specifically covenantal. This is the "covenant justice" or "covenant faithfulness" because of which, in Daniel 9 and many other passages particularly in the Psalms and Isaiah, Israel's God will both punish his people for their multiple misdeeds and idolatries and also rescue them after the severe covenantal punishment of exile—a scheme of thought which goes back to the "covenant" passage in Deuteronomy 27-30. Indeed, it would be a plausible suggestion that *the reason Paul provides such a long and detailed law court scenario is because it is suggested by, and held in place exegetically and theologically by, his vision of God's covenant with Israel, and the strange way that has worked out through the Messiah and the Spirit.* And the covenant, precisely as in 2:17-20 and then again, more positively, in chapter 4 with its exposition of the covenant with Abraham in Genesis 15, was indeed put in place to deal with the sins of the whole human race—and with the effects of that problem in the wider world over which humans were made to be stewards. It is not the case, then, that Paul simply sets up a *iustitia distributiva*, still less a blind "retributive" justice, in 2:1-16, only to replace it with something quite different in 3:21-26. Nor is it the case (against Douglas Campbell in particular) that Romans 1-4 as a whole offers a "justification theory," on a kind of contractual model, which has to be replaced as a whole with the theme of "apocalyptic deliverance" in chapters 5-8. If people have read Romans 1-4 like that, they have misread it. Rather, from scenes such as Daniel 7 we have a rich mixture on which Paul appears to be drawing: an *apocalypse* or revelation of God's sovereign *judgment*, as in a law court with God as the judge and the whole world and all history ranged before him, with the *covenant* between God and Israel finally if strangely fulfilled, as the human figure, "one like a son of man," is lifted up to sit beside God and to exercise judgment over the monsters who have tyrannized the world, thus putting the whole world right at last. Paul does not make explicit use of Daniel 7, but as many have seen it is a narrative like this that he seems to have in mind. If we in the modern West find it hard to hold together apocalypse, law court, and covenant that is our problem, not Paul's.

But as soon as we see this point we ought to recognise that a very similar scenario is being played out in Romans 8, for which of course the intervening chapters, Romans 5, 6, and 7, have been preparing the way. Reading Romans at a run—as one should always do alongside the necessary attention to exegetical detail—one can hardly miss the way in which 8:1 appears to give a direct answer to 2:1-11: *ouden ara nyn katakrima tois en Christō Iēsou*, "So, therefore, there is no condemnation for those in the Messiah, Jesus!" The *katakrima* announced in chapter 2, and emphasized in 5:16-18, has somehow been dealt with, set aside, to be replaced with the *dikaiōma*, the positive verdict which declares that one is "in the right." Thus 8:1-4, introducing this spectacular and many-sided chapter, picks up the forensic language of chapters 2 and 3, not as an accidental echo but as the focus and substance of what Paul wants to say:

> So, therefore, there is no condemnation [*katakrima*] for those in the Messiah, Jesus! Why not? Because the law of the spirit of life in the Messiah, Jesus, released you from the law of sin and death. For God has done what the law (being weak because of human flesh) was incapable of doing. God sent his own son in the likeness of sinful flesh, and as a sin-offering; and, right there in the flesh, he condemned sin. This was in order that the right and proper verdict [*dikaiōma*] of the law could be fulfilled in us, as we live not according to the flesh but according to the spirit.

Instead of the *katakrima*, the *dikaiōma*—exactly as in 5:16, and echoing the language of 2:1-11. This is not the moment to explore the route by which Paul has arrived at that point—the route that passes through the valley of the shadow of Romans 7 in particular. But arrived he has, and with the triumphant *and still clearly forensic* announcement that God has condemned "sin" (not just individual "sins," but the dark force or power which seems to have taken over the world, holding all humans in its deadly grip and even using the holy, just and good law as its base of operations) in the flesh of the Messiah. We might note, both to affirm and radically to modify one normal reading of Paul's "atonement" theology, that this is both penal (*katakrima...katekrinen* can hardly be anything but penal) and substitutionary (the sentence of condemnation has been both passed and carried out in the Messiah's flesh, therefore the Messiah's people are not condemned), but that Paul does not say here that God condemned the Messiah. He condemned *sin* in the Messiah's flesh, the place where (we might say, echoing 5:20-21), sin had grown to full height through the law, so that in the place where sin increased grace might increase all the more. This is what happens when we allow the covenantal and apocalyptic meanings, not to replace forensic ones, but to hold them in proper (and biblical) context and balance.

But this flourish of forensic imagery at the start of chapter 8 is not the end of it. Paul returns to the point again, once he has built on the foundation of 8:1-4 his remarkable picture of the whole creation restored under the glori-

ous rule of resurrected humanity in the Messiah (8:17-27). The final vision of
the overwhelming, all-conquering love of God in 8:31-39 holds at its heart a
reprise of the "forensic" statement of 8:1-4: "Who will bring a charge against
God's chosen ones? It is God who declares them in the right [*theos ho dikaiōn*].
Who is going to condemn [*tis ho katakrinōn*]?" (8:33-34). Romans 8 does
not celebrate the completion of a train of thought radically different to that
of Romans 1-4. Rather, it has drawn out of those chapters the *forensic* setting
of the divine action in the Messiah through which the larger saving purpose,
the establishment of the "reign of grace" and the victory of divine love (5:21;
8:31-39), is now revealed.

The mid-point of this whole argument, summing up the effect of chapters 1-4 and pointing forward to chapters 6-8, is without a doubt the dense
but all-embracing summary in 5:12-21, which again highlights the *katakrima*
and *dikaiōma* in verse 16 and then the *katakrima* and *dikaiōsis* in verse 18.
(Paul seems to intend a subtle and interesting difference between *dikaiōma* and
dikaiōsis: the former appears to be the *act* of "putting right," and the latter the
verdict that results from this act, though that distinction owes as much to the
context as to any definite shades of meaning in the Greek words themselves.)
Once again we may say: Romans 1-8 forms a single argument about the revelation in action of the divine "righteousness," whose covenant overtones bring
it very close to the divine love (5:8-11, pointing forward to 8:31-39), and
whose purpose is put into effect through the cosmic law court in which God,
the judge, declares the verdict. This explains, were explanation necessary, the
persistence of the language of *dikaiosynē* and its cognates at several points in
chapters 6-8 where the normal sharp division would have left it behind (five
times in 6:13-20; 8:4; 8:10).

Romans 2 and 8 thus show every sign that they are talking about the same
thing. Paul has not abandoned the language of the law court for something
else, any more than he has allowed it to become free-standing, divorced from its
wider setting in the biblically rooted saving plan of God. But by now it ought
to be clear that in both Romans 2 and Romans 8 Paul is talking about the *final*
day of judgment, "the day when God judges all human secrets" through the
Messiah, Jesus (2:16). The "condemnation" which is done away for those "in
the Messiah" in 8:1 and 8:33-34 is the ultimate condemnation spoken of in
2:1-11, the death-sentence which follows the negative verdict. That is why the
positive verdict issued in its place cannot be merely a verbal announcement.
It will be the resurrection of the Messiah's people from the dead. That is the
underlying logic which binds 8:4 to 8:9-11. "What the law was incapable of
doing" (8:3) was to give life, as it had wanted to do (7:10) but could not because of the "flesh," the weak and rebellious human nature which was shared
even, paradoxically and tragically, by "Israel according to the flesh." Israelites,

not least zealous Jews such as Saul of Tarsus had been, rightly embrace the To-rah but find that it condemns them (7:13-25, spelling out the dense advance summary in 5:20-21).

Notice what has happened. Romans 7:1–8:11 turns out to be not just a large-scale expansion of 5:20-21. It also follows on closely from Romans 2:17-29, read in the way I have proposed above. It is about *the vocation of Israel*; about *the failure of that vocation* because the law itself, which gave shape to that vocation, necessarily accused Israel of sin, and indeed of being under the power of sin; and about *God's faithfulness in creating nevertheless a people in whom that vocation would be carried forward.* This leads into the central section of Romans 8, in which those who are led by the Spirit are on their way to the "inheritance" in which they will share the "glory" of the Messiah—which is not so much his heavenly radiance as his rule over the whole world. This theme, regularly ignored, is what Paul says explicitly in the advance statement of 5:17: "those who receive the abundance of grace, and of the gift of *dikaiosynē*, reign in life through the one man Jesus the Messiah."[13] The idea, which undoubt-edly goes back to the biblical theme of "the saints of the most high" who are given sovereignty over the world, as in Daniel 7:22, 27, emerges elsewhere in Paul in, for instance, the otherwise bewildering passage in 1 Corinthians 6:2-3 where Paul suddenly asks, "Don't you know that God's people will judge the world?...Don't you know that we shall be judging angels?"

Two vital conclusions follow from all this, both of which could be stated at much greater length. First, it is thoroughly misleading to separate out chapters 1-4 and 5-8 and ascribe a different "soteriology" to each. The two sections are tied together in dozens of ways, large and small. Second, Romans 8 shows every sign of being a fresh statement, developed in the light of the intervening chapters with all their complexity, of what Paul had said briefly in advance in Romans 2:25-29. (This is backed up by the fact that 2:17-29 forces him to ask the questions of 3:1-9, which are to be virtually identical to the ones which chapter 8 forces him to ask in chapter 9.[14])

This provides strong encouragement to resist even the arguments of Klyne Snodgrass, and to understand 2:25-29 as an advance statement, puzzling at the time but now explained, concerning those whom Paul describes in 8:5-16, who belong to the Messiah, who are indwelt by the Spirit—and who are given the surprising role of "judging" (2:27: see below). The cryptic suggestion in 2:26 that there may be uncircumcised people who "keep the law's requirements," restated in 2:27 in terms of uncircumcised people "fulfilling the law" (an oxy-moron, of course, like 1 Corinthians 7:19, since circumcision was itself one of the law's commandments, and thus pointing teasingly towards a fuller resolu-tion), is hinted at again in 3:27 ("the law of faith") and 3:31b ("we establish the law"). I have elsewhere argued that a similar point underlies 10:5-11, though we cannot pursue this here.[15] But in 8:1-8 we are faced, not with hints and guesses, but with strong statements about a new kind of "fulfilling" of the law: it is "the law of the spirit of life in the Messiah" that has effected liberation from "the law of sin and death," since, through God's action in the Messiah and by the spirit, "the right and proper verdict of the law could be fulfilled in us" (8:2, 4). How does this work out?

In developing the contrast between "flesh" and "spirit" in 8:5-8 Paul points to the answer: "The mind focused on the flesh … is hostile to God. It doesn't submit to God's law; in fact, it can't. Those who are determined by the flesh can't please God" (8:7-8). He does not draw the explicit conclusion, but it is staring us in the face: those who are "not people of flesh, but people of the spirit," as in 8:9, *do* submit to God's law, and *do* please God. However much this is obviously a radically redefined sense of "submitting to the law," it is one that Paul is determined not to lose. *And it corresponds more or less exactly to what Paul says in 2:25-29.* A further obvious link is made by 7:6, regularly taken as an anticipation of chapter 8, where Paul speaks of "the new life of the spirit" as opposed to "the old life of the letter": exactly the same contrast as in 2:29. We might also compare 2 Corinthians 3:4-6.

Paul does not, to be sure, speak of Christians in 1:18–2:16 (leaving aside the question of 2:7, 10, 14-15) or 3:1-20. But the significantly different subject-matter of 2:17-29, and the way in which that section so closely anticipates the later argument of 7:1–8:11, means that it requires no "stretch of the imagination" to see Christians in 2:25-29.[16] To the horror of some, no doubt, Paul not only gives them the name *Ioudaios* in verse 29; he transfers to this people the role assigned in ancient Jewish apocalyptic writing to "the saints of the most high," namely, that of judge (2:27). And this chimes interestingly with the much harder passage in 2:14-16. By being "a law to themselves" (2:14), the Gentiles there spoken of are, as it were, placed in judgment over themselves, as they approach the day when God will judge the secrets of the heart—another link with 2:29.[17] But this, too, cannot be pursued here. Enough for the moment to have established a bridgehead into Romans 2 by demonstrating— I think the word is not too strong—that Paul does indeed envisage Gentile Christians in 2:26-29, though, since the argument of 2:17-29 is different to what is normally supposed, their presence there plays a subtly different role to that which is normally supposed.

How then does Paul's argument fit together? In Romans 8, above all, Paul draws together into a single theology of justification two vital elements which are regularly overlooked by those who think he has fully expounded that doctrine in chapters 1-4—both those who hail those chapters as the center of his theology and those who downplay them as secondary, or worse. It is in Romans 8 that he states most fully *both* the role of the Spirit *and* the relation of the moral life to final justification. To *final* justification, we note; because, though we have not here expounded it, in between Romans 2 and Romans 8 comes, of course, 3:21–4:25, and indeed 5:1-11, in which Paul makes it clear beyond any cavil that those who believe the gospel are reckoned, *in the present time* (3:21, 26), to be "in the right." *Justification by faith in the present truly anticipates the final verdict and thus provides the foundation for the united believing community without the boundary-markers of Jewish life.* I have argued elsewhere that 3:21-26 carries simultaneously the *forensic* meaning demanded by the immediate context and the *covenantal* meaning demanded by the wider context, not least Romans 4, and indeed by the proper meaning of *dikaiosynē theou*. This is the "apocalypse" in which the gospel "reveals" that God is in the right, that he is faithful to the covenant: the death and resurrection of the Messiah have brought forward the verdict of the last day into the present time, so that now, "in the Messiah," that verdict is pronounced not only over the Messiah himself but over all those who are "in him." (Paul, unlike many of his interpreters, has no difficulty combining talk of justification and incorporation, as Romans 3:24, Galatians 2:17, and Philippians 3:9 make clear.) But the gospel-believers over whom this verdict is thus pronounced (see too Romans 10:9-10) are precisely those in whose hearts the Spirit has worked to produce faith.[18] That same Spirit will now complete the task by producing, in the present time, not indeed a complete legalistic obedience to every jot and tittle of Torah (Paul frequently makes that clear), nor indeed, as some today want to argue, a renewed Torah-observance which would include a pure-food code, Sabbath-keeping, and so on,[19] but a way of life which corresponds to the divine intention of the life-giving Torah. This, I believe, is what Paul meant when he wrote, "When people patiently do what is good, and so pursue the quest for glory and honour and immortality, God will give them the life of the age to come" (2:7). It is what he meant when he wrote at least half a dozen other similar passages.[20] It is what he meant when he said, in Philippians 1:6, that "the one who began a good work in you will thoroughly complete it."

All this rules out the view, which one still meets, that what Paul said in Romans 2 is purely hypothetical, describing a class of people whom Paul will then declare to be non-existent. The most recent exponent of this that I have seen is Stephen Westerholm.[21] Westerholm sees that justification cannot be an excuse for moral carelessness, though saying that Paul, thinking of the judgment still to come, "found the thought sobering" is quite an understatement. Only in the final few lines of his discussion does Westerholm even mention the Spirit, without whose work the whole doctrine of justification (as expounded by Paul in Romans 1-8, not merely in 1-4!) cannot be understood; and there too we have a remarkable understatement, that "the Spirit's presence cannot but make a difference." Westerholm drives a wedge where none should go. "It is inconceivable," he writes, "that [Paul] meant to distinguish an anticipatory justification based on faith—one that allows for 'no condemnation' (Rom 8:1)—from a final justification based on a different criterion (performance of 'works of the law') that can call in question the original divine declaration. In the end, the decisive criterion for sinful humankind remains that of faith."[22] But this is attacking a straw man. Neither I, nor Klyne Snodgrass, nor anyone else I know who takes seriously Paul's language about a final judgment in accordance with deeds, is saying that this can "call in question the original divine declaration." The whole point of that original declaration is precisely that it is the true and valid advance statement of what will be said on the last day. By the time Paul reaches chapter 8, he has explained, though Westerholm in his new book has not, how the two verdicts will match. And here is the irony. Westerholm says that "believers' justification, first and last, rests on faith." I have sometimes been accused of saying that the final judgment has its "basis" in "the totality of the life led," and I plead guilty.[23] But my critics then ignore what I say later in the same paragraph, that the whole thing is "utterly dependent on the basic gospel events of the Messiah's death and resurrection." Westerholm would probably say the same thing; but by speaking of present and final justification "resting on faith," he tends, despite everything, to sound as though the verdict does after all depend on something within the human being, namely faith. And that, in turn, can lead only too easily into the kind of theology against which Douglas Campbell, rightly in my view, has reacted—though as I have said I believe Campbell to be wrong in seeing this view, put into the mouths of opponents, in parts of Romans 1-4. A robust theology of the Spirit's work, both in the initial call of the gospel and in the totality of the life led, avoids this problem, and ties together the whole of Romans 1-8 in a way which does justice both to the different emphases of different subsections and to the sweep and flow of the entire letter.

Has the Spirit, then, taken the role played by Phyllis Snodgrass in my earlier parable? Is it the Spirit that has brought together the two apparently divided sections of the letter? No. The Spirit is not mentioned in 1:16—4:25, apart from 2:29 which is part of the question. The theme that brings together the first two sections of Romans, and enables them at last to meet up as always intended, is God's plan for Israel, the plan *through Israel for the world*, the plan announced to Abraham and now fulfilled in the Messiah. Despite the continuing chorus of nay-sayers, the best word for this plan is "covenant." And that, both in Paul's epistle and in my own parable, seems somehow appropriate.

Endnotes

1. K. R. Snodgrass, "Justification by Grace—to the Doers: An Analysis of the Place of Romans 2 in the Theology of Paul," *New Testament Studies* 32/1 (January 1986): 72-93.

2. Ibid., 73.

3. Ibid.

4. See chapter 9 of my *Pauline Perspectives* (London and Minneapolis: SPCK and Fortress Press, 2013) (originally published in 1996); also the relevant section of my commentary on *Romans*, pages 393-770 in New Interpreters Bible vol. 10, ed. L. E. Keck (Nashville: Abingdon, 2002); and several passages in *Paul and the Faithfulness of God* (= *PFG*) (London and Minneapolis: SPCK and Fortress Press, 2013). References to the principal secondary literature will be found there, as well as in recent commentaries, e.g. R. Jewett, *Romans*, Hermeneia (Minneapolis: Fortress Press, 2007).

5. A. Schweitzer, *The Mysticism of Paul the Apostle*, ET (London: A. & C. Black, 1931), 225. See, recently, G. Macaskill, *Union with Christ in the New Testament* (Oxford: Oxford University Press), 2013.

6. E. P. Sanders, *Paul and Palestinian Judaism: A Comparison of Patterns in Religion* (London: SCM Press, 1977), 552; see the two essays in the Sanders *Festschrift, Redefining First-Century Jews and Christian Identities*, ed. F. E. Udoh et al. (Notre Dame: University of Notre Dame Press, 2008). The two essays are "What Is 'Real Participation in Christ'?" by Richard B. Hays (336–51) and "What Is 'Pauline Participation in Christ'?" by Stanley K. Stowers (352-71).

7. D. A. Campbell, *The Deliverance of God: An Apocalyptic Rereading of Justification in Paul* (Grand Rapids: Eerdmans, 2009). I understand that Campbell has modified his position somewhat, but still sees a great disjunction between Romans 1-4 and Romans 5-8.

8. See chapter 30 in *Pauline Perspectives*. Original publication in *Journal for the Study of Paul and His Letters* 1/2 (2012): 1-25.

9. See Jewett, *Romans*, here at 219-37.

10. Snodgrass, "Justification by Grace," 76. The Paul of Philippians 3:4-6 might have answered, "Yes."

11. Translations from the New Testament are, unless otherwise noted, from my own *The Kingdom New Testament* (= *KNT*) (English Title *The New Testament for Everyone*) (London and San Francisco: SPCK and HarperOne, 2011).

12. On "covenant" in Paul see *PFG* 780-82 and frequently; and my article, "Translating *dikaiosynē*," forthcoming in *Expository Times*.

13. In my translation at this point I have given two paraphrases for *dikaiosynē*: "those who receive…the gift of covenant membership, of 'being in the right'…"

14. See, e.g., my *Romans*, New Interpreter's Bible vol. 10, 454f.

15. See ibid., 658-65; and *PFG*, 1165-76.

16. Against Snodgrass, "Justification by Grace," 74.

17. I am grateful to my colleague Dr. Scott Hafemann for interesting discussions of this point, which he is developing in a forthcoming work for Mohr Siebeck in Tübingen, provisionally entitled *Paul: Eschatological Theologian of the New Covenant*.

18. See *PFG*, 952-6, 1028-32.

19. For this question see *PFG*, 1434-49.

20. Snodgrass, "Justification by Grace," 74, cites Romans 14:10-12; 1 Corinthians 3:13-15; 2 Corinthians 5:10; 9:6; 11:15; Galatians 6:7; and notes also Colossians 3:25; Ephesians 6:8; 1 Timothy 5:24-25; and 2 Timothy 4:14.

21. S. Westerholm, *Justification Reconsidered: Rethinking a Pauline Theme* (Grand Rapids: Eerdmans, 2013), 83-5.

22. Ibid., 84.

23. See *PFG*, 1028; and *Pauline Perspectives*, 434f.

INNER-BIBLICAL INTERPRETATION

The Man in Golgotha Street by Jan A. du Rand

On the artist's inspiration for the painting:
"Figuratively, in a theological sense, I found Klyne thirty-six years ago in the vivid rays of light at the foot of the cross. From there we departed as colleagues, proceeded to become sincere friends, and are now cruciformed brothers."

To Adore God's Identity through Theodicy
Reading Revelation 6:9-11 in Theological Coherence with a Remarkable Classical Example, 4 Ezra

Jan A. du Rand

Understanding and explaining the problem of evil and death in this world remains a crucial and difficult theological issue. In theological terms it is called theodicy, which can be defined in a rational (Eichrodt) or a social-religious (Berger) way. The answers lie on a rational-irrational continuum. Selected moments from Old Testament theodicy provide a comparable framework to evaluate and understand the occurrence of evil and death in 4 Ezra and Revelation 6 as part of the righteous person's life on earth. The answers of God through the angel Uriel on the problem of evil and misfortune of the righteous, as well as the message of Revelation, bring inspiring insights through theodicy that provide new perspectives on the identity of God.

The Issue under Discussion

According to Revelation 6:9-11, the martyrs who had been slain cried out with a loud voice: "I saw under the altar the souls of those who had been slain for the word of God and for the witness they had borne. They cried out with a loud voice: 'O Sovereign Lord, holy and true, how long before you will judge and avenge our blood on those who dwell on the earth?'"[1] The martyrs are crying out to God for justice. Their cry sounds like a dramatization of the rhetorical question attributed to Jesus in Luke 18:7 within the context of theodicy: "And will not God give justice to his elect, who cry to him day and night? Will he delay long over them?"

Revelation 6:10 essentially sounds like a prayer for vengeance with precedents in the Old Testament imprecatory psalms (35, 55, 58, 59, 69, 79, 83, 109, and 139). Such prayer or wish for divine vengeance also occurs in Nehemiah 4:4-5, Jeremiah 11:20, and Amos 7:17. Leaving aside the exegetical problems around the location of the martyrs or the type of altar, our focus falls on the understanding of the problem of evil and death that persist in this world. The altar can be seen as the point of contact between earth and heaven. The martyrs' cry can be interpreted within a context of theodicy and not as a cry for mere revenge. The theme of theodicy is directly or indirectly echoed in Revelation 12:10-12; 16:5-7; 19:1-2 and 20:3-4. We can trace through these passages an interweaving thread of the struggles of God's people to come to terms with the issue of hardship, evil, and death as realities in this world. The defeat of the dragon and the victory of Christ emphasize the dawning recognition of the exclusive reign of God and the Lamb. Such a perspective leads to a more tempered view of God in Revelation because the book provides the answers to the cry of the martyrs. And this brings us back to the inspiring story of theodicy in 4 Ezra.

The classical formulation of the problem of evil and death certainly comes from David Hume who translated the Greek philosopher Epicurus: "Is He (= God) willing to prevent evil, but not able? then is He impotent. Is He able, but not willing? then is He malevolent. Is He both able and willing? whence then is evil?"[2] The earlier answers given to the problem of evil and death were greatly influenced by the Old Testament and early Jewish writings. Fourth Ezra is an example. This effort to understand and explain the problem of evil and death is, as we have seen, called *theodicy*.[3] Walther Eichrodt, the Old Testament scholar, insisted that theodicy must be understood in a rational way according to the Old Testament, "to balance the present state of the world, with its physical and moral evils, with the all-inclusive government of a just and beneficent God"[4] From the field of sociology of religion, Peter Berger calls every attempt to explain evil and death in terms of its religious framework a theodicy.[5] And the subject of the theodicies in the Old Testament varies from the specific— Why did this evil happen to me?—to the more general—Why does there have to be evil? Some theodicies are used to explain moral evil (sin) and some natural evil (the curse of Genesis 3). In other words, a theodicy can range from a rational explanation to the complete opposite of a rational explanation. We may speak of a rational-irrational continuum.[6]

Selected Moments of Old Testament Theodicy

Before analyzing the theodicy and apocalyptic eschatology of 4 Ezra, we briefly give attention to some Old Testament examples to construct a comparable framework. In the Old Testament we may say that retribution occupies the rational pole, explaining evil by declaring that people get what they deserve.[7] The wisdom literature particularly emphasizes the doctrine of retribution, as in Proverbs 3:33-34: "The LORD's curse is on the house of the wicked, but he blesses the dwelling of the righteous. Toward the scorners he is scornful, but to the humble he shows favor." God's answers to Job are preferably categorized under the irrational theodicy. Other theodicies promised that retribution would happen in the future, or explained suffering as redemptive, probationary, or disciplinary.[8] The theory of retribution can be applied to many forms in the typical Israelite thought. The prophets used the theory of retribution in their writings about sin and the wisdom literature in their contrasting of the righteous and the wicked. A couple of examples will illustrate.

In the wisdom literature the general rule is that the righteous inherit good and the wicked evil in a world in which a moral order is maintained by Yahweh. For the wise, retribution explained the present state of evil and death in the world in the face of apparent injustices. In Proverbs 10:27 this principle is illustrated: "The fear of the LORD prolongs life, but the years of the wicked will be short."[9] The wise interpreted retribution as a vehicle whereby human creatures could shape their own destinies.

On the other hand, the prophets stressed that the reason for misfortunes lies with the nation's sin.[10] They operated from a more religious attitude. Therefore, misfortunes result from the injustices of the people and not the injustice of God. Both Genesis 3 and 6 tried to explain the origin of sin as connected to humanity and not exclusively as God's responsibility. The idea that sin is the reason for misfortune produced the conception that misfortune implied sin.[11] This becomes obvious in the discourses of the friends of Job. Instead of comforting their friend Job, the friends condemned him, trying to convince him that the cause of his misfortunes was his own sin. Eliphaz said to Job: "Is not your wickedness great? There is no end to your iniquities" (Job 22:5). Often evil was explained as the result of the collective sin of the nation. The untimely death of Josiah was interpreted as the result of the past sins of the nation (2 Chronicles 35:20-24).

Suffering could also be interpreted as a disciplinary procedure (Leviticus 26:14-18) or even as a test of the sufferer's faith or integrity. Consider the prologue of Job or Deuteronomy 8:2: "And you shall remember the whole way which the LORD your God has led you these forty years in the wilderness, that he might humble you, testing you to know what was in your heart, whether you would keep his commandments, or not." *Vicarious suffering*[12] as a form of redemptive suffering still held the idea of retribution in its background. That is to say, the vicarious sufferer, like the suffering servant in Deutero-Isaiah, is standing in for the other's sin.[13]

A prominent perspective on theodicy in the Old Testament is *future retribution*. Individual future retribution particularly appears in the wisdom psalms, which admit that the righteous may indeed suffer now, but that they are to believe in retribution for evil done them in the future.[14] We have to be wary of pinpointing other-worldly futuristic retribution within the prophets. In Isaiah 24, for example, the cosmic references ("heaven," "earth," "LORD of hosts") were only used as mythical language to describe the coming victory of Yahweh.

Theophany could be interpreted as another form of theodicy. The classic example, the book of Job, sketches theodicy as an overwhelming religious experience. Job could initially not find the meaning of his suffering, but later on he found meaning in his overwhelming religious experience of God's theophany. This answer to the problem of theodicy gives no logical explanation of suffering but constitutes a religious answer.[15] The psalmist found rest in "the sanctuary of God" (Psalm 73:17) and in the presence of God, according to Psalm 73:28: "But as for me it is good to be near God; I have made the Lord God my refuge, that I may tell of all thy works."

Early Jewish theodicy followed the same lines of theodicy than the Old Testament.[16] The wise man Sirach interpreted theodicy as discipline and testing. In Sirach 27:27 he says: "If a person does evil, it will roll back upon him, and he will not know where it came from."

The idea of an other-worldly future retribution really developed in early Jewish writings. According to the Wisdom of Solomon 3:18-19, death and suffering through sickness may seem unfair for the righteous but they will receive their reward after death through immortality.[17] "If they die young, they will have no hope and no consolation on the day of judgment. For the end of an unrighteous generation is grievous." Theodicy and eschatology have now been intimately linked. In the future life, in transcendental terms, the righteous will receive eternal immortality and the unrighteous eternal punishment. In future life the justice of God and the righteousness and unrighteousness of humanity will become known.

Apocalyptic Eschatology as Framework for Theodicy

The term *apocalyptic eschatology* refers to a particular type of eschatology, emphasizing the consummation of history. Two major biblical influences have contributed to apocalyptic eschatology: prophetic and wisdom influences.[18] H. H. Rowley has distinguished between apocalyptic and prophecy as follows: "That apocalyptic is the child of prophecy, yet diverse from prophecy, can hardly be disputed."[19] The differences between prophecy and apocalypticism have also centered on their different conceptions of history. The prophets usually expect God to intervene in history; therefore they have a positive view of history. On the other hand, the apocalyptists expect God to act beyond history;

therefore they have a negative view of this history.

Apocalypticism developed within a particular sociological setting. Otto Plöger identified the Hasidîm, who joined the Maccabees to oppose Antiochus IV Epiphanes (1 Maccabees 2), as the possible party out of which apocalypticism arose.[20] However, the Hasidîm did not belong to the mainstream of Judaism. Certain concerns in the apocalypses betrayed the views of a social class like the Hasidîm.[21] The only fitting conclusion would be to say that apocalyptic was not to be found in any one party within Judaism but throughout many parties. Concerning the possible social setting of apocalypticism, the indications are that it could have been a crisis-ridden post-exilic community living under a new threat.[22] The common element within apocalypses is described by Christopher Rowland as follows: "To speak of apocalyptic, therefore, is to concentrate on the theme of the direct communication of the heavenly mysteries in all their diversity."[23] It seems clear that an apocalyptic text like 4 Ezra could have been influenced by a variety of apocalyptic traditions. The possible connection to the wisdom tradition and its concern for theodicy provides a comparative and interpretative framework for a better understanding of theodicy.

4 Ezra: Structure and Content

Background. According to the Latin manuscripts, 4 Ezra (Esdrae liber IV) comprises chapters 3-14 of an extended form, known to the Apocrypha of mainly English Bibles as 2 Esdras. We also know of an expanded form in a Christian framework, adding chapters 1-2, known as 5 Ezra, and 15-16, known as 6 Ezra. The focus in this study falls on the known 4 Ezra, chapters 3-14.[24] 4 Ezra could be understood as a Jewish work, written soon after the fall of Jerusalem, 70-100 CE. The Latin manuscript presupposes a Greek text underlying it and suggests a Semitic original. The literary world of this text places the events in Babylon after the fall of Jerusalem in 587 BCE.

Chapters 3-14 of 4 Ezra consist of a series of conversational encounters between Ezra the scribe and God, through God's angel, Uriel. Ezra is struggling to understand Israel's misfortune and tragedy with Jerusalem's fall and the devastating captivity—a real theodicy situation. Ezra attempted to understand the problem of evil and death, describing it in terms of apocalyptic eschatology. The author's inner struggle is movingly sketched as he tries to reconcile the recent state of his world with his faith in God. Such inner struggle is reflected in the unfolding of the theodicy story. The pathos, according to 4 Ezra, is Ezra's wrestling with the question, why has God delivered his people into the hands of their enemies? The enemies live in prosperity while his own people are left behind to perish. Theodicy in this context tries to justify the ways of God to humankind.

Structure of its content. The general consensus is to analyze 4 Ezra as a seven-part structure.[25] The first three sections sketch Ezra's serious questions about God's justice and goodness in such difficult misfortunes. The last three sections portray Ezra as favored by God and report his experience of special revelation. The seventh section narrates the epilogue, Ezra's calmness of mind. The following outline can be helpful in the further analysis of the development of the issue of theodicy and apocalyptic eschatology in 4 Ezra. In the structural build-up lies definite meaning.

Introduction (1-2). The opening two chapters (also known as Ezra 5) contain a divine call to Ezra, a man of priestly descent (1:1-3) and the waywardness of the Jewish people, despite God's goodness (1:4-2:32). Then Ezra turns to the Gentiles (2:33-41) and he experiences a vision of a great multitude on Mount Zion (2:42-48). This is the Christian introduction to the book.

Section 1 (3:1-5:20). This section sketches Ezra within the context of captivity in Babylon, thirty years after the destruction of Jerusalem in 586/587 BCE. Ezra passionately pours out his heart to God in prayer because of the injustice of the current situation (3:4-36). But Israel's heart is full of evil. One of Ezra's questions is, why is Babylon doing so well while Israel is suffering so much? The angel Uriel replies that Ezra cannot comprehend God's ways and therefore should not question God (4:1-11). Uriel turns Ezra's attention to the future and speaks about the approaching end (4:26-5:13) and the signs of the end. Ezra's problem is that Israel has an evil heart that prevents them from being blessed.

Section 2 (5:21-6:34). This section has the same themes as section 1. Ezra is distressed (5:21-22) and complains about God's treatment of Israel. The angel Uriel answers Ezra that he is unable to understand God's ways (5:33-40). Ezra questions God's creation (5:41-45) as well as God's role at the end of time (6:1-6). Again, Ezra is told to wait until the end times and the end signs. To Ezra, Israel's suffering is unjust compared to the other nations.

Section 3 (6:35-9:25). Section 3 is parallel to the first two sections, starting with Ezra's passionate grief (6:35-37) and prayer (6:38-54), asking God why Israel does not possess the world made for her: "If the world has indeed been created for us, why do we not possess our world as an inheritance?" (6:59). Uriel, on behalf of God, answers that Israel must pass through tribulation to reach their inheritance (7:3-17). Then the angel talks about the end events. The wicked deserve what they get (7:19-25). Uriel tells Ezra about the Messianic kingdom and the end of the world (7:26-44). What about humanity (universalism), for all have sinned?[26] And the answer: "Many have been created, but only a few shall be saved" (8:3). God will bring judgment upon the wicked (8:48-62). This section also ends with a description of the end time: "there are more who perish than those who will be saved, as a wave is greater than a drop of water" (9:15-16).

Section 4 (9:26-10:59). Ezra is still distressed and has moved from his house to the field called Ardat, breaking his fast. He receives a vision of a grieving woman (9:38-10:27). The woman has lost her son. Ezra encourages her to rely on God's justness. After the vision, Uriel interprets the woman as representing the heavenly Zion, her son the earthly Zion, and the death of the son as the destruction of Jerusalem (10:29-59). Ezra has come to a turning point in the narrative. He is comforting the woman over the loss of her son (Jerusalem) over which he has been so angry and in anguish.

Section 5 (11:1-12:51). Section 5 starts with a dream vision (11:1-12:3) and the explanation of the dream is in divine monologue (12:10-39). Gone is the dialogue, replaced by monologue, indicating Ezra's unquestioning acceptance. Ezra's people again accuse him of abandoning them (cf. 5:16-19), but he offers comfort: "Take courage, O Israel; and do not be sorrowful, O house of Jacob; for the Most High has you in remembrance, and the Mighty One has not forgotten you in your struggle" (12:46-47).

Section 6 (13:1-58).[27] This section also begins with a dream vision (13:2-13), followed by Ezra's request for the interpretation of the vision. Ezra laments but also speculates about the future, asking God to clarify some questions. The meaning of the dream vision is that God is in control of history. This becomes clear in the following words: "Then I got up and walked in the field, giving great glory and praise to the Most High for the wonders that he does from time to time, and because he governs the times and whatever things come to pass in their seasons" (13:57-58).

Section 7 (14:1-48). In the epilogue no mention is made of Ezra's questions and problems. Instead, Ezra is satisfied that God did the right thing to bring destruction upon Zion and his law is efficacious in the saving of the people (14:34). Ezra is now full of praise for God.[28]

Summarizing the content. Sections 1 and 2 describe Ezra's sorrow over the people in captivity (3:1-3; 5:21-22), followed by a prayer of complaint by Ezra (3:4-36; 5:23-30). Ezra is worried about the inability of his people to do right. Ezra accuses God for abandoning his own people to benefit other nations. Uriel convinces Ezra that he cannot understand God's ways (4:5-11; 5:33-40). These dialogues are accompanied by visions and a description of the signs of the end times (5:1-13; 6:11-28). The signs function as final answer to Ezra's complaints.

Sections 3 and 4 are crucial in understanding theodicy in 4 Ezra. In section 4 Ezra has changed his attitude. Section 3 also begins with a prayer, just like the previous two sections. Ezra no longer fasts to prepare for a meeting with God, and Ezra's complaints and arguments are more and more absent.

Sections 5 and 6 both begin with visions, followed by a prayer, asking for an interpretation of the vision. The complaints of Ezra are absent, and the end times predominate.

Section 7, the last section, is parallel to the first section in structure but in opposite in content. Ezra has no more complaints, he only sings God's praise and of God's justice. In section 1, Ezra was negative towards the law; now he supports the restoration of the law.

Theodicy and Apocalyptic Eschatological Moments in 4 Ezra

Through all seven sections the reader is helped in the process of understanding the problem of evil and death by following Ezra's development of thought. The author of this dramatic narrative endeavors to reconcile the present situation with his faith in God. This reconciliation can be called the author's theodicy.[29] Ezra's theodicy starts with the posing of the problem of evil and death in sections 1 and 2: "I was troubled as I lay on my bed, and my thoughts welled up in my heart, because I saw the desolation of Zion and the wealth of those who lived in Babylon" (3:1-2). In his anxiety Ezra prays and recounts Israel's history up to the Babylon captivity. The present distress is the result of sin, coming from Israel's evil heart. Therefore, God is erring to punish his people, because they are incapable of doing right. Why did God not punish the Babylonians in the same manner as the Israelites? The angel Uriel discusses the problem by making use of a parable, telling Ezra that he is actually incapable of understanding God's ways. Such an answer only accentuates the problem. And when Uriel does not satisfy Ezra, he turns toward the eschaton, emphasizing that the righteous will only receive their rewards at the end of time (4:27-32). The certainty of the end and the signs of the end should soothe Ezra in the meantime. He will only understand God's ways at the eschaton. The eschaton has become the key element in the angel's answers to Ezra's questions. But the talk of the eschaton does not completely satisfy Ezra. In comparison to other nations Israel has received "special mistreatment" (5:28-30). Again, Ezra is told that all the inequities will be straightened out in the eschaton: "For evil shall be blotted out and deceit shall be quenched; faithfulness shall flourish, and corruption shall be overcome, and the truth, which has been so long without fruit, shall be revealed" (6:27-28). The eschaton is the destined time when the righteous and wicked will receive their rewards.

In sections 3 and 4 Ezra states his complaints in a prayer to God. He uses creation to accuse God of unfairly dealing with Israel. Was Israel not chosen by God? The angel Uriel's replies are constituted in two theodicy concepts: present evil is the result of sin and present inequities will be redressed in the future. This connects theodicy and apocalyptic eschatology in a very intimate way. Ezra accepts the future retribution for the righteous but is still uncertain of justice being done for the wicked. Such a view has turned theodicy and eschatology into a universal issue: "For who among the living is there that has not sinned, or who among mortals that has not transgressed your covenant?" (7:46; cf. 7:68).

Ezra has deepened his complaint: In the light of such universality of sin, what good are the promises of the future? In such a way the theodicy argumentation has shifted from concern over present evil to the future destiny of humankind. One can ask, is the future the solution to the present situation? Remarkably, the wicked for whom Ezra is pleading are the Israelites (8:15-16). He, however, recognizes that God's own people have sinned (8:35). Observance of the law alone is not enough for inheriting the future glory.

In an angry reply, God tells Ezra never again to compare himself to the unrighteous: "Never do so!" (8:47). God considers Ezra praiseworthy, not because he has obeyed the law, but because he is so humble: "But even in this respect you will be praiseworthy before the Most High, because you have humbled yourself…and have not considered yourself to be among the righteous. You will receive the greatest glory" (8:48-49). The only reaction Ezra can show is to plead for mercy.

According to section 4, the fate of Israel remains central. Ezra's loyalty toward God is reflected in his attitude toward the law (9:36). Ezra has completely changed, from being consoled to consoling the woman who lost her son (10:24). The deepest truth about theodicy is God's grace and mercy.

In sections 5 and 6 the issue of theodicy is illustrated through visions and their interpretations. The vision of an eagle and a lion represents the last world ruler and the Messiah. The last ruler will suffer demise and the remnant of God's people be delivered in God's mercy. Although they suffer, God has not abandoned his own people. The vision of the man rising out of the sea, according to section 6, represents another vision of the end times. This man being sent by God has the task to deliver the chosen people and to gather them again. Because of this vision Ezra declares that God governs the times. Ezra has changed. His accusing complaints have become assurances that God has not abandoned his own. The typical apocalyptic disasters of nature remind us of the eschatological meaning of the fire, wind, and the great storm (13:11). When the natural disasters and the war have passed "and the signs occur that I showed you before, then my Son will be revealed, whom you saw as a man coming up from the sea" (13:32). The Most High's interpretation of the vision within an apocalyptic eschatological context is remarkable and recollects Revelation 16:16 and 19:19: "Then he, my Son, will reprove the assembled nations for their ungodliness (this was symbolized by the storm)…" (13:37). Ezra is overwhelmed by the sign and the Most High's interpretation. He is the only one that has been enlightened about the vision (13:53).

In the final section Ezra is busy admonishing his people: their present misfortunes are the result of sin, but they will be rewarded in future if they can now rule over their hearts and minds. God is a righteous judge (14:32). Ezra has to go and gather the people. "For after death the judgment will come, when we shall live again; and then the names of the righteous will become manifest, and the deeds of the ungodly will be disclosed" (14:35).[30]

The overall eschatological message of 4 Ezra departs from the two-age eschatology: the present time is full of evil and will increase until the end but in the future age, the righteous will receive what they deserve (4:27). The wicked will be punished for their sins in the future and the humiliation of Zion will be complete (6:18-19). At the end of this age the heavenly Jerusalem and paradise, the land now hidden, will appear along with the Messiah (7:26). The Messiah will reign for four hundred years. The Messiah will overthrow the last evil political kingdom and a period of peace will commence, lasting until the final judgment (12:33-34).[31]

The vision of the eagle, coming up from the sea (11:1) has to be understood eschatologically and not only politically. The Messiah will judge the nations and bring the ten tribes together again. He is the eschatological focus at the end of time. The closeness of the end is emphasized in the last part of 4 Ezra (cf. 14:11-13). It is all about judgment and resurrection: "For after death the judgment will come, when we shall live again; and then the names of the righteous shall become manifest, and the deeds of the ungodly shall be disclosed" (14:35).

Conclusion

Fourth Ezra has to bring hope to the Jewish people after the fall of Jerusalem in 70 CE. It elaborates on the tradition of the prophets that sinfulness was the cause of all their misfortunes. Ezra complains that God is unfair with Israel because in general the people are unable to refrain from sin. The angel Uriel, on behalf of God, convinces Ezra that he does not understand God's ways and offers an apocalyptic eschatological solution to the problem of evil, death, and sin. The problem intensifies even further: How can anyone inherit the future while being so full of sin? The eschatological solution is only viable if the issue of sin is solved. From all the visions, dialogues, monologues, prayers, and interpretations, Ezra ultimately gathers the resolution of the sin problem in the mercy of God. The mercy of God, however, would neither alleviate the present misfortunes nor offer retribution to the righteous.[32]

Applied to the cry of the martyrs in Revelation 6, the righteous will receive their rewards in the eschatological future because of the mercy of God. In the meantime, while they do not understand the present evils, they should not give up hope but live from their belief. And the Jewish people have to look forward to the end of time when God's promises to Israel will be fulfilled.

This essay is dedicated to Klyne Snodgrass at his retirement—highly honored academic, passionate teacher, church-conscious theologian, and exceptional esteemed friend of integrity, like a brother, for many years.

Endnotes

1. Old and New Testament translations are from the ESV, Apocrypha translations are from the NRSV.

2. See David Hume, *Dialogues Concerning Natural Religion* (New York: Hafner, 1948), 66. Other valuable efforts to understand evil and death are: John Hick, *Evil and the God of Love* (London: Macmillan, 1977); Austin Farrer, *Love Almighty and Ills Unlimited* (New York: Doubleday, 1961). On the exegesis of Revelation 6:9-11, see D. Aune, *Revelation 6-16* (Nashville: Thomas Nelson, 1998), 402-10 as well as S. Pattemore, *The People of God in the Apocalypse* (Cambridge: Cambridge University Press, 2004), 68-116; G. R. Osborne, *Revelation* (Grand Rapids: Baker, 2002), 286-89.

3. Cf. Tom W. Willett, *Eschatology in the Theodicies of 2 Baruch and 4 Ezra* (Sheffield: JSOT Press, 1989), 11-13; Hartmut Gese, "The Crisis of Wisdom in Koheleth," in J. L. Crenshaw, ed., *Theodicy in the Old Testament*, Issues in Religion and Theology 4 (Philadelphia: Fortress, 1983).

4. Walther Eichrodt, "Faith in Providence and Theodicy in the Old Testament," in *Theodicy in the Old Testament*, 27.

5. See Peter Berger, *The Sacred Canopy: Elements of a Sociological Theory of Religion* (New York: Doubleday, 1967), 54-55.

6. There is definitely enough applicable material on theodicy (e.g., Job) in the Bible. This contribution only focuses on a very interesting and gripping extra-canonical parallel. We may even find such a continuum in our own day: H. S. Kushner, in *When Bad Things Happen to Good People* (New York: Schocken Books, 1981), declares that God must be limited in power, else he would have stopped evil—a rational explanation. On the other hand Robert Gordis, "A Cruel God or None—Is there No Choice?" *Judaism* 21 (1972): 277-84, moves away from rationality, despairing of a resolution of evil in this life.

7. Klaus Koch's article, "Gibt es ein Vergeltungsdogma im Alten Testament?" *Zeitschrift für Theologie und Kirche* 52 (1955): 1042, denies a doctrine of retribution in the Old Testament. This thesis has to be tested again. See G. K. Beale, *The Book of Revelation* (Grand Rapids: Eerdmans), 50-87.

8. Cf. Willett, *Eschatology in the Theodicies*, 13.

9. Cf. also Proverbs 10:3; 10:16 and Psalm 37:10-11.

10. The prophets Haggai and Zechariah, for example, were convinced that the misfortunes of those who returned from exile were connected to their failure to rebuild the temple. Cf. Haggai 1:7-11.

11. This concept was not only confined to the prophetic literature but also to the Deuteronomic literature. Cf. J. G. Gammie, "The Theology of Retribution in the Book of Deuteronomy," *Catholic Biblical Quarterly* 32 (1970): 6-10; J. K. Kuntz, "The Retribution Motif in Psalmic Wisdom," *Zeitschrift für die alttestamentliche Wissenschaft* 89 (1977): 228-32. Retribution in apocalyptic literature played a prominent role: cf. W. S. Towner, "Retributional Theology in the Apocalyptic Setting," *Union Seminary Quarterly Review* 26 (1971): 203-14.

12. Cf. Isaiah 53:4-6 and Jeremiah 18:20.

13. See Willett, *Eschatology in the Theodicies*, 25.

14. Cf. Psalm 34:19-22 as an example of a this-worldly retribution. In Psalm 49:15 we have a clear example of an other-worldly retribution.

15. Cf. Job 40:8: "Will you even put me in the wrong? Will you condemn me that you may be justified?"

16. See R. J. Williams, "Theodicy in the Ancient Near East," *Canadian Journal of Theology* 2 (1956): 14-26.

17. Cf. Willett, *Eschatology in the Theodicies*, 32. See the excellent argumentation of this subject by G. W. E. Nickelsburg, *Resurrection, Immortality and Eternal Life in Intertestamental Judaism* (Cambridge: Harvard University Press, 1972), 170-76, as well as H. C. C. Cavallin, *Life After Death: Paul's Argument for the Resurrection of the Dead in 1 Cor 15, part 1: An Enquiry into the Jewish Background* (Lund: Gleerup, 1974), 211-14.

18. Cf. P. D. Hanson, *The Dawn of Apocalyptic: The Historical and Sociological Roots of Jewish Apocalyptic* (Philadelphia: Fortress, 1975), 9-10.

19. See his *The Relevance of Apocalyptic: A Study of Jewish and Christian Apocalypses from Daniel to the Revelation* (Greenwood: Attic, 1963), 15. Cf. further M. E. Stone, *Scriptures, Sects and Visions: A Profile of Judaism from Ezra to the Jewish Revolts* (Philadelphia: Fortress, 1980), 46-47.

20. Cf. O. Plöger, *Theocracy and Eschatology*, trans. S. Rudman (Oxford: Blackwell, 1968), 106-7.

21. See B. Reicke, "Official and Pietistic Elements of Jewish Apocalypticism," *Journal of Biblical Literature* 79 (1960): 137-50, in this regard as well as R. G. Hamerton-Kelly, who elaborated on this in his "The Temple and the Origins of Jewish Apocalyptic," *Vetus Testamentum* 20 (1970): 1-15.

22. The view of P. Hanson, *The Dawn of Apocalyptic*, 9-10, and D. N. Freedman, "The Flowering of Apocalyptic," *Journal for Theology and the Church* 6 (1969): 166-74.

23. C. Rowland, *The Open Heaven: A Study of Apocalyptic in Judaism and Early Christianity* (New York: Crossroad, 1982), 14.

24. Cf. B. M. Metzger, "The Fourth Book of Ezra: A New Translation and Introduction," in J.H. Charlesworth, ed., *The Old Testament Pseudepigrapha, Vol 1: Apocalyptic Literature and Testaments* (New York: Doubleday, 1983), 516-59; J. M. Myers, *I and II Esdras: Introduction, Translation and Commentary* (New York: Doubleday, 1974), 107-13.

25. See Willett, *Eschatology in the Theodicies*, 54-57; A. F. J. Klijn, ed., *Der Lateinische Text der Apokalypse des Esra* (Berlin: Akademie, 1983), 131; and M. E. Stone, "A New Manuscript of the Syrio-Arabic Version of the Fourth Book of Ezra," *Journal for the Study of Judaism in the Persian, Hellenistic, and Roman Periods* 8 (1977): 183-96.

26. Cf. the clearcut argumentation by A. L. Thomson, *Responsibility for Evil in the Theodicy of IV Ezra* (Missoula: Scholars Press, 1977), 188-218.

27. There exists strong argumentation that sections 5 and 6 come from the hand of a final redactor and not from the author of 4 Ezra. Cf. E. P. Sanders, *Paul and Palestinian Judaism: A Comparison of Patterns of Religion* (Philadelphia: Fortress, 1977), 416-18.

28. Cf. Willett, *Eschatology in the Theodicies*, 64.

29. Cf. Willett, *Eschatology in the Theodicies*, 66; Thompson, *Responsibility for Evil in the Theodicy of IV Ezra*, 332-39.

30. The eschatological analysis of Leon Vaganay at the beginning of the previous century (1906) still remains remarkable: *Le Problème eschatologique dans le IV Livre d'Esdras* (Paris:

Picard). He considered 7:15-16 the major pivot: "And why are you moved, seeing that you are mortal? And why have you not considered in your mind what is to come, rather than what is now present?" Vaganay sees 3:1-7:14 as national salvation and 7:17-9:25 as personal salvation. Cf. also J. Keulers, *Die eschatologische Lehre des vierten Esrabuches* (Berlin: Herder, 1922).

31. M. E. Stone discusses the issue of the Messiah in 4 Ezra, placing emphasis on the interpretation of the eagle vision in 11:1-46 in his "The Concept of the Messiah in IV Ezra," in J. Neusner, ed., *Religions in Antiquity: Essays in Memory of Erwin Ramsdell Goodenough* (Leiden: Brill, 1968), 295-312.

32. See Willett, *Eschatology in the Theodicies*, 75.

Reading through the Rearview Mirror
Inner-Biblical Exegesis and the New Testament

Robert L. Hubbard Jr.

The genesis of this paper goes back to a course that Klyne Snodgrass and I taught at North Park Theological Seminary in the fall of 2011 entitled "The Old Testament in the New." Klyne and I had the privilege of leading students in exegeting in considerable depth a number of Old Testament texts that New Testament writers invoke. We probed their exegetical techniques, the uses to which they put the texts, and the theological implications of their written results. At one point, I introduced the class to a method of exegesis called inner-biblical exegesis (IBE), a new approach that in recent decades has provided an exegetical tool for serious readers of the Old Testament. I tentatively proposed that the literary phenomena that IBE explores within the Old Testament itself seem analogous to the interpretive process evident in the New Testament's use of the Old. This essay follows up and expands on that earlier lecture, and it is a very great personal pleasure to honor my dear friend and colleague with it. Its goal is to take advantage of Old Testament phenomena to cast new light on the use of the Old in the New Testament.

Inner-Biblical: Its Origins

The intellectual forerunners of inner-biblical exegesis appeared in French in the 1950s,[1] soon to be followed in 1963 by an exegesis in English of Psalm 89 by Nahum Sarna of Brandeis University.[2] The following decade saw early scholarly explorations of the method in several publications,[3] but it was the publications of Sarna's former student and faculty colleague, Michael Fishbane, then of Brandeis and now of the University of Chicago, that put the method on the map.[4] A string of publications followed as scholars sought to apply it to a variety of Old Testament themes, texts, and interpretive problems,[5] as well as to the Septuagint and rabbinic and medieval Jewish exegesis.[6] The inclusion of articles on IBE in recent major reference works on the history of interpretation affirms the method's general acceptance as an important exegetical tool.[7] Indeed, Jean-Pierre Sonnet applauded the method's uniqueness as "a critical exegetical model … developed within the intellectual tradition of Judaism" rather than in nineteenth-century Protestant Germany, twentieth-century America, or the twenty-first-century post-modern West.[8]

Inner-Biblical Exegesis According to M. A. Fishbane

Fishbane's main thesis is that the roots of what we know as post-biblical exegesis (e.g., the midrashic thought, rabbinic commentaries, the New Testament, etc.) lie within the Hebrew Bible itself.[9] In his view, biblical text itself grew out of a series of rewritings guided by a hermeneutical principle and sensitive exegesis.[10] This thesis is what makes his work relevant for consideration of how the New Testament uses the Old Testament. According to Fishbane, inner-biblical exegesis occurs when later writers revise, update, amend, or rewrite an authoritative source text so that it addresses the new challenges and new realities faced by their own generation and perhaps future ones.[11] The writers then copy and pass on their exegetical reworking to the next generation of scribes and their contemporaries.[12]

Fishbane stresses that the rationale driving the reworking is not grammatical or lexical but theological—and that it specifically results from the scribe's exegesis. The authority of the later text, however, still derives from its connection with its authoritative source. Indeed, argues Fishbane, the ultimate purpose of the rework is to reinforce the authority of its source by clarifying the latter's meaning, making it theologically more acceptable, or expanding the scope of its contents.[13] At a later point, readers come to accord the reworked text itself the same authority as its source—in other words, the scribe ceases to be purely a redactor and becomes an actual author.[14] Indeed, we would know nothing about it were it not included in the present canon of the Hebrew Bible.

As one might expect, Fishbane's approach has stimulated an engaging scholarly discussion of methodological issues.[15] For my purpose, the key issue concerns whether or not what Fishbane does is in reality "exegesis."[16] The examples treated below clearly reflect interpretive moves by the scribe(s) in reworking the source text, but in many of Fishbane's examples, the only connection between source and later text is shared vocabulary. The problem is that such recurrences may just as easily be explained as accidental or simply the use of common terminology on a given subject rather than as scribal exegesis per se. This and other observations have led some scholars (myself included) to reclassify what Fishbane calls "inner-biblical exegesis" as "inner-biblical allusion" (IBA).[17] In my view, "allusion" describes the umbrella phenomenon—that a later text simply "evokes…the memory of an older text"—whereas "exegesis" describes texts that intend "to apply the meaning of an earlier text to a later setting, in some cases also to modify its meaning."[18]

Two Examples of IBA

Two examples illustrate what IBA looks like in practice. First, observe in the table below what happens to the fallow year law in the Covenant Code (Exodus 23:10-11) when the later Holiness Code adapts it (Leviticus 25:3-7).[19]

Exodus 23:10-11 (Covenant Code)	Leviticus 25:3-7 (Holiness Code)
[10] "For six years you are to sow your fields (*'artseka*) and harvest (*we'asapta*) the crops, [11] but during the seventh year let the land lie unplowed and unused. Then the poor among your people may get food from it,	[3] For six years sow your fields (*sadeka*), and for six years prune your vineyards and gather (*we'asapta*) their crops. [4] But in the seventh year the land is to have a year of sabbath rest, a sabbath to the LORD. Do not sow your fields or prune your vineyards. [5] Do not reap what grows of itself or harvest the grapes of your untended vines. The land is to have a year of rest. [6] Whatever the land yields during the sabbath year will be food for you—for yourself, your male and female servants, and the hired worker and temporary resident who live among you, [7] as well as for your livestock
and the wild animals may eat what they leave.	and the wild animals in your land. Whatever the land produces may be eaten. (TNIV)
Do the same with your vineyard and your olive grove. (TNIV)	

Clearly, the main elements of the earlier and simpler text form the basic skeleton of the later and longer text. Both texts contrast the cultivation and harvest (*we'asapta*) of crops for six years with their non-cultivation during the seventh year. Interestingly, the editor of the Holiness Code has reordered the text slightly, integrating the last line of Exodus 23:11 ("Do the same with your vineyard"), itself probably an expansion added at some prior time, into the first line of the revised text. The revised line ("sow your fields... [prune] your vineyards"), thus, establishes the boundaries to which the new law applies.[20] It is particularly striking how much more detail Leviticus 25 provides compared to its Covenant Code antecedent. Its prime concern apparently is to answer questions that might arise concerning the use (if any) of fields and vineyards during the required fallow year.

The land is to enjoy "a year of sabbath rest" (v. 4a)—release from the typical annual labor cycle of sowing, pruning, and reaping—to grow as it wills (Leviticus 25:4b-5). Its produce that year comprises Israel's food supply. Indeed, the juxtaposition of the prohibitions against labor (vv. 4b-5) with the permission for consumption (v. 6) implies that the interim growth is *only* for food, not for sale, barter, storage, or other purposes. Finally, the Holiness Code version lists four categories to whom the new law applies: the landowner (and his family), his servants (male and female), workers-for-hire, and resident aliens who temporarily reside with him. The fallow land also supplies food for the owners' livestock and any wild animals thereabout. Interestingly, Exodus 23:11 understands the fallow year to provide food for both the poor and wild animals, but only the latter make the list in Leviticus 25:7. This omission may presume either the continuing validity of the Covenant Code version or perhaps awareness of other Holiness Code laws (e.g., Leviticus 19:9-10; 23:22) that require provision for the poor in both sabbatical and non-sabbatical years.[21]

In sum, later rewriting has transformed the original law. Originally, it guaranteed the poor access to food during the fallow year, but now, driven by the theology of the Sabbath, it reframes the fallow year law around the theme of "sabbath rest" (Leviticus 25:4). It also legislates explicitly what was implicit in its Covenant Code antecedent: the land itself is also to enjoy its "Sabbath rest" (Leviticus 25:4)—not to stop growing but to grow unbothered by human intervention. It also frees landowners and their households to rest—to enjoy food without the usual toil of cultivation, preservation, and distribution. Implicitly, the law's appeal to the sabbatical principle also evokes memories of God's example at creation. Thus, besides bestowing benefits on those who keep it, it portrays obedience as ultimately God-pleasing and, hence, God-blessed.

The second example considers what Jeremiah 29:10 and the Chronicler (2 Chronicles 36:21) do with Jeremiah's prophecy of the seventy years (Jeremiah 25:11-12; 29:10).[22] Notice that the opening formula of Jeremiah 25:1 frames what follows in the third person ("the word came to Jeremiah"),[23] and the introduction dates the receipt and proclamation of the oracle to 605 BCE ("the fourth year of King Jehoiakim"). These two observations present the report as a retrospective episode—a backward glance by a writer other than Jeremiah from a later point in time concerning an oracle received earlier by Jeremiah.[24] Further, a comparison of the Masoretic Text (MT) and Septuagint (LXX; see the table) suggests that the latter is probably the earlier of the two versions.

Jeremiah 25:1-14 MT (TNIV)	Jeremiah 25:1-13 LXX (Breton translation)
[1] The word came to Jeremiah concerning all the people of Judah in the fourth year of Jehoiakim son of Josiah king of Judah, *which was the first year of Nebuchadnezzar king of Babylon.*	[1] The word that came to Jeremias concerning all the people of Juda in the fourth year of Joakim, son of Josias, king of Juda;
[2] So Jeremiah the prophet said to all the people of Judah and to *all* those living in Jerusalem:	[2] which he spoke to all the people of Juda, and to the inhabitants of Jerusalem, saying,
[3] For twenty-three years—from the thirteenth year of Josiah son of Amon king of Judah until this very day—*the word of the LORD has come to me* and I have spoken to you again and again, *but you have not listened.*	[3] In the thirteenth year of Josias, son of Amos, king of Juda, even until this day for three and twenty years, I have both spoken to you, rising early and speaking,
[4] And though *the LORD* has sent all *his* servants the prophets to you again and again, you have not listened or paid any attention.	[4] and I sent to you my servants the prophets, sending them early (but you did not hearken and listen with your ears)
[5] They said, "Turn now, each of you, from your evil ways and your evil practices, and you can stay in the land the LORD gave to you and your ancestors forever and ever.	saying, [5] Turn every one of you from his evil way, and from your evil practices, and you shall dwell in the land which I gave to you and your fathers, of old and forever.
[6] Do not follow other gods to serve and worship them; do not arouse my anger with what your hands have made. Then I will not harm you."	[6] Go not after strange gods, to serve them, and to worship them, that you not provoke me by the works of your hands, to do you hurt.
[7] "But you did not listen to me," *declares the LORD, "and you have aroused my anger with what your hands have made, and you have brought harm to yourselves."*	[7] But you did not hearken to me.

Jeremiah 25:1-14 MT (TNIV)	Jeremiah 25:1-13 LXX (Breton translation)
[8] Therefore the LORD *Almighty* says this: "Because you have not listened to my words, [9] I will summon *all the peoples* (pl.) of the north *and my servant Nebuchadnezzar king of Babylon," declares the LORD,* "and I will bring them against this land and its inhabitants and against all the surrounding nations. I will completely destroy them and make them an object of horror and scorn, and an everlasting *ruin.*	[8] Therefore thus saith the Lord: Since you did not believe my words, [9] behold I will send and take *a family* (sing.) from the north, and will bring them against this land, and against the inhabitants of it, and against all the nations round about it, and I will make them utterly waste, and make them a desolation, and a hissing, and an everlasting *reproach.*
[10] I will banish from them the sounds of joy and gladness, the voices of bride and bridegroom, the *sound of millstones* and the light of the lamp.	[10] And I will destroy from among them the voice of joy, and the voice of gladness, the voice of the bridegroom, and the voice of the bride, the *scent of ointment,* and the light of a candle.
[11] This whole country will become a desolate wasteland, and these nations will serve *the king of Babylon* seventy years.	[11] And all the land shall be a desolation; and they shall serve among the Gentiles seventy years.
[12] "But when the seventy years are fulfilled, I will punish *the king of Babylon and his* nation, *the land of the Babylonians, for their guilt," declares the LORD,* "and will make it desolate forever.	[12] And when the seventy years are fulfilled, I will take vengeance on that nation, and will make them a perpetual desolation.
[13] I will bring on that land all the things I have spoken against it, all that are written in this book *and prophesied by Jeremiah against all the nations.* [14] *They themselves will be enslaved by many nations and great kings; I will repay them according to their deeds and the work of their hands."*	[13] And I will bring upon that land all my words which I have spoken against it, *even* all things that are written in this book. [i.e., the words of Jer. 32:13.]

Clearly, the LXX is the shorter and stylistically simpler of the two. MT noticeably has wording absent in LXX, while the latter completely lacks vv. 13b and 14.[25] Rather than rehearse scholarly discussion of the text's perplexities, for our purposes it is enough simply to observe the kind of extra material that MT has. LXX describes the enemy in vague, general terms,[26] while MT explicitly identifies the frightening foe as Nebuchadnezzar and his Babylonian army.[27] Textually, the harder-reading principle convinces me (and others) that it is more likely that these additions found their way into the MT than that they once were in the LXX but later removed. If so, behind the LXX translation stands an earlier, simpler Hebrew text than that behind MT,[28] and the plusses in MT represent the first phase of IBA of Jeremiah 25. It bears mention also that in MT the seventy years mark both the length of time that Judah will suffer destruction and exile at Nebuchadnezzar's hands and the endpoint of exile through divine judgment on Babylon.

Jeremiah 29:10 repeats the seventy-year motif of 25:11-12 within Jeremiah's letter to the exiles in Babylon sometime after 597 BCE, the year Nebuchadnezzar sent them there. Again, the narration addresses the reader in the third person, implying an editor other than Jeremiah, but in this case a detailed introduction (vv. 1-4) specifies when the prophet sent the letter and by what means it reached the exiles. As just noted, the letter reuses the seventy-year motif, but in this case apparently the prophet Jeremiah himself, not an editor, reuses it. Interestingly, the reuse of the motif involves two clever, subtle changes. First, it omits the phrase "for Babylon," a signal that in the context of Jeremiah 29 the reuse now concerns Judah not Babylon. Second, it repeats the key word *paqad* ("punish [Judah, Babylon]" in Jeremiah 25:11-12) but cleverly plays on another of its meanings ("come to help [exiled Judah]" in Jeremiah 29:10).[29] From a pre-exilic perspective, Jeremiah 25:11-12 proclaims a seventy-year punishment of Judah that would end with Babylon's punishment, too. By contrast, Jeremiah 29:10 takes a more conciliatory stance toward Judah. It addresses their exilic concern concerning when the exile would end and the postexilic return home begin. In short, an original prophecy of disaster has now become a prophecy of hope for release and return—a different genre that also applies the prophecy to a new audience (the exiles) and extends its fulfillment into the future.[30]

The closing chapter of Chronicles (2 Chronicles 36:21) also interprets the seventy-year motif of Jeremiah in a new way.[31] The author/editor addresses a new audience living in a new context—in Israel's homeland, now the Persian province of Yehud, nearly two centuries after what Jeremiah 25 and 29 foresaw had taken place (ca. 400-350 BCE). For Jeremiah, the exile would end with Babylon's destruction by unspecified events, but for the Chronicler its end coincides specifically with the establishment of Persian imperial hegemony.[32] Although Judah's pre- and postexilic situations lay in the distant past, the Chronicler recontextualized Jeremiah's seventy-year motif by reading it through the lens of another authoritative text, Leviticus 26:34-35. The excerpts below in italics (Leviticus 26:34-35; 2 Chronicles 36:21) show his novel interpretation:

Leviticus 26:34-35 (TNIV)	2 Chronicles 36:19-21 (TNIV)
²⁷ "If in spite of this you still do not listen to me but continue to be hostile toward me, ²⁸ then in my anger I will be hostile toward you, and I myself will punish you for your sins seven times over. [...]	
³² I myself will lay waste the land, so that your enemies who live there will be appalled.	¹⁹ They set fire to God's temple and broke down the wall of Jerusalem; they burned all the palaces and destroyed everything of value there.
³³ I will scatter you among the nations and will draw out my sword and pursue you. Your land will be laid waste, and your cities will lie in ruins.	²⁰ He carried into exile to Babylon the remnant, who escaped from the sword, and they became servants to him and his successors until the kingdom of Persia came to power.
³⁴ Then *the land will enjoy its sabbath years all the time that it lies desolate* and you are in the country of your enemies; then *the land will* rest and *enjoy its sabbaths.*	²¹ *The land enjoyed its sabbath rests; all the time of its desolation* it rested, until the seventy years were completed in fulfillment of the word of the LORD spoken by Jeremiah.
³⁵ *All the time that it lies desolate, the land will have the rest* it did not have during the sabbaths you lived in it."	

The Chronicler has strung together three sentences taken from Leviticus 26 (the first two lines) and from both Jeremiah 25:12 and 29:10 (the last line).[33] Though cobbled together, the three comprise a grammatically coherent whole (two parallel main clauses + purpose clause) and, apart from several slight modifications, are verbatim quotations.[34] I would assign the genre of conflated quotation to the chronicler's tidy reuse of Leviticus 26 and Jeremiah 25 and 29. The former text sounds very much like a prophetic warning, and thus connects well thematically and stylistically with Jeremiah 25. The Chronicler's wider preoccupation with land probably accounts in part for the interest in Leviticus 26 and, more importantly, suggests that the writer specifically has Jeremiah 25 (not 29) in mind. Leviticus 26 holds a bitter irony for Israel: the land is better off with Israel gone (Leviticus 26:35, 43); free of agricultural taskmasters, the land may now enjoy its long-overdue restorative rest.[35] Obviously, the chronicler wishes to echo the prophetic threats of doom in Jeremiah 25 and Leviticus 26 so that his contemporaries, now back in the land, may concern themselves with avoiding another seventy-year national debacle.

Rhetorically, the juxtaposition of the two motifs—Jeremiah's seventy years and the Sabbath rest of Leviticus 26—implies, first, that the exile marks a necessary but limited interim period for Judah and, second, that restoration to the land—a return to normal, non-sabbatical life-routines—will follow its expiration. Thus, in the Chronicler's prophetic warning also echoes a hopeful strain, one implicit in the seventy years of Jeremiah 25 and explicit in Jeremiah 29.[36] On the other hand, by ending Chronicles with Cyrus's statement which itself ends with an exhortation, the chronicler addresses Jews still living abroad, emphasizing that the seventy years have long expired and urging them to come home. His message might imply something like: "For Israel, the rest period is over. Time to get back to work—time to rebuild our country."[37] Finally, up to now I have referred to the seventy years as a "motif" or "typology" rather than as a chronological figure. In my view, the figure is symbolic, meaning something like "a lifetime" (cf. Psalm 90:10; Isaiah 23:15 ["the span of a king's life"]) or, more generally, "a very long time."[38] Here I suggest that from Leviticus 26 the Chronicler may have understood the figure "seventy" to mean "ten sevens"—ten sabbatical years that Israel failed to celebrate. The use of those two numbers, both symbolic of completeness, would hint that the "very long time" might in reality mean "just the right time."

In sum, the afterlife of Jeremiah's oracle about the seventy years illustrates Fishbane's main thesis, that exegesis of the sort described above can address later generations—in this case, audiences in the pre-exilic, exilic, postexilic, and Persian periods.[39]

Conclusions and Reflections

This brief sampling of several Old Testament texts that allude to and exegete earlier ones has proved fruitful. It has put on display the main elements at work in inner-biblical allusion: an earlier text of well-established authority; a new audience living in a new situation and confronting new challenges; a scribe who desires that that earlier text somehow addresses that new situation and its challenges; a new (potentially authoritative) text, the creative recontextualization by the scribe of the earlier text to realize the scribe's desires.

In two cases (Leviticus 25 and 2 Chronicles 36), the scribes drew on a central Israelite theological theme, the Sabbath, to revise and update earlier texts. The former mandates rest for the land and humans and clarifies details about the fallow year law. In the latter, the Sabbath law (Leviticus 26) provides an interpretive lens through which to reinterpret and reapply an earlier prophetic motif to address an audience nearly two centuries after its first two fulfillments (Jeremiah 25). The long-remembered prophecy explains the exile and also frames the Chronicler's closing exhortation for scattered Jews to come home. In Jeremiah 29:10, the prophet himself reuses a motif originally set in an oracle of doom addressed to pre-exilic Judah within an oracle of hope addressed to exilic Judah.

If I may reflect briefly, I am particularly struck by the cultural framework that undergirds the practice of IBA. Ongoing religious life over time requires the collection of authoritative (though not yet canonical) texts and their recontextualization into new circumstances. The community apparently sustains the scribes and their work, believing it to be of great benefit to that ongoing religious life. Interestingly, IBA does not feature fresh, new revelation but the reworking of divine revelation already received, which eventually itself becomes received revelation. I marvel, further, at the freedom the scribes apparently enjoy to revise, update, rework—and even rewrite—their source materials. Theologically, they must understand what we call "word of God" not as "fixed" or "unalterable" texts but as an invisible dimension that ensures continuity between the texts over time. I might call that dimension "the voice of God," but the point is that God speaks through those texts—and scribal work aims to ensure that God receives the clearest hearing possible from generation to generation.

Finally, the parallels between IBA and what New Testament writers do with the Old Testament seem clear. New Testament writers take authoritative (indeed, canonical) texts and reinterpret them for new audiences, Jewish and Gentile, in light of the writers' theology—the gospel and the theme of the New Israel. They share that same scribal freedom to adapt, combine, recontextualize, exegete, etc., in light of that theology. In a sense, they represent one branch among several that descend from and continue the work of the ancient scribes of Israel. Indeed, this essay argues that the writings of their many anonymous ancestors offer cultural background that illumines the use of the Old Testament evident in the New.

Endnotes

1. R. Bloch, "Écriture et tradition dans le Judaïsme. Aperçus sur l'origine du Midrash," *Cahiers Sioniens* 8 (1954): 9-34; and A. Gélin, "La question des 'relectures' bibliques à l'intérieur d'une tradition vivante," *Sacra Pagina* 1 (1959): 303-15.

2. N. Sarna, "Psalm 89: A Study in Inner-Biblical Exegesis," in A. Altmann, ed., *Biblical and Other Studies*, Brandeis University Studies and Texts 1 (Cambridge: Harvard University Press, 1963), 29-46.

3. I. Willi-Plein, *Vorformen der Schriftexegese innerhalb des Alten Testaments*, BZAW 123 (Berlin: Walter de Gruyter, 1971); R. A. Mason, "The Use of Earlier Biblical Material in

Zechariah 9-14: A Study in Inner Biblical Exegesis" (unpublished PhD dissertation, University of London, 1973), published thirty years later in M. J. Boda and M. H. Floyd, eds., *Bringing Out the Treasure: Inner Biblical Allusion in Zechariah 9-14*, JSOTSup 370 (London; New York: Sheffield Academic Press, 2003), 2-208. E.g., L. M. Eslinger, "Hosea 12:5a and Genesis 32:29: A Study in Inner Biblical Exegesis," *Journal for the Study of the Old Testament* 18 (1980): 91-99; W. C. Kaiser, Jr., "Inner Biblical Exegesis as a Model for Bridging the 'Then' and the 'Now' Gap: Hos 12:1-6," *Journal of the Evangelical Theological Society* 28/1 (1985): 33-46.

4. M. A. Fishbane, *Biblical Interpretation in Ancient Israel* (Oxford: Clarendon, 1985); idem., "Revelation and Tradition: Aspects of Inner-Biblical Exegesis," *Journal of Biblical Literature* 99/3 (1980): 343-61. R. Mason also published "The Relation of Zech 9-14 to Proto-Zechariah," *Zeitschrift für die alttestamentliche Wissenschaft* 88 (1976): 227-39, and later "Why Is Second Zechariah so Full of Quotations?" in C. Tuckett, ed., *The Book of Zechariah and Its Influence* (Aldershot: Ashgate Publishing, 2003), 21-28.

5. E.g., T. B. Dozeman, "Inner-Biblical Interpretation of Yahweh's Gracious and Compassionate Character," *Journal of Biblical Literature* 108 (1989): 207-23; R. Mason, *Preaching the Tradition: Homily and Hermeneutics after the Exile* (Cambridge: Cambridge University Press, 1990), S. E. Loewenstamm, *The Evolution of the Exodus Tradition*, trans. B. Schwartz (Jerusalem: Magnes, 1992), B. Rosenstock, "Inner-Biblical Exegesis in the Book of the Covenant: the Case of the Sabbath Commandment," *Conservative Judaism* 44/3 (1992): 37-49; E. Greenstein, "An Inner-biblical Midrash of the Nadab and Abihu Episode," in D. Assaf, ed., *Proceedings of the Eleventh World Congress of Jewish Studies, Div A: The Bible and Its World* (Jerusalem: World Union of Jewish Studies, 1994), 71-78 (Hebrew); J. Maier, "Early Jewish Biblical Interpretation in the Qumran Literature," in M. Saebo, ed., *Hebrew Bible/Old Testament: The History of Its Interpretation* vol 1, From the beginnings to the Middle Ages (until 1300), Pt 1, Antiquity (Göttingen: Vandenhoeck & Ruprecht, 1996), 108-29; idem., "The Use of Earlier Biblical Material in Zechariah 9-14: A Study in Inner Biblical Exegesis," 2-208; W. Schniedewind, "Are We His People or Not? Biblical Interpretation during Crisis," *Biblica* 76 (1995): 540-50; B. D. Sommer, *A Prophet Reads Scripture: Allusion in Isaiah 40-66* (Stanford: Stanford University Press, 1998), J. Schaper, "Rereading the Law: Inner-Biblical Exegesis of Divine Oracles in Ezekiel 44 and Isaiah 56," in E. Otto and B. M. Levinson, eds. (with W. Dietrich), *Recht und Ethik im Alten Testament: Beiträge des Symposiums 'Das Alte Testament und die Kultur der Moderne' Anlässlich des 100. Geburtstags Gerhard von Rads (1901-1971), Heidelberg, 18-21. Oktober 2001* (Münster: LIT Verlag, 2004), 125-44; D. Rom-Shiloni, "Facing Destruction and Exile: Inner-Biblical Exegesis in Jeremiah and Ezekiel," *Zeitschrift für die alttestamentliche Wissenschaft* 117/2 (2005): 189-205; D. Rothstein, "The Book of Proverbs and Inner-Biblical Exegesis at Qumran: the Evidence of Proverbs 24:23-29," *Zeitschrift für die alttestamentliche Wissenschaft* 119/1 (2007): 75-85.

6. J. Harris, "From Inner-Biblical Interpretation to Early Rabbinic Exegesis," in M. Saebo, ed., *Hebrew Bible/Old Testament: The History of Its Interpretation* vol 1. From the beginnings to the Middle Ages (until 1300). Pt 1, Antiquity (Göttingen: Vandenhoeck & Ruprecht, 1996), 256-69; J. Jacobs, "Inner-Biblical Exegesis in the Commentary of Rashbam on the Bible: Rashbam's Terminology in Referring to a Cited Verse," *Revue des Études Juives* 167/3-4 (2009): 465-482; M. Smith, "Texts Between Their Biblical Past, Their Inner-Biblical Interpretation, Their Reception in Second Temple Literature, and Their Textual Witnesses," in S. Tzoref and L. H. Schiffman, eds., *The Dead Sea Scrolls at 60: Scholarly Contributions of New York University Faculty and Alumni,* Studies on the Texts of the Desert of Judah 89 (Leiden and Boston: Brill, 2010), 271-98.

7. Not surprisingly, Fishbane himself has written two such entries; cf. M. A. Fishbane,

"Inner-Biblical Exegesis," in Saebo, ed., *Hebrew Bible/Old Testament*, 33-48; idem., "Inner Biblical Exegesis: Types and Strategies of Interpretation in Ancient Israel," in G. H. Hartman and S. Budick, eds., *Midrash and Literature* (New Haven: Yale University Press, 1986), 19-37; cf. also E. Menn, "Inner-Biblical Exegesis in the Tanak," in A. J. Hauser and D. F. Watson, eds., *A History of Biblical Interpretation. Volume 1: The Ancient Period* (Grand Rapids; Cambridge: Eerdmans, 2003), 55-79.

8. J.-P. Sonnet, "Inscribe the New in the Old: Inner-Biblical Exegesis (M. Fishbane) and the Hermeneutics of Innovation (B. Levinson)," in T. F. Michel, ed., *Friends on the Way* (New York: Fordham University Press, 2007), 128. One of Fishbane's former students, Professor Bernard M. Levison of the University of Minnesota, has researched how Deuteronomy uses materials from the Covenant Book (Exodus 21-23). He concludes that Deuteronomy's writers/editors applied the "hermeneutics of legal innovation" (his term), the adaptation of laws from the former in order to incorporate them into the latter; cf. B. M. Levinson, *Deuteronomy and the Hermeneutics of Legal Innovation* (Oxford: Oxford University Press, 1997); idem., "The Birth of the Lemma: The Restrictive Reinterpretation of the Covenant Code's Manumission Law by the Holiness Code (Leviticus 25:44-46)," *Journal of Biblical Literature* 124 (2005): 617-39. His recent studies of biblical law have led him to propose that biblical writers evoke what he calls "a rhetoric of concealment" (i.e., "the break with tradition validates itself in the vocables of tradition"); cf. B. M. Levinson, *Legal Revision and Religious Renewal in Ancient Israel* (Cambridge: Cambridge University Press, 2008), 48-49 (quote p. 48).

9. Fishbane, *Biblical Interpretation in Ancient Israel*, 23-32. In his view, Israelite scribal practices compare to the widely practiced and well-attested roles of scribes in the ancient Near East. Fishbane (29-31) plausibly argues, for example, that the terminology of Ecclesiastes 9:9-12, the book's ending, may actually reflect activities typical of scribes in ancient Israel.

10. Sonnet, "Inscribe the New in the Old," 128, who observes (129) that IBE antedates later exegesis that applied its tools to the canon of Scripture from outside it.

11. Interestingly, Fishbane (*Biblical Interpretation in Ancient Israel*, 32-37) argues that the Bible associates scribal activities with intense periods of national revival and religious reform—for example, the pre-exilic reigns of Hezekiah (2 Kings 18-20; cf. Proverbs 25:1) and Josiah (2 Kings 21-23; cf. 2 Kings 22), and the work of the priest-scribe Ezra during Israel's postexilic restoration (Ezra 7).

12. The tell-tale fingerprints of scribal activity include: a host of literary phenomena reflect the tell-tale fingerprints of scribal activity throughout the Hebrew Bible: editorial colophons (e.g., Leviticus 14:54-57), lexical and explanatory comments (e.g., Genesis 14:17; Joshua 18:13), and theological corrections (e.g., the substitution of Heb. *bosheth* ["shame"] for *ba'al* ["Baal"] in proper names; Hosea 9:10; Jeremiah 11:13); cf. Fishbane, *Biblical Interpretation in Ancient Israel*, 28-32, 44-77.

13. Fishbane, *Biblical Interpretation in Ancient Israel*, 86-87.

14. Ibid., 85-88. In other words, at that point the scribe moves across the continuum from purely scribal-redactional activity to actual authorial-compositional activity.

15. E.g., L. M. Eslinger, "Inner-Biblical Exegesis and Inner-Biblical Allusion: The Question of Category," *Vetus Testamentum* 42/1 (1992): 47-58; M. Floyd, "Deutero-Zechariah and Types of Intertextuality," in *Bringing Out the Treasure*, 225-44; E. P. McGarry, "The Ambidextrous Angel (Daniel 12:7 and Deuteronomy 32:40): Inner-Biblical Exegesis and Textual Criticism in Counterpoint," *Journal of Biblical Literature* 124/2 (2005): 211-28; D. L. Petersen, "Zechariah 9-14: Methodological Reflections," in *Bringing Out the Treasure*,

210-24; K. Weyde, "Inner Biblical Interpretation: Methodological Reflections on the Relationship between Texts in the Hebrew Bible," in K. Syreeni, ed., *Nomen et Nomina: Festkrift till Stig Norin*, *SEÅ* 70 (2005): 287-300.

16. E.g., Weyde, "Inner Biblical Interpretation," 291.

17. E.g., Eslinger, "Hosea 12:5a and Genesis 32:29," 91-99; B. D. Sommer, "Exegesis, Allusion, and Intertextuality in the Hebrew Bible: A Response to Lyle Eslinger," *Vetus Testamentum* 56 (1996): 479-89; idem., *A Prophet Reads Scripture*, 11-12, 23, 30. Cf. Weyde, p. 293. See also his fn. 26: "For example, Dan. 9:2 ff. in relation to Jer. 25:11ff; 29:10 (new interpretation) and 2 Chr. 35:13 in relation to Exod. 12:8f and Deut 16:7 (precision)"; cf. Weyde, 292.

18. Weyde, "Inner Biblical Interpretation," 300. I question his claim that "allusion does not include the notion of interpretation" but accept his distinction between exegesis as the "application or actualization of an earlier text" and exegesis as the "giving [of] new meaning to or transforming [of] an earlier text."

19. Fishbane, *Biblical Interpretation in Ancient Israel*, 180-81. The historical assumption is that the Covenant Code predates the Holiness Code, an assumption that I share.

20. This move makes it unnecessary to retain the expansion formula "Do the same with …" from the Covenant Code original. Inexplicably, however, the Holiness Code scribe omitted "your olive grove" (Exodus 23:11b), leaving a focus in the revised law exclusively on "fields" and "vineyards." Alternatively, the pairing of "sow" and "prune" may be a merism for all labors on the land; cf. J. M. Milgrom, *Leviticus 23-27*, Anchor Bible 3B (New York: Doubleday, 2001), 2158.

21. Milgrom, *Leviticus 23-27*, 2160, favors the latter but also summarizes the discussion of the matter by the rabbis (2160-61).

22. Though the motif also recurs in three other texts (Zechariah 1:12; 7:5; Daniel 9:2), brevity precludes my discussing them here; but see Fishbane, *Biblical Interpretation in Ancient Israel*, 479-85. Fishbane observes (480) that "a seventy-year period of destruction or subjugation was an established typological motif in the ancient Near East"; cf. Isaiah 23:15-17 (= "the span of a king's life") and the Black Stone of Esarhaddon, the latter available in translation at http://www.kchanson.com/ANCDOCS/meso/blackstone.html).

23. Cf. Jeremiah14:1; 28:12; 29:30; 32:26; 33:1,19,23; 34:12; 35:12; 36:27; 37:6; 39:15; 42:7; 43:8; 46:1; 47:1; 49:34. The bulk of these preface the book's two biographical sections (Jeremiah 26-29; 34-45) and the concluding oracles against other nations (Jeremiah 46-51). For introductory formulae in which Jeremiah speaks in the first-person (e.g., "The word of the LORD came to me … "), see Jeremiah 1:4, 11, 13; 2:1; 13:3, 8; 16:1; 18:5; 24:4; cf. 25:3; 32:6.

24. It may even imply that at the time of writing Jeremiah himself had already died. That would make the writer a later scribe, perhaps the prophet's secretary Baruch (Jeremiah 36; 45) or one of Jeremiah's disciples. Among others, K. M. O'Connor, *The Confessions of Jeremiah: Their Interpretation and Role in Chapters 1-25*, SBLDS 94 (Atlanta: Scholars Press, 1988), 146, believes that Jeremiah 21-25 presuppose that the fall of Judah has already occurred.

25. V. 13b, however, appears verbatim in Jeremiah 32:13. As is well known, the contents of LXX Jeremiah are not only on the whole shorter than MT but also present the same materials in different order. In LXX, MT 25:15-29:15 appears at 32:15-36:15 (less 34:1, 17, and 21).

26. E.g., "a family from the north" [v. 9], "that nation" [v. 12a], "them" [v. 12b]), a

vagueness also evident in other of Jeremiah's early announcements in MT of a terrible invader from the north (1:13-16; 4:6; 6:1, 22; 10:22; 13:20; 15:12). Elsewhere in Jeremiah, disasters overwhelming other nations (e.g., Egypt [46:20, 24]; Philistia [47:2]; Babylon [50:3, 9, 41; 51:48]) also come from the north. The exiles who eventually return to Judah also come from "the north" (16:15; 23:8).

27. MT comments that Jehoiakim's fourth year (605 BCE) equals "the first year of King Nebuchadnezzar of Babylon" (25:1). Twice it identifies Judah's destroyer by name ("Nebuchadnezzar king of Babylon" [vv. 1, 9]) and by title ("the king of Babylon" [vv. 11, 12]), and once by "his nation, the land of the Babylonians" (v. 12).

28. Fishbane, *Biblical Interpretation in Ancient Israel*, 479; and W. L. Holladay, *Jeremiah 1*, Hermeneia (Philadelphia: Fortress, 1986), 665.

29. For an overview of the root's senses, see G. André, "*paqad*," *Theological Dictionary of the Old Testament*, ed. G. J. Botterweck and H. Ringgren, trans. J. T. Willis, G. W. Bromiley, and D. E. Green, 8 vols (Grand Rapids: Eerdmans, 1974–) 13: 50-63, especially pp. 51-52, 54-55. The Exodus from Egypt offers a classic example of the same positive sense as in Jeremiah 29:10 (e.g., Exodus 3:16; 4:31; 13:19); cf. also Ruth 1:6; Jeremiah 5:7-9.

30. Fishbane, *Biblical Interpretation in Ancient Israel*, 479-80.

31. Ibid., 480-81.

32. Cf. L. C. Jonker, *1 & 2 Chronicles*, Understanding the Bible Commentary (Grand Rapids: Baker Books, 2013), 309.

33. Syntactically, the first two listed below (2 Chronicles 36:21a +b) are parallel and contextually bracketed by two purpose clauses (Hebrew *le* + infinitive constructs of *male'* qal); the first subordinates v. 21 to v. 20, while the second states the purpose of the two parallel lines just noted. Cf. Jonker, *1 & 2 Chronicles*, 310 ("The terminological similarities…are obvious").

34. The modifications include: a) the change from imperfect ("the land will enjoy…") in Leviticus 26:34a to perfect ("the land enjoyed …") in 2 Chronicles 36:21a; b) different prepositions with the infinitive forms of root *male'*; and c) a piel (vice qal) form of *male'* in 2 Chronicles 21a.

35. Fishbane, *Biblical Interpretation in Ancient Israel*, 481 ("the seventy years of doom in the Jeremian oracle were recompense *to the land*" [his italics]; cf. Jonker, *1 & 2 Chronicles*, 310 ("Possibly, in his view Judah's exile gave the land its restoration, something the people had denied it"). This does not mean, of course, that the land was totally vacant—what some call the myth of the empty land. In fact, those exiled were mainly the country's political and religious leaders, while people in rural areas apparently survived the national catastrophe of 587 BCE pretty much unscathed (cf. Jonker, *1 & 2 Chronicles*, 310). Certainly, when the exiles returned, they found themselves in conflict over land and national priorities with people who had never left.

36. Jonker, *1 & 2 Chronicles*, 310. One wonders whether the positive message of Jeremiah 29:12 may have subtly influenced the Chronicler here, although the writer leaves behind no linguistic signals to confirm that connection.

37. I.e., "Any of his people among you—may the LORD their God be with them, and let them go up" (2 Chronicles 36:23, TNIV).

38. Elsewhere, in my view, the number "seventy" also seems to connote "large quantities" (Numbers 11:16; Judges 1:7; 9:5; 12:14; 2 Kings 10:1). According to S. Japhet, *I and II Chronicles*, Old Testament Library (Louisville: WJKP, 1993), 1076, the Chronicler's seventy years marks "not a chronological datum which may be explained by various calculations, but

a historical and theological concept: a time limit for the duration of the land's desolation, established by a divine word through his prophet."

39. As Menn observes ("Inner-Biblical Exegesis in the Tanak," 71-72), "The presence of multiple interpretive layers of a single scriptural passage in the Tanak points to the adaptability of traditional texts to the ongoing life of religious communities."

WOMEN AND MINISTRY

Father Images and Women Pastors
How Our Implicit Ecclesiologies Function

Jo Ann Deasy

In 2009, I spent several months interviewing and meeting in focus groups with young women in a white suburban evangelical congregation in the Midwest that was open to women serving in ministry and as senior pastors. My goal was to better understand how these women were being formed by this congregation, especially in regard to their understanding of pastoral ministry and gender roles, both in the church and the family. My hope was to gain some tools to help congregations who want to support and advocate for women pastors. Instead, what I found was a group of women struggling with their identity as women, as ministers, and as children of God. As I analyzed the data I had gathered and compared their experiences to my own and to those of the young women I worked with while serving as the dean of students at North Park Theological Seminary, it became clear that their experiences were not unique. What was it about evangelical congregations that left so many women struggling in these areas?

The answer to this question is, of course, complicated. Our identities, including our pastoral identities, are shaped by so many factors: our families, our social class, our ethnicity, our regional and national cultures, our gifts and abilities, our experiences, our religions, and our communities of worship. Each of us is constantly receiving messages about who we are and who we are supposed to be, and one of the ways we form identity is by negotiating these various discourses both individually and together in the various communities that shape us. In this essay, I want to begin answering the question of women and pastoral identity by looking more deeply at two of those discourses. I will be exploring how evangelicals understand the pastoral role, both theologically and functionally, and how that intersects with their understanding of gender. As we will see, evangelicals have negotiated the relationship between these two discourses in a number of ways that have varied from denomination to denomination and over time. More conservative evangelicals have often claimed that their discourses regarding gender and pastoral identity are shaped solely by the Bible. As we will see, however, the changing and varied ways that evangelicals, including more conservative evangelicals, have negotiated these two discourses suggests that the broader culture has had a much more significant impact than they might like to believe. Many have concluded that this is a result of the church allowing the culture to shape their understanding of gender more than the Bible. I would argue, though, that perhaps even more significant is the way evangelicals have allowed the culture to shape their understanding of pastoral identity. The lack of a clear ecclesiology of the pastoral role contributes significantly to the struggle women have developing a pastoral identity in evangelical congregations.

Young Women, Gender, and Ministry

Broad understandings of ministry. During my interviews and focus groups, the young women and I explored issues related to ministry and pastoral identity. Most of the young women understood the word "ministry" quite broadly. Lisa,[1] a young married woman in her late twenties, described ministry this way:

> It depends on the person because I think that could be done in several ways. For some people it's speaking [and] voicing the gospel. For others it's serving and helping others....I know I've struggled with that growing up because I always felt in order to be a true minister of the gospel you had to talk about it, which is something I didn't like to do. But I think as I've gotten older [I've] realized that it can be through the smaller things that you do, not necessarily what you say, that can make you a minister of the gospel.[2]

To these young women, being a minister of the gospel meant sharing one's faith, both verbally and through acts of service. Amy, a young single professional woman, highlighted how this understanding of ministry was something that had to develop over time. As a young child, she thought of ministry as "up on a pulpit somewhere and speaking the word of God through the Bible or being a pastor." As she got older her understanding of ministry broadened to include both what one says and what one does.

Amy's comments about her general understanding of ministry as a young child highlighted a common theme among the women in their specific understanding of pastoral ministry. For most of them, pastoral ministry was connected to a pulpit and publicly sharing the word of God with others. Several of the young women, when asked what a pastor was, indicated that the obvious response was someone who is "up front, a preacher, a teacher of the gospel." They did realize that pastoral ministry was a much broader calling. They saw relational skills as essential in a pastor, and when asked about their most significant experiences with pastors, almost all of them related a time when they received pastoral care. This was not surprising—the pastor of the congregation they grew up in was known for his gentle spirit and the amount of time he spent caring for his parishioners.

A gendered interpretation of pastoral care. While it seems that a broad understanding of ministry and of the pastoral role would be empowering to the women, both as Christians living out their faith and as those who might consider pastoral ministry, many of the women admitted to being intimidated by the word "minister," even in a general sense, and to being fearful of speaking in public or having to articulate their faith. In addition, although they believed that women had stronger relational skills than men, they often downplayed women's ways of caring and relating. They rarely equated their ways of relating or caring with ministry and they almost never connected it with the pastoral care done by someone in the pastoral office. Male pastors who acted in nurturing and caring ways were seen as coming down off a pedestal to reach out to them while women pastors performing similar acts were seen as "mothering" rather than "pastoring."

Negotiating Mixed Messages

Women who take on the role of senior pastor or other forms of leadership in the church are often in a double bind when it comes to performing pastoral acts. When they attempt to lead or care in stereotypically male ways, they are often criticized for acting too masculine and failing to embrace their own gender. Yet, as these women reported, when women do use stereotypically feminine strengths, relational and nurturing skills, those very acts are often devalued as "mothering" rather than providing "pastoral care." I am not implying that the act of "mothering" is not valuable. I am arguing that the women I interviewed used the term "mothering" as a way to devalue the very same pastoral acts when they were performed by a woman rather than a man. This same devaluing occurs throughout our society in relationship to various roles performed by men and women. We see it most clearly in the way similar roles are given different titles, respect, and economic value when performed by men versus women. Cooking is often seen as a woman's job. Women who cook are called cooks. Men who cook, however, are often seen as having unique gifts and are called chefs, and are paid accordingly. Women who provide medical care are often nurses while men are doctors. Women who educate are teachers while men are professors. On the flip side, men who are strong leaders are often called powerful and assertive while women who are strong leaders are called bossy, demanding, or inflexible.

Did the women I interviewed not value the role of being a wife and mother? Did they see the act of mothering and nurturing as less than any care provided by a man? The answer to this is actually quite complicated. These women deeply valued the role of mother and believed that it was the right of every woman to be a mother and, if they so desired, to devote their full time and attention to the role. They saw mothering and the related skills of nurture and care as women's strongest gifts and something they contributed to society. At the same time, they often devalued these gifts and skills as less important than those of the men in their lives. They at times felt silly, overly emotional, or silenced when sharing relational concerns with their spouses and significant others. This seemed to be part of a trend with several of the women who seemed to have lost their voice after they graduated from college. There were several women in the group who had considered pastoral ministry as a career when they were in high school. Several had even completed bachelor's degrees in ministry-related fields. Yet, when I talked to these women just a few years after graduation, they felt that they had little Bible knowledge and would not be able to defend themselves rationally in a discussion about Christianity.

The women I interviewed were attempting to negotiate the various messages they were receiving about gender roles and pastoral ministry from the church and the culture around them. At times their negotiated understandings equipped and empowered them. They recognized their strengths as mothers, as caregivers, and as those with strong relational skills and a compassion for others. Yet, when these acts were performed outside of the traditional roles of wife and mother, they were often devalued, not recognized as potential skills in ministry or other professional callings. Even when these acts were performed within traditional roles, they did not consistently equip and empower the women. At times, these same strengths were interpreted as weaknesses and the women who possessed them as being overly emotional and unable to think or act rationally. The women were receiving mixed messages from the world around them regarding their own gifts and potential as well as the roles of mother and pastor. This left them often ambivalent about their own strengths and about the possibility of serving in ministry.

How women negotiate meaning and identity. Belenky, Clinchy, Goldberger and Tarule's groundbreaking work, *Women's Ways of Knowing*, studied women in a variety of formal and informal educational settings and developed five categories to describe how women understand knowledge, truth, and authority. They found a small group of women living in silence, having lost or having never developed their own voice with the ability to speak with any sort of confidence or authority. More common were women who had a voice, but it was a voice that was always reflective of knowledge received from others, knowledge that was received rather than imparted with any sense of authority. While the writers of *Women's Ways of Knowing* initially thought that these categories were universal for all women, further work highlighted how voice and silence operate differently in various cultural settings. In more oppressive conditions, silence may not mean lack of voice, but may instead be a way of holding on to control and protecting a sense of self in a hostile environment.[3] This suggests that silence and voice may be ways of negotiating the various messages one is receiving from the culture around them.

Mary McClintock Fulkerson has done significant work in the area of discourse analysis, studying how various communities of women negotiate the variety of messages they are receiving about themselves and the world around them. In *Changing the Subject,* her research focused on the call stories and worship practices of a group of female Pentecostal ministers and the practices of Presbyterian Women, the historic women's ministry of the Presbyterian Church, U.S.A. Fulkerson found both of these groups living within a patriarchal system, a system that they at times resisted. More often, though, Fulkerson found these women living within the system, but subverting it or making use of it for their own benefit. Fulkerson highlights the empowering nature of such choices, partly to counteract some feminist and liberation literature that has ignored or marginalized conservative women as victims or as irrational. In doing so, though, Fulkerson at times seems to ignore the damage to self that can also take place when making such choices.

The women in my research study were trying to negotiate between various messages they were receiving from the congregation of which they were a part and the culture around them. As they shared their understanding of themselves, of pastoral ministry, and of their role as women in the church, it became clear that there were various discourses shaping their understandings of themselves as women and as ministers of the gospel as well as various discourses shaping their understanding of the pastoral office. At different times in the conversation, different discourses would emerge. For example, as cited above, during a discussion of the strengths and unique gifts of women, relational skills were listed. Relational skills were also seen as important in pastoral ministry. Yet, the women were not able to make a connection between their own relational skills and the relational skills that were a part of pastoral ministry. Women's relational gifts and skills were seen as a detriment in pastoral ministry, signifying lack of strength and an inability to think rationally. Two different discourses regarding women and relational skills emerged: one that was empowering and liberating for women who wanted to embrace their nurturing qualities, and one that was diminishing and silencing as those very strengths were reinterpreted as weakness and ignorance.

Evangelicalism and Women Pastors: A History of Mixed Messages

Evangelical women have been receiving mixed messages and conflicting discourses regarding their identities and the call to ministry since the beginning of the evangelical movement in the eighteenth century. Barry Hankins, writing about the history of American evangelicals, says: "Evangelicals are deeply divided on the issue of gender and are in the midst of a serious debate over proper roles for men and women in the family, in churches, and in society. Moreover, this division has always existed."[4] Jonathan Edwards, a significant leader during the first Great Awakening of the early 1700s, was publicly against women preaching, but strongly encouraged them to become involved in personal evangelism and to speak boldly about their faith.[5] John Wesley, co-founder of the Methodist movement, encouraged women to organize class gatherings, teach, and exhort others, but warned them not to overstep their bounds or to speak with authority. Wesley felt that women should remain silent unless under "an extraordinary impulse of the Holy Spirit."[6] It does seem, though, that for Wesley and his followers there were quite a few women under an extraordinary impulse. Several of these women, such as former slave Amanda Berry Smith, became world-renowned evangelists. Others, such as Catherine Booth and Phoebe Palmer, eventually left the movement to start their own. Booth and her husband, William, founded the Salvation Army, and Palmer was one of the primary leaders of the Holiness movement. Though told that women should be silent, these women also heard that the Holy Spirit could equip and empower them to share their faith in extraordinary ways. Although they heard conflicting messages, these women negotiated these conflicts by either leaving the Methodist movement or exercising their gifts outside the framework of formal authority.[7]

In theory, the women in the congregation I studied were only receiving one message about ministry. They were hearing that women could be pastors. They were hearing that they were to use their gifts. Their theology should have empowered them to consider themselves ministers of the gospel. Those who felt called to be pastors should have been able to move forward with confidence rather than gradually losing their voice in their early twenties. What other discourses within the congregation were shaping them? What explicit and implicit theologies were working against the evangelical premise that we are all called to the priesthood of all believers? What was counteracting the theology of a congregation that believed that the Bible supported women serving in pastoral ministry? While this is clearly a complicated question, I'd like to suggest two possible areas to consider. The first is the diffuse theology of the pastoral office that was present in this congregation and has been part of the ecclesiology of the evangelical movement since the eighteenth century. The second is an implicit theology of God as male that impacts the congregation's expectations of a pastor and the self-identity and image of the young women in the congregation.

Evangelical ecclesiology. In the introduction to the book *Evangelical Ecclesiology*, John Stackhouse writes: "We evangelicals have implied an ecclesiology more than we have articulated one....We evangelicals have acted out our convictions about the church more than we have set them out."[8] Evangelicals do hold to some central theological beliefs about the nature of the church. Over against a Catholic or Eastern Orthodox ecclesiology that understands a local church to be derived from a priest or bishop, evangelical ecclesiologies define a church by the people gathered. Wherever two or more are gathered in the name of Christ, there is the church. This understanding of church is grounded in two key convictions: first, the conviction that everyone who believes in Christ has unmediated access to God through the presence of the Holy Spirit in their lives; and second, the doctrine of the priesthood of all believers which understands that all Christians are called to live as ministers of the gospel. Within evangelical ecclesiology, the pastoral office is no longer necessary for the constitution of a church. Rather, the pastoral office becomes a function of the church, a role that emerges to meet the leadership needs of the congregation. Since evangelicals did not see a particular church structure as part of the essence of the church, various forms of church emerged within evangelical congregations in the eighteenth century and continue to emerge to this day.[9] As a result, the pastoral office has been a rather fluid role within evangelical congregations. It has been defined pragmatically more than theologically, and its function has shifted as cultural understandings of leadership and the mission of the church have shifted over the years.[10]

Karl Olsson, in his history of the Evangelical Covenant Church, *By One Spirit*, comments on the shifts that took place regarding the role of the pastor in the late nineteenth century. Writing in particular about the early Swedish Pietists who formed the foundation of the denomination, Olsson says:

> In the period between 1885 and 1925 the pastor was primarily the preacher. Let us remember that he was stripped of his role as a theological teacher by the drying up of the creeds; he had no liturgy to master and hence needed no liturgical com-

petence except a strong voice; his leadership in the economy of the church (and I use economy here in a very large sense) had been taken from him by the laity; he was in no sense a canonist who made pronouncements upon the conduct of the church....His status, if he had any status, he achieved by being articulate, persuasive, and at worst engrossing and entertaining. It was, as we have pointed out elsewhere, an aristocracy of talent.[11]

Olsson's comments highlight the changes that took place in the theology and practice of the pastoral office as state churches imported to the United States became free churches, voluntary organizations that no longer relied on the authority of the state to define the authority of the pastor. These state churches were also faced with the changing relationship between geography and pastoral authority. Most state churches operated on a parish model. As the United States pushed westward and European immigrants began settling on this new frontier, churches could not supply enough ordained clergy to serve these large spread-out territories. Church became pragmatically separated from the pastoral office and authority passed into the hands of lay leaders. This shift from state church to free church, from a parish model to a frontier faith, and the impact of the Great Awakenings that swept across the United States during the eighteenth and nineteenth centuries all contributed to a fluid and changing understanding of the pastoral role.

In many ways, this fluidity of structure and in the pastoral office opened the door for a more diverse group of people to serve as pastors. Nathan Hatch, in writing about the early history of evangelicals, highlights how the Second Great Awakening, a key factor in the development of the evangelical movement, opened the door for people from different classes to serve as ministers. The Second Great Awakening allowed "ordinary" people to serve as clergy, overthrowing class hierarchies and authoritarian state church structures.[12] Clergy were no longer a distinct order of people defined by their education and social class. Instead, clergy became those people who could lead, who could persuade, and who could organize.

The church as family. It would seem that such an overthrow of social order would open the door for women pastors. However, instead of creating a new church structure that was truly more egalitarian and reflective of this concept of the priesthood of all believers, congregations created new authoritarian structures centered on charismatic personalities who were mostly male.[13] One of the reasons for this new male-centered authoritarian structure was its connection to the image of the family. As Sally Gallagher argues in her book *Evangelical Identity and Gendered Family Life*, the family became the central metaphor for the church and was tied in evangelicalism to a gendered order of creation that shaped both family and church. This connection between ecclesiology and gender roles is most clearly seen in arguments for all-male ruling elders in congregations.

On his website, "Grace to You," John MacArthur, in an article arguing that only men can serve as pastors and elders, points to 1 Timothy 2 as the clearest biblical teaching on this issue.[14] MacArthur translates 1 Timothy 2:12 as "but I do not allow a woman to teach or exercise authority over a man, but to remain quiet." He then points out that Paul supports this statement by referring back to the created order, "For it was Adam who was first created, and then Eve." Paul's connection to the created order, MacArthur argues, means that Paul's command in this passage applies universally to all churches and is not something that was unique to the context of the letter. "This proves," MacArthur writes, that "God wants his created design of male leadership and female submission in the family to extend into the functioning of the church." For MacArthur and others who believe that only men can be pastors and elders, this is not seen as devaluing women. Women are seen as equally created in God's image with an equally valuable role to play in the world as wives, and ministers of the gospel, but they are to do so in submission to men in the same way that men are to submit to God.

Implicit patriarchies in churches that advocate for women. While the connection between ecclesiology and gender roles is explicit in congregations and denominations that do not support women serving in the pastoral role, it is much more implicit in congregations that do support women pastors. In my focus groups with the young women I was interviewing, I asked if their church, which was open to women pastors, would ever hire a woman as a senior pastor. As they began to reflect on this question, they were surprised at their own feelings around this issue. While a few felt that younger members of the congregation might be open to a woman pastor, they did not see a need for a woman senior pastor. In fact, several of them voiced their own reluctance to have a woman serving as a senior pastor.[15]

Carly, a single mother and student in her late twenties, commented: "I find that the male lead pastor for me personally is like…I know it's weird cause I'm like the biggest feminist, but it's a necessity in a way. I like the strength of a male pastor." Elizabeth, a single woman in her early twenties who grew up in the congregation, shared her reflections: "It's not that I'm against having a woman head pastor, but there is something about [it]…like I view the male role as being like protective and as a leader and like that.…We've always had male head pastors and so there's something that's very comfortable about having a male as a head pastor." Later in our focus group, Elizabeth made a more explicit connection between her feelings about a male pastor and the role of the men in the family stating, "the pastor is like a role model for how men should be leading like in their own marriages." Britta, a married mother and part-time educator in her late twenties, wondered if men had a hard time having women as senior pastors because then they cannot see themselves as leaders.

Despite the fact that several women had served as associate pastors at this church, that the congregation had a position supporting women serving in all pastoral roles, that they were part of a denomination where women served as senior pastors in several churches, and that they themselves would argue that women can serve in any role they desire in the church, these women still found it hard to consider the possibility of a woman serving as a senior pastor in their congregation. I would argue that one of the reasons for their struggle to accept and want women pastors was an understanding of the pastoral role that was shaped more by their cultural expectations of leadership than their theology of the pastoral office. Their theology of the pastoral office was not strong enough to overcome their cultural assumptions about gender roles.

Sally Gallagher argues that evangelicals are faced with mixed messages about gender, pointing out both the egalitarian and patriarchal messages central to many evangelical theologies.[16] She sees these two theologies as part of the evangelical tool kit. Evangelicals choose which tool to use, egalitarianism or a patriarchal gendered-order, in any given situation. It would seem that evangelicals who support women's ordination would choose the tool of egalitarianism when defining both church and family, but the truth is much more complicated than that. Evangelicals often choose egalitarianism in their explicit theology of the church and family, but as these young women illustrate, their implicit ecclesiology is often quite patriarchal in nature.

The implicit patriarchal theology of both church and family in this particular congregation was also supported by a broader cultural discourse regarding the benefits for women of a benevolent patriarchy. The church that was studied was primarily a white middle- and upper-middle class congregation in the suburbs of a large city. While founded by a group of immigrants, often single men and women who worked as servants, chauffeurs, and gardeners, they grew significantly in the 1950s when they began to focus on young families from their denomination who were moving into the suburbs. Their sixtieth anniversary booklet talks about their "rags to riches" story which is connected both to the economic advancement of those within the congregation and a new emphasis on family-centered ministry.[17] Success in the life of the congregation became implicitly connected with a church that ministered to and embodied a family consisting of a father, a mother, and children.

Not only did the implicit understanding of a successful church become tied to the image of family, it became tied to the image of an upper-middle-class family in which the father was the financial provider and the mother's main responsibility was raising children and caring for the home. This family structure was not seen as oppressive. Rather, it was a benevolent patriarchy, one that most of these women strived to become a part of. It was also a benevolent patriarchy that could only be sustained if the family could afford to live on the father's salary alone. Anna, an eighteen-year-old high-school senior, made a direct connection between economic privilege and the desire for a male pastor by saying, "Like financially they're…everyone's comfortable and…all our needs are provided for so we can let men be the ministers in general."

The young women who participated in my research study were all quite well educated, had grown up in churches that supported and modeled women as pastors, at least in the role of associate pastor, and all believed that women should be able to serve in any ministerial role they felt called to. Yet none of them would have been vocal advocates for women senior pastors and they did not experience their church as intentional advocates for women serving in these roles. Despite their belief that women can and should be able to do anything they want in this world, they didn't desire a woman pastor and they didn't understand why a woman would want to serve in such a role. Why would a woman want to step out of a benevolent patriarchy that promised to take care of them and provide for them, giving them the freedom to choose how to live their lives, either as stay-at-home moms, part-time working moms, or moms that worked full-time outside the home? This was implied despite the fact that several them had been raised in or experienced situations where men were clearly not benevolent or able to provide everything the family needed. Still, they connected their understanding of the role of the pastor with that of an idealized father figure, one few of them had ever experienced.

Father God, Father Pastor

What are the implicit theologies in our congregations that continue to support the desire among women for a benevolent patriarchy, one that limits their ability to recognize their own potential, or for the congregation to recognize their potential, to serve in the pastoral office? Let me suggest two possible areas for further reflection: our language for God and hierarchical approaches to leadership.

Elizabeth Johnson, in her work *She Who Is: The Mystery of God in Feminist Theological Discourse*, writes about how our language for God shapes our understanding of the world. She observes that the "Christian community ordinarily speaks about God on the model of the ruling male human being."[18] While such language for God is appropriate—after all, men as well as women are created in God's image—the language becomes problematic when these terms are used exclusively. It turns out they are also problematic when used in conjunction with gender-neutral language for God. When the only gendered language for God used in a church is male, it implicitly conveys a male image for God, an image that then often gets superimposed on our image of the senior/solo pastor of a congregation. Fulkerson puts it like this: "While officially it is rightly and consistently said that God is spirit and so beyond identification with either male or female sex, yet the daily language of preaching, worship, catechesis, and instruction conveys a different message: God is male, or at least more like a man than a woman, or at least more fittingly addressed as male than as female."[19]

In the congregation I observed, a sustained effort was made to use gender-inclusive language for God, but when God was spoken of in specifically gendered terms, it was always male. This is true for most evangelical congregations that speak primarily of God the Father, Jesus the Son, and a nebulous Holy Spirit that reminds us that God transcends human categories. Using exclusively male-gendered language for God implicitly implies that men are more like God than women. Arguments are often made that female language for God is more associated with Gnosticism or pagan religions, but one might also argue that male language for God is central to many non-Christian religions and sects. It is not about using male or female language for God if we all agree that God transcends these categories. The question is how our language for God functions. With respect to women pastors, predominately or exclusively male language for God tends to convey that men are more like God and more appropriate pastoral leaders for congregations.

Male language, especially the language of God the Father, is often implicitly connected by those in the congregation with pastor as father. While the image of pastor as father can provide some useful resources for pastoral identity, there are also some significant drawbacks. Let me suggest two. First, when pastors are seen as the father of the congregation, especially when connected with male images of God the Father, the pastor is often seen as representing God to the congregation and acting as an intercessor between the congregation and God. In the early centuries of the Christian church, such understandings of the pastoral role led to a separation between clergy and laity, a separation that raised the image of clergy to that as greater than other human beings, as closer to the angels.[20] Clergy were seen as spiritual beings who did the work of ministry. Laity were seen as incapable of relating directly to God or doing the work of God's mission here on earth. In reaction to such a devaluing of laity, Martin Luther made the priesthood of all believers a central tenet of the Protestant Reformation. Ministry belonged to the people, not just to the clergy, and all human beings were granted the privilege of being able to interact directly with God. Clergy did not stand between human beings and God. This does not mean that clergy do not act on behalf of the congregation or speak to the congregation on behalf of God, but God does not only speak through clergy.

Clergy are not God. Clergy are not the head of the church. Christ is the head of the church and we are all a part of the body of Christ.

This idea of clergy as the head of the church in place of or as representatives of Christ is also implicitly communicated when churches are structured as a strict hierarchy with the pastor at the head. Churches are often modeled after a benevolent patriarchal family structure. Many churches want their pastors to act in such a way. They want their pastors to take care of them and to take responsibility for all the ministries of the church, but this often has negative consequences. First, both pastor and congregation begin to understand the laity as children, as immature and incapable of becoming mature followers of Christ. Yet what is the goal of pastoral ministry? Is it not to help our congregations to become mature followers of Christ? To equip and empower them for the work of the church? If a pastor perpetually treats the members of the congregation as if they are children, then they begin to think they are not capable of growing up, not capable of becoming a minister, not capable of living out their calling as ministers of the gospel. Second, pastors become overwhelmed with the work of ministry. Granted, pastors often relish the overwhelming responsibility of pastoral ministry. It makes them feel indispensable, needed, loved. However, a patriarchal or hierarchical structure puts a tremendous amount of pressure on the one at the top to provide, to produce, to be present for everyone at all times. It adds to the isolated and lonely nature of ministry by placing the pastor above and apart from the rest of the congregation. It also sets up new younger clergy for failure. Most young clergy learn how to be young clergy from the congregations that they serve. It is in the act of the ministry that they are formed into the pastoral office. Yet how does a young clergyperson learn from a congregation, and how does a congregation accept the responsibility of forming young clergy, if a structure is set up in which the clergy must always act as the parent and the congregation as the child? Shared models of ministry, including fully empowered leadership teams, preaching teams, pastoral teams, and pastoral-care ministries, convey to the congregation that they to do the work of ministry. They, too, are capable of and expected to grow into mature followers of Christ.

Conclusion

One of the more fascinating aspects of my research was the hunger to talk about these issues among the young women interviewed. Most of them felt that while the church communicated an implicit theology of gender and ministry, it had rarely been explicitly communicated, and they themselves had never had an opportunity to process what that might mean for their daily lives. I found a similar response among students in a class that Klyne Snodgrass and I taught for many years at North Park Theological Seminary entitled "Women, the Bible, and the Church." Those from conservative backgrounds certainly had a clear understanding of the church's theology of gender, but those from churches that were more egalitarian in their approach to gender found that their churches rarely talked about their positions on these matters. Instead, they were assumed. Even those who had a more clear understanding of gender often lacked a clear theology of pastoral ministry. There were certain key passages that were cited regarding gender and the role of elders or authority within the church, but few could articulate a clear theological understanding of authority, leadership, ordination, or the pastoral role. The same was found among students in my courses on leadership at North Park. Few of them could articulate a biblical understanding of ordination or the pastoral role other than its connection to leadership or authority. Of course, Klyne, being a Southern Baptist, would argue that ordination is never mentioned in the Bible! However, he would also argue for much more serious reflection on the biblical meanings of leadership and authority as they relate to the nature of church leadership.

We in the Evangelical Covenant Church need to do more theological reflection on the meaning of ordination and pastoral ministry. Too often we have allowed our understanding of the pastoral office to be shaped by popular understandings of charisma, power, and leadership rather than by the Bible. We have often failed to ask, "Where is it written?" As a result, we have often allowed the prejudices of our society and the false promises of our culture to shape an understanding of pastoral ministry that limits the potential for young women to recognize and live into the call of God upon their lives into these roles. As many early evangelicals pointed out, the work of the church is too urgent to allow this to happen. Arguments regarding women's ordination have often focused on the issue of gender alone, on the relationship between gender and authority in the church. Having proven our position biblically, we have considered the conversation closed, as if this proof was all that was needed to equip and empower women to serve. I would argue that the conversation is far from over. There is so much more for us to learn, so much deeper for us to go in this discussion, perhaps beginning with the basic question, what is a pastor? As we clarify our understanding of the pastoral office, we leave room for more intentional discussions about how we call and equip pastors to serve in this role, allowing our biblical convictions to speak louder than the messages of our culture.

Endnotes

1. Names of the young women in the study and information about their congregation have been changed to preserve their anonymity.

2. Data from this research was originally published in my PhD dissertation, *Called to This Image? How Discourses about Gender and Ministry Impact the Potential for Young Women to Develop a Pastoral Identity* (Ann Arbor: ProQuest LLC, 2010).

3. See Patrocinio P. Schweickart, "Speech Is Silver, Silence Is Gold: The Asymmetrical Intersubjectivity of Communicative Action," 305-34, and Aída Hurtado, "Strategic Suspensions: Feminists of Color Theorize the Production of Knowledge," 372-92, in Nancy Goldberger, Jill Tarule, Blythe Clinchy, and Mary Belenky, eds., *Knowledge, Difference, and Power: Essays Inspired by Women's Ways of Knowing* (New York: Basic Books, 1996).

4. Barry Hankins, *American Evangelicals: A Contemporary History of a Mainstream Religious Movement* (Plymouth, UK: Rowman & Littlefield, 2008), 105-6.

5. Ruth A. Tucker and Walter L. Liefeld, *Daughters of the Church: Women and Ministry from New Testament Times to the Present* (Grand Rapids: Zondervan, 1987). Also Jo Ann Deasy, "Women Leaders in Evangelical Congregations," in *Religious Leadership: A Reference Handbook*, ed. Sharon Henderson Callahan (Thousand Oaks: Sage Publications, 2013), 277.

6. Tucker and Liefeld, *Daughters of the Church*, 240.

7. For more on this topic, see Deasy, "Women Leaders in Evangelical Congregations," 276-81.

8. John G. Stackhouse, Jr., ed., *Evangelical Ecclesiology: Reality or Illusion?* (Grand Rapids: Baker Academic, 2003), 9.

9. Bruce Hindmarsh, "Is Evangelical Ecclesiology an Oxymoron?" in Stackhouse, *Evangelical Ecclesiology: Reality or Illusion?* 32.

10. See the section on free church ecclesiologies in Veli-Matti Kärkkäinen, *An Introduction to Ecclesiology: Ecumenical, Historical and Global Perspectives* (Downers Grove: InterVarsity Press, 2002), and Miroslav Volf, *After Our Likeness: The Church as the Image of the Trinity* (Grand Rapids: Eerdmans, 1998). While focusing more broadly on the global free-church movement, their work is applicable to evangelicalism which began as a free-church movement in the United States.

11. Karl A. Olsson, *By One Spirit* (Chicago: Covenant Press, 1962), 515-16.

12. Nathan Hatch, *The Democratization of American Christianity* (Yale University Press, 1991), 5-10.

13. Ibid., 9-10.

14. John MacArthur, "Can women serve as pastors and elders in the church?," Grace to You, http://www.gty.org/resources/questions/QA127, Copyright 2014, accessed March 12, 2014.

15. For the data connecting male pastors and father figures, see Deasy, *Called to This Image?,* 154.

16. Sally K. Gallagher, *Evangelical Identity and Gendered Family Life* (New Brunswick: Rutgers University Press, 2003), xi, 15.

17. Information about the sixtieth anniversary booklet is not cited here to preserve the anonymity of the congregation. More information about this congregation can be found in Deasy, *Called to This Image?,* 124-33.

18. Elizabeth A. Johnson, *She Who Is: The Mystery of God in Feminist Theological Discourse* (New York: Crossroad Publishing, 2005), 33.

19. Mary McClintock Fulkerson, *Changing the Subject: Women's Discourses and Feminist Theology* (Minneapolis: Fortress Press, 1994), 5.

20. In the sixth century, John Chrysostom wrote in *Six Books on the Priesthood* of priests who were exalted above all others "as if they were already transported to Heaven and had transcended human nature."

Women and Ancient Mortuary Culture(s)

Ekaterina Kozlova

A cursory survey of biblical scholarship on the appearance of Mary Magdalene at Jesus's empty tomb in John 20 shows that she is frequently chastised by exegetes for her failure to grasp the miracle of resurrection. Admittedly, the evangelist had a number of important truths to address in this chapter, and the reality of resurrection is by far the most prominent one. Arguably, however, Mary's persistent inquiry regarding the location of Jesus's body (John 20:2, 13, 15) could prove to be of paramount significance as well when it is considered against the heightened concern of the ancients with proper funerary protocol. In fact, some scholars do see Mary's distress as legitimate, mentioning that around this time the robbing of tombs and desecration of corpses were rather common and necessitated serious legal actions against these practices.[1] Furthermore, a few recent studies on the empty tomb narratives and other traditions have demonstrated that they are saturated with allusions to mourning rituals performed for Jesus, and that the Gospel of John is especially emphatic about the role of female disciples in matters related to his death, burial, and subsequent mortuary rites.[2]

This essay will attempt to show that Mary's query stands in the long tradition of ancient anxieties regarding the suspension of burial and attendant rites that are addressed in laments and, more specifically, in funerary laments. To that end this discussion will briefly consider the violation of funerary etiquette in the ancient Near East as an act of dishonor and the prominence of women in ancient mortuary culture(s). To illustrate the importance of proper ritual responses to deviant treatment of the dead it will then examine a lament uttered during the Babylonian invasion of Judah in Jeremiah 9:16-21 (Masoretic Text, MT hereafter). In conclusion, it will briefly comment on mourning rites used by collapse societies (e.g., Judah)[3] as tools of their social preservation and restoration.

Suspension of Burial Rites in the Ancient Near East and Women in Ancient Mortuary Culture(s)

Rooted in concepts about afterlife on the one hand, and processes of generational succession and inheritance distribution and maintenance on the other, burials and adjacent mourning rituals in the ancient world were generally sophisticated and required participation of both individual mourners and larger communities. Holding significant socio-religious weight, these procedures were meticulously followed and, at times, carried out over extended periods of time (cf. Genesis 50:10-11). Violations of funerary conventions, such as privation of burial or interment in an unknown location, exhumation of bodies with no subsequent reburial,[4] or mutilation of corpses,[5] were naturally regarded as individually dishonoring and socially damaging and as such were prominently featured in ancient Near Eastern curses, implemented in invasion and conquest accounts,[6] guarded against in funerary inscriptions, and protested in laments and associated mourning rites.[7]

As care for the dead and mourning for them in the ancient world, as in traditional modern societies, were primarily the duties of women—expert mourners and those closely related to the deceased[8]—these aggressive policies towards the dead were also addressed by female populaces. Even though ancient sources do preserve evidence of private ceremonies performed by women in cases of deviant treatment of the dead (e.g., 2 Samuel 21:10), the public dimension of female participation in death and mourning rituals on such occasions is more pronounced.[9] In the Hebrew Bible, for example, it is not unusual to hear laments over the downfall of communities and the mistreatment of their dead chanted both by men and women (Amos 5:16-17, Zechariah 12:10-14), yet the predominant use of feminine forms in summonses to wail and sing laments (Jeremiah 4:8; 6:26; 9:16-21 MT; 49:3, Ezekiel 32:16; Lamentations 1) and to accompany them with attendant rites in such contexts (Jeremiah 7:29; Isaiah 32:9-12) shows the prominence and skill of women in these matters.[10] Thus, for example, in regard to the lament over the demise of Judah in Jeremiah 9 it is observed that for the first and only time in the Hebrew Bible the messenger formula, "hear the word of the Lord," appears in the feminine plural. "How ironic that the masculine address is so frequently a summons to hear an appeal to repentance (e.g., [Jeremiah] 2:4), while the only feminine address is to help bury the covenant people!"[11]

The material culture of the ancient Near East, which is significantly richer on the subject, too validates women's expertise in this sphere. While in the broader context of ancient war imagery Egyptian and Assyrian reliefs locate ritual wailing performed by women at a variety of stages of military campaigns—siege, conquest, plunder, deportation—the latter inject the semiotics of mourning into depictions of both deportations and manumissions and portray women with their heads craned skyward, their hands placed on their foreheads and with their breasts partially or fully exposed.[12] The iconographic evidence of female mourners from the Levant from the late Bronze and early Iron Age is not as rich as from Egypt and Mesopotamia, yet a few pertinent artifacts do exist. The well-known sarcophagus of King Ahiram of Byblos, for example, is decorated with reliefs that depict four women in mourning—two beating their breasts and two holding their hands on their heads. From Palestinian sites—Azor, Tell Jemmeh, Tell Ashdod, Tell Etun—come several clay figurines of wailing women all exhibiting postures and gestures prescribed in contexts of loss and grief.[13]

This somewhat scarce archaeological evidence from the twelfth and eleventh centuries BCE can be complemented by a rich corpus of terra-cotta statuettes with disc-shaped objects discovered from many sites of Iron Age settlements. Due to the lack of written records the identity and function of these figurines have been widely debated,[14] yet there are strong reasons to identify at least a fraction of them with mourning women. Given that music and dancing were integral parts of funerary rites in the ancient world, it is not unlikely that some of the statuettes represented women skilled in solemn music and choreography.[15] Another factor in connecting these figurines with contexts of mourning is their nudity, which in many ancient cultures, including Israel, was a legitimate and conventional expression of grief.[16] Finally, in addition to other archaeological contexts some plaque figurines were found in tombs, where they could have been deposited to provide continuous mourning rituals in the afterlife. In fact, in his discussion of illustrations of musicians from tombs in the Mareshah necropolis, Joachim Braun points out the ancient Near Eastern belief that the deceased were to be accompanied in the afterlife and entertained by music and feasting (cf. Isaiah 14:10-11).[17] He also observes that terra-cotta reliefs from Beth Nattif from the Roman period, which bear striking resemblance to the Iron Age female drummers, may represent priestesses, or temple servants, or lamenting women, dancers, or funeral brides.[18]

To better illustrate the indisputable prominence of women in matters related to care for the dead this discussion will now turn to an Old Testament text, Jeremiah 9:16-21 MT, that deals with a series of funerary violations and the series of ritual responses occasioned by them.

Jeremiah 9:16-21 (MT) with Special Reference to Verse 18c

Funerary laments and their socio-religious value have received much scholarly attention in ethnography, musicology, ethnomusicology, social anthropology, and biblical studies. Based on the preserved ancient evidence and comparative ethnographic research, scholars have been able to produce a registry of themes addressed in funerary songs cross-culturally, one of which is the *circumstance* of one's passing—when eulogizing the dead person's character mourners often underscore their moral excellence and social prominence by bemoaning the *specifics* of their death.[19] Dealing with the Babylonian crisis in the seventh and sixth centuries BCE, which in Jeremiah's representation holds the highest concentration of deviant mortuary practices,[20] the communal lament in chapter 9 is also constructed according to the conventions of the genre, containing both formulaic language[21] and addressing the specifics of the national collapse. And it is the *specifics* of Judah's downfall in Jeremiah 9:16-21 (MT) that will be the focus of the remainder of this discussion.

The rationale for a lament in Jeremiah 9 is articulated as follows (Jeremiah 9:18 MT):

> *kî qôl nĕhî nišma' miṣṣiyyôn*
> *'êk šuddādnû bōšĕnû mĕ'ōd*
> *kî 'āzabnû 'āreṣ kî hišlîkû miškĕnôtênû*

> For a sound of wailing is heard from Zion:
> "How we are ruined! We are utterly shamed,
> Because we have left the land, because they have cast down
> our dwellings."

As is seen from the variety of renderings of the verb *hišlîkû* (Jeremiah 9:18c MT) in the ancient versions, and as has been rightly noted by many, the last part of verse 18 presents a number of text-critical issues.[22] The MT has *hišlîkû miškĕnôtênû*. Vulgate, Peshitta, and Targum render *hišlîkû* as "demolish" and understand it as an impersonal form, that is, "our dwellings have been demolished (or: thrown down)."[23] The Septuagint (LXX), however, has *aperripsamen ta skēnōmata hēmōn*, "we have thrown down (or: abandoned) our houses." Apparently reading *hišlaknû*, first person plural, the LXX continues the series of verbs in the first person plural that precede in the Hebrew Text: *šuddādnû*, "we are ruined"; *bōšĕnû*, "we are put to shame"; and *'āzabnû 'āreṣ*, "we have forsaken the land." William Holladay, however, observes that even though *aperripsamen* in the LXX may smooth out the inconsistency of verbal forms by making Judeans the subject of "throw down, demolish" and not the nondescript Babylonians, the oddity in this clause still remains. The active form *hišlaknû*, "we have thrown down (or: abandoned) our homes," is awkward, since in the meaning "abandoned, rejected" *hišlîk* "takes objects which are repellent (unacceptable meat, Exodus 22:30 MT; cords of bondage, Psalm 2:3). It is dubious to see the verb used by the people here of their own homes…in a lament."[24] Therefore, understanding the verb as either designating demolition of houses or rejection of them as equally problematic, a number of scholars accept the reading in the MT as straightforward and follow it without emendations. Thus Jack Lundbom, for example, says that even though "the LXX reading, 'we have thrown aside our dwellings,' makes for a more exact parallelism with 'we have forsaken our land'…the MT reading is perfectly acceptable and probably correct. The Babylonians and their allies, in subjugating Judah, have destroyed houses in the outlying villages, and the owners in the city are lamenting the loss."[25] The difficulty with this reading, however, is that apart from Jeremiah 9:18 (MT) the verb *šlk* is used only once in the context of destruction of an architectural structure in the Hebrew Bible (Daniel 8:11),[26] and the book of Jeremiah itself reserves this verb for governing human objects (discussed below).[27]

Another suggestion, however, has been proposed by Wilhelm Rudolph, and subsequently followed by a few, and that is to treat the consonants presupposed by the LXX as a first person plural form of *šlk* in the *hopʿal*, *hošlaknû*, "we have been cast out," and to assume a case of the haplography of *m* and read *mimmiškěnôtênû*, "from our homes."[28] The majority of commentators, however, understand that Jeremiah 9:18 (MT) had Judah's *general* devastation in mind, and thus the identity of the subject and object of the verb *šlk* as well as its form, passive or active, is irrelevant to the discussion of Jeremiah's lament. Thus, for example, Peter Craigie et al. state that "no reading substantially changes the meaning."[29] Seeing that the versions exhibit some uncertainty about this clause and given the abrupt switch of persons in a series of pleas coming from Zion, Rudolph's hypothesis that the LXX might have had *hšlknw* in its vorlage warrants further consideration. If Rudolph's suggestion is accepted and additional enquiry is made into the use of *šlk* in the Hebrew Bible and into the details of Judah's downfall in the immediate and larger settings of Jeremiah 9:18 (MT), a more specific reading of the outcry from Zion can emerge. Building on Rudolph's proposal, therefore, this essay will demonstrate that two semantic layers could be detected in the puzzling statement in verse 18c: (1) the eviction of Judeans from their homes and their subsequent demise and post-mortem desecration as recorded in Jeremiah 9:20-21 (MT); and (2) the exhumation of Jerusalem's citizens—aristocrats and commoners—from their graves in Jeremiah 8:1-3.

ŠLK ("to Cast") in the Hebrew Bible and Jeremiah

As has already been noted, the meaning of *šlk* (*hipʿil* and *hopʿal*) as "demolish (an architectural structure)" can be established with certainty only in one passage, in Daniel 8:11. Using the verb quite frequently, however, Jeremiah habitually uses it with either individual Judeans as its object, or society as a whole.[30] Of significance for such a feature of *šlk* in Jeremiah is that in the Hebrew Bible and in the Dead Sea Scrolls, when this verb is used of human beings, it usually denotes either their death or lethal endangerment.[31] In fact, at least five categories of such usage of *šlk* in the Hebrew Bible may be established:

1. dishonorable deposition of dead bodies into their final place of "rest" (not necessarily graves) following an unnatural death (Joshua 8:29, featuring the noun *nĕbēlâ*, "corpse"; 10:27; 2 Samuel 18:17; 2 Kings 13:21; Jeremiah 41:9, used with *peger*, "corpse"[32]

2. the execution of people and some form of interment of theirbodies (Exodus 1:22; Nehemiah 9:11; 2 Chronicles 25:12)

3. the execution without interment, or exhumation (2 Samuel 20:21, 22; Amos 8:3, again used with *peger*, "corpse"; Isaiah 14:18ff, 34:3 (used with *ḥalĕlêhem*, "their slain" in parallel with *peger*, "corpse"); Jeremiah 14:16; 22:19; 36:30 (again specifically featured with *nĕbēlâ*, "corpse"); 1 Kings 13:24, 25, 28 (used with the noun *nĕbēlâ*, "corpse"); 2 Kings 9:25-26, 10:25

4. the lowering of a person into what might become their grave (Genesis 37:22, 24; Jonah 2:4 MT; Jeremiah 38:6, 9)

5. the destruction of a nation or fatal endangerment of a nation (Deuteronomy 29:28 MT; 2 Kings 13:23; 17:20; 24:20; 2 Chronicles 7:20; Amos 4:3; Jeremiah 51:63; Ezekiel 16:5)

In the Dead Sea Scrolls the verb is used again explicitly with dead bodies as its object, *lhšlyk kl pgr[yhmh]* (4QMᵃ14-15 9).[33] The book of Jeremiah, too, conforms to these conventions in the use of *šlk*. Its first occurrence in the book, Jeremiah 7:15, threatens Judah with exile and formulates this ominous promise in the manner of Israel's earlier relocation and destruction: *wĕhišlaktî ʾetkem mēʿal pānay kaʾăšer hišlaktî ʾet kol-ʾăḥêkem*, "and I will cast you out of my sight, as I cast out all your kinsmen." In the epilogue to Jeremiah, the verb again, in retrospect, speaks of Judah's rejection by God: Jeremiah 52:3, *kî ʿal ʾap yhwh hāyetā bîrûšālaim wîhûdāh ʿad hišlîkô ʾôtām mēʿal pānāyw*, "for because of the anger of the Lord things came to the point in Jerusalem and Judah that he cast them out from his presence." Within this frame, the rest of the uses of *šlk* in Jeremiah consistently appear in the contexts of deviant manipulations of dead bodies as part of Judah's overall disintegration—from abandonment of the starved and slain Judeans with no subsequent interment (Jeremiah 14:16) to execution of individuals followed by their posthumous desecrations (22:19, cf. 36:30; see also 22:28; 26:23; 38:6, 9; 41:9). Admittedly, in Jeremiah 22:28 and 38:6, 9 the verb governs human objects—King Coniah and Jeremiah—while they are still alive. Yet even here the king's demise, that is, his deportation, is presented as his and his dynasty's complete annihilation. First, Coniah is depicted as being handed over into the hands of those who seek his life (Jeremiah 22:25) and being expelled into the land where he will die (Jeremiah 22:26). Second, the oracle envisages Coniah as childless, *ʿărîrî* (Jeremiah 22:30), and states that none of the king's descendants will prosper as his successor in Judah. In short, as far as the oracle is concerned Coniah is as good as dead.[34] Having been thrown into a cistern, Jeremiah too faces starvation and thus is lethally endangered (Jeremiah 38:6b, 9b, 10b).

The first semantic layer of *hošlaknû mimmiškĕnôtênû* (*"we have been cast out of our dwelling places"*). Given the nature of crimes against Judah as envisaged via the verb *šlk* and distributed within Jeremiah's *inclusio* (Jeremiah 7:15, 52:3), reading a human object of the verb in Jeremiah 9:18 MT (i.e., Judeans) as opposed to an inanimate object (their dwellings) accords better with Jeremiah's overall presentation of Judah's downfall and the role of *šlk* in it.[35] This reading could be further supported by the immediate context, which, in turn, will suggest the first semantic layer of *hošlaknû mimmiškĕnôtênû*, "we have been cast out of our dwelling places."

The first semantic layer, as proposed by this essay, emerges from the immediate setting of Jeremiah 9:18 (MT), namely the extension of the lament in verses 20-21 (MT). When the services of professional mourners are conscripted (vv. 16-17, 20 MT) and the elements of their lament are outlined (v. 21 MT), the rationale for the lament is further explained: the mass extermination of Judeans. The gruesome depiction of Judah's collapse in Jeremiah 9:20-21 (MT) starts with the grotesque image of a violent invasion of people's residences; death climbs through the windows and evicts tenants from homes: *kî ʿālâ māwet bĕḥallônênû / bāʾ bĕʾarmĕnôtênû* (9:20a). It then proceeds to destroy children playing in the streets and adults gathered in the squares (9:20b). Due to the pandemic nature of this tragedy the deceased are denied proper burial: *wĕnāpĕlâ niblat hāʾādām kĕdōmen ʿal pĕnê haśśādeh... wĕʾên mĕʾassēp*, "human corpses will fall like humus on the open field... no one will gather them" (9:21; cf. 14:16, *yihyû mušlākîm bĕḥūṣôt yĕrûšālaim... wĕʾên mĕqabbēr*, "[the people] will be thrown out into the streets of Jerusalem... there will be no one to bury them"); their exposed bodies are left to decompose in the fields (see verse 21 above).[36] With the *hopʿal* of *šlk* and the restored *min* in 9:18, *hošlaknû mimmiškĕnôtênû* will have Judeans as the main focus of attention and their dwellings as a secondary one, that is, "we have been thrown out (or: evicted) from our dwelling places," and, by extension, denied further deposition into graves. This reading will then have verses 20-21 (MT) as its primary referent

and the fatal displacement of the current generation of Judah as the first semantic layer of the dirge in verse 18 (MT).

The second semantic layer of *hošlaknû mimmiškĕnôtênû* (*"we have been cast out of our dwelling places"*). The inclusion of a second layer in verse 18
(MT), namely, "we have been cast away/exhumed from our (final) dwelling
places/graves," could be justified by (1) a broader context of the lament and
(2) the sufficiently wide semantic field of the vocabulary used in its formulation. As noted before, Judah's destruction in Jeremiah is marked by pervasive
sacrileges carried out through a combination of agencies—foreign and local
oppression, natural and divinely inflicted catastrophes (e.g., 8:1-3; 9:20, 21
MT; 14:16; 16:1-11; 22:19; 34:19-20; 36:30, and 41:9). With such vehement
hostility towards the Judean dead it would only be natural to have these desecrations included in the lament. With these mortuary deviances in the background and the semantic thrust of *šlk* in Jeremiah, the word *miškān* in 9:18
could also be understood as having a double duty meaning: both "a dwelling
place" and "a grave." In fact, this noun is attested in parallel with the more
explicit designation for a burial place, *qeber*, "grave," in Isaiah 22:16 and possibly has the meaning "grave" or "tomb" in a text from Qumran (3QTr 6:11).[37]

Of pertinence for this point is that such domestic representation of a grave
as one's (final) residence, one's house, is well-attested in the ancient Near Eastern sources and is quite frequent in the Hebrew Bible as well. Isaiah 14:18,
for example, speaks of the *dead* kings of the nations all lying in glory, residing
each in his own house, *bĕbêtô*. In Isaiah 14:19 these royal dwellings, tombs,
are contrasted to the grave, *qeber*, of the king of Tyre from which he is cast
out (*hošlaktā*). Similarly, in its description of a funerary procession Ecclesiastes
12:5 speaks of a grave as the deceased's eternal home, *bêt ʿôlāmô*, and in an
extended lament Job 30:23 describes death as the house appointed for all the
living, *bêt môʿēd lĕkol-ḥay*. Formulations similar to Ecclesiastes's *bêt ʿôlāmô* have
also been discovered in Phoenician, Palmyrene Aramaic, and Syriac inscriptions.[38] Given such frequent conceptualization of graves as houses/dwelling
places in both biblical and extra-biblical sources and given the semantic do-
main of *šlk* that encompasses a wide range of mortuary violations, it is not
implausible to detect an additional semantic facet, namely "disinterment,"
in *hošlaknû mimmiškĕnôtênû* in Jeremiah 9:18 (MT). In fact, Jeremiah 8:1-3
that contains a promise of mass exhumation of the bones of Judah's religio-
political leaders and less prominent citizens can serve as a perfect antecedent
of the outcry in 9:18 and further strengthen the layered reading of *hošlaknû
mimmiškĕnôtênû* suggested here.

After the indictment of practices at Tophet in the Ben Hinnom Valley (Jeremiah 7:30-34), the Lord tells the prophet that the remains of the city's past
inhabitants will be brought out from their graves and exposed to the elements.

Although their disinterment is pictured via a different verb, *hiphil* of *yṣ'*, their treatment closely parallels the demise of the current generation of Judah in Jeremiah 9:20-21 (MT). Both incidents include an imagery of violent dislodgment in the context of mortuary abuses (8:1; 9:21 MT).[39] They both employ similar formulations for the privation of re-burial in one case and burial in the other: *lō'yē'āsēpû wēlō'yiqqābērû*, "they will not be gathered or buried" (8:2) and *wē'ên mē'assēp*, "no one will gather (them)" (9:21c). Finally, they both envisage decomposition as the final destiny for their respective populaces, *lēdōmen 'al pēnê hā'ădāmāh*, "they will be like humus on the surface of the earth" (8:2) and *kēdōmen 'al pēnê haśśādeh*, "like humus upon the open field" (9:21b). Of interest for this point is that, against traditional renderings of the word *dōmen* as "dung" or "excrement," it has been recently demonstrated that *dōmen* "is always a simile for a body part left exposed to decompose on the earth" (e.g., 2 Kings 9:37; Psalm 83:11 MT), and thus should be viewed as decomposition of organic matter spread over the ground.[40] Therefore, having both 8:1-3 and 9:20-21 as referents of the dirge in 9:18c, *hošlaknû mimmiškĕnôtênû* fuses generations of Judeans, otherwise differentiated by time and class, into a unified group, forging a horrid solidarity in their experience of exile. The most recent casualties of the Babylonian invasion follow the destiny of their dead predecessors, and the complete disintegration of the former is expedited by means of circumventing the interment stage.

In light of the widespread violations of funerary conventions in Judah, such a double reading of Jeremiah 9:18 (MT) does better justice to the nature of the lament occasioned by Judah's collapse. The dirge in Jeremiah 9:18, then, "we have been thrown out of our dwelling places," addresses the eviction of all segments of the Judean community from their respective homes. On the one hand, and in retrospect, it mourns the punitive exhumation of the past generations from their graves in Jeremiah 8:1-3 and, on the other, it anticipates relocation of the living from their residences and their subsequent death in Jeremiah 9:21 (MT). Such a layered reading of the second part of verse 18c can be then viewed as a gloss on the first part of verse 18c, *kî 'āzabnû 'āreṣ*, "we have abandoned the land," with *'āreṣ* encompassing both domains—that of the living and that of the dead. The land of Judah, in its entirety, was subjected to a comprehensive and forcible ejection of its inhabitants. Having surrendered its people, the land is forsaken and thus it, too, is effectively dead (Jeremiah 4:23-27; 9:10-11 MT).

Mourning Rites as Socially Restorative Practices

The dirge over the cessation of the Judean community depicts the expulsion of its citizens by means of maltreatment and decomposition of its members. Dishonoring the dead, depriving the living of their land claims, and culturally defiling the terrain, such handling of the Judeans would have been viewed as a socially damaging practice[41] and as such naturally called for a series of ritual responses carried out, for the most part, by women. Regarding the presence of the messenger formulae, kōh 'āmar yhwh (thus says the LORD), dĕbar yhwh (the word of the LORD), ne'um yhwh (the oracle of the LORD), in 9:6, 17, 20 and 22 it is observed that they elevated the Jeremian dirge to the status of a prophetic word that was to be taught and chanted by women across generations.[42] In fact, its subject matter—punitive exhumations and privation of burial—is revisited in the traditions that address later stages in Judah's history, that is, its manumission from the Babylonian exile and resettlement in the land.

Since the precedent of placing laments and adjacent mourning rites in accounts of restoration of collapse societies was well attested in the ancient Near East, the Book of Consolation (Jeremiah 30-31) also commands the nation of Judah in its repatriation to build burial markers, ṣiyyunîm (Jeremiah 31:21; cf. 2 Kings 23:17; Ezekiel 39:15) and tamrûrîm (Jeremiah 31:21a) and to accompany its return to the homeland with ritual wailing, 'ōlāh[43] (Jeremiah 31:21c; cf. the LXX's penthousa).[44] Representing reconstitution of a nation as an amalgamation of ritualized purgation of the defiled Judah via erection of grave markers and mourning, the Book of Consolation again genders the repatriated group as feminine, that is, Virgin Israel (Jeremiah 31:21), which coheres well with the ancients' conceptualization of gender roles. Incidentally, various manipulations of the dead in the ancient Orient were viewed either as acts of violence or acts of benevolence.[45] If in prophetic thought Judah's exile is envisioned as a violent act of displacing its dead (Jeremiah 8:1-3), and its return is cast as a benevolent act of their revivification (cf. Ezekiel 37:12-14) or memorialization (Jeremiah 31:21), then Jeremiah's mourning rites, which are richly attested at every step of the Babylonian crisis, can also be viewed as part of God's benevolent scheme of Judah's preservation and reestablishment.[46]

Conclusions

Seeing that mortuary violations in the ancient Mediterranean world were not taken lightly, and given that beliefs and customs pertaining to burial were rarely innovations,[47] it might be possible to exonerate Mary's anxiety regarding Jesus's missing body in John 20. Although studies on cross-cultural funerary conventions show that laments and mourning for the dead could be carried out even without the knowledge of the place of burial or the presence of the body in a grave,[48] the tomb narratives (Mark 16:1; cf. 15:42-47; Matthew 28:1; Luke 23:56- 24:1; John 20:11; the Gospel of Peter 12:50-54) preserve a high number of rituals performed for Jesus after crucifixion—from "the preparation of the corpse (Mark) to delayed rituals for the dead (Gospel of Peter), mourning at the tomb (John), watching at the tomb (Matthew), and finally care for the tomb after burial (Luke)"[49]—and thus indicate that his posthumous honor maintained through the *proper* funerary protocol was a high priority for his disciples. Therefore it could be possible to understand Mary's tenacious query concerning Jesus's body (John 20:2,13,15) as an attempt to give her Lord secondary burial and thus salvage his honor, first compromised in the shameful mode of his execution and further tainted in the disturbance of his remains.

Endnotes

1. A decree of the emperor Claudius (CE 41-54), a copy of which was found at Nazareth, ordered capital punishment for violating the tombs, exhuming bodies, or displacing the sealing. G. Beasley-Murray, *John* (Waco, TX: Word Books, 1987), 371. Andreas J. Köstenberger, *John* (Grand Rapids: Baker Academic, 2004), 562, n. 13.

2. Carolyn Osiek, "The Women at the Tomb: What Are They Doing There?" *Hervormde Teologiese Studies* 53 (1997): 108; Antoinette Clark Wire, "Rising Voices: The Resurrection Witness of New Testament Non-Writers," in Alice Bach, Esther Fuchs, and Jane Schaberg, eds., *On the Cutting Edge: The Study of Women in Biblical Worlds. Essays in Honor of Elisabeth Schüssler Fiorenza* (New York/London: Continuum, 2004), 221-29; Angela Standhartinger, "'What Women Were Accustomed to Do for the Dead Beloved by Them' (Gospel of Peter 12.50): Traces of Laments and Mourning Rituals in Early Easter, Passion, and Lord's Supper Traditions," *Journal of Biblical Literature* 129 (2010): 559-74.

3. "A collapse or post-collapse society" is a society that displays a "significant loss of an established level of socio-political complexity." Joseph A. Tainter, *The Collapse of Complex Societies* (Cambridge: Cambridge University Press, 1988), 4. This term was applied to the mid-sixth-century BCE Judah by A. Faust in Avraham Faust, "Social and Cultural Changes in Judah During the 6th Century BCE and Their Implications for our Understanding of the Nature of the Neo-Babylonian Period," *Ugarit Forschungen* 36 (2004): 157-76.

4. On the hierarchy of dishonorable forms of burial and other manipulations of dead bodies, see Saul M. Olyan, "Some Neglected Aspects of Israelite Interment Ideology," *Journal of Biblical Literature* 124 (2005): 606-7.

5. For extra-biblical examples of this see, for instance, S. Richardson, "Death and Dismemberment in Mesopotamia: Discorporation Between the Body and Body Politic," in N. Laneri, ed., *Performing Death: Social Analyses of Funerary Traditions in the Ancient Near East and Mediterranean* (Chicago: Oriental Institute of the University of Chicago, 2007), 189-208. For comparable biblical practices, see Tracy M. Lemos, "Shame and Mutilation of Enemies in the Hebrew Bible," *Journal of Biblical Literature* 125 (2006): 225-24.

6. For Mesopotamian practices of disturbing the dead see William W. Hallo, "Disturbing the Dead," in Marc Z. Brettler, Nahum M. Sarna, Michael A. Fishbane, eds. *Minḥah le-Naḥum: Biblical and Other Studies Presented to Nahum M. Sarna in Honour of His 70th Birthday* (Sheffield: Sheffield Academic Press, 1993), 185. On non-burial as punitive measures in treaties and oaths see Donald J. Wiseman, *The Vassal Treaties of Esarhaddon* (London: British School of Archaeology in Iraq, 1958), 60-80; Delbert R. Hillers, *Treaty-Curses and the Old Testament Prophets,* Biblica et orientalia 16 (Rome: Pontifical Biblical Institute, 1964), 68-69; W. Boyd Barrick, *The King and the Cemeteries: Toward a New Understanding of Josiah's Reform* (Leiden: Brill, 2002), 178-81; Saul M. Olyan, "Unnoticed Resonances of Tomb Opening and Transportation of the Remains of the Dead in Ezekiel 37:12-14," *Journal of Biblical Literature* 128 (2009): 491-501, 492.

7. For a moving representation of a downfall of a community presented as a land covered

in human debris, see, for example, the Sumerian lament over the destruction of Ur: "Its people, not potsherds, filled its sides" (line 211). The reference is to broken pieces of pottery typically covering ancient mounds as the one that the city of Ur stood on. Lines 212-13 continue the imagery of non-burial: "On its walls they lay prostrate, To its lofty gates where they were wont to promenade dead bodies were lying about." Samuel N. Kramer, *Lamentation Over the Destruction of Ur* (Chicago: University of Chicago Press, 1940), 39. For comparable biblical examples see, for example, Jeremiah 9:18, 21 (MT) discussed in the main body of this essay. For the example of a dirge over an unburied individual see Bib. Ant. 9:12-13 that records a lament over the wife of Job: "the poor of the city made a great lamentation, saying, 'Look! This is Sitis, the woman of pride and splendour! She was not even considered worthy of a decent burial!'" Meir Bar-Ilan, *Some Jewish Women in Antiquity* (Atlanta: Scholars Press, 1998), 67.

8. Phyllis Bird, "The Place of Women in the Israelite Cultus," in Patrick D. Miller et al., eds., *Ancient Israelite Religion Essays in Honor of Frank Moore Cross* (Philadelphia: Fortress Press, 1987), 400, 410; Silvia Schroer, "Häusliche und ausserhäusliche religiöse Kompetenzen israelitischer Frauen am Beispiel von Totenklage und Totenbefragung," *Lectio difficilior* 1 (2002), accessed August 23, 2010, http://www.lectio.unibe.ch/02_1/schroer.htm.

9. Ibid.; see also Silvia Schroer, "Gender and Iconography from the Viewpoint of a Feminist Biblical Scholar," *Lectio Difficilior* 2 (2008): 10-14, accessed August 26, 2013, http://www.lectio.unibe.ch/08_2/Silvia_Schroer_Gender_and_Iconography.html; Bar-Ilan, *Some Jewish Women*, 52-77.

10. Of interest here, however, is the fact that the Old Testament does not preserve any actual laments or collection of laments composed by women. See David's laments composed for Saul, Jonathan, and Abner (2 Samuel 1:19-27; 3:33-34) or Jeremiah's lament for Josiah (2 Chronicles 35:25).

11. William Holladay, *Jeremiah 1: A Commentary on the Book of the Prophet Jeremiah, Chapters 1-25* (Philadelphia: Fortress Press, 1986), 314. On the importance of professional mourners in Jeremiah from the perspective of trauma theory, see L. Juliana Claassens, "Calling the Keeners: the Image of the Wailing Woman as Symbol of Survival in a Traumatized World," *Journal of Feminist Studies in Religion* 26 (2010): 63–77, and the bibliography cited there.

12. For a helpful catalogue of iconographic representations of mourning women in contexts related to warfare see, for example, Schroer, "Gender and Iconography," 10-14.

13. Carol Meyers, "Mother to Muse: An Archaeomusicological Study of Women's Performance in Ancient Israel," in Athalya Brenner and Jan Willem van Henten, eds., *Recycling Biblical Figures: Papers Read at a NOSTER Colloquium in Amsterdam*, 12-13 May 1997 (Leiden, Netherlands: 1998), 66.

14. Carol Meyers, "Of Drums and Damsels: Women's Performance in Ancient Israel," *Biblical Archaeologist* 54 (1991): 17; Carol L. Meyers, "Drum-Dance-Song Ensemble: Women's Performance in Biblical Israel," in Kimberly Marshall, ed., *Rediscovering the Muses: Women's Musical Traditions* (Boston: Northeastern University Press, 1993), 234-38; Sarit Paz, *Drums, Women, and Goddesses: Drumming and Gender in Iron Age II Israel* (Fribourg: Academic Press; Göttingen: Vandenhoeck & Ruprecht, 2007), 86ff., 121-22.

15. For a discussion on funerary dances in ancient Israel see, for example, W. Oesterley, *Sacred Dance in the Ancient World* (Mineola, NY: Dover, 2002).

16. For a discussion of nudity as a mourning rite in Israel and the Ancient Near East see, for example, Alexander Rofé, "Zechariah 12:12-14 and Hosea 10:5 in the Light of an Ancient Mourning Practice," in Chaim Cohen et al., eds., *Birkat Shalom Studies in the Bible,*

Ancient Near Eastern Literature, and Postbiblical Judaism: Presented to Shalom M. Paul on the Occasion of his Seventieth Birthday (Winona Lake, IN: Eisenbrauns, 2008), 299-304.

17. Joachim Braun, *Music in Ancient Israel/Palestine, Music in Ancient Israel/Palestine: Archaeological, Written, and Comparative Sources*, trans. Douglas W. Stott (Grand Rapids: Eerdmans, 2002), 209.

18. Ibid., 238. But some think that the figurines were deposited in graves for protection of the deceased from the evil eye. Others think that their presence assured the deceased of their continuing fertility in the afterlife. Paz speculates that they were deposited alongside women who used them in their domestic cults. Paz, *Drums, Women, and Goddesses*, 121-22.

19. For a list of basic themes in funerary laments see Standhartinger, "'What Women Were Accustomed to Do,'" 561-62 and the bibliography cited in n. 12-19.

20. Regarding the parallels to ancient Near Eastern treaty-curses that promise privation of burial, the deceased becoming food for vultures and animals and/or refuse on the face of the earth, Hillers observes that the number of these in Jeremiah is "remarkable, especially as contrasted with the few (and not especially close) parallels in the rest of prophetic literature." Hillers, *Treaty-Curses*, 68.

21. On suggestions regarding Ugaritic parallels to the imagery of death climbing through the window in verse 21 see, among others, John Day, *Yahweh and the Gods and Goddesses of Canaan* (Sheffield: Sheffield Academic Press, 2000), 188-90.

22. William McKane, *A Critical and Exegetical Commentary on Jeremiah* (Edinburgh: T & T Clark, 1986-1996), 209-10.

23. See NEB: "our houses have been pulled down"; NIV: "we must leave our land because our houses are in ruins"; NASB: "because they have cast down our dwellings"; KJV: "because our dwellings have cast us out."

24. Holladay, *Jeremiah 1*, 310.

25. Jack R. Lundbom, *Jeremiah 1-20: a New Translation with Introduction and Commentary* (New York: Doubleday, 1999), 557. See Craigie et al. who also follow the MT and translate v. 18 as "because they have cast down our dwellings." Peter C. Craigie, Page H. Kelley, and Joel F. Drinkard, Jr., *Jeremiah 1-25* (Dallas: Word Books, 1991), 148-49.

26. Leslie Allen is the only one who notes Daniel 8:11 and admits that the verb in Jeremiah 9:18 has to have a developed sense, that is, "demolish." Leslie C. Allen, *Jeremiah: a Commentary* (Louisville: Westminster John Knox, 2008), 118. Note that *DCH*, too, recognizes the oddity in Jeremiah 9:18 and, listing this occurrence in a separate entry, identifies it as "overthrow, demolish place by enemies." David J. Clines, ed., *The Dictionary of Classical Hebrew* (Sheffield: Sheffield Phoenix Press, 2011), vol. 8, 398.

27. Of pertinence here is also the absence of the direct object marker before *hišlîkû miškĕnôtênû* in the MT, although its omission in a poetic section is not that problematic.

28. Wilhelm Rudolph, *Jeremia* (Tübingen: Mohr Siebeck, 1947), 68. Cf. Bright's translation: "how we are ruined, how covered with shame! For we must leave the land, be hurled from our homes." John Bright, *Jeremiah: Introduction, Translation and Notes* (Garden City, NY: Doubleday, 1965), 69-70; Holladay: "'Oh, we have left the land!' and 'Oh, we are thrown from our tabernacle!'" Holladay, *Jeremiah 1*, 310; McKane: "we have been evicted from our homes." McKane, Jeremiah, 208. Holladay further suggests that *min* from *miṣṣiyyôn* can do double duty in 9:18, that is, it also goes with *miškĕnôtênû*. Holladay, Jeremiah, 310.

29. Craigie, Kelley, and Drinkard, *Jeremiah*, 149.

30. Out of fifteen occurrences of *šlk* in Jeremiah only three govern inanimate objects: hair (7:29), scroll (36:23), and stone (51:63). Although in 51:63 the stone, too, represents the destruction of a nation, Babylon.

31. To my knowledge there are only a few exceptions to such usage(s): Psalm 22:10 (MT); 51:11 (MT); 71:9; 102:10 (MT); 2 Kings 2:16; Ezekiel 28:17; Job 18:2, etc.

32. On categories of burial and more specifically on dishonorable forms of burial, which almost without exception feature the verb *šlk*, see Olyan, "Some Neglected Aspects," 606-7.

33. Maurice Baillet et al., *Discoveries in the Judaean Desert* (Oxford: Oxford University Press, 1982), vol. 7, 38-39.

34. Note that others also observe that Coniah's expulsion from the land is depicted through disinterment imagery. Francesca Stavrakopoulou, *Land of Our Fathers: the Roles of Ancestor Veneration in Biblical Land Claims* (New York; London: T & T Clark, 2010), 112, n. 31.

35. Cf. Stavrakopoulou's observation regarding the use of *ṭûl* in Jerermiah 16:13. "The same interrelated themes of non-burial and social disintegration are presented in very similar terms in Jer. 16:1-13, which culminates in the exile of the people, who will be 'hurled' (*ṭûl*) from the land (vs. 13)." Ibid., 110, n. 24.

36. In addition to the explicit imagery of death in verse 21, it has been observed that the statement about people being "cut off" is frequently used of "the socio-cultic abandonment, displacement or annihilation of the dead, or of dynastic destruction … or of exile from the homeland." Ibid., 124, and 124, n. 74. See also Olyan who shows that this image is taken from representations of the state of the dead in the underworld and that the experience of the exile was perceived as comparable to that of the dead. Saul M. Olyan, "'We Are Utterly Cut Off': Some Possible Nuances of וגל ונרזגנ in Ezek. 37:11," *Catholic Biblical Quarterly* (2003): 47-51.

37. Baillet et al., *Discoveries*, vol. 3, 249, 290. See also Psalm 49:11 (MT) where *Biblia Hebraica Stuttgartensia* suggests *qibrām*, "their grave," instead of *qirbām*, "their midst" in parallel with *miškĕnôtām lĕdôr vādôr*, "their dwelling places to all generations."

38. Paul Joüon, "Glanes palmyzéniennes," *Syria* 19 (1938): 99-103; James L. Crenshaw, "Youth and Old Age in Qohelet," *Hebrew Annual Review* 10 (1986): 9, n. 33.

39. For the discussion of *šlk* in the sense of exhumation see Saul M. Olyan, "Was the 'King of Babylon' Buried Before His Corpse Was Exposed? Some Thoughts on Isa 14.19," *Zeitschrift für die Alttestamentliche Wissenschaft* 118 (2006): 423-26. If Olyan is right then *šlk* can represent a wide range of directional "movement" of corpses—*toward* their final places of rest, past them, from them.

40. Ziony Zevit, *The Religions of Ancient Israel: a Synthesis of Parallactic Approaches* (London: Continuum, 2001), 543, n. 97; Stavrakopoulou, *Land of Our Fathers*, 112.

41. On the displacement of the dead as a form of social destabilization see chapter 4 in Stavrakopoulou, *Land of Our Fathers*, 81-102.

42. Pamela J. Scalise, "The Way of Weeping: Reading the Path of Grief in Jeremiah," *Word and World* 22 (2002): 417, n. 5.

43. For the MT's *'ēlleh*, "these."

44. In my thesis I explore this poem in detail and show that it contains a few mourning rituals—ritual wailing/mourning (vv.15, 19, 21c), erection of burial markers (v. 21a), funerary dances (v. 22b).

45. See note 6.

46. Claassens, "Calling the Keeners," 73, and the bibliography cited there.

47. Gary A. Anderson, *A Time to Mourn, a Time to Dance: the Expression of Grief and Joy in Israelite Religion* (University Park: Pennsylvania State University Press, 1991), 60.

48. Standhartinger, "'What Women Were Accustomed to Do,'" 565 and the bibliography in footnotes 28 and 29.

49. Ibid., 564.

IDENTITY

The Lord's Claim on
Our Identity

James K. Bruckner

T̲he church is having a spirited conversation about human identity, Christian identity, and sexual identity. The distinctions, in part, center on the question, to what extent is Scripture still relevant to the understanding and formation of our identity?[1] For those who consider Christian life to be rooted in Scripture as the revealed word of God—and an active, living word whose interpreted words still bear words of life—this essay may be clarifying.

Identity and the Lord God

Who Do You Think You Are? is a television dramatization (on TLC) of genealogical research into celebrities' family trees. The show's research rightly ties human identity both to genetics and historical narrative. The stories we hear and tell about ourselves matter. Our particular biology and experiences are certainly an important source of self-understanding, awareness, and sense of belonging as sentient mammals.

The Christian claim, however, includes a farther-reaching story concerning our identity. Because we belong to the Lord, God's remembrance of us and the stories God tells about us are the source of our ultimate identity. God's word precedes us and will survive us. God's claim on us is cosmic, yet intimate, and it constitutes a very personal source of our being and hope.

The stories we tell about God in relation to ourselves matter, for they reveal whether we think that we construct and can marginalize God, or whether we believe the increasingly radical notion in our society that God has created and does sustain us. Who is, ultimately, the subject of the sentence that begins the story, and who is the object?

Who we think we are and who God says we are often conflict. God's revealed word demonstrates a deeply embedded human penchant for self-referential idolatry concerning "who we are." This is why the apostolic faith has been grounded in confession of the revealed word, where ontology precedes epistemology: "In the beginning, God…" and "In the beginning was the Word," rather than, "In the beginning, Israel" or "In the beginning, we…" God is the primary actor, and the culmination of all things, including each of us.

"God" can, of course, mean many things in contemporary theological conversation. But there is only one "god" that Christians can speak of with any warrant—the LORD God, revealed in the Old and New Testaments as God's word about the true God. For the purposes of Christian identity, the confession of covenanted faith and discipleship is carried in the word "LORD."[2] The connection between Jesus and Yahweh—made by Jesus—is retained in the term "LORD."[3] The word "LORD" implies a claim of personal allegiance, and thus, is the specific external personal referent and source of our identity.

While any interpreter of Scripture worth his or her salt will acknowledge the layers of meaning in Scripture (e.g., historical, cultural, linguistic, intertextual, canonical), the Christian claim is that the Bible is *also* the living word of the LORD, capable, by means of the creating Holy Spirit, of the ultimate transformation of human lives. Moses makes a present-tense claim in the deuteronomic sermon on the Plains of Moab: "Not with our fathers did the LORD make this covenant, but with us, who are all of us here alive today" (Deuteronomy 5:3; see also Hebrews 4:7-9). He challenges the later, surviving younger generation to choose God's revealed word as a way of living.

This word may be accepted and interpreted, or rejected. Until the revealed word and its covenant of the LORD's unrelenting love is accepted by a person or a community, any person's search for identity remains a weightless and temporary endeavor, trapped in the updraft of genetics and personal experience.

Identity is created and may be transformed by the revealed word. The incarnation—that may transform our created identities—is accessible primarily through the ancient witness of Scripture. The incarnation, revealed in God's word, is the Word made flesh; the LORD, Christ Jesus, whose agency and witness give us access to the ineffable Trinity of God. Through the witness of Israel and the apostles, by means of the living Spirit of God, Christ transforms people. We are not prisoners of our present biology, neurology, or sociology. The full testimony of identity transformation was declared by Paul when he wrote: "All scripture is inspired by God and is useful for teaching, for reproof, for correction, and for training in righteousness, so that everyone who belongs to God may be proficient, equipped for every good work" (2 Timothy 3:16-17). The Scripture to which the author refers is the Old Testament—the New Testament had not yet been completed. The Old Testament is, in large relief, a testimony of the formation of the identity of a people formed *as a people* by a redeeming LORD.

The whole created world, however, is in view in the first twelve chapters of Genesis. Human beings are created, proclaimed "very good," given freedoms and boundaries, violate those boundaries, are broken in relation to God and each other, and are blessed by God in the midst of their brokenness. This fundamentally paradoxical identity has formed the basis of Jewish and Christian understanding and theologies, that is, identity in relation to God, the Creator.

Created Identity and Genesis

Genesis describes us, from the outset, as good, but dependent, animals. Like the other animals, humans are made from the earth, given the breath of life, and blessed (Genesis 1). God's word concerning human life begins with basic claims that human beings are declared "good" by God, embodied from the earth, and are filled with the breath of God. Most contemporary discussions of human identity naturally stop using Genesis at this point because these are life-affirming concepts that do not challenge our parlor goodness. Yet the *goodness* of creation is not a self-evident fact. Worldwide mythologies of creation begin with chaos and violence, not the Creator's declaration of goodness.

Goodness is bounded first by God's assertion that it *is* good. Each of the following three claims about human identity is set in context of its dynamic boundary: (1) Our goodness is established by and dependent on God's spoken and written word. (2) Our good embodiment from the earth comes with mortality; we come from the earth and return to the earth. 3) Our divine breath (Genesis 2:7) is a temporary gift. The goodness of our embodied creation can also be experienced as *bad* news, because it comes with restrictions. We are *not* autonomous, inherently immortal, or independent of God for our breath. In Genesis 1, no one is created as a self-sustaining immortal.

Dependence on God is presented as a common good for the human creation: dependence for breath, for access to the tree of life, for embodiment, and for Eve as "a suitable corresponding partner" (*'ezer kenegdo*) for Adam (Genesis 2:18). Our life, as with all animal life, is declared fundamentally good in relation to the LORD. God's declaration, however, does not end here.

The image of God and dominion. "In the image of God…male and female he created them. God blessed them…and God said…'Have dominion'" (Genesis 1:27-28). The relational goodness of our embodied lives is not the end of God's word about us in Genesis. God declares and God's people are called to remember that we are also: made in the image (*tselem*) of God, with the potential to make our image an idol (*tselem*); and given dominion (*radah*)—the potential to manipulate the created world for good or ill. Some contemporary discussions of human identity and spirituality focus on the positive side of the concept of the "image of God" in us. It is a good revelation. "The image of God is the universal value that Scripture places on human existence, as the innate dignity of being human in relation to the Creator. The child with Down's syndrome and the child prodigy both bear the image of the Creator by virtue of their human existence. The image persists without regard to intelligence, wealth, virtue, particular mystical gifts, or beauty."[4] Yet, the image of God also comes with the potential to use the *image* as an *idol.* The Hebrew word for "image" is also the word for "idol" (*tselem*). This paradoxical possibility of two truths in one word provides a thicker understanding of identity. "The image of God is also the created capacity of any person either to manifest the glory of God or to divert that glory for their own purposes. This is what we experience as the ability to make genuine decisions. Animals make decisions too; but typically they make decisions which are instinctive and predictable."[5] The image is given in relationship, by God, and can be borne within that created relationship. It is also possible to refuse or misuse that relationship and to manipulate our own identities. That is the freedom of the embodied image. The typical culprits for this twisting in Scripture are wealth, power, and sexuality.[6] God's image in us is the capacity to be self-determining or self-transcendent. God's "image" (*tselem*) provides the capacity to do what is "right in your own eyes." It is the agency to will to cross the boundaries established by God. Paul Tillich notes that the image of God provides the possibility for people to reject God; to use one's "image of God" in an idolatrous way.[7]

The New Testament declares that Jesus the Christ is the incarnate image of God (John 1). By extension, a transformed humanity is formed around this newly revealed Christocentric anthropology.[8] Christ is called the "image of God" and believers are called to participate in the image of God in Jesus Christ by putting on or "bearing" that image in anticipation of the new creation. A choice is necessary. How we act in the world reveals whether we choose to embody only "the image of the man of dust" or also the image of Christ (1 Corinthians 15:49).[9] This is the freedom of the image of God in us.

The second paradoxical assertion of Genesis concerns dominion (Genesis 1:26).[10] God gives men and women dominion: the power to manipulate the created world, for good or ill. That includes the power to manipulate our own identities and to reject God. Since we bear both the image of *dust* and the potential to bear the image of *Christ*, decisions and actions are taken. When the image of dust is used for idolatry, and is not transformed by the image of Christ, our dominion is self-serving and self-destructive. The personal practice of dominion is real relational power in the world.

The English word "dominion" has acquired negative connotations, largely because of the exercise of bad dominion by people with political power. In Scripture, however, dominion may be good or bad. The psalmist celebrates and describes the nature of good dominion in a royal song: "May he have dominion from sea to sea.... For he delivers the needy when they call, the poor and those who have no helper [*'ezer*]. He has pity on the weak and the needy, and saves the lives of the needy.... May there be abundance of grain in the land…and may people blossom in the cities like the grass of the field" (Psalm 72:8a, 12-13, 16; see also Psalm 97). Good dominion includes servant-leadership, justice for the poor, thriving cities, and care for the earth so that all will flourish. The deuteronomist declares, in the books of Kings, which rulers did and which did not exercise good dominion in Judah. Servant-ruler language culminates in Isaiah 52-53, where the practice of good dominion is declared by God's vindication of the servant-leader. [11]

Jesus's good dominion follows this trajectory of kingship in his teaching about the "kingdom of God," typified by the Sermon on the Mount (Matthew 5-7). It follows the vindicated suffering servant as a description of the work of Jesus as a dying and rising king. The ultimate act of dominion and rule was to bear the sins of the world, defeating sin and death and inaugurating hope in a new creation. [12]

For human identity and dominion, the question is, what will you do with your mortal life? Jesus's defeat of death provided the possibility that anxiety about personal mortality would not remain the controlling factor in the exercise of human dominion. The difference between good and bad dominion vis-à-vis identity is only resolved when the question of mortal life and death in relation to God are faced.

Adam and Eve had daily access to a tree of life that guaranteed the continuation of their lives. There, good dominion is finely illustrated, where the earth is ever viewed as a garden to be cared for as God's special creation, in partnership with humanity. [13] God instructed Adam and Eve to "serve and protect" (Genesis 2:15, Heb: *'eved, shamar*). Yet, even there, a casual conversation about identity and mortality with a snake changed everything (Genesis 3:1-5).

Many contemporary interpreters prefer to stop with a one-sided positive reading of human empowerment: *created good, given divine breath, given God's image, given dominion.* But dominion, given by God, may be used apart from God and God's command. In fact, the first exercise of bad dominion is the decision to eat from the forbidden tree. Genesis 3 demonstrates that we are perpetually handicapped by our tendency to falsify our stories of identity through rationalization.

Rational and rationalizing beings. A third paradox in the Genesis narrative is that we have the ability to use reason independently, as well as the ability to obey God's command simply because the LORD makes the command—even when God holds back some of the information about our lives and deaths. In Genesis 2-3, the limit of human reason is presented as God's command with a reason that only God has determined: "but of the tree of the knowledge of good and evil you shall not eat, for in the day that you eat of it you shall die" (Genesis 2:17).

The serpent, however, offers a very reasonable alternative version of God's word: "You will not surely die. For God knows that when you eat of it your eyes will be opened, and you will be like God, knowing good and evil" (Genesis 3:4-5, ESV). We cannot reason our way through or past our own mortality. This is the presenting problem in Genesis 3. Death is the ultimate human limitation: "You shall surely die" is God's earliest threat. Turning away from the idea of death to an alternative narrative construct is pretty good logic if you do not trust God, who holds back the nauseous details about death. As poet Christian Wiman says, "And that is the issue, isn't it? Death? That crashing cataract that comes to us, from this distance, as the white noise of life, that *ur*-despair that underlies all the little prickly irritations and anxieties that alcohol is engineered to erase."[14]

The couple has no way to verify the authenticity of God's word about death. It is simply a command of God, to be kept or not. As long as they kept the command it functioned as a reminder that they could trust God for their future and for what God knew about death and would not tell them. God had created a physical limit; a boundary at the center of the garden, not the perimeter, so that the center of their identity would be their relationship with God.

Reason was necessary for them to decide, each day, to trust and walk with the LORD and not eat from the tree. Each day, their restraint was an act of reason and of worship (Heb. *'eved*; or "obedience"). The alternative to this paradox of rationality is a half-truth. The serpent has the logic that does not require obedience or worship: "God knows" and "You don't!" (Genesis 3:5). And it is *correct*. The crux of the temptation offered is "Your eyes will be opened." It offers them sugar mixed with the poison. Their eyes would be opened—to their human vulnerability! They would, like God, be painfully aware of that fact. The temptation was, and is, to try to grasp what God reserves to God; to try to grasp what cannot be grasped.

A classic Christian reading of the "original sin" is pride: attempting to live *as if* they were autonomous; *as if* they were creatures with no limitations; *as if* the solution to the mortality problem is to come out with a rationalized challenge to the LORD's word about the tree. In the words of Babel, "Let us make a name *for ourselves*" (Genesis 11:4). The biblical claim is that God's love, call, and command all *precede* our awareness and knowledge of them. Again, in

Scripture and apostolic witness, ontology precedes epistemology, not the reverse—that is, God's existence and self-revelation precedes human knowledge and articulation of God.

In sharp contrast, one current tendency in Christian interpretation of the "original sin" actually elevates Adam and Eve's *contextualized proclivity* in Genesis 3, calling it an "upward" fall—or a fall forward into sophistication and experience. After all, Adam and Eve were "only" attempting to live *as if* they could competently manage their lives solely from within their *contextualized* experience—by following their created and embodied *proclivities*; *as if* God was mistaken, lying, exaggerating, or badly motivated concerning the prohibition "You must not eat from it"; *as if* God didn't really care or understand their situation. It was easy for them to consider second-guessing the command. The garden was so full of life, in their experience, why should they worry about mortality or God's commands?

The serpent, Eve, and Adam blithely construct their own new contextualized theology on the false premise that God's word probably overstated the connection between the tree and death, especially since the fruit of the tree was: "good (*tov*) for food," "a delight (*ta'awah*; 'a boundary') to the eyes," and "to be desired (*khamad*; 'covetable') to make one wise." The double meaning of *ta'awah* ("delight" and "boundary") is indicative of the subtlety of the text. Its homonym is *to'evah* ("confusion" or "perversion"), which is used in Sinaitic law for actions that pervert a godly good by pursing the wrong object (usually an idolatry of power, sex, or money). The emotional progression of the three descriptors (good, a delight, covetable) masterfully pictures the increasing intensity of the temptation. They took refuge from God within the creation that God had called "good" (see Psalm 10:11, 22:24, 69:5; Hosea 5:3; Isaiah 40:27).[15] They replaced God's word with an alternate *raison d'être*.

Using the freedom of their created dominion, they constructed a rationalized theology that deconstructed God's word, declaring the forbidden to be good—a typical ancient *and* postmodern form of original theological sin.[16] "She took…she ate…she gave.…He ate…then they knew." Genesis 3 describes the "fall" in terms of broken relationships across the board: with God, with each other, with the non-human creation, and in confusion about their own embodiment (Adam and Eve are ashamed, cover themselves, and attempt to hide their naked bodies from God).

Our fallen tendency is to falsify both our story and the LORD's story for our own satisfaction and to our own detriment. We are constantly at risk of twisting or rationalizing the nature of our created reality, including the postmodern claim that "there is no one truth or overarching story." Scripture rehearses the most common placebos—rationalized idolatries (money, sex, and power)—in its narratives, laws, and wisdom. Awareness of this human factor is an important component of identity formation.

Within the apostolic Christian faith, both pride and making excuses for our personal contextual proclivities are considered sin. Both are unhealthy responses to the ideal possibility of trusting God for both our limitations and our freedom. Both are attempts to live *sui generis* ("of his/her own kind"), that is, as authors of our own stories, without reference to God.[17] Wiman puts it this way, "If God has no relation to your experience, if God is not *in* your experience, then experience is always an end in itself, and always, I think, a dead end. Not only does experience open into nothing else, but that ulterior awareness, that spirit-cleansing whiff of the ultimate, never comes into the concrete details of existence either. You can certainly enjoy life like this; you can have a hell of a time."[18]

In an increasingly secular age, the doctrine of creation and human identity reminds us that we are both God's good creation and limited, fallen creatures. To say that we are simply "good" is only a partial truth. Deriving our vocation from our "created self," as one certainly must do, can also easily lead to the destruction of God's shalom and salvation in our lives. Transformation of the created self is the heart of the gospel of God's intervention and revelation in both Testaments. Israel is transformed by God's action and word, in the midst of its culturally diverse neighbors. Gentile Christians are transformed in faith and practice by that same word, written and made flesh, through being grafted into Christ.

The doctrine of the church and of Scripture is a counter-cultural narrative: that an external personal reality—the LORD God—made us and cares about the violent mess of the world; made us good and gave us the freedom to flourish and to fall; has intervened in history to reveal another way, first with the creation of the Jewish people and then in Jesus the Christ; came down to redeem and transform a self-poisoned people; and came down to provide for the possibility of a blessed eternal life with God in a renewed creation.

Identity Crisis and Transformation

Christian identity, at its center, is grounded in whom you love and in who loves you. This love is measured in whom you suffer for and who suffers for you. "I am loved by God, who suffered and died for me, therefore I am loved" is a crucial biblical perspective on identity formation. The LORD's love is unconditional in the sense that it lifts guilt, forgives sin, and ever stands and waits for our prodigal repentance and return. Conversely, it is conditional on human choice (dominion), including the choice to reject God's law, reject the suffering of the LORD, and reject the gospel of the Christ. Human love for God is embodied by keeping the LORD's commandments: "Abide in my love (*agapē*). If you keep my commandments, you will abide in my love, just as I have kept my Father's commandments and abide in his love....You are my friends if you do what I command you" (John 15:9b-10, 14). The commands to love indicate the complexity of this love (Heb. *'ahav, khesed*; Gr. *agapē*). We are commanded to love God (the *Shema*; Deuteronomy 6:4-9) and to love our neighbor in relation to the Lord (Leviticus 18:19). The Lord insists that self-identification of a person or community as *God's* people will include that kind of love which cares for the widow, orphan, and immigrant. Jesus extends this command to "Love your enemies, and pray for those who persecute you" (Matthew 5:44).

There are no limits on love or on whom we love. Yet this love does not conflate love for a person with love for their deeds. For example, sex does have clearly delineated limits in Scripture, and observing them is also revealed as an expression of the commanded love for God and neighbor. In the Scripture, love and intimacy are not sexualized, but rather are protected and made safe from such a conflation.

We are loved by God, but an identity "crisis" is created in us by the transforming presence of the Lord and our accompanying awareness of our disabilities in regards to love. God's presence and God's word are an external word about us—we are, Scripture tells us, by nature, broken, vulnerable, and in need of the Lord.

The Old Testament and New Testament credos, baptismal liturgies, and Jesus's Gethsemane prayer, speak of a relationship with the Lord founded in human disability to self-create authentic independent identity and futures.[19] In the Old Testament, a transformed human identity means trusting in God's love and promises in the midst of suffering (e.g., in the midst of Egyptian slavery, Assyrian crisis, and Babylonian captivity). Vitality of life in the New Testament comes through death—Jesus's death and the death and rebirth of human identity in Christ.[20] Christian identity is constituted by the presence of the Lord and the true "stories" God tells in his word.

The word of the Lord creates his people through commands that bear promise. In the Exodus-Deuteronomy Sinaitic *torah*, the formulations live within the command-promise mystery. "You will love the Lord your God" is both a promise and a command, especially indicated by the grammar, which is *not* imperative, but an indicative promise: "You will." By definition therefore, *our identity as the people of God depends on the presence and love of the Lord.*

The Lord's introductory comment in Leviticus 18 sets the context for the laws: "if a person does them, he shall live by them: I am the Lord" (Leviticus 18:5, ESV). If a person wants to live as a part of God's people, that person will live by God's command-promise.[21] "Speak to the people of Israel and say to them, I am the Lord your God. You shall not do as they do in the land of Egypt, where you lived, and you shall not do as they do in the land of Canaan, to which I am bringing you. You shall not walk in their statutes. You shall follow my rules and keep my statutes and walk in them. I am the LORD your God" (18:2-4, ESV). God's people are constituted by God's word as command-promise. The centerpiece of Old Testament *torah* is the *shema*: "You shall love the LORD your God with all your heart and with all your soul and with all your might. And these words that I command you today shall be on your heart. You shall teach them diligently to your children, and shall talk of them when you sit in your house, and when you walk by the way, and when you lie down, and when you rise" (Deuteronomy 6:5-7, ESV). At Sinai, the people enthusiastically accepted the command-promise: "All that the LORD has spoken, we will do" (Exodus 19:8, 24:7, RSV). Moses's extended sermon in Deuteronomy offers the possibility of choosing life and love by keeping the commandments.

For Christians, keeping the commands is a key measure of Christian identity, faith, doctrine, and conduct—with God and the revealed word at the center. Jesus does not destroy this paradox of command-promise, but repeatedly sustains it. "If you love me, you will keep my commandments" (John 14:15, 21; 15:10). This relationship of voluntary loving friendship is only possible in the presence of the LORD, as creator of the identity of his own people. The presence of the LORD who calls us to "come and die" and his word are the guides to grace-filled Christian identity formation.[22]

Identity, Vulnerability, and Trust

Christian identity lives in a bilateral relationship of vulnerability and trust in the presence of the LORD. The Presence is always encountered in a living tension between two potentials: threat and blessed transformation. In the early narratives of the LORD's presence in the wilderness, the pillar of fire represents this two-sided Presence: a threat to the Egyptians, but a protection and comfort to the escaping slaves. In the tabernacle, that Presence is a transforming blessing for Israel's identity, but also a deadly threat to the self-aggrandizing sons of Aaron and Korah's clan of Levitical priests. The experience of the bilateral Presence depends solely on the choices of God's people in relation to God's revealed word concerning their identity.[23] Key grammatical word-concepts illustrate this bilateral relationship between the Presence and human choices made about God's word.

Visit-punish (*paqad*). God's visitation of his people can result in either the LORD's help (e.g., Exodus 13:19) or in plague and punishment (e.g., Exodus 32:34-35). The same word is used. Its translation correlates to the situational identity of the people involved.[24] In Exodus, the visitation is a series of plagues that simultaneously punish the Egyptians and help the Hebrews. This paradoxical Presence is replete in identity formation texts, from God's presence with Cain to the exile in Babylon (e.g., Jeremiah 29:8-12).

Transform-destroy (*hapak*). Being *transformed* in the Hebrew Bible means being *overthrown* by God.[25] This may mean repentance and new life, or it may mean catastrophic destruction.[26] Various forms of *hapak* can mean "destroy," "transform," "turn," or "overthrow."[27] God "changed (*hapak*) Saul's heart" from self-serving to serving the people (1 Samuel 10:6-9).[28] The most well-known example is Jonah's short prophetic word: "Forty more days and Nineveh will be overturned-destroyed" (*hapak*; Jonah 3:4b, author's translation).[29] The Ninevites assumed it meant "destruction," as it had in violent Sodom (Genesis 19:21, 25, 29). Jonah knew the second possibility, however. Through repentance they were "overthrown" (*hapak*; Jonah 3:8-10). They were transformed in a way that "destroyed" their way of life by transforming their identity.[30]

Fear of the Lord-afraid (*yara'*). The "fear of the Lord" is a feature of identity based on a choice to actively trust in the Lord.[31] The juxtaposition of the active *fear of the Lord* and the passive *being afraid* is most obvious at Sinai.[32] Moses said to the people, "*Do not fear*, for God has come to test you that *the fear of him* may be before you that you may not sin" (Exodus 20:20, ESV). The positive "fear of the Lord" or "fear of God" is an essential feature of a person in right relation with God. In Exodus, the midwives were the first to "fear the Lord," demonstrated in saving babies in Egypt (Exodus 1:17, 21).[33] A primary basis of the fear of the Lord is God's *torah*, given at Sinai. The *torah* psalms (e.g., Psalm 19, 119) celebrate the wisdom that is given in God's law.[34] Proverbs declares that the law is "living water" and the source of knowledge of God.[35] The primary application in the New Testament is embodied personal ethics: "Since we have these promises, beloved, let us cleanse ourselves from every defilement of body and spirit, bringing holiness to completion in the fear of God" (2 Corinthians 7:1, ESV).[36] On the other hand, being afraid of God is the result of rejecting the parameters of God's word. In the New Testament, the cup of blessing/cup of death illustrates a similar juxtaposition (Mark 10:38-39, 14:36; Luke 22:20, 42; John 18:11). Jesus's blood is a cup of blessing through his death, in which his disciples share.

Justice-judgment (*mishpat*). Finally, the bilateral possibility of God's justice-judgment (*mishpat*) shares in the dynamic of Christian identity in relation to God. "Justice" (*mishpat*) can be rendered either "justice" or "judgment."[37] Its meaning depends on the identity of the people in relation to God in each context. The familiar text of Amos 5:24 is set in the context of a litany of God's judgment and could be translated in its context: "But let *judgment* roll down like waters, and righteousness like an ever-flowing stream" (author's translation).

When contemporary social justice articulates God's revealed preferences, biblical and social justice *may* work toward the same goals: care for the poor, unpolluted personal relationships, and protection of the non-human creation. But sometimes they are in conflict and require the hard work of discernment.

Biblical justice is not always the same as social justice (e.g., rights to abortion; rights to sex between any consenting adults). When society's decisions about the rights of groups and individuals are opposed to God's word on just judgments, the prophets call this to account: "Woe to those who call evil good and good evil" (Isaiah 5:20, RSV).[38] Often this is done in ignorance of God's law which is the basis of all biblical justice.[39]

The temptation of the broad American church, in its confident adolescence, has been to seek "relevance" by chasing the Dantean banners of contemporary culture. Both evangelical and mainline churches have been tempted to quarantine Scripture rather than interpret its difficult, acculturated, but holy witness.

The Paradox of Grace and Faith

Our personal identity in Christ is "sinners saved by the gift of grace" (see Romans 3:23-24). The context of this key text, however, is the reiteration of the enduring relevance of Old Testament law: "Do we then overthrow the law by this faith? By no means! On the contrary, we uphold the law" (Romans 3:31). Grace, all the way through life unto salvation, is provided so that we might live in God's kingdom, by God's law, for the sake of good works (Ephesians 2:8-10). The paradox of biblical faith is that salvation is through faith by grace, *and* that Christians are held accountable to the law by Jesus until the final judgment. What we do reveals the actual faith of our hearts and minds and will be measured by God's law.[40]

"Biblical law was destroyed by Jesus" is a false axiom and an antinomian fancy that is not found in the New Testament. Jesus did not destroy or bring the Old Testament law to an end. He brought a fuller revelation of it. Jesus warns against teaching the obsolescence of the law by saying it three ways.

> Do not think that I have come to abolish the Law or the Prophets; I have not come to abolish them but to fulfill them. For truly, I say to you, until heaven and earth pass away, not an iota, not a dot, will pass from the Law until all is accomplished. Therefore whoever relaxes one of the least of these commandments and teaches others to do the same will be called least in the kingdom of heaven, but whoever does them and teaches them will be called great in the kingdom of heaven (Matthew 5:17-19, ESV).

Jesus's presence and teaching transformed the law, but not in a simplistic way.[41] During his earthly ministry, Jesus *sustained, interpreted,* and *intensified* some biblical laws (the Ten and others; Matthew 5-7, 19; Mark 10; Luke 16, 18); *reapplied* Sabbath laws (Matthew 12; Mark 2-3; Luke 6); *summarized* the commandments as love of neighbor and love of God (not a replacement of all law;

see Matthew 22:36-40; Mark 12:28-31; Romans 13:9-14); and *reiterated* and *reinforced* laws of sexuality (Matthew 15:19-20; 19:9-12; Mark 7:20-23; Romans 13:13).[42] Jesus explicitly sustained and strengthened the laws concerning money, sex, and power and their attendant idolatries (Luke 16:15-18). The link between sexual immorality and idolatry in the New Testament is provided by the apostle: "Every other sin a person commits is outside the body, but the sexually immoral person sins against his own body. Or do you not know that your body is a temple of the Holy Spirit within you, whom you have from God? You are not your own, for you were bought with a price. So glorify God in your body" (1 Corinthians 6:18-20, ESV; see 1 Corinthians 3:16-17).

Throughout the New Testament, there is a consistent pattern after Jesus's death and resurrection for which Old Testament laws the LORD upholds and which are replaced or reinterpreted. The LORD replaced all the laws of levitical priests when Jesus becomes the high priest in heaven (Hebrews 7:23-28; replacing Leviticus 1-16 only); and replaced the laws of atonement for sin, once and for all (Hebrews 9:11-28; 10:1-14). After Jesus's resurrection, the leaders of the early church, reiterating Jesus's teaching, reinforced the laws of sexuality and idolatry (Acts 15:20; repeated in 15:28-29 and 21:25); and replaced the dietary laws and circumcision to open the way for the Gentiles (Acts 10-11; Jesus had declared all foods "clean" in Mark 7:15-19; but sustained other kinds of laws in verses 20-23; circumcision replaced in Romans 2:25-3:2; 1 Corinthians 7:18-20).

In his lifetime, Jesus primarily interprets the laws of *command and prohibition* ("you shall," "you shall not"). The body of *court-case laws* (casuistic; e.g., "an eye for an eye") in the Old Testament, however, also require and undergo theological interpretation in Scripture itself, in some of Jesus's discourse, and in the church.

In summary, the argument that *all* Old Testament law is rendered obsolete by Jesus is a category error (although literalistic caricatures of un-interpreted Old Testament law can be quite humorous).[43] Unfortunately, otherwise educated writers use the same literalistic examples as serious warrants for dismissing rather than interpreting the intent of biblical laws, as if caricatures of ancient contexts constitute an argument. Only priesthood, atonement, circumcision, and dietary laws can be said to be superseded or fulfilled in Christ. The others remain in place for Christians to interpret (2 Timothy 3:12-17). They will be the basis of the final judgment, not as a means of salvation, but as a means by which the authenticity of our faith will be measured.

The claim that Christian tradition is inconsistent in choosing some laws and not others can only be sustained by those who are ignorant of the New Testament texts above and three thousand years of *torah* interpretation. Christians certainly do elevate some laws as more important than others, with cues from

Jesus and Scripture itself, but the choices are not made willy-nilly. Not all laws are equal in the Old or New Testament texts, in the narratives, or in God's eyes.

Failure to grasp the relationship between gospel and law leads to legalism as well as to disregard for biblical law. Yet the call of Scripture from the vision of John is clear for those who will hear and listen: "Here is a call for the endurance of the saints, those who keep the commandments of God and the faith in Jesus" (Revelation 14:12, RSV).

All Scripture Resists Sexualized Identity

Early in the twenty-first century, "sexual identity" has become a pivotal construct and the primary ethical issue splitting apart the contemporary American church. Significant portions of the church have constructed a new theology of sexuality around our sexualized culture, based on the false premise that God's word has to be wrong in its understanding of such matters. This contextualized theology is biased by postmodern cultural understandings of proclivity, experience, and human embodiment, and its necessary methodological step is to marginalize the LORD's voice in the biblical text. Human beings are inherently sexual, but when our identity is oriented by our sexuality, the Bible calls this sexualized identity idolatry.

All of Scripture deeply resists the contemporary notion of sexuality as a social expression of identity, as solely a personal biological act, or as necessary for personal intimacy. The Torah, Prophets, Writings, and the New Testament correlate the commitments of embodied intimacy with identity as God's people and the misuse of them, conversely, with idolatry. The prophets especially resist making sexual preferences and behaviors primary referents of identity. Scripture's narrative and theology are broadly and specifically opposed, not to sex, but to the sexual *orientation* of individual and community life. This opposition does not come from a naïve or puritanical understanding of sexuality, but from an intentional resistance to the sexualized cultures that surrounded them.

Conversely, American culture is clearly oriented to the freedom of embodied sexual expression of most kinds. The incidence of sexual reference in entertainment media and advertising, profits of American sex trafficking and the pornography industry, and the statistics on the sexual activity of middle-school students border on the astounding. Even Christian adolescents are increasingly counseled to explore their sexuality as central to their personal identity, rather than an element of their fidelity to the LORD God.

The "sins of the body" are the most devastating sins regarding human identity precisely because they refocus our lives in relation to God. Sexual union, as a powerful identity-transforming action, has a unique potential to turn our minds and hearts away from God.[44] It causes our brains to "re-wire to re-fire" along new neuron pathways. Scripture recognizes this inherent power using theological language (e.g., 1 Corinthians 6:18-20).

How Leviticus became irrelevant. The book of Leviticus is often quarantined in the contemporary discussion on sexuality with the basic argument that it is archaic and irrelevant—with the oft-repeated erroneous warrant that it is only about ritual cleanness and boundaries for entrance to the tabernacle. Actually, the conclusion that its laws are of no use to us can only be reached by ignoring structural, rhetorical, and theological analyses of the text itself. Though the text is ancient, the surface narrative about the tabernacle is not the sum total of the provenance of Leviticus.

Leviticus stands prominently in the middle of the Pentateuch and the Lord's initiatives to begin to call and create a people who will choose to serve him alone.[45] The Lord calls his people to a new identity and sociality shaped by chastity and fidelity. Other natural loving relationships are to be expressed within the limitations of chastity and blessing. This revealed standard is to be the primary referent of their new identity in relation to the Lord.

Conversely, "Do not wear clothing of mixed-fabric clothing" is often cited as an anachronistic ancient prohibition that correspondingly demonstrates the irrelevance of the adjacent law against homoerotic sex (Leviticus 19:19). This is a primary example of an under-educated dismissal of Leviticus in the discussion of sexuality. This law against mixed-fabric clothing is actually a law against wearing the clothing finery signifying a prostitute of Egypt. Rather than being irrelevant, it corroborates the Lord's concern about embodied faith.[46]

Leviticus 18 is the primary source document and *ipso facto* Hebraic background for the phrase "sexual immorality and impurity" found in the prophetic corpus and in the New Testament. Unlike the Levitical purification laws of Leviticus 1-16, which Jesus's death fulfills, Leviticus 17-19 address key moral concerns that echo repeatedly in their trajectory through the prophets and the New Testament. They are set apart in the middle of Leviticus as three chapters addressed to the "people of Israel" rather than to Aaron and the priests, addressing food and blood (ch. 17), sexual practice (ch. 18), and economic injustice with idolatry (ch. 19).[47]

Chapter 17 is also highlighted by its use of the apodictic form (as a direct command from God, e.g., "You shall not"). Structurally, form-critically, rhetorically, and canonically it is reinforced.[48] Even the verb tenses work against the notion that this is not intended for the contemporary reading audience: "The tension between the past and future is a rhetorical device to contemporize the ancient law for each audience hearing this speech (of the Lord)."[49] Nowhere else in Scripture do we find a more comprehensive list of sexual immorality (Heb. *zanah*; Gr. *porneia*). It is the primary *torah* behind the New Testament admonitions.[50]

The council at Jerusalem in Acts 15 was sensitive to cultural accommodation for the Gentile Christians and the law. Yet, the content of their decision reflects Leviticus 17-19 (blood, sexuality, injustice with idolatry): "…we should not trouble those of the Gentiles who turn to God, but should write to them to abstain from the things polluted by idols, and from sexual immorality, and from what has been strangled, and from blood. For from ancient generations Moses has had in every city those who proclaim him, for he is read every Sabbath in the synagogues" (Acts 15:19-21, ESV; reiterated in 15:28-29 and 21:25). They assumed that Leviticus ("Moses") was widely known and would continue to be widely known wherever Christ was preached and Scripture read. They would have assumed, by prohibiting idolatry and fornication, that they had named the most devastating personal and communal sins and established Leviticus 18 as a standard definition of sexual morality for the Gentile church. Paul, for example, threatened to excommunicate a man in Corinth who had sexual relations with his stepmother (1 Corinthians 5:1-2; cf. Leviticus 18:8).

The reason for a defined focus on sexuality in the church and Scripture is that it is insidiously entwined with idolatry and its embedded identity issues. Sex easily becomes self-referential, in service of the created person rather than in service of God. Christianity has scrutinized sexual sin precisely because of its careful and close reading of Scripture.

The argument in Leviticus 18 is based on allegiance to the LORD with one's embodied self. It stands opposed to the dominant cultural sexual values of Canaan and Egypt. Seven times in the chapter the LORD warns them not to behave like the Canaanites or Egyptians (18:3, 24, 26, 27, 29, 30.) The LORD's direct speech and admonitions ground the prohibitions emphatically in the LORD's identity: "I am the LORD your God" (18:2, 4, 5, 6, 21, 30). "Israel's sexual morality is here portrayed as something that marks it off from its neighbors as the LORD's special people."[51] Homoerotic sex is marked off further by the emphatic *to'ebah* ("abhorrent") used here five times (18:22, 26, 27, 29, 30) to declare it as an infringement of the LORD's exclusive rights. It is not too strong to say that this word indicates that the LORD hates homoerotic sex.[52]

Leviticus 18, consistent with the rest of the *Tanak*, makes the theological argument that it is idolatrous to make sexuality your personal or cultural identity. The preface states it boldly, in God's own voice, as a matter of their identity in relation to the LORD's identity:

> Speak to the people of Israel and say to them, I am the LORD your God. You shall not do as they do in the land of Egypt, where you lived, and you shall not do as they do in the land of Canaan, to which I am bringing you. You shall not walk in their statutes. You shall follow my rules and keep my statutes and walk in them. I am the LORD your God. You shall there-

fore keep my statutes and my rules; if a person does them, he shall live by them: I am the Lord. (Leviticus 18:2-5, ESV)

Leviticus 18 delimits sexual practice, in specific contrast to their surrounding cultures. Practice leads to a transformation of cultural identity, for better or for worse, as verses 1-5 indicate. The chapter concludes in a similar way: "So keep my charge never to practice any of these abominable customs that were practiced before you.... I am the Lord your God" (Leviticus 18:30). Leviticus 18 is all about sex. It does not limit love. It limits the sexualization of love.

Leviticus 18 is about much more than the boundaries described by Mary Douglas.[53] The context here is the Lord's concern for stable community and familial relationships: No sex with "close relatives" (v. 6), nor should a man have sex with "a woman and her daughter" (v. 17), nor take "a sister as a rival wife" (v. 18; as Jacob did). At Sinai the Lord created a community of love and trust that established the Lord, rather than sexuality, as its primary referent. When Israel encountered the highly sexualized Canaanite culture, this *torah* standard stood as a severe warning. The source of the primary referent of its identity, the Lord, was at stake. The Lord's abhorrence is an allergic reaction to sin, because it is toxic to Israel's identity as the Lord's and to healthy community life.

Familial and community relationships of trust and love ought not to be sexualized. Yet, our American culture, centered in personal fulfillment and expression, is making inroads in the church. With it comes a growing view that one's personal identity can be validly and even primarily based in sexual preferences between consenting adults. This ignores the Scripture's claim that prohibited sexual unions break down the trust and love that could form the solid foundation of the Lord's community. The law is clear that such unions are toxic to families and to the non-sexual bonds of love (friendship) between adults that forms the fabric of healthy communities.[54]

For pastoral practice in the church today, two important and internally paradoxical texts are key: 1 Thessalonians 4:3-9 and Romans 1:22-2:2. Each of these texts names immorality as a sin against the Lord, but warns the reader against making him- or herself the judge, leaving room for God: "God will judge." This double admonition decries the sin, but calls for love. The faithful ought not and do not need to judge, but to love (1 Thessalonians 4:9). We are reminded from the beginning, "You are dust and to dust you shall return" (Genesis 3:19). When that happens to *our* dust, only the story that the Lord tells about us will matter.

Endnotes

1. Klyne Snodgrass's volume *Between Two Truths* sparked my imagination as a student. Human identity in relation to the God of Scripture also stands between two truths. In the

LORD's words: "You are all gods, children of the Most High; nevertheless, you shall die as mortals" (Psalm 82:6-7, author's translation). Its paradoxical nature does not give way to a simplistic conflation of boundaries and freedoms. I am grateful for this opportunity to offer some "between" words in this essay.

2. The word is a representation of the tetragrammaton, usually rendered "Yahweh" in scholarship in order to distinguish it from the Hebrew *adonai* or the Greek *kurios*.

3. John 8:58-59; 10:30-33.

4. James Bruckner, *Healthy Human Life: A Biblical Witness* (Eugene, OR: Cascade Books, Wipf & Stock, 2012), 8. See chapter two of this volume for a fuller articulation of the themes in this section. For a good articulation of this universal value perspective see the World Council of Churches Faith and Order Paper 199, published as *Christian Perspectives on Theological Anthropology: A Faith and Order Study Document* (Geneva: WCC, 2005), 11-12. For the image of God as a theme see especially Claus Westermann, *Genesis 1-11: A Continental Commentary* (Minneapolis: Fortress Press, 1984); Phyllis Bird, "Male and Female He Created Them: Genesis 1:27 on the Context of the Priestly Account of Creation," *Harvard Theological Review* 74 (1981): 129-59; and James Barr, "The Image of God in the Book of Genesis—A Study in Terminology," *Bulletin of the John Rylands University Library of Manchester* 51 (1968-69): 11-26.

5. Bruckner, *Healthy Human Life*, 8. Karl Barth describes a related twofold capacity given in the image as "addressable" (related to God and others) and "responsible" (differentiated from God and others). Karl Barth, *Church Dogmatics,* ed. G. Bromiley and T. Torrance (Edinburgh: T&T Clark, 1958), III.1.48, 196.

6. In four verses *tselem* refers to "image of God" (Genesis 1:26-27; 5:3; 9:6). After Genesis, the word *tselem* always means "idol." See Numbers 33:52; 1 Samuel 6:5,11; 2 Kings 11:18; 2 Chronicles 23:17; Psalm 73:20; Ezekiel 7:20, 16:17, 23:14; Amos 5:26; and fourteen times in Daniel.

7. "Only he who is in the image of God has the power of separating himself from God. His greatness and his weakness are identical." Paul Tillich, *Systematic Theology* (Chicago: University of Chicago Press, 1957) 2:32-33. Søren Kierkegaard argues that the freedom the image of God gives a person, even to reject God, creates tremendous anxiety that leads people into all kinds of destructive and self-destructive behavior (sin). See S. Kierkegaard, *The Gospel of Suffering* (Cambridge, UK: James Clarke & Co., 1987).

8. Stanley Grenz, *The Social God and the Relational Self: A Trinitarian Theology of the Imago Dei* (Louisville: Westminster John Knox, 2001), 204.

9. Christian Scripture draws upon this claim in Colossians 3:10-16 with a call to all cultures and ethnicities (Gentiles) to be renewed to a true knowledge of Genesis 1.

10. For a brief survey of dominion by Old Testament scholars including Clines, Wenham, and the dissenting Barr, see Grenz, 188-89. For dominion as a calling by God to life vocation, see Joel Green, *Body Soul and Human Life* (Grand Rapids: Baker Academic, 2005), 61-65. Green cites Christopher Wright, "Old Testament Ethics: A Missiological Perspective," *Catalyst* 26/2 (2000): 5-8; and Francisco J. Ayala, "Biological Evolution and Human Nature," in *Human Nature*, ed. M. Jeeves (Edinburgh: The Royal Society of Edinburgh, 2006), 46-64.

11. See Isaiah 52:13-15, 53:4-5, and 42:1-4 which includes "a bruised reed he will not break, and a dimly burning wick he will not quench; he will faithfully bring forth justice."

12. Acts 8:30-35; Romans 4:25, 5:18; 1 Corinthians 15:3; 1 Peter 2:22-25.

13. See Walter Brueggemann, "The Human Person as Yahweh's Partner," in *Theology of*

the Old Testament (Minneapolis: Fortress Press, 1997), 450.

14. Christian Wiman, *My Bright Abyss: Meditation of a Modern Believer* (New York: Farrar, Straus and Giroux, 2013), 67.

15. This alternative to trusting God's word about their lives is, in full form, the deification of personal and relational experience followed by a constructive epistemology. These contextualized theologies, based in experience and embodiment, are called idolatry in the Old Testament.

16. Some contextual theologies read these human responses within the text as a "fall *up*" from innocence to experience; as a necessary step for human growth. Modern theologies tended to regard the break with God's word in this text as a fall up to rational thought and enlightenment. Post-modern theologies tend to regard it as a fall up from innocence to experience. They share the hermeneutical move of interpreting with a double antagonism: first *against* the text in its canonical context and secondly *against* the history of interpretation.

17. See Stanley Hauerwas, *Peaceable Kingdom: A Primer in Christian Ethics* (Notre Dame: University of Notre Dame, 1983), 30-34. Hauerwas is also known for saying that living without reference to God is living as if we did not have bellybuttons but just appeared in the world without mothers, *sui generis*. See also James Bruckner, "Boundary and Freedom: Blessings in the Garden of Eden," in *The Covenant Quarterly* 57/3 (1999): 15-35.

18. Wiman, *My Bright Abyss,* 165.

19. E.g., Exodus 3:6-8; Deuteronomy 6:20-21; 2 Samuel 14:14; Psalms 73:21-24; 139:15-16; Isaiah 40:27-29; Lamentations 3:19-26; Habakkuk 3:16-19; Matthew 26:36-39; Luke 22:42; John 14:1-3; Romans 6:2-6; 2 Corinthians 12:9-10; Philippians 2:5-11.

20. Romans 6:3-5; Colossians 2:12. In 1 Corinthians 15:30 Paul can say, "I die every day."

21. See Patrick D. Miller, "The Good Neighborhood: Identity and Community through the Commandments," in *Character and Scripture: Moral Formation, Community, and Biblical Interpretation*, ed. William P. Brown (Grand Rapids: Eerdmans, 2002), 57-60.

22. Bonhoeffer wrote, "The only man who has the right to say that he is justified by grace alone is the man who has left all to follow Christ." Grace is a call to "come and die"; a call to a self-emptying cruciform life. Dietrich Bonhoeffer, *The Cost of Discipleship* (New York: Touchstone, 1995), 43-78.

23. See also many narratives that reflect this death/life experience of God's presence including Cain in Genesis 4, Moses in Exodus 3, and Lot and his wife in Sodom (Genesis 19).

24. For a fuller accounting of God's contextualized "visitation" see Bruckner, *Exodus,* Understanding the Bible Commentary Series (Grand Rapids: Baker, 2008), 127, 289-90.

25. Bruckner, *Healthy Human Life*, 139-40.

26. See Bruckner, *Jonah, Nahum, Habakkuk, Zephaniah*, New International Version Application Commentary (Grand Rapids: Zondervan, 2004), 90-96.

27. See Ludwig Köhler and Walter Baumgartner, *The Hebrew and Aramaic Lexicon of the Old Testament* (Leiden: Brill, 1994), 251-52.

28. For example, see Balaam's transformation in Deuteronomy 23:5 and Israel's in Jeremiah 31:11, 13; also see Psalm 66:6.

29. The 1978 NIV and the NLT have "Nineveh will be *destroyed*." KJV, RSV, NRSV, NASB all have "will be overthrown." The 1984 NIV "overturned" is the best word for preserving both necessary possibilities of the Hebrew text.

30. Yvonne Sherwood notes that *hapak* refers either to "evil" (catastrophe of destruction)

or "live" (new structure of a repentant life). This word play is analogous to the English "evil" and "live" which is "evil" spelled backwards. Y. Sherwood, *A Biblical Text and its Afterlives: The Survival of Jonah in Western Culture* (Cambridge: Cambridge University Press, 2000), 121, 236.

31. Exodus 14:31; Psalms 25:14; 33:18; 40:3; 115:11; 145:19; Proverbs 1:29.

32. See Bruckner, *Exodus*, 193-94.

33. The first elders were "capable men" who were trustworthy and "feared the LORD" (Exodus 18:21).

34. E.g., Psalms 19:9; 119:63; 111:10.

35. Proverbs 14:27; 19:23; 1:7, 29.

36. See also Acts 13:16, 26; Philippians 2:12; Revelation 14:7; 15:4; 19:5-6.

37. E.g., Jeremiah 21:12.

38. Isaiah 5:20. As Eugene Nida has observed, virtue in one culture is vice in another. In American popular culture, sexual freedom beyond the bond of marriage is thought to be "good." In Scripture, sexual experimentation and freedom is not considered a societal "good." Rather, it is considered toxic to healthy lives and communities. For example, see Deuteronomy 22:13-29.

39. E.g., Hosea 4:1-9; 6:4-9.

40. E.g., Mark 3:31-34; Luke 16:15-17, Romans 14:12; 1 Corinthians 3:12-15.

41. Jesus's identity as the Word made flesh and as the Son of the Father establish him as the one who can interpret and transform God's law. See John 1:1-2.

42. New Testament texts sustaining the Leviticus 18 laws of sexual immorality: Acts 15:20, 15:28-29, 21:25; Romans 13:13; 1 Corinthians 5:1; 5:11; 6:13, 18; 7:2; 10:8; 2 Corinthians 12:21; Galatians 5:19; Ephesians 5:3; Colossians 3:5; 1 Thessalonians 4:3; Jude 1:7; Revelation 2:20-21.

43. See A. J. Jacobs, *The Year of Living Biblically: One Man's Humble Quest to Follow the Bible as Literally as Possible* (New York: Simon & Schuster, 2007).

44. 1 Kings 11:3-5.

45. E.g., Genesis 12, 15, 26, 32; Exodus 3, 19, 32, 40; Leviticus 1; Deuteronomy 1, 10, 30.

46. This information on the mixed cloth "finery of a prostitute" is easily found in major commentaries on the text which cite the linguistic scholarship. The word itself, *sha'stnez*, has an Egyptian origin. This law is also found in Deuteronomy 22:11, where it is followed by the command to wear tassels as a reminder of the LORD's instructions. The LXX uses *porneia* in contrast to wearing tassels in Numbers 15:39. For discussion and deeper background see J. E. Hartley, *Leviticus*, Word Biblical Commentary (Nashville: Thomas Nelson, 1992), 508; D. Christiansen, *Deuteronomy*, Word Biblical Commentary (Nashville: Thomas Nelson, 2002), 501-09.

47. Chapter 20 is also addressed to the people, but uses the casuistic legal form as a random summary for the courts concerning capital crimes.

48. As demonstrated above and below; for example, structurally in the *torah* and in the surface structure of the chapter, form-critically as a direct command; rhetorically in God's voice and in sentence construction, and canonically by its reinforcement in the New Testament. See also Gordon Wenham, *Leviticus*, New International Commentary on the Old Testament (Grand Rapids: Eerdmans, 1979), 250.

49. Hartley, *Leviticus*, 290.

50. Matthew 5:32; 15:19; 19:9; Mark 7:21; John 8:41; Acts 15:20, 29; 21:25; Romans 13:13; 1 Corinthians 5:1, 11; 6:13, 18; 7:2; 10:8; 2 Corinthians 12:21; Galatians 5:19; Ephesians 5:3; Colossians 3:5; 1 Thessalonians 4:3; Jude 1:7; Revelation 2:14, 20-21; 9:21; 14:8; 17:2, 4; 18:3, 9; 19:2. The identical "shameless" (*asxemosynen*) of Romans 1:27 and the repeated Hebraic "uncover the nakedness" (*asxemosynen* 24 times; Heb. *galah 'ervah*) of Leviticus 18 are another obvious connection.

51. Wenham, 250.

52. "Abhorrent" is used in parallel with "hate" in Proverbs 6:16 and 11:1. See E. Gerstenberger, *Theologisches Wörterbuch zum Alten Testament*, ed. G. J. Botterweck and H. Ringgren (Stuttgart, 1970–), 2:1051-55; Wenham, *Leviticus*, 259. See the wider ancient Near East literature on *to'ebah* in Hartley, *Leviticus,* 283.

53. Mary Douglas, *Purity and Danger: An Analysis of Concepts of Pollution and Taboo* (London: Routledge & K. Paul, 1966).

54. Leviticus 18:19-24 shares the general theme of vv. 6-18, of trust and non-sexualized love and relationships. The Molech law seems out of place, but is included precisely because of the issue of bonds of trust and love that ought not to be corrupted. Parental love is a bond of trust and integrity with a child that ought not be violated and carries a similar weight of importance to embodied sexuality. The other prohibitions that stand with it (homoerotic sex and bestiality) reflect God's concern for integrity in bonds of love between men and for relationship of integrity with animals. Sexualizing either kind of relationship diminishes the community's integrity and identity as God's people.

Identity and Identification in the Book of Lamentations

Paul E. Koptak

Nearly two decades ago a five-thousand-pound truck bomb explod-ed outside the Alfred P. Murrah Federal Building in Oklahoma City. Now designated the worst terrorist act in the United States prior to September 11, 2001, the attack and the news that it was carried out by two former American soldiers shook the nation. One hundred sixty-eight people were killed, nine-teen of them children.[1]

Four days later, on April 23, 1995, a memorial service was addressed by President Bill Clinton, the Rev. Billy Graham, community leaders, and local clergy. Rabbi David Packman of Temple B'nai Israel in Oklahoma City read selections from the Book of Lamentations prefaced with a short introduction, the beginning of which was lost in the telecast. When the sound returned, the rabbi spoke of ancient cities

> covered with the sands of time to be excavated thousands of years later by archaeologists—Babylon, Nineveh, Haran, and Ur. But one city came back from desolation, more beauti-ful, more holy, more together than even before. The name of that city was Jerusalem. And so our city, our community, our Oklahoma City will come back, with greater closeness, greater beauty, greater love. A citizen of that Jerusalem wrote

these words of poetry in the day of Jerusalem's agony. We call this volume of poetry the Book of Lamentations. On that day he wrote: "How lonely sits the city that was full of people! How like a widow she has become, she that was great among the nations, she that was a princess among the cities! ... Behold, O LORD, how we are in distress; our soul in tumult, our heart wrung within us (1:1, 20)....I called on your name, O LORD, from the depths of the pit; you did hear my plea, 'Do not close your ear to my cry for help!' You did come near when I called on you; you did say, 'Do not fear!' (3:55-57)...Restore us unto yourself, O LORD, that we may be restored! Renew our days as of old!" (5:21)[2]

Packman's text selection corresponds to the Jewish liturgical practice of reading or singing the entirety of Lamentations on the evening before the Ninth of Ab, a memorial to the destructions of the Jerusalem temple in 587 BCE and 70 CE.[3] His reading ended with the penultimate verse 5:21, a request for restoration that sounds a note more hopeful than the divine rejection of verse 22. It also adapts synagogue custom that repeats verse 21 after verse 22 is read (as do Bibles such as the Jewish Publication Society's *Tanakh*).

Clearly Packman sought to generate hope by analogy, claiming that Jerusalem's fall and rise (and its testimony that it did so by the hand of God) was a sign that Oklahoma City would not only survive its tragedy but "come back, with greater closeness, greater beauty, greater love." Packman expressed confidence in the words of a book that is cited selectively for inspiration (mercies new every morning, 3:21-22), or expressions of despair and confrontation ("Whom have you ever treated like this?" 2:20), or ignored completely. By bringing these three excerpts together, the reading gave voice to the book's cries of lament, moments of confidence, and concluding petition.

This historic appropriation also takes its place in the current interpretive discussion. Robin Parry reviews the traditional synagogue practice and related Christian readings in the Tennebrae service to invite identification with the sufferings of Christ and the world.[4] Biblical scholar and hospital chaplain Leslie Allen highlights the themes of grief, guilt, and grievance.[5] Others like Carleen Mandolfo[6] highlight words of protest and calls for compassion.[7] In its message of encouragement, Packman's reading not only made identification between the conquest of the ancient city and the contemporary attack, it implied that the same Lord who heard the cries recorded in Lamentations would hear and act to bring restoration to a city overwhelmed with grief. Implied throughout are questions of identity, such as those Klyne Snodgrass puts before the biblical interpreter: "A hermeneutics of identity will be aware that the text is about identity, will keep seeking from specific texts in Scripture insight into the identity God desires and gives, and will both seek and allow transformation of identity with every reading."[8]

This combination of lament and hope is significant for the identity of any citizenry faced with trauma, and I would argue, for any individual who chooses to believe and call on the name of the LORD in times of crisis. Is there a portrait, a model of identity that comes through the five poems of the book, and might it speak to the personal identity of Christians and the corporate identity of the church, universal and local? In other words, what recommendations for self-understanding is the reading community given? How is this depiction of community designed to form identity for individuals and the communities they join? One avenue of approach will look to the work of Kenneth Burke (1897-1993), best known for his exploration of rhetoric as identification.

Kenneth Burke and Identity

Burke's life work could be summarized as the investigation of "language as symbolic action" that includes his inventions of dramatism, logology, and the rhetoric of identification.[9] Always rooted in his analysis of literature, Burke's rhetorical criticism sought to go behind the symbols of human relations to both understand those relations and "purify" them: he wrote "The Rhetoric of Hitler's Battle" to provide an "antidote" to *Mein Kampf*'s "poison"[10] and prefaced his *Grammar of Motives* with the epigram *Ad Bellum Purificandum* (toward the purification of war). Speaking of his method, he wrote:

> The study is thus built pedagogically about the "indexing" of some specific "symbolic structure," in the attempt to study the nature of a work's internal consistency and of its unfolding. But in contrast with courses in "literary appreciation," the generalizations at which we aim are not confined to a concern with the work's "beauty." Our question concerns its linguistic nature in general; and then, beyond that, the insight it may afford into man's ways as a symbol user.[11]

Rhetorical critic Barry Brummett said it well: "Kenneth Burke's work was written some years ago but is evergreen in its constant usefulness for scholars."[12] In his early works, Burke explored matters of identity and identification in "symbol using," part of his definition of what it means to be human.[13]

Burke's first book of criticism and theory, *Counter-Statement* (1931), examined the rhetorical appeals of literary form and symbol. Here Burke defined form as "the creation and fulfillment of desire," the sense of being led along as one hears a limerick or follows a hero's quest. Literary symbol gives shape to human experience, and to the extent that experience is common, or shared, the symbol becomes persuasive and transformative. Burke believed that "[i]ntensity in art may be attributed sometimes to form, sometimes to the Symbol, sometimes to both. Symbolic intensity arises when the artist uses subject-matter 'charged' by the reader's situation outside the work of art."[14] So also of eloquence: "That work is most eloquent in which each line had some image or statement relying strongly upon our experience outside the work of art, and in which each image or statement had a pronounced formal saliency."[15] Here "poetry contributes to the formation of attitudes, and thus to the determining of conduct."[16] In sum: "The Symbol is perhaps most overwhelming in its effect when the artist's and the reader's patterns of experience closely coincide," and those effects in turn shape attitude and action.[17]

Permanence and Change (1935), written as Burke witnessed the social metamorphosis of the American Great Depression, moved beyond individualized effects to the historical and social dimensions of literature. He observed that society was coping with a crisis caused in part by the rapid and widespread change from an agrarian to an industrial society.[18] The book examined three "orientations" based on the shared meanings of a society, their transition, and the principles of a revised orientation.[19] Throughout, he said, the poet is the midwife of the process, highlighting two functions of speech: "Speech is communicative in the sense that it provides a common basis of feeling—or it is communicative in the sense that it serves as the common implement of action."[20] Often it does both, as when one calls a person friend or enemy, recommending attitude and action at the same time. Also, the poet renames situations, or in Burke's words, "mis-names them, just as one calms a child's fears by misnaming as a coat in the corner what a child called a monster."[21] Not only is the poetic process a form of exorcism through mis-naming, the process is like a conversion: "The artist is always an evangelist, quite as the religious reformer is. He wants others to feel as he does."[22] The poet enters into a social system of shared meanings and attitudes to offer another vision.

In *Attitudes Toward History* (1937), Burke claimed that societies take on the characteristics of epic, tragedy, and comedy, each displaying its own attitude of rejection or acceptance of material and cultural conditions. Here individual identity is a social concern: "Our emphasis is not upon the individual strategy, but upon the productive and mental patterns developed by aggregates. The two emphases are not mutually exclusive, since the individual's frame is built of materials from the collective frame, but the change from one to the other shifts the emphasis from the *poetic* to the *historical*."[23] Even as Burke turned his attention to the problems of history, he continued to explain his ideas through the case of the poet who "organizes the complexity of life's relationships," "chooses alignments," and "builds frames of acceptance or rejection by overt or covert acts of 'transcendence.'"[24]

Here Burke began to speak directly about identification and identity, calling it the problem in which all the matters he examined come together. Personal identity is not an individual matter, but a social process by which individuals find or shape identity by linking themselves with "all sorts of manifestations" outside of the self. Burke traced a movement through which one set of corporate symbols is replaced by another in order to introduce a new sense of corporate identity. Thus, "the so-called 'I' is merely a unique combination of partially conflicting 'corporate we's.'"[25] States, financial corporations, and churches all stand as symbols of the "we's" that may come into conflict: a person may feel torn between love (in a partnership of two) and duty (in allegiance to a larger body). As a result, an ongoing sense of individual identity requires changes of that identity as conflicts call for and enact symbolic rituals of rebirth. In other words, a shift in social coordinates requires a redefinition of the self-orientation used to adjust to them. "Thus 'identification' is another name for the function of sociality."[26]

One could summarize *Attitudes Toward History* by noting that both collectives (societies, historical movements) and individuals within that collective also act as poets in formulating attitudes of acceptance or rejection. Individuals are socialized or "join in" by transforming their own sense of identity to adjust to the larger identity of the group with which they choose to affiliate. In *Attitudes Toward History* Burke took the link between poet and audience and extended it to the realm of relations between individual and societies, highlighting both the presence of some shared "attitude" and the use of that attitude as a resource of "appeal." Here more than any other work, Burke seemed more concerned with identification as a process of building a personal/corporate identity than as a strategy of persuasion. Here identification is an end in itself, more than a means of persuasion that recommends a "strategy for coping," as Burke developed in his later works.[27] Thus he became attuned to the processes of identification at work in all use of language, as humans use their words to define their relation to their societies, other individuals, and themselves, and he drew attention to the conflict between competing associations of identity.

In these early works Burke insisted, against then current literary trends, that symbol-mediated communication not only joins individuals to their social environments, it does so by providing means to adjust and adapt. Some, like Burke's friend Ralph Ellison, saw it as a means of survival: "'Language is equipment for living,' to quote Kenneth Burke. One uses the language which helps to preserve one's life, which helps to make one feel at peace in the world, and which screens out the greatest amount of chaos. *All* human beings do this."[28] Today others find a basis of social concern: "what Kenneth Burke terms identification with, an altruism based on reciprocity, may be found to be more adaptive, or 'natural,' by way of enlightened self-interest if nothing else, than the egocentrism and narcissism propounded in Freudian models."[29] In all, it functions as what Burke called a "rhetoric of rebirth," a transformation that adjusts individuals to their societies and vice versa.[30] Connections between the situation that gave rise to the literary work and the varied situations of its reception make sense of the world by taking form in similar patterns, what Brummett calls "homology."[31] For example, a study of the words and music of the hymn "Amazing Grace" found that the hymn's appeal extends beyond the church because it offers "equipment for living with life's trials through the homology of the grace anecdote."[32] The basic narrative form that depicts help coming from outside the self links with a wide variety of lived experiences.

Therefore the biblical interpreter watches for links and signs of association, noting key words and forms that may yield insights about the implied or desired identity of receptors. This approach looks to explain how the "I" is formed out of a series of competing "we's" and to articulate the vision of personal and corporate identity offered to the reading and listening audience. The verbal and thematic links between the final chapter of Lamentations and earlier chapters call for a study of its vision of identity.

Identity and Identification in Lamentations 5

The fifth chapter of Lamentations both stands apart from and is connected with the four poems that precede it. First, chapter 5 repeats words and themes from the previous four, especially chapter 1, that grieve Jerusalem's reversal of status from secure glory to devastated shame. Second, although chapter 5 does not follow the pattern of the alphabetic acrostic form of the previous four poems, its twenty-two verses do correspond to the number of letters in the Hebrew alphabet. In addition, just as the acrostic in chapters 2, 3, and 4 reverses the typical order of the letters 'ayin and pê, so 5:17 begins with the letter 'ayin as it would if it were following the acrostic reversal: three of its four half-lines begin with that letter. Third, the book's central passage of 3:34-39 contains the only two uses of 'elyôn ("Most High") found in the book, each prefaced with a word that begins with the letter pê, following the reversed sequence (pěnê "face," in 3:35b and pê "mouth," in 3:38). Together, these three "reversals" signal formal and symbolic links between these five distinct compositions.

Reversal as restated theme. The first words of the book draw the contrast: "How lonely sits the city that was once full of people.... She that was a princess among the provinces has become a vassal" (1:1). The city is personified as a woman (Zion) whose friends have become enemies (1:2); her crowded streets and gates are empty, even at feast time (1:3-4); there is no one to comfort her (1:2, 7, 16, 17, 21). Zion calls out to anyone who will listen, and contemporary readers may sense the "fourth wall" coming down to include them: "Is it nothing to you, all you who pass by? Look and see if there is any sorrow like my sorrow, which was brought upon me, which the LORD inflicted on the day of his fierce anger" (1:12). She hopes for someone, anyone, to "look and see" the causes of her grief. The many aspects of this reversal are summed up in a single word as Zion pleads that YHWH too would look and not pass by: "See, O LORD, how distressed I am; my stomach churns, my heart is *wrung* within me…" (1:20). Zion's heart is literally turned "upside down": the root for this reversal (*hpk*) is repeated in each of the five poems except the second, but it used twice in the fifth.

> Against me alone he *turns* his hand, again and again, all day long. (3:3)

> For the chastisement of my people has been greater than the punishment of Sodom, which was *overthrown* in a moment, though no hand was laid on it. (4:6)

> Our inheritance has been *turned over* to strangers, our homes to aliens. (5:2)

> The joy of our hearts has ceased; our dancing *has been turned* to mourning. (5:15)

Everything has been overturned, and the five poems offer no promise like that from Jeremiah: "I *will turn* their mourning into joy, I will comfort them, and give them gladness for sorrow" (Jeremiah 31:13; cf. Amos 8:10 and Isaiah 24:7-8).[33] The double appearance of the term *hpk* at the start and near middle of this fifth poem bears watching, for the occupation of the conquering army means that everything is still out of order, even though wartime has passed. Citizens must pay for their own water and wood, they are ruled by underlings, there is no respect for elders, and the young work in humiliating circumstances carrying heavy loads. Surely "the crown has fallen!" (5:2-16).

Additional verbal and thematic links in chapters 1 and 5 indicate a significant development. Terms and images of this reversal of Zion's fortunes in both chapters include "days of old," desolate gates, awful fate of princes, desperation to acquire bread, pursuers who allow no rest, and the admission of sin, with prayer for God to "look upon" their plight.[34] These correspondences between the pleadings of woman Zion in chapter 1 and the prayer of the community in chapter 5 show a movement from the lone figure's desolation to community solidarity; the various voices of the poems have become one in the last chapter, the different "I"s coming together into the repeated "we."[35]

The parallels in vocabulary are even more striking. Woman Zion begs both YHWH and those passing by to "look and see" (*nbṭ* and *r'h* in 1:11-12, sometimes translated, "pay attention and see"), and the same phrase appears in the second line of the community's prayer in 5:1, "look and see our disgrace!" Here the community joins with Zion to ask for a reversal of the previously stated judgment: "The LORD himself has scattered them, *he will regard them* (*habbîṭām*) no more" (4:16). The reversal of fortunes and status appears again in 5:2 as the community laments, "our inheritance has been turned over to strangers," just as Zion asked YHWH to "see" her distress of a heart disturbed or "turned over within me" (*nehpak libbî*, 1:20). So also the community cries that "joy of our hearts has ceased" (*libbēnû*) and that their dancing has been overturned (*nehpak*) to mourning (5:15). Zion names her heart as faint because of her sins (*libbî dawwāy*, 1:22), even as the community states that "our hearts are faint" (*dāweh libbēnû*, 5:17). A chart lays out the parallels.

Zion	Community
Look and see (my suffering, 1:11-12)	Look and see (our disgrace, 5:1)
My heart overturned (1:20)	Joy of our hearts ceased, dancing turned (5:15)
My heart faint (1:22)	Our heart faint (5:17)

So the laments of woman Zion have become the words of lament for the community, naming both the situation of reversal and the reaction of heart sickness. This recovery of Zion's language becomes a sign of the community's identification with her suffering, but also her inclusion in the community. She who had no one to comfort her is now symbolically linked with this praying community as they use her words, perhaps even giving the sense that she is among them praying.[36] The repeated "we" states again and again that others *have* taken note of her suffering but, as the final prayer of 5:19-22 asks, will YHWH?

Reversing the acrostic sequence. Chapter 5 is distinct from previous chapters in that its lines are shorter, it does not use the *qinah* rhythm of mourning, and it does not follow an alphabet acrostic.[37] Previous attempts to discover an organizational pattern for the book also tried to explain these distinctive features. William Shea thought the different lengths of the five chapters mimic the 3+2 *qinah* rhythmic pattern of the dirge verses (however, the presence of the *qinah* meter in Lamentations and lament in general has been questioned).[38] Others have proposed a concentric structure for the book based on recurring words and motifs.[39] Casper Labuschangne offers a seven-part "menorah" concentric structure but also notes that there are an equal number of alphabetic and non-alphabetic lines in the book. Therefore, the non-alphabetic sequence of twenty-two verses in chapter 5 may be attributed to "deliberate design for the sake of balance."[40] Phillipe Guillaume finds a different sort of acrostic in verses 19-22; the first letter of the book's last four lines spells out *'lhk*, which he reads as *'elohêkā*, "your God." The "hidden acrostic," he claims, is highlighted by the use of the letter *'ayin* that comes at the start of three of the four half-lines of 5:17-18: one would expect to find *'ayin* in verse 17 if chapter 5 were an alphabet acrostic that followed the reversed order of *pê 'ayin* in chapters 2, 3, and 4.[41] Verse 17 stands as yet another way that chapter 5 is associated with the poems that have come before.

The *Midrash Rabbah* notes the reversal of the *'ayin* and *pê* in 2:16-17, 3:46-51, and 4:16-17 and offers an explanation based on the Hebrew meaning of the letters: "Why does the verse beginning with the letter *peh* precede that beginning with the letter *'ain*? Because they uttered with their mouth what they had not seen with their eye."[42] Recent commentators have revived the search for symbolic significance and move beyond historical explanations.[43] Lina Rong finds a progression in the three *'ayin/pê* reversals that highlights the running theme of status reversal. Nancy Lee believes the acrostics and letter reversals challenge the "extremity of the 'order' of God's words." The poems then mimic the experience of reversal to throw a spotlight on the oppression of the enemies and complain that God would allow it.[44]

The midrash suggests that eye and mouth are key images, so it is worth noting that references to the eyes appear throughout the book (1:16; 2:4, 11, 18; 3:48, 49, 51; 4:17, 5:17), while references to the mouth do not continue beyond chapter 3 (1:18; 2:16; 3:29, 38, 46). Early references are to eyes that weep, later to eyes that see and grieve. Moreover, a reference to the eyes or seeing appears in almost every *'ayin* verse, including Guillaume's "hidden acrostic" marker verse of 5:17. It does not appear in 2:17 where the *'ayin/pê* letter reversal begins (although references to weeping eyes do appear in 2:11 and 18).

What can be learned by observing the placement of these references to eyes and seeing? A look at the first alphabetic acrostic in chapter 1 shows that the *'ayin* verse at 1:16 repeats the word *'ênî* ("my eyes, my eyes," although some see that repetition as scribal error). Zion weeps and stretches out her hands, "but there is no one to comfort her" in verses 16 and 17, only oppressors who circle around at the command of the LORD. The *pê* and *'ayin* verses of 2:16-17 and 3:46-51 also juxtapose images of enemies who open their mouths against Zion with references to eyes or seeing.[45] The *'ayin/pê* reversal appears once more in chapter 4 with a significant variation. Both lines in the *pê* verse (4:16) repeat the sad news that the LORD will not consider/or look at Zion's plight (root *nbṭ*). Eyes fail in the *'ayin* verse, (4:17), looking for help from other nations that never comes.

As previously noted, chapter 5 only preserves the twenty-two verse sequence: otherwise lines do not follow alphabetic acrostic, except that three of the four half-lines of 5:17 begin with the letter *'ayin* (*'al*, "because" and *'ayin*, "eyes"): "*Because* this has happened, our hearts are sick, *because* of these *our eyes* are dimmed." The next verse 18 begins the same way: "*Because of* Mount Zion, lying desolate." No other verse in chapter 5 mimics the previous acrostic pattern, but 5:17 continues the letter reversal of chapters 2, 3, and 4 with an *ʿayin* verse where one might expect it. The reversal of the *ʿayin/pê* sequence in chapters 2, 3, 4 with this trace in 5:17 directs the reader's attention to the role of the mouth and eyes in the laments, especially the eyes that see, weep, and finally grow dark at the suffering of Zion.[46] It reinforces the pleas of Zion in chapter 1 that those who pass by, including readers, will look, see, and join in the prayer of chapter 5 that YHWH will "look and see" (1:11-12; 5:1).

Will YHWH look and see? We have seen that the final poem of chapter 5 echoes and summarizes all that has come before as it recommends a final "strategy for coping." It reminds readers of the eyes that see sorrow, weep endlessly, look in vain for help, and finally wear out, dark (5:17)—from shock, disappointment, exhaustion? The structure of the fifth chapter and the petition of its first verse also point to this importance of seeing. While many follow an outline that marks off the petition of 5:1, laments of 5:2-18, and final petition of 5:19-22, Allen uses the two interrupting confessions of sin to mark the end of sections 5:1-7 and 5:8-16, leaving a concluding section of 5:17-22.[47] In this outline, verses that begin with the letter *ʿayin* open the second and third sections. As noted previously, the chapter and first section begins with prayer that YHWH "look and see," in 5:1 (cf. 1:11 and 2:20). Descriptions of the catastrophe's lingering effects in 5:2-18 are similar to those laid out in chapters 1 and 2 but now are spoken either in third person or first person plural, not in first person singular.[48] And, to repeat, the "acrostic" verse of 5:17 wearily states that because of "these things" listed in 5:2-18, the eyes of those who lament are dimmed or darkened. Especially distressing is the sight of a desolate Mount Zion, empty of all but a symbol of wildness, the foxes who roam freely. YHWH may be on the heavenly throne eternally, but the throne that represents YHWH's rule among the people is vacant (5:18-19). No, YHWH has not remembered the people as petitioned, but instead has forsaken them (5:1, 20). Whatever the translation of 5:22, ("unless you have," or "for you have") the experience of this community is rejection. Its petitioners clearly see the lingering effects of the devastation, but from their point of view, YHWH does not because he refuses to look their way (4:16).

However, another reversal of the *ʿayin/pê* sequence makes a surprising appearance at the center of the book, highlighted by these signals to look for it. Even as the book's turning point at 3:22-33 reminds readers that YHWH's steadfast love and mercies never fail (the suffering man [*geber*, 3:1] recalls them at 3:21), the following section of 3:34-39 includes an *ʿayin/pê* reversal that reinforces this reason for hope. Three features stand out. First, the "*lamed*" section of 34-36 at the center of the book lists three oppressions followed by the rhetorical question: "Does the Lord not see?" Most translations of this difficult phrase affirm that God indeed sees injustice and does not approve.[49] Second, God is named "Most High" ('elyôn,) in verses 35 and 38, the only appearances the book, placed here at the center verse of both the central *lamed* and *mem* sections. Third, in both occurrences, the name is prefaced with a Hebrew word that begins with *pê*: "the face of the Most High" (*pěnê 'elyôn*, 3:35) and the "mouth of the Most High" ("*mippî 'elyôn*" the *pê* prefaced with *min*, "from," in 3:38) so that the initial letters *pê* and *'ayin* appear in the reversed alphabetical order of chapters 2, 3, and 4.

The two rhetorical questions of 3:36-38 are answered in the affirmative. Does the Lord (*'ădōnay*) not see injustice (3:36)? Of course the Most High sees what is done "before the face" (3:35). Did not the Lord command that which others—presumably the enemies—spoke so that it came to pass (3:37)? Of course, but ultimately, from the mouth of the Most High comes both good and bad (3:38). Taken together, these central lines affirm that *'elyôn* does see oppression and injustice and does speak judgment against them. This sequence of seeing and speaking that worked against the people with Jerusalem's destruction will one day work for it (see the petitions of chapter 5 and the imprecations of 1:20-22; 3:64-66; 4:21-22).

The *'ayin/pê* reversals in these appearances of *'elyôn* also signal an answer to the final rhetorical question of 3:39. Why should a man (*geber*) complain about the punishment of his sins? The Most High *'elyôn* does see and will act, so it is good to wait, as the *geber* has learned to do (3:15-26). The promise that *'elyôn* sees and speaks also stands in counterpoint with the reference to eyes in the *pê* and *'ayin* verses of chapter 3:

> [48] My eyes flow with rivers of tears because of the destruction
>   of my people.
> [49] My eyes will flow without ceasing, without respite,
>   [50] until the Lord from heaven looks down and sees.
> [51] My eyes cause me grief at the fate of all the young women
>   in my city.

Finally, the strategic central placement of *'elyôn*'s involvement provides counterpoint to YHWH's inaction as a present, but not everlasting, reality. Yes, YHWH will not look or consider (4:16), but that will not always be so: *'elyôn* sees, so as the flowing tears plead, this same God will look from heaven and see (3:50; cf. 3:55-66). In that hope, the mourner's eyes will weep until that day comes.

Lament and Identity

David Packman's memorial reading drew from the beginning, middle, and end of Lamentations to create a three-tone chord; his selection from chapter 3 centered on speaking and hearing: "I called...you did hear...you did say" (3:55-57). Perhaps the mouth does speak what the eye has not yet seen, just as the midrash claimed, even as the reversal of the letters *pê* and *'ayin* points to the Most High (*'elyôn*) who does see and will act. Although the lament of chapter 5 asks why YHWH acts as if he does *not* see, the very choice to pray is itself an affirmation of faith, to take what the human eye does see and bring it to speech.[50] Readers and hearers who make identification with this praying community accept the distance that often stands between what is said in faith and what is seen at the present time. They may take encouragement when others "look and see," joining their voices with those who may have little strength of their own to continue in prayer. Both YHWH and passersby are implored to "look and see" in 1:11-12, and the petition of chapter 5 shows how the mouth has done its work in forming a community of prayer—the one appeal left has been made to YHWH.

Contemporary readers then are among those passing by who are implored to see what Woman Zion sees and join the community whose members also look and report the suffering before their eyes. They too direct their prayers to YHWH, remembering that *'elyôn* sees and speaks. Even so, we readers and hearers who have been begged to stop and look now enter into this conversation with the one who often seems so far away. The progression of the book recruits readers and hearers to join Zion, the suffering man, and the community in lament, so that we might do the same with those who come into view today. In this way, the community's prayer that God would see and act in the face of suffering becomes ours.[51] These final prayers of the community bring together the laments that have gone before, and they do so based on the conviction that *'elyôn* does see and will act in speaking his justice into being. The book forms Christian readers as they make identification with devastated Jerusalem, holding the sorrow of lament and the hope of petition in biblical tension. Prayer and service are two ways the many "I's" become "we," sometimes voicing the group's own pain as in Rabbi Packman's reading, sometimes reaching out to others isolated in their suffering.

It begins with intentional sight, a lesson we can learn from photographer Dorothea Lange (1895-1965), who said: "A camera is a tool for learning how to see without a camera."[52] Lange, best known for her picture of the "Migrant Mother," was a portrait photographer for San Francisco's wealthy until she took her camera to the streets, documenting the effects of the Great Depression. Her work was seen by agrarian economist Paul Taylor, and together the two recorded the experience of migrant workers, first for the Farm Security

Administration and later for a jointly authored book, *An American Exodus: A Record of Human Erosion.*[53] They hoped the book would draw attention to the rural displacement that sent some 300,000 persons in search of work to the agribusiness farms of California. Recalling the day she met the "Migrant Mother," Lange said:

> I saw and approached the hungry and desperate mother, as if drawn by a magnet. I do not remember how I explained my presence or my camera to her, but I do remember she asked me no questions. I made five exposures, working closer and closer from the same direction. I did not ask her name or her history. She told me her age, that she was thirty-two. She said that they had been living on frozen vegetables from the surrounding fields, and birds that the children killed. She had just sold the tires from her car to buy food. There she sat in that lean-to tent with her children huddled around her, and seemed to know that my pictures might help her, and so she helped me. There was a sort of equality about it.[54]

This article, written with deep appreciation for Klyne's scholarly work and his life of caring (each hard to imagine without the other), argues that an important part of our identity as Christian readers of the Old Testament is based on learning to see and finding a way to speak. The progression of the Book of Lamentations leads us to long for reversal, to see that our identity in the risen Christ is bound up with exiled and restored Israel, and to move from passerby to co-sufferer with those in pain within our sight, adding our voices to pray that God will see and reverse injustice and suffering. In the fifth chapter especially that outcry and confidence coexist in uneasy but believing tension; it is this communal prayer that forms identity as we pray along with those whose eyes see, weep, and darken. We also hold lament and trust together as we worship and serve. Here is a progression of sight, compassion, and prayerful action that we are called to make our own.

Endnotes

1. The events and story of the memorial are posted at http://www.oklahomacitynationalmemorial.org/.

2. Transcribed from a video recording posted at http://www.c-spanvideo.org/clip/4464773. Packman used a paraphrase of the Revised Standard Version, substituting "we" for "I" in 1:20a and updating phrases like "thou didst," to "you did" in 3:55-57.

3. The Jewish holy day Ninth of Ab falls in late July or early August. See Elise R. Stern, "Lamentations in Jewish Liturgy," in *Great Is Thy Faithfulness? Reading Lamentations as Sacred Scripture*, ed. R. A. Parry and H. A. Thomas (Eugene, OR: Pickwick Publications, 2011), 88-91.

4. Robin A. Parry, *Lamentations* (Grand Rapids: Eerdmans, 2011), 159-236, and "Prolegomena to Christian Theological Interpretations of Lamentations," in *Canon and Biblical Interpretation,* ed. S. Bartholomew et al. (Grand Rapids: Zondervan, 2006), 393-418.

5. Leslie C. Allen, *A Liturgy of Grief: A Pastoral Commentary on Lamentations* (Grand Rapids: Baker Academic, 2011), 148-49. See also Kathleen D. Billman and Daniel L. Migliore, *Rachel's Cry: Prayer of Lament and Birth of Hope* (Eugene, OR: Wipf and Stock, 2006).

6. Carleen R. Mandolfo, *Daughter Zion Talks Back to the Prophets: A Dialogic Theology of the Book of Lamentations* (Atlanta: Society of Biblical Literature, 2007) argues that making the book's central passage the dominant voice ultimately drowns out other voices of outcry and protest. Dialogues with Mandolfo's work are collected in M. J. Boda, C. J. Dempsey, L. S. Flesher, eds., *Daughter Zion: Her Portrait, Her Response* (Atlanta: Society of Biblical Literature, 2012).

7. For a review, see Miriam J. Bier, "Theological Interpretation and the Book of Lamentations: A Polyphonic Consideration," in *Ears That Hear: Explorations in Theological Interpretation of the Bible*, ed. J. B. Green and T. Meadowcroft (Sheffield: Sheffield Phoenix Press, 2013), 204-22. Tracing the shift in scholarly focus from the trusting, penitent man (*geber*) of chapter 3 to the protest of Zion in chapters 1 and 2, Beir offers this caution: "The *geber's* statements of faith—and his negations of them—and Zion's voicing of protest—and her admissions of sin—coexist. In its representation of dialogic truth, Lamentations presents a polyphony of pain, penitence, and protest" (222).

8. Klyne R. Snodgrass, "Jesus and a Hermeneutics of Identity," *Bibliotheca Sacra* 168 (April-June 2011): 131.

9. Kenneth Burke, *Language as Symbolic Action: Essays on Life, Literature, and Method* (Berkeley: University of California Press, 1966), 16. For introductions, see William H. Rueckert, *Kenneth Burke and the Drama of Human Relations*, 2nd ed. (Berkeley: University of California Press, 1982), and Jeffrey A. Crafton, "The Dancing of an Attitude: Rhetorical Criticism and the Biblical Interpreter," in *Rhetoric and the New Testament: Essays from the 1992 Heidelberg Conference*, ed. S. E. Porter and T. H. Olbricht (Sheffield: JSOT Press, 1993), 429-42.

10. Kenneth Burke, "The Rhetoric of Hitler's Battle," *The Southern Review* 5 (1939): 1-21, reprinted in *The Philosophy of Literary Form: Studies in Symbolic Action* (Berkley: University of California Press, 1974), 191-220.

11. Kenneth Burke, "A Socioanagogic Approach to Literature," in *A Symbolic of Motives, 1950-1955*, selected, arranged, and edited by William H. Rueckert (West Lafayette, IN: Parlor Press, 2007), 275.

12. Barry Brummett, *The World and How We Describe It: Rhetorics of Reality, Representation, Simulation* (Westport, CT: Praeger, 2003), 5. "'What are the signs of what?' asked Kenneth Burke in turning on its head the usual theory of meaning in which language is a sign of the world....Our sense of reality may instead be a sign of certain ways of symbolizing, he argued" (34-35).

13. For an appreciation of the earlier works, see Ross Wolin, *The Rhetorical Imagination of Kenneth Burke* (Columbia: University of South Carolina Press, 2001).

14. Kenneth Burke, "Lexicon Rhetoricae," in *Counter-Statement* (Berkeley: University of California Press, 1968), 163.

15. Ibid., 165.

16. Ibid., 163.

17. Ibid., 153, 163.

18. Kenneth Burke, *Permanence and Change: An Anatomy of Purpose*, 2nd ed. (Indianapolis: Bobbs-Merrill, 1965), xlvii-xlviii.

19. Ibid., 69.

20. Ibid., 175-76.

21. Ibid., 133.

22. Ibid., 154, n. 1.

23. Kenneth Burke, *Attitudes Toward History*, 3rd ed. (Berkeley: University of California Press, 1984), 111.

24. Ibid., 106.

25. Ibid., 263-64.

26. Ibid., 265-67.

27. Kenneth Burke, *A Grammar of Motives* (Berkeley: University of California Press, 1945, 1969); *A Rhetoric of Motives* (Berkeley: University of California Press, 1950, 1969); *Language as Symbolic Action* (Berkeley: University of California Press, 1966).

28. Ralph Ellison, *Going to the Territory* (New York: Vintage Books, 1986), 66, quoted in Beth Eddy, *The Rites of Identity: The Religious Naturalism and Cultural Criticism of Kenneth Burke and Ralph Ellison* (Princeton: Princeton University Press, 2003), 12. For an exploration of the relationship, see also Brian Crable, *Ralph Ellison and Kenneth Burke: At the Roots of the Racial Divide* (Charlottesville: University of Virginia Press, 2012).

29. C. Jan Swearingen, *Rhetoric and Irony: Western Literacy and Western Lies* (New York: Oxford University Press, 1991), 236.

30. Rueckert, *Kenneth Burke and the Drama of Human Relations*, 27: "However it functions, the same kind of mysterious process occurs: through exploiting the psychological universals, the poet effects an identification between the auditor and the work…"

31. Barry Brummett, *Rhetorical Homologies: Form, Culture, Experience* (Tuscaloosa: The University of Alabama Press, 2004), 33-41.

32. John Katison, "The Hymn 'Amazing Grace': The Grace Anecdote as Equipment for Living," *Journal of Communication and Religion* 36/2 (Fall 2013): 146.

33. Saul M. Olyan, *Biblical Mourning: Ritual and Social Dimensions* (New York: Oxford University Press, 2004), 17.

34. The list is taken from David A. Dorsey, *The Literary Structure of the Old Testament: A Commentary on Genesis-Malachi* (Grand Rapids: Baker, 1999), 251.

35. Dobbs-Allsopp counts thirty-four occurrences of the first-person plural in chapter 5. F. W. Dobbs-Allsopp, *Lamentations*, Interpretation Commentary (Louisville: John Knox, 2002), 134-37, 145-46; Lee claims that the exchange of voices encouraging Zion to cry out is there from the beginning. "Other voices join in the wrangling in chapter 3, and by the final lament of chapter 5, there is a 'we' communal lament prayer song to YHWH." Nancy C. Lee, *Lyrics of Lament: From Tragedy to Transformation* (Minneapolis: Fortress, 2010), 161-62. Elizabeth Boase argues that Lamentations "enacts a trauma process which seeks to gather a fragmented community around a shared narrative in order to facilitate collective unity and identity." Boase highlights the communal prayers at 3:40-47, 4:17-20, and 5:1-22. "Fragmented Voices: Collective Identity and Traumatization in Lamentations," presented at Society of Biblical Literature Annual Meeting, 2013.

36. Olyan's study of ancient ritual found that comforters debased themselves with peti-

tioners in both identification and hope of increased effectiveness. Olyan, *Biblical Mourning*, 139.

37. The verses are only one line each, so it is the shortest of the poems. The consistent use of first person plural occurs in communal laments such as Psalms 44, 74, 79, 80, and 83. Paul M. Joyce and Diana Lipton, *Lamentations Through the Centuries*, Wiley Blackwell Bible Commentaries (Chichester: Wiley-Blackwell, 2013), 175-77.

38. William H. Shea, "The *qinah* Structure of the Book of Lamentations," *Biblica* 60 (1979): 103-7. R. de Hoop, "Lamentations: the Qinah-Metre Questioned," in *Delimitation Criticism: A New Tool in Biblical Scholarship*, ed. Marjo Christina Annette Korpel and Josef M. Oesch (Assen: Van Gorcum, 2000), 80-104.

39. For a review and proposal, see Dorsey, *The Literary Structure of the Old Testament*, 246-52.

40. Casper J. Labuschagne, "The Book of Lamentations: A Survey of Its Numerical Features" (2008), posted at http://theol.eldoc.ub.rug.nl/FILES/root/2012/Labuschagne/ NumericalFeaturesoft/Blessings/BookofLamentations/7.lament.pdf. See also his discussion in *Numerical Secrets of the Bible: Rediscovering the Bible Codes* (North Richland Hills, TX: BIBAL Press, 2000), 14-18.

41. Phillipe Guillaume, "Lamentations 5: The Seventh Acrostic," *Journal of Hebrew Scriptures* 9/16 (2009): 3-4.

42. "Lamentations," trans. and ed. A. Cohen, in *The Midrash Rabbah* vol. 4, ed. H. Freedman and M. Simon (London: Socino Press, 1977), 183 (Lamentations II.1-18 § 20), repeated on page 209 (Lamentations III. 44-50 § 9).

43. The commentaries that note the reversal typically mention its appearance in abecediaries discovered at Kuntillet ʿArujud (eight century) and Izbet Sartah (eleventh century); eg., Johan Renkema, *Lamentations*, Historical Commentary on the Old Testament (Leuven: Peeters, 1998), 47-49. Renkema claims the reversal is meant to distinguish chapter 2 from chapter 1 and link it with chapters 3 and 4.

44. Lina Rong, *Forgotten and Forsaken by God (Lamentations 5:19-20): The Community in Pain in Lamentations and Related Old Testament Texts* (Eugene, OR: Pickwick Publications, 2013). Nancy C. Lee, "Lamentations and Polemic: The Rejection/Reception History of Women's Lament…and Syria," *Interpretation* 67/2 (2013): 162-66.

45. Moreover, the first two words of the *pê* verse in chapters 3 and 4 also follow the new *pê*/*ʿayin* sequence: "All your enemies open wide their mouths against you" (*pāṣû ʿālayik pîhem*); "they say, 'We have swallowed her up! This is the day we have waited for…we have seen it" (2:16); "[YHWH] has made the enemy rejoice over you, and exalted the might of your foes" (2:17); "All our enemies have opened wide their mouths against us" (*pāṣû ʿālêynû pîhem*)…Rivers of water fall down from my eyes" (3:46, 48).

46. The eyes are "dark" (*ḥšk*, cf. 3:2; 4:8). Renkema, *Lamentations*, 619, thinks it is from tears (cf. 1:6; 2:11; 3:49; 4:17). Iain W. Provan, *Lamentations*, New Century Bible Commentary (Grand Rapids: Eerdmans, 1991), 132, sees it as fatigue (cf. Psalm 69:23, Ecclesiastes 12:3).

47. Allen, *A Liturgy of Grief*, 148-49.

48. These "we" passages cast the whole work as giving voice to the congregation: "All the descriptions of violence and death relate in the first place to the group, not to individual agonies." Erhard S. Gerstenberger, "Elusive Lamentations: What Are They About?" *Interpretation* 67/2 (2013):123-24.

49. Reading with JPS/Tanak: "This the Lord does not choose." Parry, *Lamentations*,

106-14, takes 3:36 as a rhetorical question with NIV and NRSV: "Does the Lord not see?" Renkema, however argues it is not a question or a figure, but a statement: "The LORD does not see." Rong, *Forgotten and Forsaken,* 85, and Dobbs-Alsopp, *Lamentations,* 121-22, do also, stressing the perceived absence of divine action.

50. Rong, *Forgotten and Forsaken,* 192: "Hope in Lamentations, however, is not based on a cause and effect view of the God- human relationship, neither is hope limited to the words of hope found in Lamentations 3:24-31; rather, it is rooted in the courage and faithfulness of the community which continues to choose God when God seems absent and silent."

51. As Parry puts it: "Using this book well in worship is not about becoming self-obsessed, miserable people but about becoming people who can respond to the pain of others in more appropriate ways (an outward-looking and missional practice if ever there was one) and who can respond to our own pain (either individual or communal) more honestly and faithfully." Robin A. Parry, "Wrestling with Lamentations in Christian Worship," in *Great Is Thy Faithfulness?,* 195.

52. Linda Gordon, *Dorothea Lange: A Life Beyond Limits* (New York: W. W. Norton, 2009), xii. Lange also said: "There is poverty within us, poverty of spirit that allows the other poverty" (412).

53. Dorothea Lange and Paul Taylor, *An American Exodus: a Record of Human Erosion* (New York: Reynal and Hitchcock, 1939; reprint, Paris: Jean Michel Place, 1999).

54. Lange, "The Assignment I'll Never Forget: Migrant Mother," *Popular Photography* (February 1960). Lange's "Migrant Mother," along with others taken for the Farm Security Administration, can be viewed at http://www.loc.gov/rr/print/list/128_migm.html.

I Am Church
Ecclesial Identity and the Apostle Paul

Scot McKnight

Paul's mission, not to reduce it to simplicities, was to get Gentiles saved and to get saved Gentiles to sit at table with saved Jews—and to like the arrangement at the table. Easier said than done, we might say, but even harder then than now, though it's not like we have mastered anything like an ethnic, gender, or ideological diversity in our local churches. The debate today over the "old" versus the "new" perspective (which frequently enough loses track of its commonalities and becomes obsessed with border disputes instead of solid examinations of what the New Testament is actually saying) misses at times the signal contribution the new perspective has offered, not only to New Testament scholarship but also to the church: namely, a stronger ecclesio-centric approach to early Christian self-perceptions and theology.[1]

In a recent study of Pauline churches based on the archaeological evidence from Pompeii, a city we know very well now (with deft adjustments once one moves the same data set to Rome, and then with more than a little nuancing for churches in places as diverse as Ephesus, Philippi, or Corinth), Peter Oakes proposes that an early Pauline house church in Rome would have looked something like this: thirty people in total, comprising

- a craftworker who rents a workshop with separate living accommodation for his family, some male slaves, a female domestic slave, and a dependent relative

- a few other householders who rent less space, with family and slaves and dependents
- a couple of members of families whose householder is not part of the house church
- a couple of slaves whose owners are not part of the house church.
- a couple of free or freed dependents of people who are not part of the house church
- a couple of homeless people
- a few people who are renting space in shared rooms (migrant workers, etc.)[2]

The genius of Oakes is that he constructed his model on the basis of space and who owned and lived and worked in those spaces, with the result that our picture of a typical house gathering—a house church—gains immediate clarity as well as concrete reality.

Now let's make it messier. The apostle Paul's brilliant insight, expressed as early as Galatians and as late as Colossians, formed those early house churches into fellowships (*koinoniai*) that brought together the previously not-brought-together. Namely, from Galatians 3:28 and Colossians 3:9-11:

> There is no longer Jew or Greek, there is no longer slave or free, there is no longer male and female; for all of you are one in Christ Jesus.

> … seeing that you have stripped off the old self with its practices and have clothed yourselves with the new self, which is being renewed in knowledge according to the image of its creator. In that renewal there is no longer Greek and Jew, circumcised and uncircumcised, barbarian, Scythian, slave and free; but Christ is all and in all!

Take Peter Oakes's house church and give labels and names to those thirty odd people, labels like Jew and Greek, male and female, ethnicity and cultural ideologies, and now we get closer to the reality of the first fellowships.

What Paul sought to create, and what resulted in no end of tension and sometimes even chaos, was a church composed of everyone. His gospel was that Jesus was Messiah and Lord, not just Messiah of the Jews, but Messiah and Lord *of all*. If Jesus is Messiah and Lord of all, then all are invited to the table. And if all are invited to the table, then everyone has a place to sit. And that means exactly what it means: they have to talk to one another, share life with one another, give to and receive from one another regardless of one's status in the Roman world—a status driven world. In the workshops, in the Roman agora, in the belly of ships, and in the villas of the citizens there were very clear distinctions. Romans were obsessed with status. Citizens were not slaves and slaves were not citizens (whose rights were protected). Martin Goodman, one of the leading scholars on the Roman world today, puts it this way: "On the public level, Roman society was highly stratified on the basis of birth and wealth. The social and political status of each adult male citizen was fixed at irregular censuses. . . . On the domestic scale . . . the only fully legally recognized person (*sui iuris*) in each family unit was its male head, the *paterfamilias*."[3]

Complicate this a bit on another scale, the political one, and we add the emperor, the senators, the cavalry (called *equites*). Then we add yet another, different kind of scale running alongside the previous scale, one concerned with the Roman world of hierarchy: first men, then women, then foreigners, and then slaves. Hierarchy and status and reputation and connections are the Empire. Complicate it once removed with synagogues and local Jewish communities, and status gets a twist and a challenge: Jews had their own hierarchies and Paul, the Jew, attempted to bring together in the house churches both the Roman and the Jewish worlds. It could get testy. Which it did in Antioch, a city on the border of Israel and therefore in need of some particularly defensive maneuvers. Here is Galatians 2:11-14, and I suggest that we read it in light of the reconstruction of a house church as proposed by Oakes:

> But when Cephas came to Antioch, I opposed him to his face, because he stood self-condemned; for until certain people came from James, he used to eat with the Gentiles. But after they came, he drew back and kept himself separate for fear of the circumcision faction. And the other Jews joined him in this hypocrisy, so that even Barnabas was led astray by their hypocrisy. But when I saw that they were not acting consistently with the truth of the gospel, I said to Cephas before them all, "If you, though a Jew, live like a Gentile and not like a Jew, how can you compel the Gentiles to live like Jews?"

What played out here—at a simple table—played out every time Paul got one of his house churches going, and perhaps it ought to be noted that it wasn't very often that Paul hung around until things were running smoothly. It was not uncommon for Paul to have founded a church, say in Philippi or Thessalonica, and then within a month or two take off for months or more. We hear echoes of this table fellowship chaos in Paul's use of terms like the "strong" and the "weak" in Romans 14-15 and in the party spirits of 1 Corinthians 1:10-12, so we can imagine our way quite accurately into the tensions between men and women, slaves and free, Jews and Greeks, and different ethnic groups whom Paul in his vision of Jesus as Lord had brought into a new kind of *koinonia*. Let us take this as the reality, but also as the very vision Paul had for his mission: he wanted to rescue Gentiles from idolatry and pull them into fellowship with already existing Jewish synagogues. However, tension with synagogues (and that tension was over more than his mission, though we can't explore that here) led Paul to form what he called the *ekklesia* (hereafter Latinized to *ecclesia*). This term was profoundly political—a group of citizens drawn into a body politic in order to discern, judge, and render decisions for a city.[4] And Paul used this term *ecclesia,* not for a new people of God but for the one, old people of God, Israel, now expanded to include Gentiles. The church, after all, is but a branch grafted onto the old tree called Israel (Romans 11:11-24). Hence, we might say the church is Israel expanded.

Identity, *Ecclesia*, and Jewishness

Right here we need to pause to reflect on something many of us have learned from Klyne Snodgrass—the issue of identity. What happens to identity when we become part of this *ecclesia*? More particularly, what happens to identity when the *koinonia* becomes a fellowship of people who are wildly different and in completely different locations when it comes to the moral journey? Paul had very much to say about identity, but the major element in this identity is that it is radically reshaped by *ecclesia* and *koinonia*; that is, Paul both embodied and gospeled an ecclesial identity. What does that look like? We begin with Galatians 2:15-21, one of the most important passages in all of Paul's writings.[5]

> We ourselves are Jews by birth and not Gentile sinners; yet we know that a person is justified not by the works of the law but through faith in Jesus Christ. And we have come to believe in Christ Jesus, so that we might be justified by faith in Christ, and not by doing the works of the law, because no one will be justified by the works of the law. But if, in our effort to be justified in Christ, we ourselves have been found to be sinners, is Christ then a servant of sin? Certainly not! But if I build up again the very things that I once tore down, then I demonstrate that I am a transgressor. For through the law I died to the law, so that I might live to God. I have been crucified with Christ; and it is no longer I who live, but it is Christ who lives in me. And the life I now live in the flesh I live by faith in the Son of God, who loved me and gave himself for me. I do not nullify the grace of God; for if justification comes through the law, then Christ died for nothing.

Paul's Jewish identity was transformed by what God was doing in the world through Christ, in particular, that God's doing was bringing Gentiles into what

Paul calls the "Israel of God" (Galatians 6:16). Some observations of mine now follow, all aiming at an ecclesial identity.

This passage is about the Jewish experience, or perhaps better yet, the consequences for Jews who are now part the Messiah's work. While I—and perhaps you—grew up memorizing Galatians 2:19-20 ("I have been crucified with Christ; and it is no longer I who live, but it is Christ who lives in me"), a more accurate reading of this passage leads us to see the "I" who here dies not as the Gentile "I" but the Jewish "I,"[6] that sense of electional privilege that gets reframed by an ecclesial identity. The fact is that Gentiles don't need to die to the Torah since they aren't identified by or in connection to that Torah. Only a Jew can die to the Torah in this way. This ought to be the natural reading since Paul opens his official reflection on the apostle Peter's behaving badly at Antioch (2:11-14) with the overt, "We ourselves are Jews by birth and not Gentile sinners" (2:15). This Jewishness is then led into ecclesialness with "yet we [Jewish believers, Peter, you and I] know that a person is justified not by works of the law [more below] but through faith in Jesus Christ [Messiah]."[7] He continues: "And we [that is, we Jews, Peter, you and I] have come to believe in Messiah Jesus, so that we [Jews, yet again] might be justified by faith in Christ [Messiah], and not by doing works of the law, because [to repeat myself, which I'm fond of doing] no one will be justified by works of the law" (2:16).

When Paul says in 2:18, "But if *I* build up…" he's referring in an inclusive way to Peter. That is, he is saying, "If you Peter, or if I were to do such a thing…" and he refers here to Peter's own storied and backtracking behavior. It works like this: Peter grew up as a Jew with a wall of separation between Jews and Gentiles, embodied and visible in the temple court itself where the wall of Gentiles prohibited Gentiles from deeper penetration into the inner courts. He lived that wall but then learned the wall had been knocked down by Jesus, and so he began to eat in total fellowship with Gentiles, though I'm not suggesting that Peter began to eat pork or shrimp. But when the "men from James," and this is either a reference to an official assembly from James, brother of Jesus, or (perhaps more likely) a claim to have come as officials from the foundational church, Peter skedaddled away from the table, out the window, and from all contacts with Gentiles. Paul sees this as building back the wall—"If I build up again the very things I once tore down"—and again the "I" is Peter but Paul includes himself to soften his rhetorical blows. That act of rebuilding, then, would prove that when Peter was acting like a Gentile or fellowshipping with Gentiles he was, as a Jew, acting sinfully.

No, Paul continues, "I [Peter and I] through the law"—here we must jump to Galatians 3:19-29 to catch Paul's story of the Torah—"died to the law, so that I [Peter and I] might live to God" (2:19). So we come to the memorized verses, now revised: "I [Peter and Paul, Jews] have been crucified with Christ" and put to death, in need of resurrection in the new creation, and with that all behind him the Jewish Paul (and Peter) can now say, "It is no longer I [as a Jew with that wall separating and holding back Gentile full entry] who live, but it is Christ who lives in me [again, a Jewish 'me']." He goes on to say, "And the life I [Peter and Paul, representative Jews] now live in the flesh [an echo perhaps of circumcision?] I live by faith in the Son of God, who loved me and gave himself for me [Jewish 'me']. I [again, the Jewish ego] do not nullify the grace of God [here Paul must be responding to the view that the borders of God's grace and Israel were the same]; for if justification comes through the law [which it doesn't, circling back to 2:16], then Christ died for nothing" (Galatians 2:20-21).

Before we get to the identity issue, here's a brief sketch of what Paul means by "works of the law" in Galatians 2:16. In the typical Lutheran and Reformed wings of the Protestant movement, "works of the law" got downloaded with Augustinian thinking about human nature and depravity, so this expression became synonymous with human pride and egocentric strivings to justify oneself before God. Hence, "works of the law" is often understood by Christians today as the attempt to do enough good works to be accepted by and acceptable to God. This anthropocentric reading of "works of the law," however, is not only contrary to what we know of Judaism—which as E. P. Sanders long ago pointed out was not a works righteousness religion but a covenant-based religion—but is not consistent with how Paul uses such a term. It is well-known that Paul reserves this term, along with justification, mostly for polemical contexts in which he's attempting to keep the wall between Jews and Gentiles from reconstruction. Hence, my professor, James D. G. Dunn, taught us—and many have become students of Dunn on this one—that "works of the law" does not refer to Torah in general but to *mitzvot* (commands) in particular. And even more particularly, for those commands that created boundaries between Jews and Gentiles, namely, Sabbath observance, food practices, circumcision, and all things pertaining to purity. The works of the law at work here then is a code expression for "Jewishness" so that in Galatians 2:16 Paul can be paraphrased as "we know that a man is justified not by *having to become Jewish* but through faith in King Jesus." Works of the law then refer to those practices that Jews observed, on the basis of Torah, that intentionally segregated them from Gentiles.

All of this changes when Paul and Peter—and other Jews (and Gentiles, too)—are "in Christ."[8] One can say Paul's theology is all contained in this expression, and within that very circle of "in Christ" is located even the doctrine of justification. If one counts all the letters attributed to Paul, the expression occurs eighty-three times, but this expands considerably when we consider "in the Lord" and "with Christ" and "into Christ" and "through Christ." As Dunn details, "in Christ" contains motifs and so Dunn himself focuses on the objective and the subjective. That is, "in Christ" from an objective perspective means that we are justified (Romans 3:24), and we have eternal life (Romans 6:23), freedom (Romans 8:2), new creation life (Romans 8:39), grace (1 Corinthians 1:4), resurrection life (1 Corinthians 15:22), the removal of the veil (2 Corinthians 3:14), reconciliation (2 Corinthians 5:19), the expansion of Israel to include Gentiles in the church (Galatians 3:14; 5:6), and a renewed mind (Philippians 2:5) as well as abundant riches (Philippians 4:19). The more subjective looks at what the saints/faithful experience: we reckon ourselves dead in Christ (Romans 6:11), under no condemnation (Romans 8:1), a one-body people (Romans 12:5; Galatians 3:28); we labor with others in Christ (Romans 16:3); we are sanctified in Christ (1 Corinthians 1:2); we enter into new creation in Christ (2 Corinthians 5:17); and we find freedom in Christ (Galatians 2:4)—that is, the churches are all "in Christ" (Galatians 1:22). In summary, Dunn: "Paul's perception of his whole life as a Christian, its source, its identity, and its responsibilities, could be summed up in these phrases."[9] This expression then is the inaugurated eschatological reality into which the Christian has been placed, and it also evokes the new creation realities that person discovers. Christ both indwells the believer (Galatians 2:19-20) and the believer dwells "in Christ." To be "in Christ" is also to be "in the *ecclesia*" though the two terms are not synonymous. As such, identity, as we can see in the sketch above and what will come shortly, is reformed in Christ and in the *ecclesia*.

In Christ, however, since Jesus is Lord of all and since the *ecclesia* is a *koinonia* for all sorts, and not just observant Jews, those elements of the Torah that segregated are now done away with. This raises yet another hot-button issue in our world: supersessionism and post-supersessionism. Without engaging this discussion in any kind of direct fashion that would take us into the next decade to sort out, a new group of Pauline scholars, spearheaded by Markus Bockmuehl and Mark Nanos, to name but two, are arguing that Jewish believers continued to observe Torah completely while Gentile believers were to observe the Torah insofar as it was for Gentiles. This argument is rooted in part in Acts 15:22-35, where we read of a fourfold Torah expectation for Gentiles (based evidently on Leviticus 18-19[10]), but also in part accommodating both contemporary religious pluralism as well as messianic Judaism's desire to be Torah observant.[11] To be called a supersessionist in today's academy is the kiss of death but, as N. T. Wright recently observed, at some point one has to be given permission to think that Paul thought things that today's market may not like. In particular, once Paul took on board that Jesus was in fact the Messiah, things in his Jewish story began to change—not by replacing Judaism but by revising Judaism, and revising not in the sense of inside out, but by making the sincere claim that Jesus fulfilled that story and was/is the fullness of Judaism. Here's how Wright said it:

We have to contend with what one can only call a revived anti-Christian polemic in which anything, absolutely anything, that is said by way of a "fulfillment" of Abrahamic promises in and through Jesus of Nazareth is said to constitute, or contribute to, that wicked thing called "supersessionism," the merest mention of which sends shivers through the narrow and brittle spine of postmodern moralism. How can we say what has to be said, by way of proper historical exegesis, in such a climate?

My proposal has of course been...that Paul's revision of the Jewish view of Election was more or less of the same type as what we find in Qumran. Call it "Jewish supersessionism" if you like, but recognize the oxymoronic nature of such a phrase. The scandal of Paul's gospel, after all, was that the events in which he claimed that Israel's God had been true to what he promised centered on a crucified Messiah. That is the real problem with any and all use of the "supersession" language: either Jesus was and is Israel's Messiah, or he was not and is not. That question in turn is of course directly linked to the question of the resurrection: either Jesus rose from the dead or he did not. Trying to use postmodern moralism, with its usual weapon of linguistic smearing, as a way to force Christians today to stop saying that Jesus was Israel's Messiah is bad enough, though that is not our current problem. Trying to use that moralism as a way of forcing first-century historians to deny that Paul thought Jesus was the Messiah, and that the divine promises to Israel had been fulfilled in him, simply will not do.[12]

Identity, to take us back to where we were and where we are headed, is formed in this very crucible for the apostle. He, the good observant Pharisee that he was, found himself "in Christ" and, being found in Christ, everything was both the same and different all at once. It's a bit like finding oneself suddenly capable of being taken in by an autostereogram, those children's books in which a superficial reading shows little more than some artist's bizarre assortment of dots but which, upon closer inspection and a simple eye permission, becomes a 3D picture that takes on depth and, in some cases, a whole new world with seeming motion. Paul was given that kind of capacity "in Christ." What was formerly flat (or flatter now that he can see anew) now had new depth, new perspective, new range, and a new (rainbow-ish) color.

So, what do we learn here about identity? Paul's identity as a Jew was given a whole new form "in Christ." What was a story about Israel became the story about Jesus as Messiah; what was once a story about Torah became a story about the faithfulness of Christ to God in the mission of God; what was once about the presence of God in the temple became the story of the Spirit now at work in the *ecclesia*. What was once, at the least, nothing but ludicrous and, at worse, the very curse of God, became for Paul—we are talking here about the cross—became the saving power of God that extends Israel's blessing and inheritance to the Gentiles (Galatians 3:10-14). What was once at the end of time, the general resurrection, has now happened in Christ's own resurrection, leading the apostle Paul to believe that in Christ everything is "new" (2 Corinthians 5:17-20).

This, I suppose, is what Paul means when he says, "There is no longer Jew or Greek" in Galatians 3:28. The Jewish identity, and we could mirror this discussion with the new identity of a Gentile because it, too, was reformed in Christ, is now formed through the death and resurrection of the faithful Israelite, Messiah Jesus. It is not that Jews ceased being Jews or that Romans ceased being Romans or anything of the sort. But what is different is that *the primary identity,* or what one might call *the ontology of identity,* shifted. From being Jewish or Roman, one saw oneself as "in Christ" and "in the church." That is, Paul became an "in Christ" or ecclesial Jew, or if you prefer, a Jewish Christian or Jewish ecclesial person. One's Judaism and one's Roman identities were now given a new orientation so that one's standing in Christ and in the church became the primary identity that reformed one's Judaism or Roman cultural outlook. But what about men and women? To this we now turn.

Identity, *Ecclesia*, and Gender

Our evangelical connections have sometimes been ripped apart by asking this question, not to mention the tattered remains of those connections when one has come to the "wrong" conclusions about the same questions. The questions, of course, are: What about women in Christ? What about women in the Bible? And what about women today in the church? My own entry into this debate occurred in my book *The Blue Parakeet*,[13] but more importantly, it occurred when teaching a course at North Park and in my preparations I landed on a slightly different (yet generally the same) question: what did women do (in the Bible)? I reasoned if we are people who keep our finger on the text, if the Bible permitted women to do X or Y then women today ought *at least* to be doing the same today. (Yet, as we all know, they don't.)

It is not possible to know all that women did in the Pauline churches, where a new identity was being formed for all those who were in the *ecclesia* and who were therefore learning how to live in a new *koinonia*. But there are some indicators that, for me, show that the principle "there is no longer male and female" had some concrete and new realities for those who were "in Christ." To use Paul's words for his own discoveries about his Jewish identity in Christ, "It is no longer my gender who lives but it is (the) Christ (who transforms gender) that lives in me."

Often forgotten, like the stories of women in the history of the church,[14] here are some women from the New Testament who reveal not only what women did but the identity issue about gender: Mary, Priscilla, Junia, and Phoebe. We must unlearn the nagging bad habit of trumping the presence of women in the ministry of Jesus and in the early churches by showing how bad Jews were when it came to the treatment of women. The fact is that Jesus was not once criticized for any of his relations with women and neither was the presence of women in the earliest churches seen as an outrage. That we show the liberation of women in the New Testament by making Judaism our foil only proves how poor we are at history.[15] We need not triumph in order to win; we need only tell the true story, and the true story is the rather unnoticed presence of women in the ministry of Jesus and in the earliest churches—fully present, to be sure, but not by way of offending either Jewish or Roman sensibilities. Of course, Galatians 3:28, when read over against the rabbinic prayer, reveals a much greater liberation for women, but the issue is whether or not that is the context for reading what Paul says about women.[16] I would hold that the jury has concluded that the rabbinic prayer was both atypical and curmudgeonly, and at the same time capable of appearing in any society, not least Judaism.

So Paul's "there is no longer male and female" is a comment as much about reversing the gendered reality and identity of Genesis 1:26-27 as it is about transcending gendered realities in the church, in Christ. What women did reveals their "in Christ" identity, and at the same time it reveals a male identity, for it shows that what both women and men do both does and does not determine identity. It is not, then, for men to teach and women to listen, or for men to prophesy and women to take it in, or for men to found churches and for women to pray for the church-planting husbands. Men and women share gifts and callings. A brief summary is all we have space for.

Mary, mother of Jesus—someone who unnerves many an evangelical—was called by God through angelic visitation to mother the Messiah, and we can hear echoes of Mary's Magnificat (Luke 1:46-55) both in Jesus's ministry, not least the Lord's prayer (Matthew 6:9-13), and in the Letter of James, and this proves her to be a woman of influence. Her significance in the early church is at least visible, if not on full display, in Revelation 12, where the woman "clothed with the sun, with the moon under her feet, and on her head a crown of twelve stars," who gives birth to the Messiah, is none other than Mary.[17] If this is Mary, or at least a glimmering echo of Mary, she had a magnificent role.

I have in another location told the story of Junia (Romans 16:7), so only a comment or two: she was converted from a woman to a man in the course of church history and only in the late twentieth century returned to full acceptance (at which time the never-did-exist man Junias was put to death). Junia was both an apostle and a great apostle, and here apostle probably means a church-planting emissary.[18]

Priscilla taught someone who already was and then became even more so a powerful orator, Apollos. Remembering her teaching posture in the church, we also ought to remind ourselves that when she is listed along with her husband, Aquila, she almost always gets mentioned first (Acts 18:3, 18, 19, 26; Romans 16:3; 2 Timothy 4:19). The point is that she taught, which proves that teaching is not simply for men: in the church, in Christ, in the *koinonia*, men and women do what God gifts them to do, not what their culture assigned them. Finally, Phoebe (Romans 16:1-2), appears to be not only a financial benefactor of the Pauline mission to gospel Gentiles into the *ecclesia*,[19] but also the courier and therefore reader-interpreter of Romans to the house churches in Rome—which brings us back to Rome, Peter Oakes, and that incredibly odd and new mix of people in the first Christian *ecclesiai* in the Roman Empire.

These first house churches were the location where brand-new Jewish-Roman identities were being formed "in Christ," and we ought to observe that these little house groups, with the altogether pretentious claims of being *ecclesiai*, were thereby making the claim that they were a political assembly of God's people. Here males would learn they stood before God on the same plane as their wives; here women would learn they stood on the same plane before God as their husbands. Here men and women, married or not, would learn that their identity was not their gender but Christ and that, in Christ, gender would be reformed into an instrument for the glory of God. How, for goodness' sake, did they pull it off?

Identity, *Ecclesia*, and Spirit

My doctoral supervisor is a world-known scholar of the New Testament, James D. G. Dunn.[20] Dunn is known for major contributions to New Testament pneumatology,[21] but it can be said that he took all that he learned from those technical studies and locked them into a memorable formula for what the Spirit does. In a slender commentary on the Book of Acts, Dunn observed: "The Spirit of God transcends human ability and transforms human inability."[22]

How so? One might answer this question in a number of ways, but the reality is that *the gift of the Spirit* ushers us into kingdom realities. One thinks, of course, of spiritual gifts. Perhaps we should be asking *why* God gave us gifts, and the answer to that question is contained in the epigram of Dunn: "the Spirit of God transcends human ability and transforms human inability." The gifts are given not so we can have something to do, nor even simply to give us an assignment to keep us from being lazy, but because the *ecclesia* is a body and for a body to work well all its parts must function well and in harmony. Gifts are given because on our own we won't work together; with the Spirit we can transcend what we previously could do and, at the same time, the Spirit transforms what we could not do so that we can now do the very thing the *ecclesia* needs. Here we are brushing up one more time on identity: we are Spirit-inspired persons called into a *koinonia* with people very unlike us, and to become a body we must overcome our inabilities and transcend our current abilities.

Again, as we move this essay to a close and closer to the ground at the church level, we remind ourselves that far too often church folks are led to ask "What is *my* gift?" Paul's question, however, looks more like this: "*Why* the gifts?" His answer: "Unity." This is seen in Romans 12:5 and Ephesians 4:16. The *ecclesia* then is a place where a new kind of unity is obtained, and our identity becomes people dwelling in unity in the *ecclesia* because we are indwelled by God's unifying Spirit—the one God of 1 Corinthians 8:4-6 is the one God who now is at work in the Spirit to make us one. The irony, of course, is that what is given for unification has become the source of fragmentation amongst Christians.

Let us think again about the importance of the Spirit in the *ecclesia*, and it can begin with this: we all need the Spirit. But our proof for this might surprise: *even Jesus needed the Spirit*. Peter explained Jesus to a Roman military leader, Cornelius, in these words: "You know what has happened throughout the province Judea, beginning in Galilee after the baptism that John preached— how God anointed Jesus of Nazareth *with the Holy Spirit and power*, and how he went around doing good and healing all who were under the power of the devil, *because God [in the Holy Spirit] was with him*" (Acts 10:37-38, NIV). We see in this text that Peter says Jesus *was empowered by the Spirit*. We might think logically: if Jesus needed the Spirit because he was human, then we surely need the Spirit. In what ways did Jesus need the Spirit? In his miracle working power, in his breathing of new life into the lives of others, when he cracked boundaries between the Torah-observant and those who were less than observant, and when he exorcised demons. We may be tempted to think Jesus did these things by virtue of his messianic vocation or status, but as Gerald Hawthorne once framed Jesus and the Spirit, "the Holy Spirit was the divine power by which Jesus overcame his human limitations, rose above his human weakness, and won out over his human mortality."[23] It stands to reason that the same Spirit was operating on the altogether "human" Peter and Paul and everyone else in the earliest churches (Acts 4:8; 10:45).

Furthermore, the Spirit was not given just to the apostles or to the apostles and the prophets. Being Christian and having the Spirit are one and the same reality. Each of us has the Spirit and each of has gifts for the sake of the church. There is an orderliness here about the Spirit: from Jesus to the apostles on into the churches: Peter and John to the new converts in Samaria (8:17) and from Ananias to Saul (9:17-19). Evidence for universal distribution of the Spirit comes from Acts 10:44-48 and 11:15-16:

> While Peter was still speaking, the Holy Spirit fell upon all who heard the word. The circumcised believers who had come with Peter were astounded that the gift of the Holy Spirit had been poured out *even on the Gentiles*, for they heard them speaking in tongues and extolling God. Then Peter said, "Can anyone withhold the water for baptizing these people who have received the Holy Spirit just as we have?" So he ordered them to be baptized in the name of Jesus Christ. Then they invited him to stay for several days.

> "And as I [Peter] began to speak, the Holy Spirit fell upon them just as it had upon us at the beginning. And I remembered the word of the Lord, how he had said, 'John baptized with water, but you will be baptized with the Holy Spirit.'"

Christian identity, then, is a pneumatologically created identity of new life in the *ecclesia* that empowers us to be part of what God is doing in this world.

This identity is an eschatological identity. Paul uses some remarkable language about the Spirit. Four different times Paul tells us that with the Spirit we have entered into the future kingdom's reality in the present order:

> But it is God who establishes us with you in Christ and has anointed us, by putting his seal on us and giving us his Spirit in our hearts as a *first installment.* (2 Corinthians 1:21-22)

> ...and not only the creation, but we ourselves, who have the *first fruits* of the Spirit, groan inwardly while we wait for adoption, the redemption of our bodies. (Romans 8:23)

> [The Holy Spirit] is the *pledge* of our inheritance toward redemption as God's own people, to the praise of his glory. (Ephesians 1:14)

> And do not grieve the Holy Spirit of God, with which you were *marked with a seal* for the day of redemption. (Ephesians 4:30)

The kingdom is a Spirit-created new world order, and the future kingdom has already begun to invade the present world order. Whoever has the Spirit is leaning already into the future reality.

This eschatological identity in the Spirit begins a work of transformation now so that we can say we are living in a new transformation or creation identity. Here is a list of the fruit of the Spirit, moral markers as it were, of this new creation kingdom reality:

> By contrast, the fruit of the Spirit is
> love,
> joy,
> peace,
> patience,
> kindness,
> generosity,
> faithfulness,
> gentleness, and
> self-control. (Galatians 5:22-23a)

Back to what Dunn said: we need transcendence and transformation, and the fruit is given to us to make Christlike and kingdom-like, and when the Spirit takes hold we become people who are transformed and who transcend our former realities. Our identity, then, is a Spirit-created, eschatologically shaped, and morally transforming identity.

One more observation: the gifts place us into a new ecclesial order. Through the Spirit's gifts we participate in the body of Christ, and the body of Christ is God's mission for the world. Our identity now is in the very people of God.

There are four lists of gifts in the New Testament, the most complete one in 1 Corinthians 12:8-10, 27-28, along with Romans 12:3-8 and Ephesians 4:11 and 1 Peter 4:10-11. The four lists of the spiritual gifts differ enough that we must conclude that *these are representative instances of Spirit-inspired acts but not a complete listing of all the Spirit does.* Our sometimes preoccupation with which gift is the one that fits us best reverses the divine order. Instead of looking at the list and wondering which one is me, a better approach is to ask "What is the Spirit gifting me to *do* in the fellowship?" The answer to that is your "gift."

When it comes to identity we are back to an ecclesial identity: the spiritual gifts are *for [unto] the good and unity of the Body of Christ.* In one of Paul's last instructions, at Ephesians 4:12-13, Paul says it this way. The gifts are given "to [unto] equip the saints for the work of ministry." Why? "[F]or building up the body of Christ [not just "me"]. And here is the teleology of the spiritual gifts: "until all of us come to the unity of the faith of the knowledge of the Son of God, to maturity, to the measure of the full stature of Christ."

Conclusion

I am church. That is, our identity is "in Christ" and Christ is at work today in the church, so that our identity is in the church. Our fundamental identity is not in our vocation or our gender or our ethnicity, but in Christ. We have probed but three elements of a Pauline sense of identity: how Paul's own identity was revised in Christ so that he learned to see the inclusion of Gentiles as the mission of God in this world, in gendered realities where gender is respected as a part of created order but reshaped "in Christ," and we have seen that the Spirit unleashed in this world reshapes our identity into a new creation, an eschatological reality through the Spirit.

When I came to North Park University in the mid-1990s Klyne Snodgrass not only served as a member of the search committee, he became for me a man of wisdom and a resource for interpreting all things Covenant. We are all indebted to Klyne, not only for his personal presence but for his academic and pastoral contributions to the church, and certainly at the center of that is his constant probing of Christian identity.

Endnotes

1. Magnus Zetterholm, *Approaches to Paul: A Student's Guide to Recent Scholarship* (Minneapolis: Fortress, 2009). For the foundational discussions, see E. P. Sanders, *Paul and Palestinian Judaism: A Comparison of Patterns of Religion* (Philadelphia: Fortress, 1977); James D. G. Dunn, *The New Perspective on Paul*, rev. ed. (Grand Rapids: Eerdmans, 2008); N. T. Wright, *Paul and the Faithfulness of God*, 2 vols., vol. 4 of *Christian Origins and the Question of God* (Minneapolis: Fortress, 2013); N. T. Wright, *Pauline Perspectives: Essays on Paul, 1978-2013* (Minneapolis: Fortress, 2013); Seyoon Kim, *Paul and the New Perspective: Second Thoughts on the Origin of Paul's Gospel* (Grand Rapids: Eerdmans, 2002); Francis Watson, *Paul, Judaism, and the Gentiles: Beyond the New Perspective*, rev. ed. (Grand Rapids: Eerdmans, 2007). For one common response, defending a classical Protestant understanding of justification, see Stephen Westerholm, *Justification Reconsidered: Rethinking a Pauline Theme* (Grand Rapids: Eerdmans, 2013). But the best discussion of the debate, covering both sides, is to be found in James D. G. Dunn, *The Theology of Paul the Apostle* (Grand Rapids: Eerdmans, 1998), 1-97.

2. Peter Oakes, *Reading Romans in Pompeii: Paul's Letter at Ground Level* (Minneapolis: Fortress, 2009), 96.

3. Martin Goodman, *The Roman World: 44 BC–AD 180*, 2nd ed., Routledge History of the Ancient World (London: Routledge, 2012), 16-17.

4. Paul Trebilco, *Self-Designations and Group Identity in the New Testament* (Cambridge: Cambridge University Press, 2012), 164-207.

5. I have long taught the vitality of Galatians 2:15-21 (and that we can perhaps begin reading Galatians with a close look at how Paul sets up his argument in 3:23-29), so I was delighted to see concurrence in Wright, *Paul and the Faithfulness of God*, 852-60. For my essay on the passage, see "The Ego and I: Galatians 2:19 in New Perspective," *Word and World* 20 (2000): 272-80.

6. A similar usage of "I" that one finds in Romans 7, which has led to endless discussions,

none of which are to be raised here.

7. On the meaning of "Christ" as "Messiah" and not simply Jesus's second name, see Matthew V. Novenson, *Christ among the Messiahs: Christ Language in Paul and Messiah Language in Ancient Judaism* (New York: Oxford University Press, 2012).

8. On the "in Christ" theme, see Dunn, *The Theology of Paul the Apostle*, 390-401.

9. Ibid., 399.

10. Richard Bauckham, "James and the Jerusalem Church," in *Palestinian Setting*, vol. 4 of *The Book of Acts in Its First Century Setting* (Grand Rapids: Eerdmans, 1995), 452-62.

11. For a recent study of messianic Judaism, see David Rudolph and Joel Willitts, eds., *Introduction to Messianic Judaism: Its Ecclesial Context and Biblical Foundations* (Grand Rapids: Zondervan, 2013).

12. Wright, *Paul and the Faithfulness of God*, 784, 810.

13. Scot McKnight, *The Blue Parakeet: Rethinking How You Read the Bible* (Grand Rapids: Zondervan, 2008), 176-85.

14. As an act of help for those who need stories for churches and families, I mention three resources that have proven helpful to me: Kirsi Stjerna, *Women and the Reformation* (Oxford: Blackwell, 2009); Catherine A. Brekus, *Strangers and Pilgrims: Female Preaching in America, 1740-1845* (Chapel Hill: University of North Carolina Press, 1998); Marion Ann Taylor and Agnes Choi, eds., *Handbook of Women Biblical Interpreters: A Historical and Biographical Guide* (Grand Rapids: Baker Academic, 2012).

15. On women in Judaism, the standard now is Tal Ilan, *Jewish Women in Greco-Roman Palestine* (Peabody, MA: Hendrickson, 1996); Tal Ilan, *Integrating Women into Second Temple History* (Peabody, MA: Hendrickson, 2001). See also Lynn H. Cohick, *Women in the World of the Earliest Christians: Illuminating Ancient Ways of Life* (Grand Rapids: Baker Academic, 2009).

16. The best study I've seen is Klyne Snodgrass, "Galatians 3:28—Conundrum or Solution?," in *Women, Authority, and the Bible*, ed. Alvera Mickelsen (Downers Grove, IL: InterVarsity Press, 1986), 161-81.

17. For your discouragement, grab ten or so commentaries on Revelation by evangelicals and see how many of them find Mary in the obvious reference in Revelation 12.

18. Scot McKnight, *Junia Is Not Alone* (Colorado Springs, CO: Patheos Press, 2011).

19. Reta Halteman Finger, *Roman House Churches for Today: A Practical Guide for Small Groups* (Grand Rapids: Eerdmans, 2007). For the more technical side, see Robert Jewett, *Romans: A Commentary*, Hermeneia (Minneapolis: Fortress, 2007), 941-48.

20. This section is rooted in a forthcoming book of mine tentatively called *A Fellowship of Differents*.

21. James D. G. Dunn, *Baptism in the Holy Spirit: A Re-examination of the New Testament Teaching on the Gift of the Holy Spirit in Relation to Pentecostalism Today* (Philadelphia: Westminster, 1970); James D. G. Dunn, *Jesus and the Spirit: A Study of the Religious and Charismatic Experience of Jesus and the First Christians as Reflected in the New Testament* (Philadelphia: Westminster, 1975); James D. G. Dunn, *The Christ and the Spirit: Pneumatology*, vol. 2 of *The Christ and the Spirit* (Grand Rapids: Eerdmans, 1998).

22. James D. G. Dunn, *The Acts of the Apostles* (Valley Forge, PA: Trinity Press International, 1996), 12.

23. Gerald F. Hawthorne, *The Presence and the Power: The Significance of the Holy Spirit in the Life and Ministry of Jesus* (Dallas: Word, 1991), 35.

Cyril of Alexandria's Hermeneutics of Identity in the *Commentary on the Twelve Prophets*

Hauna Ondrey

Historiography has not been kind to Cyril of Alexandria (d. 444), casting him as an intolerant tyrant and opportunistic politician—even suppressor of scientific progress and educated women.[1] As such, an essay on Cyril may seem an odd way to honor the person and scholarship of Klyne Snodgrass, to whom I am tempted to apply Werner Kümmel's confession that he believed in the doctrine of original sin until he met C. F. D. Moule. Yet once the anachronisms of such portraits of Cyril have been dismissed, a more nuanced, more contextualized Cyril emerges, whose varied pastoral strategies effectively held together the diverse, often volatile Christian communities of Egypt.[2] If, as Klyne writes, "pastors communicate identity,"[3] a major task of Cyril's pastoral ministry was the communication of identity to the church of Egypt at a time of intense intercommunal contestation in late antique Alexandria. Cyril refers frequently to the evangelical *politeia* (polity or way of life) in his writings[4]—a term Klyne offers as a potential New Testament equivalent to "identity."[5]

The term *politeia* signifies for Cyril not primarily individual identity but the communal identity of the Christian church. His use accords with Greek Christian usage, in which *politeia* can refer at once to a distinct group and to that group's distinctive way of life.[6] In Cyril's early *Commentary on the Twelve Prophets*[7] it serves both to designate the church's way of life and to distinguish the church from pagan and Jewish communities. I will address each of these two aspects in turn, showing how Cyril delineates both in his reading of the prophetic text in order to strengthen the identity of his Christian audience. I offer this as a patristic example of Klyne's "hermeneutics of identity."

The Evangelical *Politeia*

For Cyril Christian identity is inextricable from the social identity of the Christian church. Surprisingly little scholarly attention has focused on Cyril's ecclesiology since Hubert du Manoir's 1944 *Dogme et Spiritualité*.[8] I am aware of only a brief article by Norman Russell, surveying Cyril's elaboration of the symbolic significance of tabernacle, temple, Zion, and the body of Christ within his biblical commentaries.[9] Russell's organizing principle is that for Cyril, "the Church is presented in the Old Testament under a variety of symbols."[10] Russell is apparently interested to link Cyril to "more recent scholars" (he cites only Otto Kaiser on Isaiah) who, rather than simply dismissing patristic interpretation as anachronistic, "have recognized the need for sensitivity to poetic imagery if a Christian reading of the Old Testament is to be meaningful."[11] He does not elaborate on this. Yet more can be said. The texts of the minor prophets certainly do contain symbolic images, and Cyril is sensitive to these. But what "the prophetic books consist largely of" for Cyril is a series of prophecies regarding Israel's Babylonian captivity and restoration. Cyril goes to the text with the conviction that parallels exist between God's mighty acts in the two covenants of the economy. "By way of similarity [*hōs ex homoiotētos*] to the favors bestowed on the ancients, there is a promise of assistance to those believing in Christ."[12]

Cyril interprets the scriptural witness in a variety of ways in order to explicate the work of Christ. Robert Wilken has demonstrated how Second Adam and new creation imagery permeates Cyril's biblical interpretation.[13] Luis Armendáriz and John McGuckin have explored how Cyril illuminates Christ through the figure of Moses.[14] In his *Commentary on the Twelve Prophets* Cyril develops an additional Old Testament image to acclaim the work of Christ: Judah's restoration from captivity. Powered by the conviction that "the events of the Jews [*ta tois Ioudaiois*] would be a very clear type [*typos*] of the overall and universal economy [*tēs katholou kai genikōtatēs oikonomias*] brought into effect through Christ,"[15] Cyril develops Judah's restoration from captivity to acclaim Christ's deliverance of humanity from captivity to Satan. Of course the Pauline germ of the Exodus typology (1 Corinthians 10:2) had been well-developed in patristic interpretation.[16] Cyril too exploits the Christological potential of the Exodus narrative when he detects an allusion in the prophetic text.[17] But Cyril's sustained attention to Jewish restoration in commenting through all twelve prophets highlights his view of the church's mission as testifying to and extending Christ's mission. Through attention to this aspect we can build on Daniel

Keating's persuasive account of appropriation of the divine life in Cyril[18] to see the outworking of the divine life in the church's teaching and ethics. For Cyril the church is the sole locus of appropriation of Christ's benefits through the sacraments. It is also proof of Christ's victory and the ongoing instrument of Christ's work through its twofold *paideusis* (instruction), doctrinal and ethical.

Christ's defeat of death, sin, and Satan is not the extent of Cyril's soteriology, generally[19] or in the minor prophets commentary. It is, however, the component that prophetic themes of idolatry, captivity, and deliverance draw to the fore in Cyril's reading. Throughout the commentary, Cyril identifies Israel's national enemies as a figure of Satan, casting Satan's tyranny over humanity in strongly active terms. Satan is the "inventor of sin,"[20] the "patron of error,"[21] a tyrant who exercises despotic rule over humanity and whose power was invincible before Christ.[22] "Satan has exercised an illicit rule over everyone, and together with the evil powers he dominated the land under the sun; by putting the yoke of oppression on everyone he led the race on earth away from God."[23] Satan's oppression consists of deceit and slavery to the passions, so that virtue and knowledge of God are impossible. Prior to Christ's incarnation, "Satan ravaged us…[and] the unbearably destructive currents of various passions corrupted us" so that we "remained dry and fruitless, bare and bereft of any good, our mind set on no virtuous practice… undistinguished for doctrinal discernment… and, in a word, deprived of all fruitfulness."[24]

Correspondingly, Cyril presents the defeat of Satan as a primary aim of Christ's work: "Christ came to achieve two things: on the one hand, to destroy adversaries who led astray the whole earth under heaven…and, on the other, to rescue those who were deceived and subjected to a truly unbearable oppression."[25] The tyrannical rule of Satan now broken, those in Christ are freed from slavery to sin and ignorance. When "the oppression of those formerly in power was then undone; sin was toppled, and along with them it fell, and the force of the passions was eliminated. Christ undermined it, in fact, and brought them through faith to holiness despite their being dissipated by effete passions of various kinds and grievous polytheism."[26] Throughout the commentary Cyril celebrates not only Christ's victory but the church's participation in and extension of this victory through its gospel teaching (bringing pagans to knowledge of God) and its holy living (overcoming passions).

Christ's declaration to the seventy disciples in Luke 10:19 provides Cyril with a key image for the reversal of "power dynamics" Christ effected: "See, I have given you authority to tread on snakes and scorpions, and over all the power of the enemy; and nothing will hurt you."[27] Cyril appeals regularly to this image of the saints treading on snakes (alternately to the similar image of Psalm 91:13). For Cyril it is not merely a descriptive image but a promise that Christ's defeat of evil is extended to his successors, and so becomes a call to do battle with evil powers: "For we have overcome the world with him, and he has given us [authority] 'to walk on snakes and scorpions' (Luke 10:19)."[28] Note that in Cyril's citation, Christ's "to you [*hymin*]" becomes "to us [*hēmin*]," as he claims the text for himself.

The church continues Christ's work of delivering the nations from Satan's deceit, to knowledge of the "one who is God by nature." Cyril's interpretation of Habakkuk 2:3-6 takes Cyrus's defeat of Nebuchadnezzar as a type of Christ's defeat of Satan. As Cyril moves on through Habakkuk 2:7-10, Satan's defeat is still in view, but here the victor expands to encompass the saints, whom Christ strengthens to join his battle against Satan. It is not only Christ whom Cyril presents as the antitype to Cyrus as plunderer of Satan; it is also the disciples, followed by the saints, on the basis of Luke 10:19.

Cyril's text of Habakkuk 2:7 reads, "Because suddenly they will arise and bite him, your schemers will be on the alert, and you will be their plunder." On the one hand it is of course Cyrus who made the Babylonians his plunder. But "we shall also find the wretched Satan suffering this fate."[29] Cyril explains Satan's prey as the nations, which he had "carried off as a whole...setting the snare of the error of polytheism and spreading the nets of sin."[30] The ones who "bite" Satan are "the preachers of the Gospel oracles"; their "biting" signifies the rending from him of those who have become one with him by "choosing to adopt his attitudes."[31] Thus "schemers will be on the alert" because they know that Satan

> has now been put under the feet of the saints, since Christ said openly, "Lo, I have let you walk on snakes and scorpions and all the power of the foe" (Lk 10:19), they will snatch those adopting his attitudes and easily bring them to the knowledge of the truth, teaching them who it is who is God by nature and in truth, and by explaining the mystery of Christ, who also proved to be the first to *plunder* [the devil].[32]

Cyril links Habakkuk's mention of "plunder" to Christ's parable of binding the strong man in order to plunder his property (Matthew 12:29; Mark 3:27).[33] He finds evidence of Christ's plundering Satan's prey in the worship of the magi immediately after his birth. Cyril terms the magi "the first-fruits of the church of the nations; though they were the devil's property and the most precious of all his members, they betook themselves to Christ."[34]

Cyril's view narrows to the saints alone in his comments on the following verse (Habakkuk 2:8): "Because you despoiled many nations, all the surviving peoples will despoil you because of human bloodshed and crimes against land and city and all its inhabitants...." While it was the Babylonians who plundered *many nations*, Satan also was guilty of this. Consequently they suffered the same fate: "the Chaldeans' [Babylonians'] fortunes were plundered by Cyrus, and Satan by the saints."[35] Cyril describes Satan as the universal enemy; the "the surviving people" that despoiled him are "those justified by faith through Christ and sanctified by the Spirit."[36] Cyril traces the line of "plunderers" from the disciples, "the first-fruits of those who plundered the destructive wretch,"[37] to the ecclesiastical leaders of his own time. "Next after them the leaders of the people in addition now plunder him by correctly crafting the message of truth and bringing into paths of piety those in submission."[38] Thus the church continues Christ's breaking of Satan's deceit of the nations through its proclamation of the gospel, bringing the nations "to the knowledge of the truth, teaching them who it is who is God by nature and in truth, and explaining the mystery of Christ."[39] It is just this idea we find in Cyril's homily on the occasion of his transfer of martyrs' relics to Menouthis, to combat the lure of the Isis cult there.[40] In his homily commemorating the occasion, Cyril casts the martyrs as fulfilling the promise of Luke 10:19: "The holy martyrs Cyrus and John came out ready to do battle for the Christian religion... as their reward for their love of Christ, they received the power to trample on Satan and expel the force of evil spirits."[41]

A second front of the church's ongoing battle against Satan is the overcoming of passions by the individual believer, manifested in a *politeia* marked by "conspicuous virtue." Christ's defeat of Satan becomes in Cyril's commentary also a call to virtuous living. We see this, for example, in Cyril's interpretation of Zechariah 2:9: "For this reason, lo, I raise my hand against them, and they will be booty to their slaves, and will know that the Lord almighty sent me." Focusing on the image of "booty to their slaves," Cyril links Christ's cosmic victory with the power he gives the church, using Ephesians 6:12 and Luke 10:19. The powers of evil are made "booty" through the saints' ability to exercise virtue, having been set free from captivity to sin and "made righteous in Christ."[42] Cyril holds a high degree of virtue to be immediately possible for those delivered and justified by Christ, who "have already [*ēdē*] attained to such a degree of spiritual vigor as to be capable of displaying the luster of every virtue and of living the evangelical life in Christ."[43]

Cyril then links the virtue of the saints to their defeat of evil powers, through Matthew 10:1 ("Then Jesus summoned his twelve disciples and gave them authority over unclean spirits, to cast them out, and to cure every disease and every sickness") and Romans 16:20a ("The God of peace will shortly crush Satan under your feet"). Cyril writes: "We shall then be filled with the gifts of grace from him, given authority over unclean spirits, and inflict punishment on the unholy demons, with Christ prostrating and crushing under the feet of the holy ones Satan himself and the wicked powers subject to him."[44] He goes on, "There is also another way you could make booty of those once in power: when we resist our own passions and give the highest priority to controlling worldly and fleshly pleasures and every improper and vile desire, then it is that we have vanquished those once in power."[45] In this way the individual believer's success in the battle against the passions proves the outcome of Christ's work of strengthening weakened human nature.

Cyril identifies the single purpose (*heis ho skopos*)[46] of all the prophets as calling Israel from sin and error to obedience to the one true God. In Cyril's interpretation, the twelve prophets not only serve as moral guides to Old Testament Israel but offer enduring moral guidance to the Christian Church. Guided by Paul (1 Corinthians 10:11), Cyril holds that,

> We believers are anxious to take what happened in former times as a model for our behavior, and thus avoid offending God as productive of ruin; instead, we seek out and carefully put into action what works for his pleasure. Paul in his wisdom, remember, urges us to this in saying, "Now, these things happened to them as a type, and were recorded for our instruction, on whom the ends of the ages have come" (1 Cor 10:11). So there is need to study what happened to the ancients as a means of guiding us to virtue [*tropos oun ara paidagōgias eis aretēn*].[47]

On this basis Cyril regularly draws moral lessons from Israel's history and applies them to his Christian audience as a way of instructing the church in ethical *paideusis*.

Israel and the Legal *Politeia*

Cyril's understanding of the Christian *politeia* was, of course, not worked out in a vacuum but in reference to the strong Jewish and pagan communities of Alexandria. Cyril's episcopacy (412-444) saw the Christian community securing hegemony, but only after Jewish-Christian tension reached its climax in a series of violent altercations in 414/415, culminating in Cyril's expulsion of part of the Jewish community from the city.[48] The foci of Cyril's early pastoral activity and written output demonstrate his active identity maintenance of the Christian *politeia* in this context of intercommunal competition. We have already seen Cyril's view of the church's mandate to call pagans from the ignorance of polytheism to knowledge of the true God. What about the Jewish community of Alexandria?[49] Cyril's supersessionism has been well-established from his works on the Pentateuch and New Testament commentaries.[50] It is no less prevalent in his interpretation of the twelve, where prophetic threat of exile for Israel's disobedience offers Cyril ample opportunity to develop the theme of Jewish displacement as punishment for rejection and crucifixion of Christ. A comparable principle of similarity is operative: "Now, the ancient crimes are of a similar kind to those of the Jews against Christ [*Syngenē de ta archaia tois epi Christō tōn Ioudaiōn enklēmata*]."[51] The commentary is littered with references to Jewish guilt and rejection, but Cyril executes the theme systematically by regularly positing first-century Jews as the antitype (the reality foreshadowed by an earlier type) to Old Testament Israel's captivity (the original type).

Cyril consistently links Israel's exile to the antitype of Jewish punishment for rejecting Christ, which he can apply as easily to his contemporary Jews as the Jews of the gospel and 70 CE.[52] Though not without exception, Cyril regularly posits the church as the antitype of prophetic promises and unbelieving Israel as the antitype of prophetic threats. So much so that he holds it the "custom" of the (pre-exilic) prophets to turn to the mystery of Christ at the end of their prophecies, that is, as their vision reaches ahead from conquest to deliverance: "It is generally the custom [*ethos gar aeipōs*] for the holy prophets, you see, especially at the end of their discourse, to mention Christ and give an explanation of the mystery concerning him, even if still shrouded in obscurity."[53]

This is the case in Cyril's reading of Hosea. With its theme of spiritual idolatry, this text evokes some of the most virulent anti-Jewish rhetoric of the commentary. At several points Cyril consistently draws parallel interpretations between Old Testament Israel's spiritual apostasy and rejection with the fate of Israel in response to Christ. His interpretation of Hosea 7, for example, alternates between the guilt of Ephraim and Samaria for their spiritual adultery and the guilt of the Jews for the death of Christ.[54] But when the prophet turns to God's mercy in the final chapter, it is the church that occupies center stage in Cyril's interpretation. Following the "general custom of the holy prophets," he observes that at this point Hosea foretells "the redemption coming through Christ, and the fact that death will in due course give way, and the goad of hades will be no more."[55]

Because this is the prophet's vision, Cyril explains the benefits detailed throughout the chapter with reference to the church. He applies the promise of Hosea 14:4, "I shall heal their dwellings, I shall love them openly, because my wrath has turned from them," briefly to Israel. But then, guided by Paul's claim that "not all Israelites belong to Israel" (Romans 9:6) but those who follow Abraham's faith apart from circumcision (Romans 4:12), he relates the verse to "the calling of the nations and their relationship to God in Christ through faith and holiness."[56] His interpretation for the remainder of the chapter relates the blessings of restoration of verses 5-8 nearly exclusively to the church.[57] I give just one example from Cyril's interpretation of 14:8, "I am like an evergreen cypress; your fruit is found to come from me." Cyril names the relevant feature of the simile: the leaves of the cypress form a dense canopy. By the image, the prophet means that "those subject to God enjoy impenetrable protection or assistance."[58] The second half of the verse Cyril interprets with reference to the virtue of believers: "Now, the fact that complete fruitfulness of those subject to God would come in no other way than in Christ and through Christ he personally confirms by saying in Gospel pronouncements, 'Apart from me you can do nothing' (Jn 15:5). So let it rightly be said to each of the believers, if anyone should be conspicuous and praiseworthy and adorned with virtue, *Your fruit is found to come from me*."[59] In this way Cyril's interpretation of Israel's exile and restoration is governed by his conviction that, on the one hand, "the ancient crimes are of a similar kind to those of the Jews against Christ"[60] and, on the other, that "the events of the Jews would be a very clear type of the overall and universal economy brought into effect through Christ."[61] These key typologies provide his interpretation of the prophetic text's "frictionless tracks"[62] along which he moves with ease from the prophets' immediate concerns to New Testament events and further on to his fifth-century context, more or less consistently positing the Jewish community as the antitype of oracles predicting captivity, and the church as the antitype of oracles predicting restoration.

Is the only conclusion, then, that Cyril is the staunch supersessionist we always knew he was, engaging in a sort of exegetical confirmation bias? The judgment is tempting but lacking in subtlety. Cyril's starting point, his most basic conviction, is the universal significance of Christ's death and resurrection. God has acted finally and decisively in Christ, and after the Incarnation there is no neutral ground. For Cyril only two groups, Jews and pagans, are joined in Christ. Cyril shows a negative attitude toward both apart from Christ[63] and an equally celebratory attitude toward both in Christ. Cyril is not first anti-Jewish but "pro-Christ." His soteriology and ecclesiology are so identified that his Christocentrism is also an "ecclesio-centrism." It is less that Cyril defines the Christian *politeia* with the Jewish *politeia* as a foil (so Wilken[64]) than that his convictions of the absolute work in Christ render everything subsequent to the Christ event a simple binary: those in Christ and those outside Christ, whether they be pagans who persist in idolatry or Jews who persist in shadows and types. And it is only in the church one can appropriate Christ's restoration as first fruit through its sacraments: the Holy Spirit received in baptism[65] and Christ's life-giving flesh in the Eucharist.[66]

Conversion for both groups is possible only by faith in Christ,[67] into which they are baptized in the church. In his comments on Zechariah 13:1, Cyril affirms that a transformation is required of "everyone who is now called through faith, to both Jew and pagan."[68] Both groups enter the church through "saving baptism [*to sōtērion baptisma*]." For Jews this requires a prerequisite transference from shadow to reality (*apo skias eis alētheia*), that is, from life under the law (*ek nomikēs agōgēs*) to the *politeia* in Christ (*eis politeian tēn epi Christō*).

Pagans in turn must transfer from darkness to light (*apo skotous eis phōtismon*), that is, from unbelief and complete ignorance to faith in Christ and knowledge of God through him.[69] Here we see that Jewish "shadows" provided by the law were certainly superior to pagan darkness. But after Christ, the light and truth, has appeared, they are untimely and insufficient. On this point he is no less emphatic with respect to pagans, the prior group in which he classes himself.

> In former times, remember, when we lived in error and were styled children of wrath, the evil and hostile powers…destroyed us. But when we came to know in Christ the one who is God by nature [*en Christō ton physei Theon*], and were cleansed of the crimes of the former deception through faith, then we were saved and received authority, "to walk on snakes and scorpions and on all the power of the foe" (Lk 10:19); then we trod on snake and basilisk, walked on lion and dragon with Christ as protector, who walls his own about with unconquerable power, and admits peace into our mind.[70]

Cyril likewise affirms and celebrates that Israel will be converted to Christ through faith. At this time "they will be astonished at the magnitude of his generosity and the immeasurable grace of his clemency; they will have a share in the hope prepared for the saints and the vast numbers of the believers generally, and will be tended in a good pasture and a rich location."[71]

Cyril's supersessionism, unwavering as it is, is part of a larger account of salvation history whereby God's decisive and universal restoration of humanity has taken place in Christ. And *anyone*—pagan or Jew—who does not appropriate this restoration within Christ's body, the church, remains in captivity to Satan.

Conclusion: Cyril and a Hermeneutics of Identity

Cyril's convictions about the coherence of God's redemption in the Old and New Covenants allows him to expound Christ's victory through the prophetic text and invite his audience to take their place within it. Throughout his *Commentary on the Twelve Prophets* he expounds the restoration effected in Christ's death and resurrection and equips his Christian audience to join Christ's victory by drawing from the prophetic texts the church's doctrinal and ethical *paideusis*. Convinced that the church is the exclusive locus of God's saving economy, Cyril further summons pagans to knowledge of God in Christ and Jews to the reality to which the law pointed. In all this Cyril is engaging in a thoroughgoing hermeneutics of identity—one with which Klyne might take an issue or two.

In regard to the relationship between the church's identity and non-Christian polities, Klyne might apply to Cyril his warning against Christian triumphalism.[72] Cyril's confidence in Christ's victory on the cross extends to his ongoing victory through the church. Cyril is convinced that the church continues Christ's defeat of Satan, according to his promises to the disciples (Luke 10:19; John 15:5) and Paul's depiction of the church in Ephesians 2:11-22 and 6:10-17. For Cyril the enemy to be overcome is fundamentally spiritual and cosmic. Christ's victory is likewise cosmic, and the power Christ gives the church is over the spiritual enemies of Ephesians 6:12.[73]

That this takes political expression can be accounted for by Cyril's worldview in which spiritual realities are played out in political realities. Regardless of its contextual sense, we may well charge this presupposition a misreading of Scripture, whether on the basis of exegesis or its effective history. Yet on this very point, Cyril's reading of the biblical text raises a question for Klyne's hermeneutics of identity. Does not a hermeneutics of identity depend upon prior answers to certain theological questions, presupposing, for example, a soteriology and ecclesiology? Taking up the latter, Klyne writes that "identity formation must be the focus of the church,"[74] but what is the relationship between being *in Christ* and being *in the church*? Christ is the "center of gravity" of Cyril's thought (as Klyne says of Paul[75]), following his reading of the Pauline epistles. But Cyril's soteriology and ecclesiology coalesce so that the church is the locus where Christ's triumphant economy is realized. For Cyril what it means to be in Christ is not exhausted by what it means to be in the church, but it is nevertheless impossible outside of the church. What is the relationship between individual Christian identity and the social reality of the Christian church? Will not one's ecclesiology shape the biblical hermeneutics of identity Klyne proposes? And ecclesiology is only a single example of any number of prior theological categories that shape our hermeneutics of identity.

In the end we may justifiably reject Cyril's assumption that all outside of the church remain in Satan's grip. The church, nevertheless, can claim with Cyril its gospel identity as those rescued by Christ and restored to incorruption and communion with God, saying of Christ, along with the bishop of Alexandria:

> You became peace, by faith binding into a single people both those from circumcision and also those from nations (Eph 2:14); you became "a cornerstone, chosen, precious" (1 Pt 2:6/Is 28:16), you restored the world to the God and Father; you freed from sin those entrapped because of weakness; you delivered them from the devil's grasp; what was enslaved was enlightened by the grace of adoption [*tē tēs huithesias chariti*]; humanity [*anthrōpos*] moved from earth to become a

citizen of heaven.... [T]he one who gives life to everything has endured with us death in the flesh; but you became "firstborn from the dead" (Col 1:18), "first-fruits of those who have fallen asleep" (1 Cor 15:20), and spoils of a humanity [*anthrōpotētos*] that has been restored to incorruption [*aphtharsian*]. By returning to life as God, in fact, you have trampled on the harsh and ill-omened beast, namely, death, canceling the force of that ancient curse; an end has been put in you and through you to the sentence delivered against us: "Earth you are, and to earth you shall return" (Gen 3:10).[76]

Endnotes

1. A move to get past polemical depictions of Cyril establishes the conciliatory tone of *The Theology of St. Cyril of Alexandria: A Critical Appreciation*, ed. Thomas G. Weinandy and Daniel A. Keating (London and New York: T & T Clark, 2003).

2. John A. McGuckin, "Cyril of Alexandria: Bishop and Pastor," in Weinandy and Keating (eds), *The Theology of St. Cyril of Alexandria: A Critical Appreciation*, 205-36. For McGuckin's critique of historiography on Cyril, see pp. 205-208.

3. Klyne Snodgrass, "Paul's Focus on Identity," *Bibliotheca Sacra* 168 (July-Sept 2011): 259 [259-73].

4. Cyril makes use of the term forty times within the *Commentary on the Twelve Prophets* to refer both to the evangelical *politeia* (*hē euangelikēs politeia, Comm. Hos.* 11:5-6, 215/232; *Comm. Amos* 8:13-14, 117/525) and, especially, its conspicuous virtue (e.g., *Comm. Joel* 3:18, 314/361; *Comm. Mic.* 4:5, 226/664), and the legal *politeia* (*hē kata ton nomon politeia*, e.g., *Comm. Hos.* 8:10, 170/175). It should be noted that the latter does not always carry a negative connotation for Cyril, e.g., *Comm. Hos.* 11:10-11, 220/240.

5. Klyne Snodgrass, "Introduction to a Hermeneutics of Identity," *Bibliotheca Sacra* 168 (Jan-Mar 2011): 4, n. 6, referencing Judith Lieu, *Neither Jew nor Greek? Constructing Early Christianity* (London: Clark, 2002), 179.

6. I.e., the third usage of those outlined by Michael J. Hollerich, *Eusebius of Caesarea's Commentary on Isaiah: Christian Exegesis in the Age of Constantine* (Oxford: Oxford University Press, 1999), 114-15. See Hollerich's survey of the terms *politeia* and *politeuma* in Greco-Roman, Jewish, New Testament, and Greek Christian usage, pp. 105-16.

7. Written between 412 and 418. For issues of dating see Pierre Évieux, "Introduction," *Contre Julien 1-2*, Sources Chrétiennes 322 (Paris: Éditions du Cerf, 1985); G. Jouassard, "L'activité littéraire de Saint Cyrille D'Alexandrie jusqu'a 428: essai de chronologie et de synthèse," *Melanges E. Podechard* (Lyon: Facultés catholiques, 1945), 159-74. The critical edition of the Greek text is in Phillip E. Pusey, ed., *Sacti Patri patris nostri Cyrilli archiepiscopi Alexandrini in XII prophetas*, 2 vols. (Brussels: Culture et civilization, 1965). English translation by Robert C. Hill, *Commentary on the Twelve Prophets*, 3 vols., The Fathers of the Church, 115-17 (Washington, D.C.: The Catholic University of America Press, 2007-2008, 2012). Citations in this paper reference Hill's translation, followed by the corresponding Pusey reference.

8. Herbert du Manoir, *Dogme et Spiritualité chez saint Cyrille d'Alexandrie* (Paris: J. Vrin, 1944).

9. Norman Russell, "The Church in the Commentaries of St. Cyril of Alexandria," *Inter-*

national Journal for the Study of the Christian Church 7, no. 2 (2007): 70-85.

10. Russell, "The Church," 73.

11. Ibid.

12. *Comm. Zech.* 10:11-12, 209/444; cf. *Comm. Joel* 1:1-3, 305/349; *Comm. Mic.* 6:3-4, 248-49/695-96; 7:14-15, 274/734.

13. Robert L. Wilken, *Judaism and the Early Christian Mind: A Study of Cyril of Alexandria's Exegesis and Theology* (New Haven: Yale University Press, 1971).

14. Luis M. Armendáriz, *El Nuevo Moisés. Dinámica christocéntrica en la tipología de Cirilo Alejandrino* (Ediciones Fax, Madrid, 1962); John A. McGuckin, "Moses and the 'Mystery of Christ' in St. Cyril of Alexandria's Exegesis, Part 1," *Coptic Church Review* 21, no. 1 (2000): 24-32; "Moses and the 'Mystery of Christ' in St. Cyril of Alexandria's Exegesis, Part 2," 21, no. 2 (2000): 98-114.

15. *Comm. Hag.,* 1:5-6, 3:67/249, modified.

16. Tertullian, *De Baptismo* 8.9; Didymus, *De Trinitate* 1.11; Cyril of Jerusalem, *Catech. Myst.* 1. Cf. Armendáriz, *El Nuevo Moisés*, 46-48 for interpretations of the Exodus in Philo, Origen, and Gregory of Nyssa.

17. See, e.g., *Comm. Joel* 3:19-21, 316-17/363-65; *Comm. Mic.* 6:34, 248-49/695-96; 7:14-15, 273-74/733-34; *Comm. Hab.* 3:8-9, 384-85/143-45; *Comm. Zech.* 4:7, 133-34/337-38; 10:11-12, 209/444.

18. Daniel A. Keating, *The Appropriation of Divine Life in Cyril of Alexandria* (Oxford: Oxford University Press, 2004).

19. Cf. Lars Koen, *The Saving Passion: Incarnational and Soteriological Thought in Cyril of Alexandria's Commentary on the Gospel According to St. John* (Stockholm: Alqvist & Wiksell International, 1991); Daniel A. Keating, *The Appropriation of Divine Life in Cyril of Alexandria* (Oxford: Oxford University Press, 2004).

20. *Comm. Nah.* 3:19, 328/67.

21. *Comm. Amos* 7:7-9, 101/502.

22. *Comm. Nah.* 1:4, 289/12.

23. *Comm. Mic.* 4:2-3, 224/661.

24. *Comm. Joel* 2:25-26, 292/332.

25. *Comm. Hab.* 3:4, 377/132.

26. *Comm. Nah.* 1:14, 300/29.

27. Cyril only once (*Comm. Mal.* 3:16–17, 335/616) cites the following verse in Luke, "Nevertheless, do not rejoice at this, that the spirits submit to you, but rejoice that your names are written in heaven."

28. *Comm. Joel* 2:25-26, 292/332, modified. Hill's rendering of the finite verbs reduces the force of the Greek: *gar syn auto ton kosmon, kai dedōken hēmin patein apanō opheōn kai scorpion.*

29. *Comm. Hab.* 2:7, 353/99.

30. *Comm. Hab.* 2:7, 353/100.

31. *Comm. Hab.* 2:7, 353/100.

32. *Comm. Hab.* 2:7, 353-54/100.

33. As he had in *Comm. Nah.* 2:8-9, 312/44-45, where he cited Habakkuk 2:7, attributing it to Jeremiah. "Now Satan was also *plundered*, first by Christ the Savior, then after

him by the holy apostles." In this context Cyril names the "plunder" as those who once worshiped Satan coming to the fear of God.

34. *Comm. Hab.* 2:7, 354/100-101.

35. *Comm. Hab.* 2:8, 354/101.

36. *Comm. Hab.* 2:8, 355/102.

37. Ibid.

38. Ibid.

39. *Comm. Hab.* 2:7, 353-54, 100.

40. John A. McGuckin, "The Influence of the Isis Cult on St. Cyril of Alexandria's Christology," *Studia Patristica* 24 (1992): 191-99; "Cyril of Alexandria."

41. *Hom.* 18.3, PG 77.1105, qtd, trans. McGuckin, "Cyril of Alexandria," 223, n. 58.

42. *Comm. Zech.* 2:9, 112/308.

43. Ibid.

44. *Comm. Zech.* 2:9, 112/308-309.

45. *Comm. Zech.* 2:9, 112/309.

46. *Mic. Pref.*, 181/599.

47. *Comm. Hos.* 2:15, 81/66. Cf. *Comm. Mic.* 7:4, 263/718.

48. See the balanced discussion of Christopher Haas, *Alexandria in Late Antiquity: Topography & Social Conflict* (Baltimore: The John Hopkins University Press, 1997), especially 278-330, 333. The exchange is narrated in Socrates, *EH* 7.13. On the events and the consequent power struggle between Cyril and Orestes, the augustal prefect, see Haas, *Alexandria*, 302–308; McGuckin, *St. Cyril of Alexandria: The Christological Controversy, Its History, Theology, and Texts* (Crestwood, NY: St. Vladimir's Seminary Press, 2004; orig. Leiden: Brill, 1994), 8-13; Wilken, *Judaism*, 54-58, who includes the full account from Socrates, pp. 54-56.

49. On which see Haas, *Alexandria*, 91-127; Wilken, *Judaism*, esp. 39-53.

50. See especially Wilken, *Judaism*; B. Lee Blackburn, Jr. *The Mystery of the Synagogue: Cyril of Alexandria and the Law of Moses* (PhD dissertation; University of Notre Dame, 2009).

51. *Comm. Hos.* 6:11/7:1, 150/151.

52. Cf. *Comm. Hos.* 7:4, 155; 9:16-17, 193; and *passim*; *Comm. Joel* 1:11-12, 272; *Comm. Amos* 8:9-10, 112-13; 9:1, 119; 9:8-10, 127; *Comm. Mic.* 1:15-16, 198; 2:10, 207/637-38; 2:12-13, 211; 3:1-4, 213; 3:5, 214; 3:9-10, 217; 3:11-12, 219; 5:12-15, 244-45; *Comm. Hab.* 2:12-13, 357-58; 15-16, 360; 2:16-17, 36; *Comm. Zech.* 1:2, 95-96/285-86; 3:9, 123-24; 10:6-7, 216/454; 11; 12:11-14, 246/495-96.

53. *Comm. Amos* 8:9-10, 111/517.

54. *Comm. Hos.* 6:11-7:1a, 150-51/151; 1-2, 153/153, v. 3, 153/154; v. 4-5, 155/157.

55. *Comm. Hos.* 14:1-3, 249/276.

56. *Comm. Hos.* 14:4, 252/280.

57. *Comm. Hos.* 14:5 through 14:7, 252-54/280-83.

58. *Comm. Hos.* 14:8, 255/285.

59. Ibid.

60. *Comm. Hos.* 6:11/7:1, 150/151.

61. *Comm. Hag.,* 1:5-6, 3:67/249, modified.

62. Keating, "Supersessionism in Cyril of Alexandria," *Studia Patristica* 68 (2013): 119-124.

63. Take, for example, Cyril's contrasting lament that Israel "though instructed by the Law, remained fruitless," the nations "were a hive of wild wasps, their minds full of demons and completely fruitless," Cyril, *Comm. Zech.* 4:11-14, 140/346.

64. Cf. Wilken, *Judaism,* 75-77.

65. Cf. Daniel A. Keating, *The Appropriation of Divine Life*; "The Twofold Manner of Divine Indwelling in Cyril of Alexandria: Redressing an Imbalance," *Studia Patristica* 37 (2001): 543-49; "The Baptism of Jesus in Cyril of Alexandria: the Re-Creation of the Human Race," *Pro Ecclesia* 8 (1999): 201-22. Within the context of Cyril's *Commentary on the Twelve* see *Comm. Joel* 2:28–29, 295–97/336-40.

66. See especially, Henry Chadwick, "Eucharist and Christology in the Nestorian Controversy," *Journal of Theological Studies* n.s. 2 (1951): 145-64; Ezra Gebremedhin, *Life-Giving Blessing: An Inquiry into the Eucharistic Doctrine of Cyril of Alexandria* (Uppsala: Borgströms, 1977); Ellen Concannon, "The Eucharist as Source of St. Cyril of Alexandria's Christology," *Pro Ecclesia* 18, no. 3 (2009): 318-36. Within the context of Cyril's *Commentary on the Twelve* see Cyril, *Comm. Amos* 9:6, 2:124/535.

67. Cf. Keating, "Supersessionism in Cyril of Alexandria."

68. *Comm. Zech.* 13:1, 249/499.

69. *Comm. Zech.* 13:1, 248-49/498-99.

70. *Comm. Hos.* 2:18, 86-87/72-73.

71. *Comm. Hos.* 3:4-5, 100/89.

72. Klyne Snodgrass, "Pauline Perspectives on the Identity of a Pastor," *Bibliotheca Sacra* 168 (Oct-Dec 2011): 391 [387–401].

73. Cf. *Comm. Nah.* 1:6, 292/17; *Comm. Zech.* 2:9, 3:112-13/308-309.

74. Snodgrass, "Introduction," 5. Cf. "Pauline Perspectives," 387.

75. Snodgrass, "Paul's Focus on Identity," 261.

76. *Comm. Hab.* 3:2, 367–68/119-20, modified.

Identity in the Fourth Gospel

John Painter

Klyne Snodgrass and I have been friends for almost twenty-five years. We first met and became friends when, following the Dublin Society of New Testament Studies Meeting of 1989, we met and spent time together in Cambridge where three of us had arranged a short period of research and writing. During that time we spent many hours in the evenings sharing our common interests in theology. The conversation continues, and this essay is a response to Klyne's interest in and advocacy of the importance of identity for Christians. Here I begin with a Bonhoeffer-like comment. Identity may be important, but the Christian's preoccupation with it is not. Because identity is about the way others see us (at least in part), preoccupation with that aspect of identity can lead to the creation of appearances that have little to do with reality. There is ample evidence in the Jesus tradition of this problem and of Jesus's rejection of such behavior (see Matthew 6:1-18). Distinguishing appearance from reality is a serious problem because the power of self-deception is so strong that we may not distinguish the difference even in ourselves.[1]

Approaches to Identity

In contemporary discussions identity is used in many different ways so that it is important to be clear about how this essay approaches the issue.[2] Of course it is true that every person and group has an identity or perhaps multiple identities, as for example, a son who is also a brother, husband, and father, or a wife who is also a sister, mother, and daughter. This perspective makes clear that the question of identity is related to context and point of view. What context or contexts are relevant to our topic?

Consider, first of all, the implied identity of the believer in the eyes of those John's Gospel portrays as "opponents." Even here there is room to recognize a variety of identities. The same is true of the identity of Jesus from the points of view of the various characters in the Gospel. All of this would be quite interesting, but it would not engage the vital concerns of the person for whom this volume is a tribute. I suspect that he would be interested in the identity of Jesus, which could be examined in the responses of the various characters to him. But I suspect that Klyne would be even more interested in the overall presentation of the identity of Jesus implied by the completed text of the Fourth Gospel, what might otherwise be described as its Christology. This entails a resolution of a variety of traditions into one coherent, if complex, image.[3] A conviction that I have long held is that the fourth evangelist drew on the roots of various Christological traditions to produce a high-resolution image of Jesus the Christ. From the perspective of this study on identity, this might be expressed in terms of the production of a sharply focused identity from a number of fuzzy images.

But perhaps Klyne would be most interested in the bearing the Fourth Gospel has on the formation of Christian identity. While this has a correlation with the Christology of the Gospel, it is another enterprise. Consequently the identity under consideration here is the identity or implied appropriate response to the revelation in the Jesus of the Fourth Gospel.

Identity and the Love Command in the Fourth Gospel

An obvious starting point for our discussion occurs in the farewell scenes in 13:34-35. Some sort of break is implied after the enunciation of the new commandment, which is, "Love one another" (*hina agapate allēlous*), followed by a comma, semi-colon, or the like.[4] Then follows a clarification and a restatement of the commandment, "as I have loved you, love one another" (*kathōs ēgapēsa humas hina kai humeis agapate allēlous*).[5] It is notable that the Johannine Jesus finds it necessary to qualify the love command in an overt and obvious way.[6] What is meant by love cannot be clarified by the choice of the correct Greek word. For example, the verb *agapan* is used of the human love of the darkness (3:19) as well as for God's love for the world (3:16), and the Father's love for the Son is expressed using *philein* (5:20) as well as *agapan* (3:35; 10:17). Thus the meaning of the love command is here clarified in the *kathōs* clause.

Here *kathōs* has a double meaning.[7] The first meaning is exemplary, and clarifies the way the love command is to be understood. Love for one another is to be *in the same way as* Jesus loved the disciples. The nature of that love was symbolically demonstrated in a preceding scene where Jesus washed the disciples' feet. This is an act of generous self-giving love such as is essential to the meaning of the love command. It is an exemplary self-giving act of service providing an example (*hypodeigma*; see especially 13:12b-15). At the same time, the foot-washing symbolically conveys all that Jesus does to transform the lives of his disciples. In what follows, the foot-washing is shown to symbolize the giving of Jesus's life for his own, actualizing God's love for the world (3:16 and cf. 1 John 4:9-13). Thus, the love command asserts that the appropriate response to the love of God is to love one another in a Godlike way.

The meaning of *kathōs* is also *causal*. The disciples are to love one another *because* Jesus loved them. To love one another is a response to Jesus's love for them. Their response may seem surprising, because it breaks the sequence of mutual love, which is featured between the Father and the Son (3:35; 5:20 and 14:31; 15:9-10), and which might be expected between the Son and his own. But when their love of Jesus is mentioned, it is expressed in a conditional way and seems to be redirected. "If you love me, you will keep my commandments" (14:15); and "the person who has my commandments and keeps them, that person is the one who loves me" (14:21); and "if you love me you will keep my word" (14:23). The commandment that is featured in this Gospel (13:34; 15:12, 17; and cf. 1 John 3:23) is the new commandment to love one another. According to Jesus, the keeping of this commandment marks the disciples, identifying them as his disciples (13:35). But it is *not because* this will identify them as Jesus's disciples that they love one another. It is because Jesus first loved them in a generous, self-sacrificing giving way, and in a way that changed their being/lives. Nevertheless, loving one another identifies them as disciples of Jesus.

The Synoptics and the Love Command

It is commonly noted that the Synoptics transmit the broader command to love *your neighbor* (Matthew 5:43; 19:19; 22:34-40, especially 22:39; with partial parallels in Mark 12:28-34, especially 12:31; Luke 10:25-28). In all three Synoptics, the command to love your neighbor is clarified. It is to "love your neighbor *as yourself.*" This assumes, but does not command, self-love. What is commanded is "love your neighbor," while the nature of the love commanded is clarified by "as you love yourself," assuming that people love themselves—that is, they look after their own well-being. While this gives information about what is required, it provides no incentive or inspirational source to motivate loving the neighbor as is found in the command of John 13:34.

In contrast, in Matthew 5:38-48 and Luke 6:27-36 (Q?), where Jesus pointedly calls for the love of *enemies*, there is some motivational ground. The Jesus of Matthew pointedly notes that his command goes beyond love of neighbor: "You have heard that it was said, 'Love your neighbor and hate your enemy.' But I say to you, Love your enemies...." He then characterizes the sort of action that constitutes such love, and pointedly notes that such actions reflect the action of God and express their relationship to God: "Love your enemies, pray for those who persecute you, so that you may be sons of your heavenly Father, because he causes the sun to rise on the evil and the good and the rain to fall on the righteous and the unrighteous....But you be perfect as your heavenly Father is perfect." In Luke also, Jesus clarifies the nature of the command to "Love your enemies" by listing specific actions that are grounded in the character and action of their (heavenly) Father: "Do good to those who hate you, bless those who curse you, pray for those who abuse you...and you will be sons of the Most High; for he is kind to the ungrateful and the wicked. Be merciful as your Father is merciful." Though Matthew and Luke have arranged the Jesus tradition differently, much of it is common to both. Interestingly, each concludes with a Jesus command grounded in the way God acts: where Matthew has "heavenly Father," Luke has "Father," and where Matthew has "You be perfect," Luke has "You be merciful." My suspicion is that Luke is true to the Jesus tradition on both counts.

The comparative analysis of Matthew 5:43-48 and Luke 6:27-36 extends the Johannine love command in two directions, taking the source of the love back to God, the Most High heavenly Father, and extending the love beyond the mutual love of the disciples to the love of enemies, because God is indiscriminate in loving the good and the bad, the just and the unjust (Romans 2:11; Matthew 5:45, 47; Luke 6:35-36). Thus, Matthew and Luke describe appropriate loving actions that ultimately find the exemplary and motivational source in Jesus's teaching about God as the compassionate and merciful heavenly father. This comes close to John 13:34-35 in providing a motivating and inspiring source for loving. But does the Jesus of the Fourth Gospel identify the source of love with God (the Father) and extend the range of that love and the command to love as widely as the Jesus of Matthew and Luke?

God and the *Logos,* the Father and the Son

The form of the love command in the Fourth Gospel implies that Christian identity is grounded in Christology. Those who love one another as Jesus loved them are revealed as his disciples.[8] But Jesus's love arises from being the Son in relation to the Father and the mutual love between the Father and Son, which is the source of the love of the Son for "his own" and their love for one another. God's love nurtures mutuality and has a gracious downward or condescending momentum through God's Son to the world. When used of God in relation to the creation, including humans, the notion of condescension is not tainted by arrogance but bears a sense of graciousness.

In the Gospel as well as in 1 John, God (the Father) is the source of gener-ous, gracious giving-love, and the love of the Son is responsive. The love of the Father for the Son involves endowing and empowering the Son in all that he does (1:3-4; 5:20, 26), and the love of the Son for the Father is expressed in doing only what he sees the Father doing, speaking only what he hears from the Father, doing only the will of the Father (4:34; 5:19-29, 30; 8:26, 40). So there is a unity of being and action in the Father and the Son (5:17; 10:30). Likewise, the love of the Son for his own endows and empowers mutual love. This love has its source in God (the Father), becomes effective in mutual love, and yet remains open, unfulfilled, ever seeking the resolution of unfulfilled mutuality in the world.

God (the Father) as the Source of Gracious Love for the World

That this is true of the love revealed in Jesus in the Fourth Gospel becomes clear in one of the foundational texts that embodies the message in a nutshell: "For God loved the world in this way ['thus' *houtōs*], God *gave* God's only be-gotten Son, so that whoever believes in him may have eternal life" (John 3:16).[9] Gracious giving is also stressed in 6:32-33 where Jesus asserts that "[It was] not Moses who *has given* [*dedōken*] to you the bread from heaven, but my Father *gives* [*didōsin*] to you the true bread from heaven; for the bread of God is the one who comes down from heaven [*estin ho katabainōn ek tou ouranou*] and *gives* [*didous*] life *to the world*." Jesus's response makes two corrections to the assertion he answers: Not Moses, but my Father was the giver; not the manna, but the true bread from heaven is the gift. In this text Jesus uses God's giving of the manna as a symbol of the gift of God's Son and the life-giving benefits that continue to flow from it for the life of the world.

The indiscriminate nature of the love is seen in the universal scope, "the world" which (in 3:16) includes "whoever," thus also the good and the bad, the just and the unjust of Matthew. It also takes love back to its ultimate source in God, in "my Father (6:33)," for here Jesus is the speaker, not the narrator as in 3:16. What is stated simply in 3:16 is complex, and the nature of the love is clarified. God's love is shown to be generous, giving-love: "God loved the world like this, God gave...." Thus it is clear that love has its source in God (the Father) and has an unrestricted, universal scope. The text implies more than it actually says, because what God gave was "his only begotten Son [*ton huion ton monogenē*]," a phrase used with slight variation in 3:18, which refers to those who fail to believe "*in the name* of the only begotten Son of God [*to onoma tou monogenous huiou tou theou*]." Elsewhere in the Fourth Gospel *monogenēs* is used only in the concluding paragraph of the prologue.

The *Logos* and the Only-Begotten Son

The final paragraph of the prologue begins with the announcement of the incarnation, and witnesses attest the revelation of glory in the incarnate *logos,* "We beheld his glory, glory as of an only begotten from the Father [*doxan hōs monogenous para patros*]…" (John 1:14). At the end of the prologue, the impersonal voice of the narrator concludes, "No one has ever seen God, only begotten God [*monogenēs theos*][10] who is in the bosom of the Father [*eis ton kolpon tou patros*], he has made God known [*ekeinos exēgēsato*]" (John 1:18). In this way the last verse of the prologue returns to the first, the beginning, the *logos* with God (1:1).

But there is a difference. Between the beginning and the end of the prologue, God has brought into being all things through the *logos* and has made God's-self known in the *logos* made flesh before returning to the bosom of the Father. In the beginning the *logos* was with God (*pros ton theon*). By the end of the prologue the only begotten God is in the bosom of the Father. Thus 1:1 and 18 form an *inclusio,* and it has become clear that both the *logos* and the Father may be designated *theos,* God.

In the prologue the *logos* is designated *theos* (1:1), and in 1:14 the glory revealed in the incarnate *logos* is described as "glory as of an only begotten from the *Father.*" Yet, in the prologue, there is no reference to the *Son,* even if it seems to be suggested by the reference to the Father, as it is also in 1:18. But, in the prologue, the focus is on the *logos*—first in the beginning, then in the course of history including the incarnation, and finally in the return to the Father. But in the body of the Gospel that tells the story of Jesus, the reference is to the Son and, in 3:16, to God's only begotten Son (*ton huion ton monogenē*). Surprisingly, in 3:16, 18 where the only references to "the only begotten Son" occur, "Father" is not used, but "God." Yet the use of "Son" there in 3:16, 18 suggests "Father," just as the use of "Father" in the prologue suggests "Son." Elsewhere in the Gospel the idiom is of the Father *sending* his Son, and Jesus refers to God as "the Father who *sent* me [*ho pempsas me patēr*]."[11] Only in 3:16 does *God give* his only begotten Son.[12] Even here the Gospel immediately reverts to the sending image, but retains the reference to God, "For God did not *send* his Son into the world to judge the world, but to save the world through him" (3:17).

Only-Begotten (*monogenēs*) as the Christological Connection Between the Prologue and the Body of the Gospel

While the man called John is an historical connection (1:6-8, 15, and 19-36), the two uses of "only-begotten," together with the two references to God as *Father* (1:14, 18; 2:16; 3:16, 18; 3:35 and see note 10), form an important Christological and theological connection with the body of the Gospel. The glory revealed in the incarnate *logos* is "glory as of an only-begotten from the *Father*" (1:14), and "the only-begotten God" is "in the bosom of the *Father*" (1:18). "Father" is characteristic of the language of Jesus about God in the body of the Gospel. There, the only two uses of *monogenēs* occur with "Son" and "God," not "Father" (3:16, 18). In 3:16 "only-begotten Son *of God*" is implicit and explicit in 3:18. But neither "Son" nor "God" occurs in 1:14, 18. The choice of "God," rather than "Father" in 3:16 is appropriate because the focus of this statement is on God and the world. Though involved, the Son is the means by which God acts in love for the world. Though 3:16 says, "God loved the world," the Gospel avoids any suggestion that God's relationship to the world is comparable to the Father-Son relationship. Thus, it is Father-Son and God-world and, although the Father-God is said to love the Son and the world, there are differences in the way this is expressed. The *Father's* love for the *Son* is expressed using verbs in the present tense (3:35; 5:20) but *God's* love for the *world* is expressed using the aorist tense *ēgapēsen*. The one describes a loving relationship, while the other expresses an act of love, which the aorist *edōken* clarifies as *an act of giving* the priceless, gracious gift.

The description of the act as "giving," not "sending," is crucial to clarify the nature of God's love for the world. It is generous giving love. For this purpose the more characteristic sending motif would not do, because the force of its use is to endow the one sent with the authority of the sender. What was needed in 3:16 was an idiom that would powerfully evoke the graciousness of God's love for the world. Interestingly, in the bread of life discourse delivered to the crowd that had followed Jesus across the lake, he asserts: "It was not Moses who *has given* to you the bread from heaven, but my Father *gives* to you the true bread from heaven. For the bread of God is the one coming down from heaven and giving [*didous*] life to the world" (6:32-33). Though God's love is not the subject here, the use of the present participle implies that the gift of the Son (3:16) has opened the continuing possibility of life for the world.

Underlying the Revelation Is the Unfathomable Mystery of God

The absence of the Father-Son terminology is nowhere more missed than in the opening verses of the prologue, which lack this distinction and struggle to express the relationship of the *logos* to God.

> In the beginning was the *logos*
> And the *logos* was with God
> And the *logos* was God.

What are we to make of the absence of any sign of the Father-Son language in the prologue until the announcement of the incarnation and that the full use of this matched pair of terms is found only in the body of the Gospel?

Perhaps the Gospel is warning us not to be led astray by familiarity with the human terms of father and son, even if we capitalize them. The prologue proclaims that the incarnation revealed ("we beheld," aorist tense) the "glory as of an only-begotten from the Father" and, having asserted that "no-one has ever seen God [*theon oudeis heōraken pōpote*]," goes on to proclaim that "the only begotten God, who is in the bosom of the Father, he has made him known [*ekeinos exēgēsato*]." It seems to me that the strategy of reserving the Father-Son language together with denying that any one has seen God, is designed to remind the reader that we are here face to face with the mystery of God. Language struggles with our human limitations in the face of the mystery of God that remains beyond our comprehension, even when we have been grasped by the vision of God in the face of Jesus Christ. God condescends to come down to human terms. But, as the prophet Isaiah eloquently shows (especially in chapters 40-55), the unfathomable mystery of God lies beyond human comprehension (Isaiah 55:8-9; and see Job 38-39).

I suspect that the Christian doctrine of the Trinity is but a striving for the best we humans can do to make comprehensible the mystery of the God who meets us in and through the *logos* made flesh.[13] We have already seen that the unity of God is complex, involving the *logos* and God, the Son and the Father. Because the Son always does what he sees the Father doing, and the Father shows the Son all that he does, there is a subordinate relationship but an equality/identity of action (5:17). Yet the Son is not a subordinate being, but is *homoousios* with the Father. That this is not self-contradictory can be seen if we allow that the contradiction arises from the use of a human analogy in our attempt to speak of the mystery of God. We are reminded of this when we speak of the Son as eternally begotten of the Father. So qualified, begetting has no beginning or end, and can only describe a relationship, a relationship within God (the Godhead).

The Love of God as the Generative Source of All Things

The prologue begins by establishing the status and being of the *logos* in the beginning already in intimate relationship with God (*ēn pros ton theon*). That relationship generates the creation of all things. God creates through the agency of God's *logos*. Only through the connections between the prologue and the body of the Gospel does it become clear that where the prologue speaks of the relationship of the *logos* to God, the body of the Gospel speaks of the relationship of the Son to the Father. Discussion of the last five verses of the prologue draws the lines of connection between the use of *monogenēs* in 1:14, 18 and in 3:16, 18. Where the prologue speaks of the *logos* and God, the body of the Gospel speaks of the Father and the Son. The references to the Father in 1:14, 18 are exceptional, as are the references to God giving and sending his

Son in 3:16-17. God's gracious love for the world is the source of God's gift of his only-begotten Son, the *logos* incarnate whose incarnation reveals the glory of God, the "*glory* as of an only begotten from the Father [*doxan hōs monogenous para patros*]." The incarnate *logos* reveals the glory, the source of the glory is the Father, and the character and content of the glory is the "fullness of grace and truth" (*plērēs charitos kai alētheias*). This phrase, generally recognized as a translation of the Hebrew *chesed weemeth* qualifying the divine love revealed in the incarnation, might be translated as "gracious loving-kindness." Combined with 3:16, it defines God's love for the world as gracious-giving love, which has its source in the Father, and is mediated and made effective in the Son, the *logos* made flesh (1:14).[14]

The unique reference to God *giving* his Son in the Gospel in 3:16 calls for explanation.[15] In this reference God's love for the world is being defined. To paraphrase; "God *loved* the world like this: God *gave* God's unique Son." God's love for the world is generous and giving and is expressed with a clarity that would not exist simply using the verb "to send." Further, though the Father-Son relationship is involved, the focus is actually on *God's* relationship to the *world*, as it is in the prologue in 1:3. There the focus is on the way God brings about the creation of "all things" through God's *logos* (1:3). Only in 1:10 do we learn that *panta* ("all things") is an alternative for "the world," or at least, the "world" is included in *panta*. Just as 1:3 says that "all things came to be by" the *logos*, so too 1:10 asserts that "the world came to be by" the *logos*. In each case the creation is expressed in terms of the agency of the *logos* and we should understand God acting through the agency of God's *logos*.[16]

The connection between the last paragraph of the prologue and John 3:16 has an indirect influence on the opening of the prologue because of the *inclusio* created by 1:1 and 18. The only-begotten God, the *logos* made flesh, has returned to be *pros ton theon*, indeed the relationship is further defined as "in the bosom of the Father" (*eis ton kolpon tou patros*). God's action in creation, like the incarnation, arises out of the relationship of the *logos* to God. In the case of the incarnation the gift of the Son is God's act of love for the world and arises out of the Father's love for the Son and the Son's love for the Father. That love is creative rather than locked up in mutuality. Though the prologue offers no explicit motive for the creation, the connection between God creating through the agency of the *logos* and God saving through the agency of the Son, the *logos* made flesh, suggests that creation and redemption are generous loving acts of the God of gracious love. If creation gives the world its possibility, the loving gift to save the world can be seen as renewing or completing what creation began. The world that has long been ruled by dominating and oppressive power is now called to a new and better way (1 Corinthians 12:31b–13:13).

Creation and Discipleship

From the beginning the struggle for life has favored the survival of the fittest, but humans have been so successful in subduing the earth and all its creatures (Genesis 1:26-28) that this very success now threatens the survival of all life on earth. That threat is exacerbated by the human struggle, often at a national level, for power and possession. Selfish exploitation of the resources of the earth by the rich and powerful (the fittest?) has brought about this dire situation. A more generous and caring response is required, not only for the poor and oppressed humans (Galatians 5:13-14), but also for the other creatures and for the earth itself.[17]

Discipleship is *marked* by the recognition of *life* as the gift of unmerited love, a recognition that involves living out of that love, which is the foundation of Christian identity according to the Fourth Gospel, a foundation that is reaffirmed in 13:34-35. This is implied already in the prologue's account of creation (1:3-4). Whether the original reading placed a major break before or after *ho gegonen,* the life is the light for humans. While I favor the reading, "In him [the *logos*] was life, and the life was the light of/for humans," I think that "what became in/by him was life" can support the position I argue here. Given the use of agency in 1:3, an instrumental use of *en* seems to be called for in reading *ho gegonen en autō.* Creation by the *logos* was directed towards the creation of life. But I think it more likely and it makes better sense if, having spoken of the creation of all things (*panta*) by the *logos,* the prologue retains focus on the *logos* and asserts that life-giving power resides in the *logos.* This reading is supported by 5:26, "For in the same way as [*hōsper*] the Father has life in himself, thus [*houtōs*] also he has given to the Son to have life in himself." Certainly this does not merely mean that the *logos* is alive. Rather it means that the *logos* is the mediator of the life-giving power of God and, in 1:4, that life-giving power was the *light* for humanity. In what follows I aim to show that the life-giving power, which is symbolized as the light, is the love of God.

In 1 John, God is identified by two affirmations, "God is light" (1:5), and "God is love" (4:8). The first affirmation is clarified by the contrast, "in whom there is no darkness at all." The same contrast is crucial for the Fourth Gospel: "the light shines in the darkness" (1:5), and "This is the judgment, light has come into the world, but people loved the darkness rather than the light" (3:19-21).[18] In 1 John 1:5-7 and 2:7-11 it becomes clear that light and darkness are symbols: the one of God's love and the other of hatred of God; of love of the brother and hatred of the brother. I consider that in this 1 John draws on the Fourth Gospel. Thus "God is light" and "God is love" are overlapping affirmations, but "God is light" also emphasizes that the love is self-revealing, self-communicating, and brings to light what is hidden in the darkness by way of contrast with the love revealed (John 3:19-21).[19] The emphasis on the self-communicating character of love is related to the essential generosity and creative power of the love of God that underlies the creation and is the power for the renewal or completion of the creation. In this renewal we humans have been called to share in a special way.[20]

In the creation story of Genesis 1:28, God blesses the humans and says: "Be fruitful and multiply, and fill the earth and *subdue* it; and have *dominion*… over everything that moves on the earth." By and large we might say that humans have done this. The growth in the number of humans on earth (1 billion in 1800, now at 7 billion) has exacerbated the conflict between humans who struggle to control the earth's "scarce" resources, and have accelerated the destruction of the habitat of many of earth's creatures, leading to the extinction of many species, and in many places have contaminated the earth, the once fresh water, the oceans, and even the atmosphere.[21] Through science and technology it has been possible to subdue the earth and, in one sense, to have dominion over it. It has not been possible to annul the consequences of our own actions.[22] Perhaps partly for this reason Rudolf Bultmann wrote: "By the means of science [and technology] men try to take possession of the world but in fact the world gets possession of men."[23] But his point is more about the way possessions become an obsession so that "enough is never enough," which he attributes to uncontrolled human desire (*epithymia*). Such obsession is destructive of the earth and the web of life of which we humans form a part. Here we have the power to lead ourselves astray, denying the destructive effects of our actions for the sake of possessions, without concern for other life forms, or indeed for future generations. And it is God's world, the creation of the generative love of God.

Identity and the Mission of God in John 17

The form of the new commandment made the way Jesus loved the disciples (*kathōs*) the basis of the way they were to love one another. Now, in the great "prayer" of John 17, Jesus lays out a panoramic vision. In the first section (17:1-5), although trial and crucifixion await him, Jesus looks back on his mission as already completed. He says, "I have completed the work that you gave me to do; and now Father, you glorify me with the glory I had with you before the world came to be" (17:4-5).

Jesus then turns to pray for his chosen disciples whom he guarded and cared for, but who are about to be left alone in the world (17:6-19). Jesus prepared the disciples to maintain his presence in the world, and to this end, he prays for them (17:9). Though Jesus notes that he does not pray for the world, the world is not overlooked. Everything depends on the disciples maintaining Jesus's presence in the world. As Jesus was, so the disciples are to be in the world, and Jesus prays, "Holy Father, keep them in your name, [the name] which you gave to me, that they may be one as we [are one]" (17:11).[24]

The prayer for oneness with the Father and the Son recurs (17:22-23 and cf. 17:19, 26) and is about identity. The Johannine Jesus represents the Father to the world, or perhaps it is better to say that he mediates the Father's presence in the world. God's love for the world was made present in him. The new commandment expresses the intent that the disciples continue that presence, and that their love for one another would identify them with Jesus (13:35). Indeed it is implicit that the mutual love of the disciples, like the mutual love of the Father and the Son, will be an over-spilling generous love for the world. Thus Jesus does not ask that the disciples be taken out of the hostile world, but that the Father would sustain them, and sanctify them by the truth of the Word.

This part of the prayer culminates in the commission of the disciples, "*In the same way* [*kathōs*] as the Father sent me into the world so I also sent them" (17:18 and cf. 20:21). This means quite explicitly that the mission of the disciples is an extension of Jesus's mission from the Father. But unlike 3:16, where giving exemplifies the nature of God's love for the world, here sending stresses the relation between the sender and the one sent. The sender is present in the one sent. This is already stressed in the prayer of 17:11, "Holy Father, keep them in your name, which you gave to me, that they may be one as we [are one]" (cf. 17:12, 19). Given the focus already on Jesus's role in keeping the disciples from the corrupting power of the world (17:12), his prayer that the Father would now, at his departure, keep the disciples, not just from the corrupting power of the world, but keep them as one just as the Father and the Son are at one (17:11). In this way the revelation of the Father in the Son is to be maintained in the disciples, preserving the presence of the Father through the Son in the disciples.

But the story does not end with the disciples. The third section of the prayer turns to those who, down through though the ages, on the basis of the *logos* of the disciples will come to believe and to embody the message (17:20-26). As Jesus prayed for his disciples, so now he prays for those who identify the presence of God in those commissioned by the Son to maintain his mission. All this is possible because the love with which the Father loved the Son is in/among them as Jesus is present in/among them (17:26).

The mission envisaged here is quite different from a conventional evangelistic mission focused on a spoken message which the hearers accept or reject. Here the message Jesus embodied is now embodied in the lives of his disciples, and through them in all whose lives manifest the light of God's generous love in a world that remains in the dominion of the darkness. The success of this mission remains totally dependent on the oneness of those who are sent with the source of divine love, which may yet transform the world from a place of darkness and terror. The final words of Jesus's prayer hold out the hope:

"Righteous Father, the world does not know you, but I know you, and these [disciples-believers], they know that you sent me, and I made known to them your name and I will make it known, that the love with which you loved me may be *in/among* them and I *in/among* them" (John 17: 25-26).

I take "in them" (*en autois*) in each case to mean, "among them." The love that has its source in the Father is present among them through the presence of the living Jesus among them. Hope for the world, the entire created order, rests on the presence of God's love, embodied in those who love one another and the world in the same way as Jesus loved them and God loved the world.

Endnotes

1. The power of self-deception is a neglected issue: see James 1:22; 1 John 1:8 and my commentary on James in John Painter and David de Silva, *James and Jude* (Grand Rapids: Baker Academic, 2012), 4-5, 79, 81, 86.

2. See David G. Horrell, "'Becoming Christian': Solidifying Christian Identity and Content," in *Handbook of Early Christianity: Social Science Approaches,* ed. Anthony J. Blasi, Jean Duhaime, and Paul-Andre Turcotte (New York and Oxford: AltaMira Press, 2002), 309-35.

3. See John Painter, *John: Witness and Theologian* (London: SPCK 1975, and subsequent editions), 53-58; and *The Quest for the Messiah*, 2nd edition (Edinburgh and Nashville: T&T Clark and Abingdon, 1993), 224-52, especially 244-49.

4. All translations are the author's.

5. Each use of *hina* in 13:34 is epexegetical, signifying that the content of the commandment follows.

6. On the place of love in the Fourth Gospel see Painter, *John: Witness and Theologian*, 92-100; and Francis J. Moloney, *Love in the Gospel of John* (Grand Rapids: Baker Academic, 2013).

7. See F. Blass and A. Debrunner, trans. and R. W. Funk, ed., *A Greek Grammar of the New Testament and Other Early Christian Literature* (Chicago: University of Chicago Press), 1961, §453; and John Painter, *1, 2, and 3 John: Sacra Pagina*, vol. 18 (Collegeville, MN: The Liturgical Press, 2002), 124 and see *kathōs* in the subject index, 406.

8. The formula of John 13:34-35 like 1 John 4:7-12 makes embodied love like God's love for the world and Jesus's love for his disciples the mark of the presence of Jesus and God's love in the world (17:25-26). Does this mean that love like this, wherever it appears, is evidence of the presence and power of God?

9. See Painter, *The Quest for the Messiah*, 224-52. 1 John 4:9-10 echoes John 3:16-17 and uses *apesteilen* from 3:17 in place of *edōken* in 3:16. By so doing 1 John fails to build on the implied generous, gracious nature of the gift of love expressed in *edōken*.

10. This is almost certainly the correct reading, being much more strongly attested than "the only-begotten Son" (*ho monogenēs huios*). Had the latter been original it is unlikely another "corrective" reading would have been made. The variant is an attraction to John 3:16.

11. In the body of the Gospel, God is the "sending Father" and Jesus "the sent one." See Painter, *The Quest for the Messiah*, 227 and note 54, 246-49.

12. In 1 John 4:9-10, where 1 John echoes John 3:16, the idiom is twice of God *sending* his son, even in 4:9, which refers to "his only begotten Son."

13. Integrity rejects easy recourse to the mystery of God as a way of avoiding difficult

problems, but it is foolish to deny human ignorance and fallibility even when the pervasive human bias of self-interest is not involved.

14. See Painter, *John: Witness and Theologian*, 58.

15. Characteristic also of 1 John is the reference to God sending his Son, using *apostellein* (4:9, 10, 14). The Gospel frequently used both *apostellein* and *pempein* to speak of God (the Father) as the sender and the Son as the sent one.

16. On the use of this motif in the Fourth Gospel see Painter, *The Quest for the Messiah*, 244-49.

17. See John Painter, "Earth Made Whole: John's Reading of Genesis," in *Word, Theology and Community in John*, ed. John Painter, R. Alan Culpepper, and Fernando F. Segovia (St. Louis: Chalice Press, 2002), 65-84; "The Incarnation as a New Testament Key to an Anglican Public and Contextual Theology," *St Mark's Review* 203/2 (2007): 61-70; "An Anglican Approach to Public Affairs in a Global Context," *St Mark's Review* 213/3 (2010): 9-31; Sally McFague, *A New Climate for Theology: God, the World, and Global Warming* (Minneapolis: Fortress, 2008).

18. See John Painter, "John and Qumran," in *The Quest for the Messiah*, especially 35-47, and "Monotheism and Dualism: John and Qumran," in *Theology and Christology in the Fourth Gospel: Essays by the Members of the SNTS Johannine Writings Seminar*, ed. G. Van Belle, J. G. Van Der Watt, P. Maritz (Leuven: Peeters, 2005), 225-43.

19. In 16:8, which I have identified as part of the third version of the farewell discourse, Jesus attributes to the Spirit, described as "another Paraclete," the same function as the Gospel earlier ascribes to the coming of the light into the world as the judgment of the world. Those who reject the light do so to avoid the exposure (*elegchthē*) of their evil works (3:19-21). In 16:8, Jesus says that when the Paraclete comes, "He will expose/reveal (*elegxei*) the sin of the world by revealing the righteousness of God, thus bringing about the judgment of the world." It is implied that this work is mediated via Jesus's disciples to those who believe through their *logos*, thus continuing the work of the light of the world. See John Painter, *The Quest for the Messiah*, 428-35, which is based on "The Farewell Discourses and the History of the Johannine Community," *New Testament Studies* 27 (1981): 525-43, especially 537-39.

20. See note 17 above.

21. In the ancient world the notion of the "limited/finite good" was common. Today there is a strong sense among many people that humans have the ability to cope with any problem we may face. Yet there may now be evidence of planets that show signs of once supporting life. A warning?

22. See note 17 above.

23. Rudolf Bultmann, *Jesus Christ and Mythology* (London: SCM, 1960), 40, and cf. 42-43. Bultmann notes unintended consequences.

24. Perhaps on the basis of this text the *Gospel of Truth* asserts: "The name of the Father is the Son." Nag Hammadi Codex XII, column 38.5-9.

BIBLIOGRAPHY

Bibliography of the Works of Klyne R. Snodgrass

Stephen R. Spencer

Books

Between Two Truths: Living with Biblical Tensions. Grand Rapids: Zondervan, 1990. Translated into Korean, Spanish, and Turkish. Reprint, Eugene, OR: Wipf & Stock, 2005.

Ephesians. The NIV Application Commentary. Grand Rapids: Zondervan, 1996. Translated into Chinese and Spanish.

The Parable of the Wicked Tenants. Wissenschaftliche Untersuchungen zum Neuen Testament 27. Tübingen: J. C. B. Mohr (Paul Siebeck), 1983. Reprint, Eugene, OR: Wipf & Stock, 2011.

Stories with Intent: A Comprehensive Guide to the Parables of Jesus. Grand Rapids: Eerdmans, 2008. Translated into Portuguese.

Pamphlets and Papers

A Biblical and Theological Basis for Women in Ministry: An Occasional Paper. Chicago: Covenant Publications, 1987.

Divorce and Remarriage: An Occasional Paper. Chicago: Covenant Publications, 1992. Updated ed., 2008.

"An Explanation of the Message to the Church in Pergamum (Revelation 2:12-17)." Paper presented to meeting of the International Federation of Free Evangelical Churches, 1996.

Articles

"1 Peter 2:1-10: Its Formation and Literary Affinities." *New Testament Studies* 24, no. 1 (1978): 97-106.

"After Death, What? Biblical Perspectives." *The Covenant Companion* 71, no. 18 (October 15, 1982): 4-5.

"Amen." In *Baker Encyclopedia of the Bible*, ed. Walter A. Elwell, 1:69. Grand Rapids: Baker, 1988.

"*Anaideia* and the Friend at Midnight (Luke 11:8)." *Journal of Biblical Literature* 116, no. 3 (Fall 1997): 505-13.

"Between Text and Sermon: Mark 4:1-20." *Interpretation* 67, no. 3 (July 2013): 284-86.

"Can Seminaries Hold Piety and Intellect Together? Reflections on Glenn T. Miller's *Piety and Intellect*." *Perspectives in Religious Studies* 20, no. 1 (Spring 1993): 71-79.

"A Case for the Unrestricted Ministry of Women." *The Covenant Quarterly* 67, no. 2 (May 2009): 26-44. Translated into Norwegian as "Et forsvar for kvinners ubegrensede tjeneste." In *Her er ikke mann eller kvinne: Om kvinnelige pastorer og ledere i evangelikale menigheter*, ed. Ingunn Fokestad Breistein, Astri T. Anfindsen Dragrød, Anne Wenche Hellem, and Reidar Salvesen, 139-56. Oslo: Ansgarskolen, Misjonsforbundet, 2009.

"The Centrality of the Word of God: Theological Reflection." In *Living Faith: Reflections on Covenant Affirmations by the Faculty of North Park Theological Seminary*, ed. James K. Bruckner, Michelle A. Clifton-Soderstrom, and Paul E. Koptak, 31-47. Chicago: Covenant Publications, 2010.

"Church and Law." In *Mercer Dictionary of the Bible*, ed. Watson E. Mills, 153-55. Macon, GA: Mercer University Press, 1990.

"Common Life with Jesus: The Parable of the Banquet in Luke 14:16-24." In *Common Life in the Early Church: Essays Honoring Graydon F. Snyder*, ed. Julian V. Hills, 186-201. Harrisburg, PA: Trinity Press International, 1998.

"Computer-Assisted Biblical Study." *Theology, News and Notes* 42, no. 3 (October 1995): 20-22.

"Divorce." In *Mercer Dictionary of the Bible*, ed. Watson E. Mills, 218-19. Macon, GA: Mercer University Press, 1990.

"Do We Need Another Pentecost?" *The Covenant Companion* 64, no. 10 (May 15, 1975): 6-7.

"Elemental Spirits." In *Baker Encyclopedia of the Bible*, ed. Walter A. Elwell, 2:684-685. Grand Rapids: Baker, 1988.

"Eli, Eli, Lama Sabachthani." In *Baker Encyclopedia of the Bible*, ed. Walter A. Elwell, 2:686-87. Grand Rapids: Baker, 1988.

"Encouraging Presence." *The Covenant Companion* 101, no. 5 (May 2012): 16-18.

(Editor) *Ex Auditu: An International Journal of the Theological Interpretation of Scripture* 8 (1992)-.

"Exegesis." In *Dictionary for Theological Interpretation of the Bible*, ed. Kevin J. Vanhoozer, 203-6. Grand Rapids: Baker, 2005.

"Exegesis and Preaching: The Principles and Practice of Exegesis." *The Covenant Quarterly* 34, no. 3 (August 1976): 3-29.

"From Allegorizing to Allegorizing: A History of the Interpretation of the Parables of Jesus." In *The Challenge of Jesus' Parables*, ed. Richard N. Longenecker. Grand Rapids: Eerdmans, 2000. Reprinted in *The Historical Jesus in Recent Research*, ed. James D. G. Dunn and Scot McKnight, 248-68. Winona Lake, IN: Eisenbrauns, 2005.

"From Faith to Faith." *The Covenant Companion* 72, no. 15 (September 1, 1983): 12.

"Galatians 3:28: Conundrum or Solution?" In *Women, Authority and the Bible*, ed. Alvera Mickelsen, 161-81. Downers Grove: InterVarsity Press, 1986.

"Gnosticism." In *Holman Bible Handbook*, ed. David S. Dockery, 724. Nashville: Holman Bible Publishers, 1992.

"The Gospel in Romans: A Theology of Revelation." In *Gospel in Paul: Studies on Corinthians, Galatians and Romans for Richard N. Longenecker*, ed. L. Ann Jervis and Peter Richardson, 288-314. Journal for the Study of the New Testament Supplement Series 108. Sheffield: Sheffield Academic Press, 1994.

"The Gospel of Jesus." In *The Written Gospel*, ed. Markus Bockmuehl and Donald A. Hagner, 31-44. Cambridge: Cambridge University Press, 2005.

"The Gospel of Thomas: A Secondary Gospel." *The Second Century: A Journal of Early Christian Studies* 7, no. 1 (Spring 1989-1990): 19-38. Reprinted in *The Historical Jesus*, vol. 4: *Lives of Jesus and Jesus Outside the Bible*, ed. Craig A. Evans, 291-308. London: Routledge, 2004.

"Guiding Values Concerning the Teaching of Preaching at North Park Theological Seminary." *The Covenant Companion* 81, no. 12 (December 1992): 22.

"'Head': What Does It Mean?" *Daughters of Sarah* 2, no. 4 (July 1976): 1-6.

"A Hermeneutics of Hearing Informed by the Parables with Special Reference to Mark 4." *Bulletin of Biblical Research* 14, no. 1 (2004): 59-79.

"Hidden Treasures." *The Covenant Companion* 93, no. 3 (March 2004): 20-22.

"How Shall We Respond to Wrongdoing? Is Moral Indignation Permissible for Christians?" In *Judgment Day at the White House*, ed. Gabriel Fackre, 72-83. Grand Rapids: Eerdmans, 1999.

"Identity in Colossians." *Miqra* 9, no. 4 (Fall 2010): 9-15.

"Introduction to a Hermeneutics of Identity." *Bibliotheca Sacra* 168, no. 669 (January-March 2011): 3-19.

"Jesus and a Hermeneutics of Identity." *Bibliotheca Sacra* 168, no. 670 (April-June 2011): 133-45.

"Jesus and Money: No Place to Hide and No Easy Answers." *Word & World: Theology for Christian Ministry* 30, no. 2 (Spring 2010): 135-43.

"Junia the Apostle." *The Covenant Companion* 98, no. 2 (February 2009): 16-17.

"Justification by Grace—to the Doers: An Analysis of the Place of Romans 2 in the Theology of Paul." *New Testament Studies* 32, no. 1 (January 1986): 72-93.

"Key Questions on the Parables of Jesus." *Review and Expositor* 109, no. 2 (Spring 2012): 173-85.

"Law." In *Holman Bible Handbook*, ed. David S. Dockery, 702-3. Nashville: Holman Bible Publishers, 1992.

"Law in the New Testament." In *Mercer Dictionary of the Bible*, ed. Watson E. Mills, 501-503. Macon, GA: Mercer University Press, 1990.

"Liberty or Legality? The Pauline Dilemma." *The Covenant Quarterly* 33, no. 4 (November 1975): 21-36.

"Matthew and the Law." In *Society of Biblical Literature 1988 Seminar Papers*, ed. David J. Lull, 536-54. Atlanta: Scholars Press, 1988. Reprinted in *Treasures New and Old: Recent Contributions to Matthean Studies*, ed. David R. Bauer and Mark Allan Powell, 99-127. Atlanta: Scholars Press, 1996.

"Matthew's Understanding of the Law." *Interpretation* 46, no. 4 (October 1992): 368-78. Reprinted in *Gospel Interpretation: Narrative-Critical and Social-Scientific Approaches*, ed. Jack Dean Kingsbury, 38-48. Harrisburg, PA: Trinity Press International, 1997.

"Modern Approaches to the Parables." In *The Face of New Testament Studies: A Survey of Recent Research*, ed. Scot McKnight and Grant R. Osborne, 177-90. Grand Rapids: Baker Academic, 2004.

"No Easy Escape." *The Covenant Companion* 77, no. 12 (December 1988): 18-19.

"Ὁ Ἀπόστολος Παῦλος, ἡ ἐργασία καὶ οι εργασιακές σκέσις" ["Paul, Work, and Work Relations"], Αστηρ της Ανατολής 152, no. 8 (September 2009): 246-49.

"Only Begotten." In *Baker Encyclopedia of the Bible*, ed. Walter A. Elwell, 3:1590-91. Grand Rapids: Baker, 1988.

"The Ordination of Women—Thirteen Years Later: Do We Really Value the Ministry of Women?" *The Covenant Quarterly* 48, no. 3 (August 1990): 26-43.

"Parable." In *Baker Encyclopedia of the Bible*, ed. Walter A. Elwell, 4:1606-14. Grand Rapids: Baker, 1988.

"Parable." In *Dictionary of Jesus and the Gospels*, ed. Joel B. Green, Scot McKnight, and I. Howard Marshall, 591-601. Downers Grove: InterVarsity Press, 1992.

"The Parable of the Wicked Husbandmen: Is the Gospel of Thomas Version the Original?" *New Testament Studies* 21, no. 1 (October 1974): 142-44.

"Parables and the Hebrew Scriptures." In *To Hear and Obey: Essays in Honor of Fredrick Carlson Holmgren*, ed. Bradley J. Bergfalk and Paul E. Koptak, 164-77. Chicago: Covenant Publications, 1997. [*The Covenant Quarterly* 55, nos. 2-3 (May/August 1997)].

"Parables as Stories with Intent: The Contextualization of Jesus' Parables." In *Hermeneutik der Gleichnisse Jesu: Methodische Neuansätze zum Verstehen urchristlicher Parabeltexte*, ed. Ruben Zimmermann with Gabi Kern, 150-64. Wissenschaftliche Untersuchungen zum Neuen Testament 231. Tübingen: Mohr-Siebeck, 2008.

"The Parables of Jesus." *The Covenant Companion* 68, nos. 15-19 (September 1–November 1, 1979): 13-15; 6-7; 8-9; 8-9; 17-19.

"Paul and Women." *The Covenant Quarterly* 34, no. 4 (November 1976): 3-19.

"Paul's Focus on Identity." *Bibliotheca Sacra* 168, no. 671 (July-September 2011): 259-73.

"Pauline Perspectives on the Identity of a Pastor." *Bibliotheca Sacra* 168, no. 672 (October-December 2011): 387-401.

"Preaching Jesus' Parables." In *Preaching the New Testament*, ed. Ian Paul and David Wenham, 45-58. Downers Grove: InterVarsity, 2013.

"Preface to the 1992 Reprint." In *Chiasmus in the New Testament: A Study in the Form and Function of Chiastic Structures*, by Nils Wilhelm Lund, vii-xxi. Peabody, MA: Hendrickson, 1992. (Co-authored with David Scholer.)

"Prophets, Parables, and Theologians." *Bulletin of Biblical Research* 18, no. 1 (2008): 45-77.

"Providence is Not Enough." *Christianity Today* 32, no. 2 (February 5, 1988): 33-34.

"Quotations of the Old Testament in the New Testament." In *Baker Encyclopedia of the Bible*, ed. Walter A. Elwell, 4:1808-1813. Grand Rapids: Baker, 1988.

"Reading and Overreading the Parables in *Jesus and the Victory of God*." In *Jesus and the Restoration of Israel: A Critical Assessment of N. T. Wright's* Jesus and the Victory of God, ed. Carey C. Newman, 61-76. Downers Grove: InterVarsity Press, 1999.

"Reading to Hear: A Hermeneutics of Hearing." *Horizons in Biblical Theology* 24, no. 1 (June 2002): 1-32.

"Recent Research on the Parable of the Wicked Tenants: An Assessment." *Bulletin of Biblical Research* 8 (1998): 187-215.

"Reconciliation: God Being God with Special Reference to 2 Corinthians 5:11-6:4." *The Covenant Quarterly* 60, no. 2 (May 2002): 3-23. Translated and published as "Versöhnung—das charakteristische Handeln Gottes." *Theologisches Gespräch* 26, no. 4 (2002): 3-22.

"A Response to Hans Dieter Betz on the Sermon on the Mount." *Biblical Research* 36 (1991): 88-94.

"Response to N. T. Wright's 'Jesus and the Identity of God.'" *Ex Auditu* 14 (1998): 57-58.

"Responsible Christian Freedom." *North Park Bulletin: Seminary Review* 13, no. 2 (June 1975): [4-5].

"Resurrection Ecclesiology." *North Park Theological Seminary: Seminary Review* 27, no. 1 (Fall 1988): 2-3.

"Rock." In *A Dictionary of Biblical Tradition in English Literature*, ed. David Lyle Jeffrey, 668. Grand Rapids: Eerdmans, 1992.

"Spheres of Influence: A Possible Solution to the Problem of Paul and the Law." *Journal for the Study of the New Testament* 32 (February 1988): 93-113. Reprinted in *The Best in Theology*, vol. 3, ed. J. I. Packer, 81-96. Carol Stream, IL: CTI, 1989. Reprinted in *The Pauline Writings*, ed. Stanley E. Porter and Craig A. Evans, 154-74. Sheffield: Sheffield Academic Press, 1995.

"Stone." In *A Dictionary of Biblical Tradition in English Literature*, ed. David Lyle Jeffrey, 736-37. Grand Rapids: Eerdmans, 1992.

"Streams of Tradition Emerging from Isaiah 40:1-5 and Their Adaptation in the New Testament." *Journal for the Study of the New Testament* 8 (1980): 24-45. Reprinted in *New Testament Backgrounds: A Sheffield Reader*, ed.

Craig A. Evans and Stanley E. Porter, 149-68. Sheffield: Sheffield Academic Press, 1997.

"The Temple Incident." In *Key Events in the Life of the Historical Jesus*, ed. Darrell L. Bock and Robert L. Webb, 429-80. Wissenschaftliche Untersuchungen zum Neuen Testament 247. Tübingen: Mohr-Siebeck, 2009.

"That Which Is Born from *Pneuma* Is *Pneuma*." *The Covenant Quarterly* 49, no. 1 (February 1991): 13-29. Reprinted as "That Which Is Born from PNEUMA is PNEUMA: Rebirth and Spirit in John 3:5-6." In *Perspectives on John: Method and Interpretation in the Fourth Gospel*, ed. Robert B. Sloan and Mikeal C. Parsons, 181-205. National Association of Baptist Professors of Religion Special Studies Series, no. 11. Lewiston, NY: Edwin Mellen Press, 1993.

"That Which Is Born from the Spirit *Is* the Spirit: Reflections on John 3:6." *The Covenant Companion* 80, no. 2 (February 1991): 12-14.

"The Use of the Old Testament in the New Testament." In *New Testament Criticism and Interpretation*, ed. David Alan Black and David S. Dockery, 409-34. Grand Rapids: Zondervan, 1991. Reprinted in *The Right Doctrine from the Wrong Texts?*, ed. G. K. Beale, 29-51. Grand Rapids: Baker Books, 1994. Reprinted in *Interpreting the New Testament: Essays on Methods and Issues*, ed. David Alan Black and David S. Dockery, 209-29. Nashville: Broadman & Holman, 2001.

"Western Non-Interpolations." *Journal of Biblical Literature* 91, no. 3 (September 1972): 369-79.

"'Where Is It Written': Slogan or Lifestyle?" *The Covenant Companion* 76, no. 12 (December 1987): 30.

"'Your Slaves—On Account of Jesus': Servant Leadership in the New Testament." In *Servant Leadership*, ed. James R. Hawkinson and Robert K. Johnston, 1:7-19. Chicago: Covenant Publications, 1993. [*The Covenant Quarterly* 50, no. 4]

Book Reviews

Review of *The Apostle of God: Paul and the Promise of Abraham*, by John L. White. *Interpretation* 55, no. 2 (April 2001): 202, 204.

Review of *Christianity According to St. John*, by D. George Vanderlip. *The Covenant Quarterly* 35, no. 1 (February 1977): 39-40.

Review of *Christology: A Biblical, Historical, and Systematic Study of Jesus*, by Gerald O'Collins. *Bulletin of Biblical Research* 7 (1997): 255-57.

Review of *Dictionary of Latin and Greek Theological Terms: Drawn Principally from Protestant Scholastic Theology*, by Richard A. Muller. *The Covenant Quarterly* 45, no. 1 (February 1987): 45-46.

Review of *The Epistle to the Romans*, vol. 1; The International Critical Commentary, by C. E. B. Cranfield. *The Covenant Quarterly* 36, no. 3 (August 1977): 40-41.

Review of *Freedom and Obligation: A Study of the Epistle to the Galatians*, by C. K. Barrett. *Interpretation* 41, no. 1 (January 1987): 100, 102.

Review of *From Plight to Solution: A Jewish Framework for Understanding Paul's View of the Law in Galatians and Romans*, by Frank Thielman. *Interpretation* 46, no. 1 (January 1992): 80, 82.

Review of *Good News Bible*. *The Covenant Companion* 46, no. 7 (April 1, 1977): 10-11.

Review of *The Gospel of Luke*; The New International Commentary on the New Testament, by Joel B. Green. *The Covenant Quarterly* 56, no. 3 (August 1998): 51-54.

Review of *Handbook of Biblical Criticism*, by Richard N. Soulen. *The Covenant Quarterly* 36, no. 3 (August 1977): 39-40.

Review of *Inerrancy and Common Sense*, ed. Roger R. Nicole and J. Ramsey Michaels; *Inerrancy*, ed. Norman L. Geisler; and *The Inspiration of Scripture: Problems and Proposals*, by Paul J. Achtemeier. *The Covenant Quarterly* 39, no. 1 (February 1981): 41-44.

Review of *Israel's Law and the Church's Faith: Paul and His Recent Interpreters*, by Stephen Westerholm. *The Covenant Quarterly* 48, no. 2 (May 1990): 36-37.

Review of *The Jewish Reclamation of Jesus: An Analysis and Critique of Modern Jewish Study of Jesus*, by Donald A. Hagner. *Theological Students Fellowship Bulletin* 9, no. 4 (March-April 1986): 23-24.

Review of *Jesus and the Gospels: An Introduction and Survey*, by Craig L. Blomberg. *The Asbury Theological Journal* 53, no. 2 (Fall 1998): 92-94.

Review of *The Letter to the Ephesians*; The Pillar New Testament Commentary, by Peter T. O'Brien. *Interpretation* 55, no. 1 (January 2001): 90, 92.

Review of *Man and Woman in Biblical Perspective*, by James B. Hurley. *Trinity Journal* n.s. 3, no. 2 (Fall 1982): 223-26.

Review of *On This Rock: A Commentary on First Peter*, by Donald G. Miller. *Interpretation* 49, no. 4 (October 1995): 420, 422, 424.

Review of *Pauline Theology and Mission Practice*, by Dean S. Gilliland. *Theological Students Fellowship Bulletin* 7, no. 5 (May-June 1984): 24.

Review of *Poles Apart: The Gospel in Creative Tension*, by D. S. Russell. *Critical Review of Books in Religion* (1992): 91-92.

Review of *The Priority of John*, by John A. T. Robinson. *The Covenant Quarterly* 47, no. 1 (February 1989): 38-40.

Review of *Reading Matthew: A Literary and Theological Commentary on the First Gospel*; Reading the New Testament, by David E. Garland. *Review and Expositor* 91, no. 3 (Summer 1994): 440-41.

Review of *Reden in Vollmacht: Hintergrund, Form und Anliegen der Gleichnisse Jesu*, by Eckhard Rau. *Journal of Biblical Literature* 112, no. 2 (Summer 1993): 344-45.

Review of *Rediscovering the Lord's Supper*, by Markus Barth. *The Covenant Quarterly* 48, no. 2 (May 1990): 34-35.

Review of *The Responsibility of Hermeneutics*, by Roger Lundin, Anthony C. Thiselton, and Clarence Walhout; *A Guide to Contemporary Hermeneutics: Major Trends in Biblical Interpretation*, ed. Donald K. McKim; and *Hermeneutics, Authority, and Canon*, ed. by D. A. Carson and John D. Woodbridge. *The Covenant Quarterly* 45, no. 6 (November 1987): 199-202.

Review of *Romans* (2 vols); Word Biblical Commentary, by James D. G. Dunn. *Christian Scholar's Review* 20, no. 3 (February 1991): 309-11.

Review of *Romans 1-8*; Wycliffe Exegetical Commentary, by Douglas J. Moo. *Themelios* 18, no. 1 (October 1992): 29.

Review of *Sacrifice and the Death of Christ*, by Frances M. Young. *The Covenant Quarterly* 37, no. 2 (May 1979): 37-38.

Review of *The Shape of Scriptural Authority*, by David L. Bartlett. *The Covenant Quarterly* 42, no. 3 (August 1984): 37-39.

Review of *Turning to Jesus: The Sociology of Conversion in the Gospels*, by Scot McKnight. *The Covenant Quarterly* 61, no. 1 (February 2003): 45-47.

Review of *Union with Christ: The New Finnish Interpretation of Luther*, ed. Carl E. Braaten and Robert W. Jenson. *The Covenant Quarterly* 58, no. 2 (May 2000): 40-41.

Review of *Women & Church Leadership*, by C. Margaret Howe, and *The Ordination of Women: An Essay on the Office of Christian Ministry*, by Paul K. Jewett. *The Covenant Quarterly* 40, no. 3 (August 1982): 39-41.

Review of *Women in Judaism*, by Leonard Swidler. *Christian Scholar's Review* 7, no. 4 (1978): 377-78.

Contributors

Darrell L. Bock is executive director of cultural engagement and senior research professor of New Testament studies, Dallas Theological Seminary, Dallas, Texas.

James K. Bruckner is professor of Old Testament, North Park Theological Seminary, Chicago, Illinois.

Stephen J. Chester is academic dean and professor of New Testament, North Park Theological Seminary, Chicago, Illinois.

Jo Ann Deasy is director of institutional initiatives and student research, the Association of Theological Schools, Pittsburgh, Pennsylvania.

Jan A. du Rand is emeritus professor of biblical studies, University of Johannesburg, and extraordinary professor, North-West University, Potchefstroom, South Africa.

Rebekah A. Eklund is assistant professor of theology, Loyola University Maryland, Baltimore, Maryland.

Jodi Mullen Fondell is pastor at Immanuelskyrkan, Stockholm, Sweden.

Robert L. Hubbard Jr. is professor emeritus of Old Testament, North Park Theological Seminary, Chicago, Illinois.

Robert K. Johnston is professor of theology and culture, Fuller Theological Seminary, Pasadena, California.

David Kersten is dean of North Park Theological Seminary, Chicago, Illinois.

Paul E. Koptak is the Paul and Bernice Brandel professor of communication and biblical interpretation, North Park Theological Seminary, Chicago, Illinois.

Ekaterina Kozlova is a DPhil candidate, University of Oxford, England.

Max J. Lee is associate professor of New Testament, North Park Theological Seminary, Chicago, Illinois.

Richard N. Longenecker is professor emeritus of New Testament, Wycliffe College, University of Toronto, Ontario.

Scot McKnight is professor of New Testament, Northern Baptist Theological Seminary, Lombard, Illinois.

Hauna Ondrey is a PhD candidate, University of St. Andrews, Scotland, and a teaching fellow, North Park Theological Seminary, Chicago, Illinois.

John Painter is professor of theology, St. Mark's School of Theology, Charles Sturt University, Australia.

John E. Phelan Jr. is senior professor of theological studies, North Park Theological Seminary, Chicago, Illinois.

Stephen R. Spencer is theological and cataloging librarian, Brandel Library, North Park University, Chicago, Illinois.

Nicholas Thomas Wright is research professor of New Testament and early Christianity, St. Mary's College, University of St. Andrews, Scotland.